Alan Watts—
in the ACADEMY

SUNY SERIES IN TRANSPERSONAL AND HUMANISTIC PSYCHOLOGY

Richard D. Mann, editor

Alan Watts—
in the ACADEMY

essays and lectures

Edited and with an introduction by
Peter J. Columbus and Donadrian L. Rice

On the cover: Portrait of Alan Watts by Fred Richards–Daishi, from the artist's collection.

Published by
STATE UNIVERSITY OF NEW YORK PRESS
Albany

© 2017 State University of New York

For information, contact
State University of New York Press
www.sunypress.edu

Production, Dana Foote
Marketing, Anne M. Valentine

Library of Congress Cataloging-in-Publication Data

Names: Watts, Alan, 1915–1973, author. | Columbus, Peter J., editor. | Rice, Donadrian L., editor.
Title: Alan Watts—in the academy : essays and lectures / by Alan Watts ; edited and with an introduction by Peter J. Columbus and Donadrian L. Rice.
Description: Albany, NY : State University of New York Press, 2017. | Series: SUNY series in transpersonal and humanistic psychology | Includes bibliographical references and index.
Identifiers: LCCN 2016031500 (print) | LCCN 2017008164 (ebook) | ISBN 9781438465555 (hardcover : alk. paper) | ISBN 9781438465548 (pbk. : alk. paper) | ISBN 9781438465562 (ebook)
Subjects: LCSH: Philosophy.
Classification: LCC B945 .W321 2017 (print) | LCC B945 (ebook) | DDC 191—dc23
LC record available at https://lccn.loc.gov/2016031500

10   9   8   7   6   5   4   3   2   1

Contents

PART ONE

LANGUAGE AND MYSTICISM

PART TWO

BUDDHISM AND ZEN

PART THREE

CHRISTIANITY

PART FOUR

COMPARATIVE RELIGION

Illustrations

Editors' Preface

The year 2015 marked the centenary of Alan Watts' birth. He lived only 58 years, and once conjectured that his relevance would fade within five decades beyond his death. Yet, nearly 45 years after his 1973 passing, interest in Watts' life and work is not subsiding. His books remain in vogue, and popular audiences in large numbers now view his audiovisual materials via YouTube. Moreover, contemporary scholars are currently mapping Watts' historical influence, and surveying his ongoing impact in a variety of academic disciplines. It is in service to this scholarly effort that we have gathered and organized, thematically and chronologically, the present anthology of writings and lectures by Watts. All materials herein, particularly endnotes, references, and figures were formatted for consistency with the American Psychological Association's publication style. Occasionally, though rarely, editorial comments were added as endnotes for clarification of subject matter.

As this manuscript reaches publication, a substantial debt of thanks is coming due. First, to everyone who generously offered permission to reprint materials. A University of West Georgia faculty grant to Don Rice helped cover any reprint fees. Jean-Claude van Itallie and the Shantigar Foundation supported Peter Columbus' writing and editing. Lisa Prolman's interlibrary loan staff at the Public Library of Greenfield, Massachusetts, helped locate, identify, and acquire materials necessary for the text. Fred Richards kindly allowed use of his artwork for the cover. Three anonymous reviewers (particularly "reviewer #3") offered critical commentaries affording important revisions to an early draft of the introduction. Another anonymous reviewer subsequently offered practical suggestions for final revision. The State University of New York Press editorial, technical, and marketing staff, including the late Nancy Ellegate,

Andrew Kenyon, Christopher Ahn, Jessica Kirschner, Dana Foote, and Anne Valentine, shepherded the manuscript to publication. Sincere gratitude to all.

—Peter J. Columbus
Rowe, Massachusetts

—Donadrian L. Rice
Carrollton, Georgia

Introduction

Alan Watts and the Academic Enterprise

Peter J. Columbus and Donadrian L. Rice

> As in some economies the rich keep getting richer and the poor poorer,
> so in the overspecialized disciplines of modern scholarship the learned get
> more learned and the ignorant get more ignorant—until the two classes
> can hardly talk to each other. I have dedicated my work to an attempt to
> bridge that gap.
>
> —Alan Watts, 1975b, p. xx

This collection of academic essays by Alan Watts serves to commemorate the centenary of his birth on the Feast of the Epiphany—January 6—in 1915. Watts was born into a middle-class family at Rowan Tree Cottage, in the village of Chislehurst, located on the outskirts of London. He was raised in the Church of England, educated at elite Anglican preparatory academies—including King's School in Canterbury (1928–1932)—and studied at Seabury-Western Theological Seminary in Evanston, Illinois (1941–1944). Receiving the Sacrament of Holy Orders on the Feast of the Ascension, May 18, 1944, Watts served as Episcopal priest, chaplain and theologian at Northwestern University (1944–1950), professor of comparative philosophy at the American Academy of Asian Studies in San Francisco (1951–1957), and freelance philosopher (1958–1973), including visiting scholar at Harvard University (1962–1964). He held a Master of Sacred Theology degree from Seabury-Western Seminary (1948), an Honorary Doctorate of Divinity from the University of Vermont (1958), and was a Fellow of the Society for Arts, Religion, and Contemporary Culture.

Watts integrated his Anglo-Catholic religious formation with knowledge of Buddhism, Daoism, and Hinduism toward resolving problems of ontological estrangement in the twentieth-century West (Morgan, 2008). His 1947 book, *Behold the Spirit: A Study in the Necessity of Mystical Religion*, was hailed by Fr. Alan

1

Griffith Whittemore (1890–1960), superior of the Order of the Holy Cross and abbot of Holy Cross Monastery in West Park, New York, as "one of the most penetrating works that ever has come from the pen of an Anglican author" (as cited in Sadler, 1985, p. 2). In the 1950s, Watts' vital counterpoints to capricious interpretations of Buddhist doctrine rendered him "the most influential figure to come out of the era of Beat Zen" (Coleman, 2001, p. 63). He subsequently offered innovative understandings of spiritual and religious consciousness amid the countercultural upheavals of the psychedelic 1960s (Roszak, 1969/1995), and was a formative influence within the "human potential movement"—the diverse association of psychotherapists and alternative education centers exploring groundbreaking approaches to psychological growth, personal insight, and creative expression in the 1960s and 1970s (Kripal, 2007). The death of Alan Watts, likely due to a combination of heart disease and work fatigue, occurred during his sleep on November 16 in 1973. It was the eve of the Feast of Saint Hugh, the patron saint of Watts' first Anglican boarding school.

Note that two book-length biographies on Watts are available. Both are informative, if sometimes unreliable. The first, by Stuart (1976/1983), emphasizes Watts' professional life but projects a rather cynical subtext (see Sadler's 1976 review). The second, by Furlong (1986/2001), places greater emphasis on Watts' personal life by capitalizing partly on salacious (but dubious) accounts of Watts' first marriage and his reputation for alcoholic excess. Perhaps the fairest biographical considerations of Watts are brief essays by Gidlow (1972), Sadler (1974a, 1974b) and, most recently, Chadwick (2015). See also Watts' (1973a) autobiography and, for a narrative account of Watts' curriculum vitae, see Columbus and Rice (2012b, pp. 2–3).

POMP AND CIRCUMSTANCE

A compilation of scholarly writings and lectures by Alan Watts may seem counterintuitive and counterfactual given his prominent and ubiquitous reputation as a nonacademic writer. Jackson's (1984) review of Watts' life and work, for example, concluded that his "most important public role is that of *popularizer* of Oriental religions to the West; it seems safe to say that no modern writer has exceeded his contributions here" (p. 99, italics added). Likewise, in the twenty-first century, Watts is remembered as "the principle popularizer of Zen Buddhism to American audiences in the 1950 and 1960s" (Kabil, 2012, p. 47) and "the great popularizer of Asian religions" (Seigler, 2010). Although "popularizing"—rendering information as accessible, comprehensible, and appreciable—is an activity professors engage regularly in college classrooms, the moniker may be the antonym of academic heft when applied to Watts. Jackson (1984) wrote:

> *Though no scholar*, he had a wide acquaintance with Asian religious thought and, what is more important, a genius for explaining and

dramatizing the Eastern concepts. . . . No recent Western writer has more successfully presented Oriental religious conceptions to a wide audience or awakened so many readers to the relevance of such conceptions to twentieth-century life. (p. 99, italics added)

The popularizer soubriquet attached to Watts is further complicated with the addition of a "guru" appellation. Watts has been called "America's guru" (Review, 1973, p. 117), "the guru of the Beat Generation" (Stuart, 1976/1983, p. 180), "guru to disenchanted youth" (Curti, 1980, p. 371), and "a guru to the counterculture of the fifties and sixties" (Ballantyne, 1989, p. 437). The two labels affixed to Watts may be conjoined in contemporary thinking, for example, "pop guru" (Oldmeadow, 2004, p. 259), "pop Zen guru" (Crocker, 2013, p. 1) and, stated more elaborately, "New Age guru famous for his popularizations of Hindu and Buddhist philosophy" (Zaretsky, 2015, p. 209). The combination of "popularizer" and "guru" tags on Alan Watts can imply or suggest a radical compromising of academic rigor. The *Dictionary of American Religious Biography* states: "There was a core of serious intention within his efforts to enhance greater understanding of Oriental religions, but Watts *succumbed to popularizing and became a guru* to various forms of counter-culture in the 1950s and 1960s" (Bowden, 1993, pp. 584–585, italics added). Versluis (2014) channels this stream of thought into the contemporary conversation by placing Watts within the category of "renegade religious figures" (p. 6) who ran afoul of traditional academic sensibilities. Watts instead became a "proto-guru," that is to say, "one of the first celebrity spiritual advisors" (p. 87).

Given the "popular guru" motif running through discussions about Alan Watts during his lifetime and after his death, some scholars view his work as virtually antithetical to the academic enterprise. As Ponce (1987) suggested, Watts is "the religious philosopher whom everybody reads at night, but nobody seems to want to acknowledge during the day" (p. 241n6). In the daylight hours of academe his accessible and prolific discussions of abstruse subject matters are seen by certain lettered factions as lacking scholarly diligence and fine distinction. Adams (1958), for example, criticized Watts for abridging Buddhist tenets so as "to trifle with the simplicities of the half-educated" (p. 630). According to Braun (1961), "the more literate of the Zen aficionados admit that Watts is the Norman Vincent Peale of Zen" (p. 180). Prebish (1978) as well referred to Watts' "somewhat amateurish attempt to explain Zen in the context of modern science and psychology" (p. 161). Others in the academy consider Watts' literary accessibility as symptomatic of a superficial and pedestrian temperament: He was "not a deep or profound thinker" (Jackson, 1984, p. 99), "not a particularly original thinker" (Fuller, 2004, p. 190), and "his mystical experiences were quite mediocre and shallow" (Nordstrom & Pilgrim, 1980, p. 387).

In the years after his death, and due much to his popularity among wide-ranging audiences, Watts was mostly marginalized by those in higher education.

Nordstrom and Pilgrim (1980), for example, acknowledged as much in their scathing review of Watts' mystical philosophy:

> Our critique of Watts' mysticism may well strike even the unsympathetic reader of his work as excessively harsh and perhaps even unbalanced. We are well aware of the fact that we have been severe with Watts in this review. At the same time, however, we are aware of the enormous contribution he has made in awakening people all over the world to the spiritual path, particularly in the area of Eastern philosophy and religion. We know as well that for many Watts is a holy man, who has been all but canonized in certain spiritual circles. It is precisely because of Watts' influence that we have been harsh. (p. 397)

Moreover, paradigmatic shifts and programmatic changes in various academic disciplines, including postcolonial studies and Buddhist studies, eventually rendered Watts' thinking as seriously suspect or largely irrelevant in the minds of many thinkers. Summarizing the ensuing reticence about Watts, D. L. Smith (2010) writes: "The current climate of academic opinion makes most readers reluctant to admit that they ever took him seriously" (p. 16). Additionally, Smith points out, "scholars still occasionally define themselves over and against him, using him as a cautionary example of just how wrong modern appropriations of Buddhism can be" (p. 35n5).

The discomfiture with Watts' academic marginalization remains palpable to some scholars in the present day. Philosophy professor Samir Chopra, for example, writes the following in his online blog dated September 24, 2014:

> I have a confession to make: I enjoy reading Alan Watts' books. This simple statement of one of my reading pleasures, this revelation of one of my tastes in books and intellectual pursuits, shouldn't need to be a confession, a term that conjures up visions of sin and repentance and shame. But it is, a veritable coming out of the philosophical closet.

Chopra continues:

> I am supposed to be "doing serious philosophy," reading and writing rigorous philosophy; the works of someone most commonly described as a "popularizer" do not appear to make the cut. Even worse, not only was Watts thus a panderer to the masses, but he wrote about supposedly dreamy, insubstantial, woolly headed, mystical philosophies. An analytical philosopher would be an idiot to read him. Keep it under wraps, son.

Adding to obfuscation of Watts' academic credibility is the personal recounting of his own educational story. Throughout his life Watts had rather tumultuous relationships with formal institutions of learning. Readers familiar with Watts' (1973a) autobiography will know of (1) his traumatic 1922 exiling at the age of seven years from the blissful Rowan Tree Cottage to his first religious boarding school: "I felt myself given over to the care of maniacal bullies" (p. 105); (2) the botched scholarship exam in 1932 that blocked his chance of attending Trinity College at Oxford: "I failed to get a scholarship to Trinity because, as I was later told, I wrote the essay examination on Courage in the style of Nietzsche, having just read his *Zarathustra*. Some theologically occidental examiner must have been offended" (p. 118); (3) the advice of Marguerite Block, editor of the *Review of Religion*, who in 1940 counseled against Watts pursuing doctoral studies: "She said . . . it isn't worth it. I simply wouldn't waste your time with all that picayune, myopic-minded, long-drawn-out, mole-eyed academic ritual" (p. 175); (4) his abrupt resignations from Northwestern University and the Episcopal Church in 1950: "I chose the priesthood because it was the only formal role of Western society into which, at the time, I could even begin to fit. . . . But it was an ill-fitting suit of clothes" (p. 214); and (5) his 1957 resignation from the American Academy of Asian Studies where, as he later wrote, "I was as much out of place in the groves of academe as in the Church, . . . I was never, never going to be an organization man" (pp. 319–320).

Calling himself "an intellectual critic of the intellectual life" (p. 5), Watts (1973a) remained, in his maturity, intensely disparaging of the academic enterprise by viewing it as rather uninspiring, humorless, and too concerned with conventional rules and details. He observed: "You cannot maintain proper status in an American university without cultivated mediocrity. You must be academically 'sound,' which is to be preposterously and phenomenally dull" (p. 132). Further along in his autobiography, Watts referred to "the dubious objective of impressing the more dreary pandits of the American Oriental Society, the in-group of academic Orientalists who, as librarians, philological nitpickers, and scholarly drudges, dissolve all creative interest into acidulated pedantry" (p. 165). Though Jackson (1984) conjectured that Watts' "sensitivities were undoubtedly inflamed by . . . J. K. Shyrock's [1937] dismissal of *The Spirit of Zen* in the *Journal of the American Oriental Society*" (p. 100n22; note also that Watts himself was a member of the Society), it may nevertheless seem unsurprising that Watts (1973a) dubbed himself a "philosophical entertainer" because, he wrote, "I have some difficulty in taking myself and my work *seriously*—or perhaps the right word is 'pompously' " (p. 252).

AIMS AND SCOPE: VALIDITY, RELIABILITY, NECESSITY

The preceding discussion calls into question the propriety of the present manuscript in three key ways. First is the question of validity: Does Alan Watts have a body of work that could reasonably and justifiably be called academic or scholarly? Watts' legacy includes a corpus that, while occasionally ignored or denied, contains learned writings published in scholastic journals and monographs, and sophisticated presentations at professional conferences and symposia. Perhaps indicative of scholarly neglect of Watts, only three extant English-language books approach his work with academic rigor, including Keightley (1986), Brannigan (1988), and Columbus and Rice (2012a). A fourth text, by Clark (1978), is a conservative defense of Christian theism vis-à-vis Watts' mystical philosophy. However, see Columbus (2015a) for a bibliographic resource of primarily academic articles and chapters on Watts' life and work plus a listing of Watts' major books, including posthumously published volumes.

Though sometimes forgotten, Watts' books were regularly and substantively reviewed in leading academic journals (see Appendix). Much of his work was recognized as ahead of its time and located at the forefront of emerging trends in Western intellectual and religious life (Columbus & Rice, 2012a). Heide (2013) notes likewise:

> The perspicacity of Watts' thinking is jaw-dropping. He was the first person in the West to write seriously about Zen . . . the first to conduct a seminar at Esalen, and one of the first to propose linking Eastern philosophy with Western psychology. . . . [He anticipated] the now-prominent distinction between spiritual quest and religious affiliation. Ingesting psychedelics two years before Timothy Leary did, Watts became a principle spokesman for their spiritual value and even proposed that their use be protected constitutionally.
>
> Watts wrote about the psychology of acceptance, one of the central issues in 21st-century cognitive behavioral psychotherapy as early as 1939. His *Nature, Man and Woman* (1958) was one of the earliest feminist critiques of Western religion, preceding most others by decades, as well as a forerunner to the modern environmental movement.

A conclusion to be drawn, in Heide's (2013) view, is that Watts was a more important and substantive thinker than is typically remembered, acknowledged, or appreciated by considerable numbers of academics. Psychologist Diane Gehart (2012) concurs with Heide. She considers Watts "an important but seldom recognized early contributor to the field of family therapy." Gehart writes:

> In his landmark book, *Psychotherapy East and West*, Watts (1961) was the first to make a connection between the premises of systemic family therapy and Buddhism, both recognizing that the perceiver and the perceived cannot be considered separately: the perceiver is inherently connected to and influences the perceived and vice versa. Watts encouraged the practice of family therapy, in which the individual is addressed—not alone—but in the context of relationships, society, and as Watts encouraged, the cosmos. Furthermore, Watts saw in family therapy techniques parallel to Buddhist traditions of koans that aim to identify and dissolve life's double binds through paradox. (p. 22)

Richards (2003) makes a similar observation regarding psychedelic research:

> When the man in the street, and even many mental health and religiously-trained professionals, hears the terms "entheogen" or "psychedelic drug," the image that comes to mind seems to be a rebellious teenager in a tie-dyed T-shirt with rose-colored glasses about to do something crazy, or waiting in an emergency room for attention. Few know about, or recall, the profound value placed upon experiences catalyzed by these substances as reported by respected academicians in the past, such as . . . Alan Watts. (pp. 145–146)

The selection of materials for the present volume was accordingly informed by four overlapping criteria, including Watts' (1) contributions to professional journals, monographs, and edited books, (2) papers presented at academic conferences and symposia, (3) works produced during periods of grant funding from the Franklin J. Matchette Foundation (1950) and Bollingen Foundation (1951–1953, 1962–1964), and (4) writings and lectures during his tenures at Seabury-Western Theological Seminary (1941–1944), Northwestern University (1944–1950), American Academy of Asian Studies (1951–1957), and Harvard University (1962–1964). The contents range from Watts' first academic journal article, published in 1941, to essays written in 1973, his final year of life. The works include materials appearing in the *Review of Religion*; *Journal of Religious Thought*; *Philosophy East and West*; *American Journal of Psychoanalysis*; *Journal of Humanistic Psychology*; *New Politics*; *The Psychedelic Review*; *California Law Review*; *Existential Psychiatry*; *Journal of Transpersonal Psychology*; *The Eastern Buddhist*; *Asian Study Monographs*; *Advent Papers*; and *Chicago Review*. Other offerings include conference and symposia presentations at Stanford University; University of California-San Francisco Medical Center; Central Washington State College; Society for the Arts, Religion, and Contemporary Culture; and Mount Saviour Monastery.

A second question, following from the first, implicates the issue of reliability: Does Watts' thinking count as a dependable voice or relevant topic of conversation within contemporary academe? There is in the second decade of the twenty-first century an identifiable renaissance of interest in Alan Watts. His work is garnering renewed attention from emerging scholars and established thinkers in psychology, philosophy, religion, history, art and literary theory. This notice includes affirmative and critical considerations of Watts in relation to transcultural studies (Chen, 2013; Wang, 2009; Williams, 2014; Wolter, 2013); Beat culture (Coupe, 2010); counterculture (Bond, 2014; Greer, 2014; Harvey & Goff, 2005; Kripal, 2007; Lasar, 2000; Lumish, 2009; Oldmeadow, 2004; Sjogren, 2013); Christianity (Copan, 2009; Dart, 2004; Keightley, 2012; King, 2001; Masi, 2015; Peach, 2011); metaphysics (Justesen & Seidler, 2013); ethics and education (Patterson, 2007); religion and film (D. L. Smith, 2014); psychology of religion (Fuller, 2008; Hood, 2012; Woodhead, 2001); religious autobiography (Duggan, 2014; Gausted, 2001); embodied spirituality (Brannigan, 2012; Gordon,

2015; Levering, 2012; Ostdiek, 2015; Rice, 2012; Spallier, 2012); psychedelics (Cunningham, 2007; Dickins, 2012; Fadiman, 2011; Fuller, 2000; Krippner, 2012; Metzner, 2012; Shipley, 2013); modern Buddhism (Denning, 2005; Lopez, 2002; McMahan, 2008); Buddhism vis-à-vis art (Munroe, 2009; L. Smith, 2011); American culture (Coleman, 2001; Garrett-Farb, 2015; Greer, 2011; D. L. Smith, 2010); psychotherapy (Columbus, 2015a; McCowen, Reibel, & Micozzi, 2010, pp. 41–48; Puhakka, 2012), and postcolonial studies (Brown, 2009; Iwamura, 2011; Masatsugu, 2008); Daoism in the West (Clarke, 2000; Cohen, 2015; Huang, 2012; Miller, 2006); peace and conflict studies (Bennett, 2014, 2015); medical history (Pickering, 2011); political thought (Guerin, 2004); phenomenology and hermeneutics (Columbus, 2012); consciousness and human development (Atsina, 2002; Gordon, 2012; LaHood, 2008, 2010; Loechel, 2014; Messerly, 2015; Pope, 2012); organizational behavior (Anderson, 2012); pagan studies (Chase, 2011, 2015); and postmodernism (Hungerford, 2010, p. 44; Shipley, 2012).

The nascence of the twenty-first-century Wattsian renaissance can be seen in such late twentieth-century works as Bartholomeusz (1998), Beidler (1994), Dunbar (1994), Helminiak, (1998, pp. 281–284), and Norrman (1999). While it is beyond the scope of this discussion to consider the above studies individually and in detail, they serve en masse to exemplify a growing body of scholarship acknowledging the current relevance—problematical and/or commendable—of Watts and his work. *In the Academy*, therefore, supplements contemporary and continuing scholarship on Alan Watts with 30 erudite offerings by Watts himself.

A third question begged from the preceding discussion concerns the issue of necessity: Is there a clear and present need for a comprehensive assemblage of Watts' academic works? *In the Academy* is organized with a view to the general arc of thinking by Watts due to prevailing disagreements concerning the developmental trajectory of his intellectual life. There are differing opinions concerning the degree of continuity versus change in comparison with his earlier and later works. One point of view is that Watts' later works were simply elaborative expressions of ideas, concepts, and categories acquired and developed early in his career (Ballantyne, 1989; Jackson, 1984; Snelling, 1987). "Surveying Watts' early writings," observed Jackson, "one is amazed at the degree to which he had already arrived at the basic ideas that he would elaborate on for the next thirty-five years. In many ways his books were to be so many variations on a limited number of themes" (p. 94). Yet Ruland (1975) described Watts' development as an "odyssey from Anglican theology, to meta-Catholic syncretism, and finally to his own version of an apophatic mysticism and Hindu pantheism" (p. 219).

Conversely, Nordstrom and Pilgrim (1980) treated the same corpus as a collection of disparate and inchoate materials hence critically implying an incomprehensible absence of trajectory: "In the works of Alan Watts one finds a bewildering array of self-ascribed epithets ranging all the way from guru, sha-man, Christian theologian, and philosopher, to mystic, showman, sensualist, and egotist" (p. 381). Some thinkers bypass the issue. Brannigan (1988), for example, emphasized a recurring theme—the transition of ego to Self—throughout the entirety Watts' work. Suligoj (1975) totalized and reduced the entirety of Watts' works down to a set of three propositions and various corollary statements. A contrasting observation made from a twenty-first-century vantage point is that Watts' mature offerings were qualitatively and creatively different from his earlier output in terms of his approach to various topics, selection of content, methods of analysis, and modes of discussion (Columbus, 2012).

Assessments differ also concerning the apex of Watts' thinking particularly with respect to when and how his philosophical vision was most vital and perceptive. Sadler (1974a, 1974b) points to the years from 1947 to 1958 when Watts was largely and readily associated with academic institutions. During this period, described by Sadler as Watts' "vintage years," he published six of his most influential books, including *Behold the Spirit: A Study in the Necessity of Mystical Religion* (1947) at the age of 32, *The Supreme Identity: An Essay on Oriental Metaphysic and the Christian Religion* (1950) at 35 years of age, *The Wisdom of Insecurity: A Message for an Age of Anxiety* (1951b) at age 36, *Myth and Ritual in Christianity* (1953c) at age 38, *The Way of Zen* (1957) at age 42, and *Nature, Man and Woman* (1958b/1970b) at age 43. Sadler (1974a) notes: "Out of the very tension between institutional conventions and his free spirit came his best work" (p. 121).

Yet Jolicoeur (2000) expands the range of Watts' "premiere periode" to include the years 1935 to 1958, and others point to Watts' freelance period in later life. David L. Smith (2010), for example, identifies the span of years from 1958 to 1966 during which Watts published the already cited *Nature, Man and Woman* (1958b/1970b), as well as *This is IT, and Other Essays on Zen and Spiritual Experience* (1960), *Psychotherapy East and West* (1961), *The Joyous Cosmology: Adventures in the Chemistry of Consciousness* (1962a), *The Two Hands of God: The Myths of Polarity* (1963c), *Beyond Theology: The Art of Godmanship* (1964a), and *The Book: On the Taboo Against Knowing Who You Are* (1966). The works produced by Watts during this phase of time, in Smith's view, "constitute his finest and most characteristic achievements" (p. 21). A fourth assessment is offered by Oldmeadow (2004) who identifies four texts (Watts, 1953c, 1957, 1961, 1975b) interspersed among Watts' total output reflecting "genuine scholarship . . . rigorous intellectual inquiry . . . [and] substance" (p. 262).

Finally, and as mentioned previously, Watts is commonly and popularly associated with Zen Buddhism. Yet of the 21 major books authored by Watts during his lifetime, including the posthumously published *Tao: The Watercourse Way* (1975b), only two texts—*The Spirit of Zen: A Way of Life, Work, and Art in the Far East* (1936) and *The Way of Zen* (1957)—concerned Buddhism per se. Most of his works focused on other topics or were much broader in scope, with various interdisciplinary emphases informing his particular subject matter. Thus in light of concerns about the arc, apex, and focus of Watts' work, *In the*

Academy is structured thematically and ordered chronologically therein. The text provides a database for readers to gauge comparisons and contrasts of Watts' developmental trajectories reflected in and across a range of topics, including language and mysticism (Part 1), Buddhism and Zen (Part 2), Christianity (Part 3), comparative religion (Part 4), psychedelics (Part 5), and psychology and psychotherapy (Part 6).

THE WHOLE AND ITS PARTS

Taken in its entirety *In the Academy* offers a compelling survey of Watts' scholarly efforts in a variety of pedagogic disciplines. The word "entirety" is here used advisedly. The intention is not to totalize the Wattsian corpus nor to suggest a complete unification of his work. This book instead brings into focus a collection of essays that are frequently, though not always, marginalized due to Watts' ubiquitous reputation as a nonacademic writer. The relegation of his academic materials to the conversational periphery has been called "the taboo against knowing Alan Watts" (Columbus & Rice, 2012b, pp. 4–6). Often upstaging Watts' more learned offerings is a dualistic dialogue of idolatry and iconoclasm reverberating in and resounding through conversations about him. Here one set of voices articulates and recapitulates Watts' "popular guru" reputation while an iconoclastic and skeptical constituency undercuts the adulation by dismissal of him in summary fashion. *In the Academy* is thus an attempt to add tone and volume to some routinely muffled aspects of Alan Watts' life and work.

PART I: LANGUAGE AND MYSTICISM

The relation of language to mysticism is central to understanding Alan Watts' mystical philosophy, and so the topic serves as a useful point of departure toward subsequent sections of the text in hand. Moreover, the role of language in structuring, expressing, and understanding first-person mystical experience is an ongoing debate within psychology, philosophy, religion and other academic specialties (Dible, 2010; Hood, 2012; Tyson, 2013). Two components of the debate are relevant here. First is the *problem of religious language*, that is to say, the extent to which human linguistic forms limit, afford, or nullify veridical claims about God and mystical transcendence (Reed, 2007; White, 2010). Second is the *problem of pure consciousness*, in other words, the extent to which mystical experiences are universally recognized (Forman, 1990, 1998, 1999) or structured by culturally determined modes of communication (Katz, 1978, 1983, 1992). Though a full accounting of Watts' position on language, consciousness, and mysticism is beyond the scope of the present discussion—see Brannigan (1977, 1988), Recoulley (1986), and Keightley (1986) for extended coverage—it may be said here that Watts employed apophatic *and* cataphatic languages toward expressing and talking about mystical experience (Keightley, 2012). Watts, furthermore, transitioned from a universal *philosophia perennis* early in his career (e.g., Watts, 1947, 1953c) to hermeneutical analyses of contextual horizons in the 1960s and beyond (e.g., Watts, 1966, 1975b; see Columbus, 2012).

The leadoff essay is a heretofore unpublished and unnamed piece written during Watts' 1950 sabbatical funded by the Franklin J. Matchette Foundation. Here it is assigned the title "On the Meaning and Relation of Absolute and Relative." Watts suggests that knowledge of what may be called "God" or "ultimate Reality" is discovered in the full embrace of finitude rather than struggling to flee the relative and finite world. Only through the most thorough acceptance of limitations and ignorance can one encounter the "mystery of the universe." Documents contained in the Franklin J. Matchette archive at the Wisconsin Historical Society indicate the piece was a work-for-hire modeled on Matchette's (1949) posthumously published *Outlines of a Metaphysics.* Early on, however, Watts radically departed from Matchette's vision, while adding supplementary pedagogic illustrations. In time, the project was terminated in favor of grant funding for *The Wisdom of Insecurity: A Message for an Age of Anxiety* (Watts, 1951).

"The Negative Way" was published during Watts' first year at the American Academy of Asian Studies. It is a brief tutorial on the meaning of "negation" in the metaphysics of Vedanta and Buddhism vis-à-vis positive affirmations of God in Christianity. The article appeared in the journal of the Vedanta Society of Southern California, *Vedanta and the West* (Watts, 1951a). The journal described Watts' essay as follows:

> Mr. Watts feels that a meeting of eastern and western religious viewpoints must rest upon a better understanding of their respective terminologies. He has attempted to help build such an understanding with his essay explaining the oriental custom of seeking to portray the infinite through negation. (In This Issue, 1951, n.p.)

"The Language of Metaphysical Experience: The Sense of Non-Sense" is a critical appraisal of logical philosophy's rejection of metaphysics as meaningless tautology. The essay was first presented at the 13th Conference on Science, Philosophy, and Religion held at Columbia University in 1952. (Watts also served as a discussant at the meeting. See Bryson, Finkelstein, Maciver, & Mckeon, 1954.) Records of the Conference, established in 1940 and continuing until 1968, are housed at the Jewish Theological Seminary in New York. An archive note reads:

> The conference constituted a response to the rise of totalitarianism in Europe. Its founding members [including Paul Tillich, Harold D. Lasswell, Franz Boas, Enrico Fermi, and Mortimer J. Adler] and their successors sought to create a framework for the preservation of democracy and intellectual freedom through the collaboration of

scholars from a wide variety of disciplines in the sciences and humanities. Conference members, many of whom blamed the development of "value-free" scholarship for the rise of European fascism, additionally hoped to synthesize traditional values and academic scholarship. (Historical Note, n.d.)

Watts' essay was subsequently published in 1953(b) by the *Journal of Religious Thought.*

"On Philosophical Synthesis" was published in *Philosophy East and West* (Watts, 1953d) as part of an ongoing series of reflections by eminent thinkers of the day (e.g., John Dewey, William Ernest Hocking, George Santayana, and D. T. Suzuki) concerning the possibility and viability of intercultural philosophy. As Chatterjee noted in 1960:

> The writers of these articles have not only expressed different but conflicting views. Some of them have held high hopes for a synthesis, or, at least for the significance of a synthesis between the philosophies of East and West. Others have contended that a synthesis between the two is impossible, and undesirable, too. (p. 99)

Watts' essay concerns problems of commensurability between Western philosophies of logic, and Buddhism, Taoism, and Hinduism, suggesting the former cannot understand the latter without admitting "that philosophy is more than logic, more than verbalization, to the point where philosophy can include the transformation of the very processes of the mind."

Concluding Part 1 is "Philosophy Beyond Words." Here Watts registers critical reflections on philosophy as rationalism, and asserts that philosophers can renew their "basic wondering" through embodied engagement and "sensuous apprehension" of existence. The essay was written circa 1972 and published posthumously (Watts, 1975a) in *The Owl of Minerva: Philosophers on Philosophy,* a text surveying perspectives of 18 prominent philosophers, including Karl Popper, Gabriel Marcel, Brand Blanchard, W. V. Quine, A. J. Ayer, and Herbert Marcuse, concerning the nature and function of contemporary philosophy. Bontempo and Odell (1975) observe that Watts' slant in this essay is less historical or pragmatic than it is reflective of an "activity approach to philosophy" as he objects to emphases placed by many academics on "philosophy as an intellectual activity" (p. 20).

PART 2: BUDDHISM AND ZEN

Alan Watts, along with D. T. Suzuki, is considered by historians of religion as a prime facilitator of Zen Buddhism for American culture in the twentieth century (Queen, Prothero, & Shattuck, 2009, p. 1048; Seager, 2013; Smith, 2010).

Watts began his studies of Zen in 1930 at the age of 15 while serving under the tutorage of a seminal figure of British and European Buddhism, Christmas (Toby) Humphreys (1901–1983). Humphreys established the Buddhist Lodge in 1924 as an auxiliary to the London office of the Theosophical Society, an esoteric religious group founded by Madame H. P. Blavatsky and Henry Steele Olcott in 1875. Humphreys later left the Theosophical Society, renamed the Lodge as the Buddhist Society, and remained president of the organization until his death. Guy (2000) notes that Humphreys, author of 15 books on Buddhism:

> made an important early attempt to take the voluminous history of Buddhist teachings and put them in an accessible and coherent form. There may be better sources of this information today, but there weren't then, and Humphreys is an important transitional figure [in the movement of Buddhism from Asia to Europe]. (n.p.)

Under Humphreys' mentorship, Watts edited the Lodge's journal, *Buddhism in England* (now *The Middle Way*), from 1936 to 1938, and wrote *The Spirit of Zen* (1936). Watts (1973a) later acknowledged: "Even though I now remonstrate, mildly, against some of Toby's interpretations of Buddhism, I shall love him always as the man who really set my imagination going and put me on my whole way of life" (p. 88).

After settling in New York City in 1938, Watts came under the sway of two formative figures in American Buddhism, Sokei-an Sasaki and Ruth Fuller (Everett) Sasaki, about whom he (1973a) wrote: "Much of what I learned from Sokei-an and Ruth has so become part of me that I cannot now sort it out" (p. 168). Sokei-an Sasaki (1882–1945) was a Zen master in the Rinzai lineage of Shokaku Shaku and Soyen Shaku. He is recognized as the first Japanese Zen teacher to reside permanently in the United States. Sokei-an founded the Buddhist Society of America (now the First Zen Institute of America) in New York City in 1930 where he offered private face-to-face teaching, public talks, and translated important Buddhist texts into English, including the *Record of Rinzai*, *The Platform Sutra*, and the *Mumonkon* made available to Watts for his early writings on Zen. Milstead (2014) described Sokei-an as "a vibrantly wise and funny man who was eager to take on the challenges of bringing Buddha's ancient teachings on no-self, impermanence, and emptiness to the materialistic, noisy, self-centered people of the United States" (p. 213). Watts (1973a) experienced Sokei-an as a kindred spirit: "I felt that he was on the same team as I; that he bridged the spiritual and the earthy, and that he was as humorously earthy as he was spiritually awakened" (p. 168).

Ruth Fuller (Everett) Sasaki (1892–1967) was second wife of Sokei-an Sasaki, mother of Watts' first wife (Eleanor Everett), and primary patron of the First Zen Institute. Ruth studied briefly with D. T. Suzuki in 1930 and with Nanshinken Roshi at Kyoto's Nanzenji monastery in 1932. She met Sokei-an in

1933, began formal Zen studies with him in 1938, and they married in 1944. Ruth moved to Japan in 1949 for further Zen training, becoming in 1958 the first Westerner (and only woman) to be a priest of a Rinzai Zen Buddhist temple. Founder of the First Zen Institute of America in Japan, she was instrumental in facilitating translations of important Buddhist texts into English (Stirling, 2006). Her book, *Zen Dust*, coauthored with Isshu Miura, "remains the single-most important English-language introduction to koan study in the Japanese manner" (Ford, 2006, p. 70).

Watts published two major books on Zen Buddhism during his lifetime: *The Spirit of Zen* (1936) and *The Way of Zen* (1957). The former text, though often criticized as simply derivative of D. T. Suzuki's work, was according to Humphreys (1994) "the first major attempt by a Westerner to write on the subject" (p. 15). The latter text was an important milestone for the field of Buddhist Studies in that Watts challenged D. T. Suzuki's ahistorical narratives by locating Zen within a temporal-developmental trajectory (Hurvitz, 1958; McCarthy, 1957). Praised by Soto Zen teacher, Shunryu Suzuki, as "a great Bodhisattva" (Chadwick, 1999, p. 381), Watts' writings and lectures framed the American conversation about Zen from the 1950s into the 1970s (Smith, 2010; Swearer, 1973). Yet the prominent status of Watts within twentieth-century American Buddhism is not without ambiguity and skepticism. Watts, for example, was criticized for not gaining firsthand experiences of Buddhism in Asia until 1961, *after* writing his major texts on Zen (Ballantyne, 1989; see Watts, 1973a, pp. 417–453, for a narrative account of his journeys to Japan). Also, the late Philip Kapleau (1912–2004), a teacher in the Sanbo Kyodon tradition of Zen, and Louis Nordstrom who continues teaching in the White Plum lineage of Hakuyu Taizan Maezumi, charged Watts with misinterpreting certain historical aspects of Zen Buddhism, and misjudging the value of *zazen* (Kapleau, 1966, pp. 21–22, 83–84; Nordstrom & Pilgrim, 1980). However, see Watts (1975b, p. 89n15) for a brief reply to Kapleau (1966), and see Columbus (1985) for a reply to Nordstrom and Pilgrim (1980).

In the twenty-first century, four perspectives on Watts in relation to Buddhism are noticeable. One critical view is that Watts' writings are informed by idealized and stereotyped constructions of "the East" which compromise their ecological validity (Iwamura, 2011). Second is the view that Watts arrogated Buddhism and constructed a philosophical commodity for consumption by an American constituency alienated from Cold War politics (Matsatsugu, 2008). Third is that Watts was signaling an Occidentalism, that is to say, he converted extant Japanese appraisals of American rationalism and materialism into therapeutic critiques of Cold War culture in America (Brown, 2009). Finally, Watts is seen as proffering a "modern Buddhism" that is divergent from tradition, but congruent with the spiritual sensibilities of contemporary Western life (Lopez, 2002; McMahan, 2008). (A fifth perspective relating Buddhist practice to a psychedelic ethos is identified in Part 5.)

The six writings by Alan Watts here compiled under the rubric of Buddhism and Zen were published between 1941 and 1963. The initial essay is "The Problem of Faith and Works in Buddhism." This 1941 article, written for Columbia University's *Review of Religion*, was the first-ever academic journal article by Watts. The essay is an exploration of self-reliance (*jiriki*) and spiritual conviction (*tariki*) in their relationship to Enlightenment in Mahayana Buddhism. As Watts (1973a) recounted in his autobiography, the essay had "momentous consequences" as it presaged his perennialist approach to Christianity:

> I saw that . . . Zen, Jodo Shinshu, and Christianity were all approaching the same point by different routes. It might thus be possible to develop a deeper and more intelligible form of Christianity which would, however, have to bypass that religion's . . . claims [to exclusivity]. (p. 177)

The second writing, dedicated to Ruth Fuller Sasaki and simply titled "Zen," is an introductory tutorial on (1) the historical background of Zen in Indian and Chinese religion, (2) the influence of Daoism on Buddhism, (3) the role of *mondo*, *zazen*, and *koans* in Zen practice, and (4) the cultural effects of Zen in Japan. The essay was an invited lecture to the Department of Religion at Beloit College in 1945, and subsequently revised and expanded in 1948 as a corrective update for *The Spirit of Zen* (1936). In a foreword to the essay, Watts (1948) noted his indebtedness to D. T. Suzuki and Sokei-an Sasaki for their English translations of Zen texts, and to Ruth Fuller Sasaki who provided and discussed with Watts various transcriptions of lectures by Sokei-an.

"The Way of Liberation in Zen Buddhism" was the first contribution to the short-lived *Asian Study Monographs* series, published by the American Academy of Asian Studies (AAAS) in 1955. Located at the intersection of Buddhism and psychology, the essay is an elucidation of how Zen practitioners resolve conflictual paradox into unity (nonduality). A preliminary to both *The Way of Zen* and *Psychotherapy East and West*, Watts wrote the essay in light of his consultations on Gregory Bateson's double-bind communication research (see Pickering, 2011), publishing it one year *before* Bateson, Jackson, Haley, and Weakland (1956) published their classic essay, "Toward a Theory of Schizophrenia." Watts' monograph is yet another example in which he was one step ahead of the cutting-edge thinkers of his era. A review in *Manas* described the essay as "the kind of thinking that may result when psychological problems and questions are approached with philosophical conviction and commitment" (Study of the Mind, 1955).

Next is the famous 1958(a) *Chicago Review* essay on "Beat Zen, Square Zen, and Zen," based on a series of lectures given by Watts at the University of Chicago in 1957. The article is a critical appraisal of problematic appropriations of Zen Buddhism in Judeo-Christian culture, and thus anticipates a genre of postmodern scholarship that deconstructs European and North American approaches to Asian cultures and histories toward uncovering hidden assumptions and biases. Due to Mahoney's (1958) erroneous impression that Watts sided with the "squares," the essay was subsequently twice revised, first as a tract for Lawrence Ferlinghetti's City Lights Books, then as chapter in *This is It, and Other Essays on Zen and Spiritual Experience* (Watts, 1960).

"Zen and Politics" is a 1962(c) commentary on political implications of Buddhist ethics. Published in *New Politics: A Journal of Socialist Thought*, this brief essay is a rebuttal to Braun's (1961) "The Politics of Zen." Braun argued that Zen Buddhism, including Watts' (1958, 1960) work, is a "mysticism that denies the reality of moral choice" and therefore supports problematic states of affairs "with dogmatic certainty" (p. 188), including, for example, World War II atrocities. Watts rejoins that Braun's is a fallacious argument that confuses categorically the moral ends of Christianity with the practice of Zen (see also, Braun's 1962 response). The debate foreshadows later controversies concerning the role of Zen in Japan during World War II. See, for example, Victoria (2003, 2006) and the reply by Sato (2008).

The final essay on Buddhism and Zen is Watts' 1963(b) "Prefatory Essay" written for a reissue of D. T. Suzuki's *Outlines of Mahayana Buddhism*. Suzuki, as is well-known, was a formative influence on Watts' early thinking about Zen. See, for example, Watts' (1967) reminiscence in the wake of Suzuki's death (see also, Watts' brief 1954 review of Suzuki's works). In the present essay, Watts identifies and elaborates consistencies between Mahayana Buddhism and certain strains of thought in twentieth-century science and philosophy. Beyond any consistencies, however, Watts suggests the main contribution of Mahayana Buddhism to Western culture is that, with committed Buddhist practice, one realizes "the compassion of one who knows that, in some way, all suffering is his own suffering, and all 'sentient beings' the disguises of his own inmost nature."

PART 3: CHRISTIANITY

Alan Watts' religious discernment and spiritual formation within the Church of England and the wider Anglican Communion are often overshadowed by his prevalent association with Zen Buddhism. Nurtured in a devout Anglo-Catholic family and educated at the kindergarten school of Saint Nicholas Church in Chislehurst (1921–1922), Saint Hugh's School in Bickley (1922–1928), and King's School at Canterbury (1928–1932), Watts "had been immersed in the Anglican tradition from birth until his late teens to a degree that is hardly imaginable today" (Keightley, 2012, p. 44; see Watts, 1973a, pp. 53–121, for autobiographical reflections on his Anglican upbringing). After relocating to New York City, Watts accepted spiritual direction from Fr. Grieg Taber at the Episcopal Church of Saint Mary the Virgin before enrolling at Seabury-Western Theological Seminary in Evanston, Illinois in 1941. Sans an undergraduate degree, Watts was admitted to the Seminary as a "special student" in the graduate school, on the strength of his previous reading, research, and writing (e.g., Watts, 1936, 1937, 1940). After one year of class attendance, he spent his remaining two years of seminary engaging tutorials and independent study where, Watts (1973a) recounts, he:

> combed through Patristics, reading Clement and Origen, the remains of the Gnostic writings, Saint Athanasius, Saint Irenaeus, Saint Gregory Nazianzus, Saint John of Damascus, and the apocryphal literature excluded from the New Testament. Then I went heavily into Russian theology—Solovyev, Berdyaev, Bulgakov, and the Hesychasts—and thereafter became fascinated with the architectural magnificence of Saint Thomas Aquinas and his modern interpreters, Jacques Maritain and Etienne Gilson.
>
> There followed mystical and ascetic theology: almost all the classics from Saint Dionysius to Leon Bloy, as well as the historians and commentators, Bremond, Underhill, von Hugel. Inge, Dom Cuthbert Butler, Dom John Chapman, and Garrigou-Lagrange. (pp. 206–207)

Watts received the Sacrament of Holy Orders on the Feast of the Ascension, May 18, 1944, and subsequently obtained a master's degree in sacred theology from Seabury-Western in 1948. After his 1944 ordination and until his resignation from the Church in 1950, Watts served Bishop Wallace Conklin of Chicago as examining chaplain for candidates seeking Holy Orders, while also stationed as priest, theologian, and spiritual counselor at Canterbury House, located on the grounds of Northwestern University. Watts rapidly became a rising star on the Northwestern University campus. According to Ellwood (1997):

> Canterbury House was the scene of nonstop bull sessions and unforgettable lectures in which Watts, as always, managed to make his listeners feel they were being let in on some wonderful cosmic secret. His Sunday liturgical enactments had the color of great theater and the mood of playful dance more than of courtly rite. (p. 169)

The signature accomplishments by Watts as priest and theologian are the publications of *Behold the Spirit* (1947) and *The Supreme Identity* (1950). The former text was lauded by reviewers for exposing neglect of Christian mysticism in mid-twentieth-century theological study and practice of Anglo-Catholicism and Protestantism (Akhilananda, 1948; Gowen, 1949; Steere, 1949). The latter text, considered by the *Dictionary of Modern American Philosophers* as "probably his most substantial work of scholarship and sustained, serious philosophical discourse" (Ellwood, 2005, p. 2539), was praised for its contributions to constructive dialogue between Christian and non-Christian religions (Keene, 1952; Morris, 1951; Waterhouse, 1953).

Part 3 of *In the Academy* contains four writings on Christianity published in the mid-1940s during Watts' tenure as an Episcopal priest. They were written prior to the publication of *Behold the Spirit* (1947) and are preliminary to that text as each essay concerns an aspect of mystical union between God and humanity. The initial offering is Watts' 1944 translation of *"Theologia Mystica, being the treatise of Saint Dionysius pseudo-Areopagite on Mystical Theology, together with the first and fifth Epistles."* "With few exceptions," Watts (1944) noted in a Foreword, the translation "follows the text given in Migne's *Patrologiae Graecae*, vol. 3. This text has been compared with the earliest version, by John Scotus Erigena, in Migne's *Patrologaie Latinae*, vol. 122." Published as a monograph by Holy Cross Press, Watts begins with an introductory tutorial on the apophatic approach to mysticism and mystical experience.

In "The Case for God," Watts establishes the premise that God is revealed in the world through evidence of the senses and reasoned argument. He suggests "it is not presumptuous to attempt to prove the existence of God by reason. It is, on the contrary, the duty of reason and the chief purpose for which this faculty is given us." Watts offers details of the five proofs of God as described by St. Thomas in *Summa Theologica*, and considers what the evidence for God suggests about God's nature. Three particularly significant facets of divine nature deduced from reason via human experience are identified: God is life, God is being, and God is love. The essay was published by Holy Cross Press in the *Roodcroft Papers* series in 1946(a).

Next is "The Meaning of Priesthood" in light of Anglo-Catholicism. The essay was published in 1946(c) in *Advent Papers*, a monograph series inaugurated in 1943 by Boston's Church of the Advent, with an editorial board including, most notably, philosopher John D. Wild, psychologist Gordon W. Allport, and theologians John B. Coburn and Adelaide T. Case. An advertisement in *The Living Church* describes the series as "designed to bring to our people the richness and depth of traditional Catholic Christianity as it has been preserved in our free and democratic Anglican Catholicism." Watts, the ad continues, "writes comprehensively though compactly of the priestly function—it's setting in the church's history and teaching, its work, its opportunities and privileges, and also its problems" (The Advent Papers, 1946, p. 5).

The final writing on Christianity is "The Christian Doctrine of Marriage." Watts suggests that "Holy Matrimony is the highest earthly analogy of that creative union of God and man, Christ and Church, which is the end and fulfillment of human life." First differentiating Agape love from erotic love, Watts then follows-up with practical applications of Agape love to three realms of marriage: body, mind, and spirit. The monograph was published in 1946(b) as a *Canterbury Club Tract* by the Episcopal Church at the University of Colorado-Boulder. Note that Watts, as an Anglican priest in 1946, was referring in this piece to marriages between men and women. See Watts (1979) for his later perspective on gay and lesbian relationships.

PART 4: COMPARATIVE RELIGION

Alan Watts was awarded an Honorary Doctor of Divinity from the University of Vermont in 1958 for *"scholarly contributions marking him as one of our country's outstanding authorities on comparative religion"* (Dykhuizen & Borgmann, 1958, p. 1, italics added). Indeed, beyond his studies of Buddhism and Christianity per se, "comparative religion" may best echo the overarching tenor of Watts' writings and lectures. His early comparative thinking was informed by a *philosophia perennis* with a priori assumptions that religion and spirituality transcend exoteric contingencies of culture and context toward esoteric and universal realms of mystical experience (Watts, 1947, 1950, 1951b, 1953c). As Watts (1973) explained in his autobiography, by adopting the approach of perennial philosophy "one could go behind the screen of literal dogma to the inner meaning of symbols, to the level at which Eckhart and Shankara, Saint Teresa and Ramakrishna, Saint Dionysius and Nagarjuna are talking the same language" (p. 180).

Watts' early *philosophia perennis* was, no doubt, influenced in part by Christmas Humphrey's theosophical leanings (Sutcliffe, 2007, p. 61) and, perhaps most notably, by the tutorage from 1934 to 1936 of Serbian philosopher Dimitrije Mitrinovic (1887–1953). A formative thinker in the pre–World War I Young Bosnia movement and subsequent New Europe Group and New Britain Movement (Rigby, 2006), Mitrinovic integrated mystical metaphysics and transformative political-social philosophy (Rutherford, 1987). Watts (1973a) especially recounts a discourse by Mitrinovic "in which he explained the complementation of the principle of unity and the principle of differentiation in the universe. . . . He showed me that acute differences positively manifest unity, and that you cannot have the one without the other" (p. 126). There is, in other words, "the mutual interdependence of all things and events (p. 126).

In the 1960s Watts transitioned away from perennial philosophy as a point of departure for comparative religion. Spurring the transition was a rising tide of relativistic thinking in academic discourse, including postmodernism and social constructionism, which challenged the veracity of absolutistic and universalistic epistemological claims. In this way of thinking, people are embedded in their particular situations—culture, history, gender, language, education, spiritual practice—which makes it difficult for them to entirely comprehend differing religious systems and texts without the distorting effects of bias and prejudice. Seeking to overcome the limited vision of contextualized knowledge, Watts (1963c, 1964a, 1966, 1975b) turned toward hermeneutical analyses exploring interconnections and disjunctions between localized narratives. Through this kind of interpretive study, one arrives at an expanded awareness and comprehension of perspectives via the dialectical rotation of differing vantage points.

Four texts are excellent examples of Watts' hermeneutical turn in the 1960s and beyond. First is *Psychotherapy East and West* (Watts, 1961/1969) in which Watts engaged transcultural comparisons between (1) psychotherapy and

(2) Buddhism, Daoism, and Hinduism toward uncovering the "philosophical unconscious" of Western therapeutic systems (Columbus, 2015b). In *Beyond Theology* (1964) and *The Book* (1966), Watts employed hermeneutical rules of analysis to explore horizons of self and cosmos (Columbus, 2012). Watts' final book, *Tao: The Watercourse Way* (1975), is an exploration of historical, cultural, and personal horizons vis-à-vis contemplative Daoism. Watts' analysis is a historical hermeneutic in that he seeks to understand what the "far-off echoes" of fifth- and fourth-century B.C. Daoism mean to the contemporary state of affairs. The analysis is a cultural hermeneutic in that he seeks to "interpret and clarify the principles of *Lao-tzu, Chuang-tzu*, and *Lieh-tzu*" in relation to Euro-American thinking. The text also is a personal hermeneutic because, writes Watts, "I am . . . interested in how these ancient writings reverberate on the harp of my own brain, which has, of course, been tuned to the scales of Western culture" (p. xvi). Note, however, that Watts was roundly criticized by perennial philosophers for his transition to hermeneutics. Vis-à-vis *Beyond Theology*, for example, Perry (1972), rejoined:

> Watts . . . sets forth the pattern of this transition in *Beyond Theology* . . . , a crazy pastiche of esoteric insights and false deductions, yet typically symptomatic of the ills to which so much of the pseudo-spiritual flesh of our times is heir. (p. 176)

The quartet of essays on comparative religion contained in Part 4 were initially presented at various symposia in the 1960s during Watts' hermeneutic phase, and subsequently published in an assortment of academic venues. "Worship in Sacrament and Silence" was offered in 1964 at the third Symposium on Human Values, an annual conference hosted by Central Washington State College. The 1964 symposium theme centered on the meaning of worship. Juxtaposing Christian worship with Hindu epistemology, Watts explored various themes and variations on the sacred character of communal liturgy. The presentation was published (Watts, 1971b) in the symposia proceedings, *A College Looks at American Values, Vol. 1*, edited by E. H. Odell.

In "Western Mythology: Its Dissolution and Transformation," Watts explores some experiential implications of paradigmatic transitions away from patriarchal-theistic myths of Judeo-Christianity toward Newtonian-mechanistic myths of natural science, and finally to quantum physics. The piece was presented at a 1968 symposium on "Myth and Dream" sponsored by the Society for the Arts, Religion, and Contemporary Culture, "a multi-disciplinary professional society which provides the occasion and the resources for bringing together persons from diverse professional backgrounds to consider basic issues of human conflict and community" (Society, 1970, p. 6). The essay was published (Watts, 1970b) in the symposium proceedings, edited by Joseph Campbell, titled *Myths, Dreams, and Religion*.

"The Future of Religion" was presented at a 1968 lecture series on "human values in a technological society" at Stanford University. The speakers were urged to consider and offer new paradigmatic norms for the approaching new century vis-à-vis the individual, technology, and society. Essays of the lecture series were published in *Toward Century 21: Technology, Society, and Human Values*, edited by C. S. Wallia. In a foreword to the text, psychologist Ernest R. Hilgard (1970) wrote:

> If this book does nothing else than give us a sense of choice, it will have served its purpose; for if we are free to choose, we shall certainly make our choice for a better world for those who will follow after us. (p. xii)

Watts (1970a) chose to consider the influx of Buddhist, Daoist, and Hindu mysticisms into American culture, and their future bearing on Christian relationships to God.

The final work on comparative religion, "Unity in Contemplation," was given at Word Out of Silence: A Symposium on World Spiritualities, sponsored by the Center for Spiritual Studies and held at Mount Saviour Monastery in 1972. Symposium essays were published in a 1974 issue of *Cross Currents*. Symposium editor, John-David Robinson (1974), called the venture "an invitation to the 'one-world spirituality' emerging in our time" (p. 133). Watts' (1974b) essay served to explore the paradox of human limitation as the juncture for spiritual insight. He contended that methods and practices of religious mysticism, either Eastern or Western, are designed to bring individuals to their human spiritual limits where Divine Wisdom is encountered. For discussion of Watts' essay, see "Responses to Alan Watts" (1974).

PART 5: PSYCHEDELICS

The *Current Biography Yearbook* (Moritz, 1963) described Alan Watts as a philosopher exploring the *catalytic impact* of Buddhism, Daoism, and Hinduism in the West. This description of Watts is perhaps most apt in relation to his writings on psychedelics where he integrated natural and social science field theory with Hindu mythology and Zen Buddhism toward understanding mystical implications of psychoactive substances such as LSD and psilocybin. According to the *New Westminster Dictionary of Christian Spirituality*, Watts was "one of the most important and influential writers" on the relations of psychedelics and spiritual growth in the 1960s (Leech, 2005, p. 255). As Krippner (2012) explains, the prevailing behaviorist, neobehaviorist, and psychoanalytic paradigms of the 1950s and 1960s were unequipped to handle altered modes of awareness inherent to psychedelic experiences beyond the categories of pathology and disorder. Watts, among others, offered nuanced phenomenological and interpretive accounts providing "optimistic and comprehensive" perspectives on psychedelic experiences while also legitimating their ontological status.

Between 1958 and 1963 Watts participated in four psychopharmacological studies on psychedelics, including research at the University of California-Los Angeles; the Langley-Porter Psychiatric Institute at the University of California San Francisco Medical Center; University of California—Irvine; and Timothy Leary's Psychedelic Research Project at Harvard University's Center for Personality Research where he served also as an editorial advisor to *The Psychedelic Review*. Based on these studies and his own personal experiments, Watts' perspective on the relations of psychedelics to spiritual growth evolved over time, from skepticism (1958/1970, p. 78n11) to mild enthusiasm (Watts, 1960/1973b, 1962a), and, finally, to guarded optimism (Watts, 1973a).

Reactions to Watts' writings on psychedelics were of a binary sort. He was, on one hand, lauded for his qualitative descriptions and interpretations of psychedelic experience (Gorham, 1963; Leary & Alpert 1962/1970; Metzner, 1968) as they proved valuable for revising psychological understandings of human affect (Collier, 1966) and personality (Unger, 1963). On the other hand, he was criticized for misinterpreting ego *regression* as ego *transcendence* (Gordon, 1970; Rascke, 1980), and for reifying Hindu and Buddhist interpretations of psychedelic experience (Masters & Houston, 1966). Watts' qualitative work on psychedelics nevertheless remains pertinent as archival data for theory, pedagogy, and research (Fadiman, 2011; Grof, 1988; Merkur, 1998; Slattery, 2011), and in contemporary analyses of psychedelic experience in relation to psychospiritual narratives (Dickins, 2012; Kripal, 2007), Buddhist practice (Cunningham, 2007), and postmodern thinking (Fuller, 2000; Shipley, 2012).

Part 5 centers on a group of four essays concerning psychedelics written by Watts between 1963 and 1971. The first essay, "The Individual as Man/ World," is an elaboration of commensurability between organism-environment field theory and subjective mystical experiences of nonduality. The essay was offered as a colloquium presentation to the Department of Social Relations at Harvard University on April 12, 1963, and published in the inaugural issue of *The Psychedelic Review* (Watts, 1963a). A *Review* editorial (1963) notes: "Philosophical studies exploring the epistemological and metaphysical implications of increased flexibility of consciousness are needed. Alan Watts' essay on the philosophical problems arising out of the possibility of increased control of the mind delineates one of the major themes" (p. 4).

The next essay is titled "A Psychedelic Experience: Fact or Fantasy?" Here Watts critically appraises psychiatric nomenclature on psychedelics, describes the phenomenology of psychedelic experience, and considers the implications of the experience in light of field theory and Hindu philosophy. The essay was written and published per the invitation of David Solomon for his edited volume on *LSD: The Consciousness-Expanding Drug* (Watts, 1964b). Cohen (1965) described Watts' essay as "an illuminating article" that "finds Watts consolidating his previous thinking and successfully shaking-up the psychiatric cosmology, always a salutary exercise." Watts, Cohen continued, "exposes all too well those acceptable myths which we, in our time-bound existence, label as truths, and our unfortunate descriptions of what is culturally unacceptable in terms of disease or aberration" (p. 408).

In "Psychedelics and Religious Experience," Watts describes qualities of consciousness evoked by psychedelic substances, and discusses objections to their use which, he suggests, arise mainly from disjunctions between the values of the mystical counterculture and the conventional, secular and religious standards of Western society. The essay was presented at the National Symposium on Psychedelic Drugs and Marijuana sponsored by the Illinois State Medical Society in cooperation with the American Medical Association in April 1968, and published in the same year by *California Law Review* (Watts, 1968) in a special issue on drugs and the law.

The final essay on psychedelics is titled "Ordinary Mind is the Way." In this brief essay, Watts describes and comments on four distinct stages in the temporal-phenomenological trajectory of a psychedelic experience. Alluding tacitly to Case 19 of *The Mumonkon* (see, e.g., Shibayama, 1974), Watts suggests that "ordinary consciousness is the supreme form of awakening." The essay was included in a literary symposium on "Drugs and Buddhism" published by *The Eastern Buddhist* (Watts, 1971a), including essays by D. T. Suzuki, Ray Jordan, Ueda Shizutsu, Richard Leavitt, and Robert Aitken. Cunningham (2007) notes the symposium marked a somewhat official divide between the psychedelic community and Zen Buddhists, as most of the essays argued that psychedelics were an obstacle, rather than an aid, to Buddhist practice.

PART 6: PSYCHOLOGY AND PSYCHOTHERAPY

Alan Watts was a trailblazer in humanistic and transpersonal psychologies. *The legacy of Asia and Western Man* (Watts, 1937) and *The Meaning of Happiness* (Watts, 1940) were among the earliest texts exploring relations between modern psychology and wisdom traditions of Asia. Watts' early psychological writings were inspired by the tutorage (1936–1938) of psychiatrist Eric Graham Howe (1896–1975), a cofounder of the famous Tavistock Clinic. Howe remarkably integrated spiritual practice and existential-phenomenology into psychoanalysis and psychotherapy, controversial moves in the early decades of the twentieth century (Stranger, 2012). Watts attended weekly discussions at Howe's Harley Street office. The meetings included Richard Arman Gregory, an astronomy professor of the University of London; Philip Metman, a Dutch psychiatrist and eventual founding member of the Society of Analytical Psychology in London who "seemed to understand everything about dreams and symbolism (Watts, 1973a, p. 132); and Frederic Spiegelberg, an Asian Studies scholar and philosopher who later hired Watts at the American Academy of Asian Studies in 1951. Watts (1973a) wrote of his relationship with Howe: "I was not his patient. He was simply a genial, dignified, and reassuring doctor who let me in on his mind" (p. 131).

While stationed at the American Academy of Asian Studies (1951–1957), Watts was among the first mid-twentieth-century thinkers offering courses and colloquia on psychology beyond the conventional models of psychoanalysis and behaviorism. The American Academy of Asian Studies, predecessor of the California Institute of Integral Studies, was founded in 1951 via financial backing from entrepreneur Louis Gainsborough as "the first graduate school in the United States exclusively devoted to a study of Asia" (Subbiondo, 2011, p. 12). In addition to Watts (who served as Dean of the Academy from 1953 to 1956), faculty included Frederic Spiegelberg, Haridas Chaudhuri, C. P. Ramaswamy Aiyar, Judith Tyberg, Tokwan Tada, and Rom Landau. According to Watts (1973a), "we were concerned with the practical transformation of consciousness, with the actual living out of the Hindu, Buddhist, and Taoist ways of life at the level of high mysticism" (p. 286). Subbiondo (2011) notes: "Through his scholarly reputation and personal connections, Watts positioned the Academy to be a principle meeting place for artists, writers, teachers, activists and practitioners of the emerging counter-culture movement of the San Francisco Renaissance" (p. 12). Moreover, Subbiondo points out, "Watts played a critical role in developing the Academy's weekly colloquia that attracted many of San Francisco's leading . . . psychotherapists and scholars as well as visiting guests like D. T. Suzuki" (p. 12).

Moreover, Watts advised Gregory Bateson's research team concerning their revolutionary studies on communicational paradox (Pickering, 2011), and he expanded the famous "double-bind theory" to cosmic levels of analysis (e.g., Watts, 1961, 1964, 1966). His *Psychotherapy East and West* (Watts, 1961), considered foundational to the emergence of transpersonal psychology (Bankart, 2003), has been called "possibly one of the most influential texts of the American psychotherapeutic counterculture" (Taylor, 2003, p. 185; see also, Columbus, 2015b). Watts presented the first-ever seminar at Esalen Institute in January 1962, thereby launching what became known as the Human Potential Movement. He was, finally, a founding editorial board member of the *Journal of Transpersonal Psychology* in 1969, and his applications of phenomenological modes of analysis (e.g., Watts, 1951b, 1966) anticipated later methodological developments in humanistic and transpersonal psychology (Columbus, 2012).

Part 6 contains seven writings by Watts on psychology and psychotherapy. The first essay, published in the *American Journal of Psychoanalysis* (Watts, 1953a), is "Asian Psychology and Modern Psychiatry." The piece contains preliminary, large-scale reflections on the similarities and differences between (1) Buddhism, Hinduism, Daoism, and (2) Western psychiatry, psychotherapy and transformations of mind. The essay is informed by an experimental seminar on "The Application of Asian Psychology to Modern Psychiatry" conducted by Watts in collaboration with Frederic Spiegelberg and Haridas Chaudhuri at the American Academy of Asian Studies in 1951.

In "Convention, Conflict, and Liberation: Further Observations on Asian Psychology and Modern Psychiatry," Watts considers processes of acculturation and psychological emancipation as understood through the lens of psychiatry in the West, Hinduism in India, and Daoism in China. Watts elaborates several conflicts arising out of socialization processes and cultural expectations in the West, while noting that certain "Asian societies provide optional means for relieving people of the warping effects of their acculturation and upbringing, which give them inward liberation (*moksha*) from the conventions which they have been compelled to learn." The essay was published in the *American Journal of Psychoanalysis* in 1956.

"Eternity as the Unrepressed Body" is a 1959 book review of Norman O. Brown's *Life Against Death: The Psychoanalytical Meaning of History*. Watts describes and elaborates Brown's effort as a meta-analysis of Freud's psychoanalytic theory—a sort of "psychoanalysis of psychoanalysis"—while adding his own critique of Freud into the mix. Freud, Watts suggests, "was at heart a moralist who, despite his brilliant diagnosis, did not like what he found and could not bring himself to that *love* of his own nature which would be the necessary condition for reconciling man to himself." The review was published in *Etc: A Review of General Semantics*.

"Oriental and Occidental Approaches to the Nature of Man" is a brief comparative analysis of Anglo-Saxon Protestant and Daoist views on human nature, values, and morality. The paper was part of "A Symposium on Human Values" organized by Lawrence N. Solomon of the Western Behavioral Sciences Institute at the 1961 meeting of the California State Psychological Association, and published by the *Journal of Humanistic Psychology* (Watts, 1962a). Other papers of the human values symposium were offered by Charlotte Buhler, Herbert Fingarette, and Wolfgang Lederer. See Maslow (1962) for commentary.

In "The Woman in Man," Watts outlines aspects of patriarchal culture preventing recognition and appreciation by men of sensibilities typically labeled as "feminine." He then considers "masculinity" and "femininity" with reference to their adaptive value for men and women. The paper was presented at a forum on "The Spectrum of Femininity" conducted at the Third Symposium on Man and Civilization hosted by the University of California San Francisco Medical Center in January 1963, and published in *The Potential of Woman*, edited by Seymour M. Farber and Roger H. L. Wilson (Watts, 1963d). For a panel discussion of Watts' presentation plus other papers in "The Spectrum of Femininity" forum, see Pribram, Howe, Money, and Watts (1963).

"An Interview with Alan Watts" was published in a 1969 issue of *Existential Psychiatry*. The conversation, with Philip D. Ungerer, managing editor of the journal, covers three primary subjects. The first topic concerns the relations of human alienation and technological development as expressed in ecological degradation and war. The second topic covers the state of clinical psychiatry circa 1969. Third, Watts expounds on the political and social upheavals afflicting America in the 1960s.

The final essay is "Psychotherapy and Eastern Religion: Metaphysical Bases of Psychiatry." Watts considers intellectual assumptions underlying Western psychotherapy affecting the understanding, fear and acceptance of death. Ironically, the essay was given as an invited address at Forest Hospital in Des Plains, Illinois, in January 1973. It was the month of his birth, in the year of his death. Watts had been living with a problematic heart condition, and may have known of his deteriorating health. The essay was published posthumously in the *Journal of Transpersonal Psychology* (Watts, 1974a).

ALAN WATTS RECONSIDERED

In the Academy offers a compendium of 30 writings and lectures by Alan Watts. The materials are divided among six pedagogic themes, including language and mysticism; Buddhism and Zen; Christianity; comparative religion; psychedelics; and psychology and psychotherapy. As the text marks the centenary of Watts' birth and serves to commemorate his life and work, it also allows an opportunity to reconsider the three epithets—popularizer, guru, and philosophical entertainer—commonly attached to his legacy. Each of the labels seems at first glance to reinforce the familiar theme that Alan Watts was a writer for the masses but not for the scholar. The popularity of Watts' books and lectures among general audiences cannot be denied, and some contemporary thinkers suggest the sustained salience over decades of the popularizer label on Watts may be due, not only to his literary acumen and charismatic personality, but also to the wide variety of media platforms extending his work beyond self-selecting readers and listeners (Iwamura, 2011; Siff, 2015). Also irrefutable is that the "popularizer" label affixed to Watts often holds pejorative connotations for academic specialists who view the accessibility and broad appeal of his writings as inherently compromising of scholarly rigor. Yet, as Roszak (1969/1995) observed, "too often such aristocratic stricture comes from those who have risen above popularization by the device of restricting themselves to a subject matter that preserves its purity only because it has no conceivable relevance to anything beyond the interests of a small circle of experts" (p. 133).

An alternative understanding of the "popularizer" epithet attached to Watts is illuminated in light of the present text. Without belaboring the point, a case can be made that Watts was a polymath inhabiting the interfacial margins of disparate academic disciplines—as between religion and psychology, Buddhist studies and theology, or philosophy and psychopharmacology—toward affording conversations between the specialists working in these and other fields of study. He was attempting, then, to employ a nomenclature accessible to scholars regardless of their pedagogic disciplines in order to stimulate between-group exchange. The epigraph at the beginning of this introduction supports such a conclusion, and it bears repeating here:

> As in some economies the rich keep getting richer and the poor poorer, so in the overspecialized disciplines of modern scholarship the learned get more learned and the ignorant get more ignorant—until the two classes can hardly talk to each other. I have dedicated my work to an attempt to bridge that gap. (Watts, 1975b, p. xx)

The "guru" tag on Watts is likewise ripe for reconsideration. Here again, the epithet is usually employed in reference to the undeniable fact that popular audiences found, and continue to find, his writings valuable to their spiritual and intellectual lives. Watts surely was (and is) a revered guide and adviser on spiritual and intellectual matters of relevance to mass audiences. However, the guru role was one he neither sought nor encouraged, and it spurred his withdrawal from the living quarters on the Sausalito houseboat, S. S. *Vallejo*, to a less-accessible cottage on Mount Tamalpais. According to Watts (1995):

> I am not trying to create disciples. I work on the principle of a physician rather than a clergyman. A physician is always trying to get rid of his patients and send them away healthy. . . . My objective is really to get rid of you so that you won't need me. (p. 2)

Still, the common pedagogical problem from the viewpoint of specialists in the academy (as well as in the seminary or monastery) is that neophytic readers of Watts' extraordinarily approachable texts often come away imagining they know and understand more than is actually the case (see, e.g., Merzel, 2003, p. 92). Hence the scathing style of review offered by Nordstrom and Pilgrim (1980) intended in part to disabuse students-in-training of any epistemological commitments or devotional affectations toward Watts and his work. It may be suggested, however, that Watts indeed informed the spiritual and intellectual sensibilities of numerous discerning scholars in a variety of academic disciplines. Convenient examples are found in humanistic and transpersonal psychologies where there are no shortages of eminent thinkers counting Alan Watts as a formative influence, including Aanstoos (2005), Haley (1992), Krippner (2012), Metzner (2012), Puhakka (2012), Singer (Singer & Roundtree, 2005), Sutich (1976), and Welwood (2000).

Finally, there is the question of Watts' self-ascription as a "philosophical entertainer." Three observations are offered here. First, the epithet initially appeared in Watts' rhetorical repertoire in the late 1950s near the fulcrum of his hermeneutical turn. Indeed, the earliest "entertainer" self-reference by Watts to be found in textual form is in a 1959 interview with *The Realist* magazine (see Krassner, 1999, p. 5). Greek folklore suggests that Hermes, often considered the etymological root of hermeneutics, was himself a kind of philosophical entertainer inhabiting and playing within the flux and flow of language and communicative processes. In this way it seems the epithet was Watts' light-hearted tactic for acknowledging his transition toward hermeneutical writing. Second, collective judgments about Watts often take the form of what may be called a *Sartrean triad* in the semblance of *No Exit*: Academic intellectuals reject Watts as a popularizer; popular audiences problematically idolize him as a guru; and gurus, that is to say, mystics, spiritual teachers, and religious practitioners criticize him as too intellectual (e.g., Krishna, 1975; Nordstrom & Pilgrim, 1980; see also Humphreys, 1994, p. 30; Pope, 2012, p. 195; Yamada, 2009, p. 221). It seems plausible to suggest that Watts' philosophical entertainer moniker was his way of "exiting" the existential dilemma. It was, in other words, an interpretive strategy intended (successfully or not) to disarm critics and fanatics alike.

Third and lastly, Watts' use of the philosophical entertainer epithet as rhetorical equipoise coincides with the countercultural revolution of the 1960s, and this correlation affords a conclusion drawn previously by Reed Baird (1988) that seems no less pertinent in the twenty-first century:

> At a time in a burning and anguished world when theologians spoke either of a "wholly other" or totally dead God, when philosophers lost themselves in intricate analyses of the meaning of meaning, and when far too many psychologists occupied themselves with experiments on rats and denied man's [people's] freedom, dignity, even his [their] very consciousness, Alan Watts sought to restore man's [people's] sense of being at home in the world. . . . Watts' great gift was his ability to contribute to the revitalization of America's intellectual and spiritual life, precisely through his remaining always a "divine amateur" who was therefore freer than most intellectuals to perceive and express healing versions of Reality not generally available to modern consciousness. (p. 74)

REFERENCES

Aanstoos, C. M. (2005). Life as a symphony. In G. Yancy & S. Hadley (Eds.), *Narrative identities: Psychologists engaged in self-construction* (pp. 131–149). London, UK: Kingsley.

Adams, R. M. (1958). Man and nothing: Earthbound comments. *Hudson Review, 11*(4), 626–631.

Akhilananda, S. (1948). [Review of the book *Behold the Spirit*]. *Journal of Bible and Religion, 16*(3), 185–186.

Anderson, J. J. (2012). *Seeing beyond the veil: Addressing the unseen barrier to socially unsustainable behavior.* Unpublished doctoral dissertation, Saybrook University, San Francisco, CA.

Atsina, C. A. (2002). *Global dialectics of narrative identity: Mediating the voluntary and involuntary* [Abstract]. Doctoral dissertation, University of San Francisco, CA.

Retrieved from: http://phdtree.org/pdf/25763997-global-dialectics-of-narrative-identity-mediating-the-voluntary-and-the-involuntary/

Baird, R. M. (1988). The influence of Oriental mysticism on American thought. In T. Sakamoto & K. Takeno (Eds.), *America's changing scene* (pp. 74–84). Tokyo, Japan: Eichosha Shinsha.

Ballantyne, E. C. (1989). Alan Watts. In C. H. Lippy (Ed.), *Twentieth-century shapers of American popular religion* (pp. 436–445). Westport, CT: Greenwood.

Bankart, C. P. (2003). Five manifestations of the Buddha in the West: A brief history. In K. H. Dockett, G. R. Dudley-Grant, C. P. Bankart (Eds.), *Psychology and Buddhism: From individual to global community* (pp. 45–70). New York, NY: Kluwer.

Bartholomeusz, T. (1998). Spiritual wealth and neo-orientalism. *Journal of Ecumenical Studies, 35*(1), 19–32.

Bateson, G., Jackson, D. D., Haley, J., & Weakland, J. H. (1956). Toward a theory of schizophrenia. *Behavioral Science, 1*(4), 251–264.

Beidler, P. D. (1994). *Scriptures for a generation: What we were reading in the '60s*. Athens: University of Georgia Press.

Bennett, J. (2014). *Narrative and peace: A "new story" to address structural violence*. Master's thesis, University of Sydney, Australia. Retrieved from http://ses.library.usyd.edu.au/handle/2123/11588

Bennett, J. (2015). Alan Watts' "dramatic model" and the pursuit of peace. *Self and Society: An International Journal for Humanistic Psychology, 43*(4), 335–344.

Bond, M. J. (2014). *Headless and homeless: Zen non-thinking awareness in American counter-cultural trip narratives post-WWI to the Vietnam War*. Doctoral dissertation, University of California-Riverside. Retrieved from http://escholarship.org/uc/item/5nb7x0hw#

Bontempo, C. J., & Odell, S. J. (1975). Introduction: Some approaches to philosophy. In *The owl of Minerva: Philosophers on philosophy* (pp. 1–40). New York, NY: McGraw-Hill.

Bowden, H. W. (1993). Watts, Alan Wilson. In *Dictionary of American religious biography* (2nd ed., pp. 584–585). Westport, CT: Greenwood.

Brannigan, M. C. (1977). Alan Watts' metaphysical language: Positivity in negative concepts. *Orientalia Lovaniensia Periodica, 8*, 341–350.

Brannigan, M. C. (1988). *Everywhere and nowhere: The path of Alan Watts*. New York, NY: Lang.

Brannigan, M. C. (2012). Listening to the rain: Embodied awareness in Watts. In P. J. Columbus & D. L. Rice (Eds.), *Alan Watts—here and now: Contributions to psychology, philosophy, and religion* (pp. 149–161). Albany: State University of New York Press.

Braun, H. (1961). The politics of Zen. *New Politics: A Journal of Socialist Thought, 1*(1), 177–189.

Braun, H. (1962). Mr. Braun's reply. *New Politics: A Journal of Socialist Thought, 1*(2), 172–173.

Brown, J. (2009). The Zen of anarchy: Japanese exceptionalism and the anarchist roots of the San Francisco poetry renaissance. *Religion and American Culture: A Journal of Interpretation, 19*(2), 207–242.

Bryson, L., Finkelstein, L., Maciver, R. M., & Mckeon, R. (Eds.). (1954). *Symbols and values*. New York, NY: Harper.

Chadwick, D. (1999). *Crooked cucumber: The life and teaching of Shunryu Suzuki*. New York, NY: Broadway.

Chadwick, D. (2015). Alan Watts at 100. *Shambhala Sun, 24*(1), 64–68.

Chase, C. (2011). *Building a California bildung: Theodore Roszak and Alan Watts's contributions to pagan hermeneutics*. Essay presented to the annual meeting of the American Academy of Religion, San Francisco.

Chase, C. (2015). Square gnosis, Beat eros: Alan Watts and the occultism of Aquarian religion. *Self and Society: An International Journal for Humanistic Psychology, 43*(4), 322–334.

Chatterjee, S. C. (1960). On philosophical synthesis. *Philosophy East and West, 10*(3), 99–103.

Chen, Y. (2013). *The fusion of ecological visions: Human beings' relationship to nature in twentieth-century Eastern and Western thought and poetry*. Unpublished Doctoral Dissertation, University of Texas at Dallas.

Chopra, S. (2014). *In praise of Alan Watts and "popularizers."* Retrieved from http://samir-chopra.com/2014/09/24/in-praise-of-alan-watts-and-popularizers/

Clark, D. K. (1978). *The pantheism of Alan Watts*. Downers Grove, IL: Inter-varsity Press.

Clarke, J. J. (2000). *The Tao of the West: Western transformations of Taoist thought*. New York, NY: Routledge.

Cohen, K. (2015). "You can tell a yogi by his laugh": Reminiscences of Alan Watts' last summer. *Self and Society: An International Journal for Humanistic Psychology, 43*(4), 299–310.

Cohen, S. (1965). [Review of the book *LSD: The consciousness-expanding drug*]. *International Journal for Group Psychotherapy, 15*(1), 408–409.

Coleman, J. W. (2001). Alan Watts: The way of the writer. In *The new Buddhism: The Western transformation of an ancient tradition* (pp. 63–64). New York, NY: Oxford University Press.

Collier, R. M. (1966). The role of affect in human behavior: A holistic-organism approach. *Journal of Individual Behavior, 22*(1), 3–32.

Columbus, P. J. (1985). A response to Nordstrom and Pilgrim's critique of Alan Watts' mysticism. *The Humanistic Psychologist, 13*(1), 28–34.

Columbus, P. J. (2012). Phenomenological exegeses of Alan Watts: Transcendental and hermeneutic strategies. In P. J. Columbus & D. L. Rice (Eds.), *Alan Watts—here and now: Contributions to psychology, philosophy, and religion* (pp. 59–82). Albany: State University of New York Press.

Columbus, P. J. (2015a). Alan Watts: A bibliographic resource. *Self and Society: An International Journal for Humanistic Psychology, 43*(4), 354–358.

Columbus, P. J. (2015b). *Psychotherapy East and West*: A retrospective review, Part I—1961–1970. *Self and Society: An International Journal for Humanistic Psychology, 43*(4), 345–353.

Columbus, P. J., & Rice, D. L. (Eds.). (2012a). *Alan Watts—here and now: Contributions to psychology, philosophy, and religion*. Albany: State University of New York Press.

Columbus, P. J., & Rice, D. L. (2012b). Introduction: A new look at Alan Watts. In *Alan Watts—here and now: Contributions to psychology, philosophy, and religion* (pp. 1–24). Albany: State University of New York Press.

Copan, P. (2009). *True for you, but not for me: Overcoming objections to Christian faith.* Bloomington, MN: Bethany House.

Coupe, L. (2010). This is it: Alan Watts and the visionary tradition. In *Beat sound, Beat vision: The Beat spirit and popular song* (pp. 22–55). London, UK: Manchester University Press.

Crocker, S. (2013). *Bergson and the metaphysics of media.* New York, NY: Palgrave MacMillan.

Cunningham, E. (2007). *Hallucinating the end of history: Nishida, Zen, and the psychedelic eschaton.* Bethesda, MD: Academica Press.

Curti, M. E. (1980). *Human nature in American thought: A history.* Madison: University of Wisconsin Press.

Dart, R. (2004). Thomas Merton and Alan Watts: Contemplative Catholic and Oriental anarchist. *Merton Journal, 11*(2), 12–15.

Denning, J. (2005). *Self-educated Buddhism and Alan Watts.* Unpublished honors thesis, Reed College.

Dible, R. T. (2010). The philosophy of mysticism: Perennialism and constructivism. *Journal of Consciousness Exploration and Research, 1*(2), 171–183.

Dickins, R. J. (2012). *The birth of psychedelic literature: Drug writing and the rise of LSD therapy, 1954–1964.* Master's thesis, University of Exeter, UK. Retrieved from https:// ore.exeter.ac.uk/repository/handle/10036/4207?show=full

Duggan, E. F. (2014). *Three lives, three paths: The spiritual quests of Thomas Merton, Alan Watts, and Annie Dillard* [Abstract]. Honors thesis, University of Hawaii at Manoa. Retrieved from http://scholarspace.manoa.hawaii.edu/handle/10125/33680

Dunbar, D. (1994). *The balance of nature's polarities in new-paradigm theory.* New York, NY: Peter Lang.

Dykhuizen, G., & Borgmann, C. (1958, June). [Presentation for the degree of Honorary Doctor of Divinity to Alan Watts]. University archives, Bailey/Howe Library, University of Vermont, Burlington.

Editorial. (1961). *The Psychedelic Review, 1*(1), 2–5.

Ellwood, R. S. (1997). *The fifties spiritual marketplace: American religion in a decade of conflict.* New Brunswick, NJ: Rutgers University Press

Ellwood, R. S. (2005). Watts, Alan Wilson (1915–73). In J. R. Shook (Ed.), *Dictionary of Modern American Philosophers* (Vols. 1–4, pp. 2539–2540). Bristol, UK: Thoemmes Continuum.

Fadiman, J. (2011). *The psychedelic explorer's guide: Safe, therapeutic, and sacred journeys.* Rochester, VT: Park Street Press.

Fields, R. (1992). *How the swans came to the lake: A narrative history of Buddhism in America* (Rev. ed.). Boulder, CO: Shambhala.

Ford, J. I. (2006). *Zen master who? A guide to the people and stories of Zen.* Boston, MA: Wisdom.

Forman, R. K. C. (Ed.). (1990). *The problem of pure consciousness.* New York, NY: Oxford University Press.

Forman, R. K. C. (Ed.). (1998). *The innate capacity: Mysticism, psychology, and philosophy.* New York, NY: Oxford University Press.

Forman, R. K. C. (1999). *Mysticism, mind, and consciousness*. Albany: State University of New York Press.

Fuller, A. R. (2008). Alan Watts. In *Psychology and religion: Eight points of view* (pp. 167–194). Lanham, MD: Rowman & Littlefield

Fuller, R. C. (2000). Psychedelics and metaphysical illumination. In *Stairways to heaven: Drugs in American religious history* (pp. 51–90). Boulder, CO: Westview Press.

Fuller, R. C. (2004). *Religious revolutionaries: The rebels who reshaped American religion*. New York, NY: Palgrave MacMillan.

Furlong, M. (2001). *Zen effects: The life of Alan Watts*. Woodstock, VT: Skylight Paths. (Original work published 1986)

Garrett-Farb, B. (2015). An aesthetic appreciation of Alan Watts. *Journal of Humanistic Psychology*. First published online May 6, 2016. doi:10.1177/0022167815584863

Gausted, E. S. (2001). *Memoirs of the spirit: American religious autobiography from Jonathan Edwards to Maya Angelou*. Grand Rapids, MI: Eerdmans.

Gehart, D. R. (2012). *Mindfulness and acceptance in couple and family therapy*. New York, NY: Springer.

Gidlow, E. (1972, April 16). Who is Alan Watts? *California Living Magazine*, 15–21.

Gordon, L. (1970). Beyond the reality principle: Illusion or new reality? *American Imago, 27*(2), 160–182.

Gordon, S. (2012). Existential time and the meaning of human development. *Humanistic Psychologist, 40*, 79–86.

Gordon, S. (2015). Alan Watts and neurophenomenology. *Self and Society: An International Journal for Humanistic Psychology, 43*(4), 311–321.

Gorham, D. R. (1963). The new world of superconsciousness. [Review of the book *The Joyous Cosmology*]. *Contemporary Psychology, 8*(1), 22–24.

Gowen, H. H. (1949). [Review of the book *Behold the Spirit*]. *Anglican Theological Review, 31*(1), 46–47.

Greer, J. C. (2011). *Pride and paradigmatic prejudice: Alan Watts and Zen scholarship*. Unpublished master's thesis, Harvard University, Cambridge, MA.

Greer, J. C. (2014). *Angelheaded hipsters: From the birth of beatnik antinomianism to psychedelic millennialism* [Abstract]. Doctoral dissertation in progress, University of Amsterdam, The Netherlands. Retrieved from http://www.amsterdamhermetica.nl/research/individual-research-projects/christian-greer-research/

Grof, S. (1988). *The adventure of self-discovery: Dimensions of consciousness and new perspectives in psychotherapy and inner explorations*. Albany: State University of New York Press.

Guerin, S. P. (2004). *The Zen of work and the Zen of leisure: The political thought of D.T. Suzuki and Alan Watts*. Unpublished master's thesis, University of Rochester, New York.

Guy, D. (2000). Christmas Humphreys. *Tricycle: The Buddhist Review, 9*(4). Retrieved from http://www.tricycle.com/ancestors/christmas-humphreys

Haley, J. (1992). Zen and the art of therapy. In J. K. Zeig (Ed.), *The evolution of psychotherapy: The second conference* (pp. 24–38). New York, NY: Brunner/Mazel.

Harvey, P., & Goff, P. (Eds.) (2005). Religion and the counterculture. In *The Columbia documentary history of American religion since 1945* (Chap. 2). New York, NY: Columbia University Press.

Heide, F. J. (2013). *A Lamp unto himself: Alan Watts and the illumination of spirit.* *PsycCRITIQUES*, *58*(1), Article 1. Retrieved from http://psqtest.typepad.com/blog-PostPDFs/201233246_psq_58-1_aLampUntoHimself.pdf

Helminiak, D. (1998). *Religion and the human sciences.* Albany: State University of New York Press.

Hilgard, E. R. (1970). Foreword. In C. S. Wallia (Ed.), *Toward century 21: Technology, society, and human values* (pp. xi–xii). New York, NY: Basic Books.

Historical Note (n.d.). *Record group 5: Conference on science, philosophy, and religion.* New York, NY: Archives of the Jewish Theological Seminary. Retrieved from http://www.jtsa.edu/The_Library/Collections/Archives/The_Ratner_Center/_Finding_Aids_to_institutional_records_of_JTS/Record_Group_5_Conference_on_Science_Philosophy_and_Religion.xml

Hood, R. W. Jr. (2012). Alan Watts' anticipation of four major debates in the psychology of religion. In P. J. Columbus & D. L. Rice (Eds.), *Alan Watts—here and now: Contributions to psychology, philosophy, and religion* (pp. 25–41). Albany: State University of New York Press.

Huang, C. (2012). Watercourse way: Still flowing with Alan Watts. In P. J. Columbus & D. L. Rice (Eds.), *Alan Watts—here and now: Contributions to psychology, philosophy, and religion* (pp. 219–232). Albany: State University of New York Press.

Humphreys, C. (1994). *Zen comes West: The present and future of Zen in Western society* (2nd ed.). Surrey, UK: Curzon Press.

Hungerford, A. (2010). *Postmodern belief: American religion and literature since 1960.* Princeton, NJ: Princeton University Press.

Hurvitz, L. (1958). [Review of the book *The Way of Zen*]. *The Journal of Asian Studies, 17*(3), 487–489.

In this issue. (1951). *Vendanta and the West, 14*(4), n. p.

Iwamura, J. N. (2011). *Virtual orientalism: Asian religions and American popular culture.* New York, NY: Oxford University Press.

Jackson, C. T. (1984). Zen, mysticism, and counter-culture: The pilgrimage of Alan Watts. *Indian Journal of American Studies, 4*(1), 89–101.

Jolicoeur, R. (2000). *Alan Wilson Watts: Spiritialite orientale en occident, un parcours, premiere periode, 1935–1958.* Doctoral dissertation, University of Laval, Quebec City, Canada.

Justesen, B. B., & Seidler, M. H. (2013). *Mistakens Metafysik.* Master's thesis, Roskilde University, Denmark.

Kabil, A. (2012). The new myth: Frederic Spiegelberg and the rise of a whole earth, 1914–1975. *Integral Review, 8*(1), 43–61.

Kapleau, P. (1966). *Three pillars of Zen: Teaching, practice, enlightenment.* New York, NY: Harper & Row.

Katz, S. T. (Ed). (1978). *Mysticism and philosophical analysis.* New York, NY: Oxford University Press.

Katz, S. T. (Ed). (1983). *Mysticism and religious traditions.* New York, NY: Oxford University Press.

Katz, S. T. (Ed.). (1992). *Mysticism and language.* New York, NY: Oxford University Press.

Keene, J. C. (1952). [Review of the book *The Supreme Identity*]. *Journal of Bible and Religion, 20*(2), 132.

Keightley, A. (1986). *Into every life a little Zen must fall: A Christian philosopher looks to Alan Watts and the East.* London, UK: Wisdom.

Keightley, A. (2012). Alan Watts: The immediate magic of God. In P. J. Columbus & D. L. Rice (Eds.), *Alan Watts—here and now: Contributions to psychology, philosophy, and religion* (pp. 43–57). Albany: State University of New York Press.

King, P. C. (2001). Roots and wings: Thomas Merton and Alan Watts as twentieth century archetypes. *Merton Journal, 8*(2), 36–44.

Krassner, P. (Ed.). (1999). *Impolite interviews.* New York, NY: Seven Stories Press.

Kripal, J. J. (2007). *Esalen: America and the religion of no-religion.* Chicago, IL: University of Chicago Press.

Krippner, S. (2012). The psychedelic adventures of Alan Watts. In P. J. Columbus & D. L. Rice (Eds.), *Alan Watts—here and now: Contributions to psychology, philosophy, and religion* (pp. 83–102). Albany: State University of New York Press.

Krishna, G. (1975). The dangers of partial awareness: Comments on Alan Watts' autobiography. In *The awakening of Kundalini* (pp. 96–105). New York, NY: Dutton.

LaHood, G. (2008). Paradise unbound: A perennial philosophy or an unseen process of cosmological hybridization. *Anthropology of Consciousness, 19*(2), 1–57.

LaHood, G. (2010). Relational spirituality, part 1. Paradise unbound: Cosmic hybridity and spiritual narcissism in "New Age" transpersonalism. *International Journal of Transpersonal Studies, 29*(1), 31–57.

Lasar, M. (2000). Three gurus and a critic. In *Pacifica Radio: The rise of an alternative network* (pp. 112–132). Philadelphia, PA: Temple University Press.

Leary, T., & Alpert, R. (1970). Foreword. In A. W. Watts, *The joyous cosmology: Adventures in the chemistry of consciousness* (pp. ix–xv). New York, NY: Vintage. (Original work published 1962).

Leech, K. (2005). Drugs. In P. Sheldrake (Ed.), *The new Westminster dictionary of Christian spirituality* (pp. 254–255). Louisville, KY: Westminster John Knox Press.

Levering, M. L. (2012). Alan Watts on nature, gender, and sexuality: A contemporary view. In P. J. Columbus & D. L. Rice (Eds.), *Alan Watts—here and now: Contributions to psychology, philosophy, and religion* (pp. 163–182). Albany: State University of New York Press.

Loechel, J. (2014). *Listening to the rain: A fresh look at the works of Alan Watts.* Honors thesis, Texas State University, San Marcos. Retrieved from https://digital.library.txstate.edu/bitstream/handle/10877/5058/LoechelJessicaFinal.pdf?seqence=1

Lopez, D. S. (Ed.). (2002). *A modern Buddhist bible: Essential readings from East and West.* Boston, MA: Beacon.

Lumish, M. W. (2009). *The human potential movement: The career of an idea in the United States during the third quarter of the twentieth century.* Doctoral dissertation, Pennsylvania State University. Retrieved from https://etda.libraries.psu.edu/paper/10451/

Mahoney, S. (1958). The prevalence of Zen. *Nation, 187*(14), 311–315.

Masatsugu, M. K. (2008). "Beyond this world of transiency and impermanence": Japanese Americans, Dharma bums, and the making of American Buddhism during the early Cold War years. *Pacific Historical Review, 77*(3), 423–451.

Masi, W. (2015). *The Gospel reinvented: A new addition to the Jesus of Alan Watts.* Essay presented at the annual Thinking Matters conference, Portland, Maine.

Maslow, A. H. (1962). Comments. *Journal of Humanistic Psychology, 2*(1), 110–111.

Masters, R. E., & Houston, J. (1966). *Varieties of psychedelic experience.* New York, NY: Dell.

Matchette, F. J. (1949). *Outlines of a metaphysics: The absolute-relative theory.* New York, NY: Philosophical Library.

McCarthy, H. E. (1957). [Review of the book *The Way of Zen*]. *Philosophy East and West, 7*(1–2), 70–73.

McCowen, D., Reibel, D., & Micozzi, M. S. (2010). *Teaching mindfulness: A practical guide for clinicians and educators.* New York, NY: Springer.

McMahan, D. L. (2008). *The making of Buddhist modernism.* New York, NY: Oxford University Press.

Merkur, D. (1998). *The ecstatic imagination: Psychedelic experiences and the psychoanalysis of self-actualization.* Albany: State University of New York Press.

Merzel, D. G. (2003). *The path of the human being: Zen teachings on the Bodhisattva way.* Boston, MA: Shambhala.

Messerly, J. G. (2015). Alan Watts: Who am I? *Institute for Ethics and Emerging Technologies.* Retrieved from http://ieet.org/index.php/IEET/more/messerly20150223

Metzner, R. (1968). *The ecstatic adventure.* New York, NY: Macmillan.

Metzner, R. (2012). From the joyous cosmology to the watercourse way: An appreciation of Alan Watts. In P. J. Columbus & D. L. Rice (Eds.), *Alan Watts—here and now: Contributions to psychology, philosophy, and religion* (pp. 103–121). Albany: State University of New York Press.

Miller, J. (2006). *Chinese religions in contemporary societies.* Santa Barbara, CA: ABC-CLIO.

Milstead, C. (2014). Shigetsu Sasaki: Zen vagabond in the United States. In A. C. Richards & I. Omdivar (Eds.), *Historic engagements with Occidental cultures, religions, powers: Perceptions from Europe and Asia* (pp. 213–232). New York, NY: Palgrave MacMillan.

Morgan, J. H. (2008). Alan Watts: "Beyond separation." In P. Mohanty & R. C. Mailik (Eds.), *Language, culture and society: Studies in honor of Acharya Bhabananda* (pp. 171–180). Dehli, India: Indian Institute of Languages.

Moritz, C. (Ed.). (1963). Watts, Alan Wilson. *Current biography yearbook: 1962* (pp. 450–452). New York, NY: Wilson.

Morris, C. (1951). [Review of the book *The Supreme Identity*]. *Philosophy East and West, 1*(1), 77–79.

Munroe, A. (2009). Buddhism and the neo-avant garde: Cage Zen, beat Zen, and Zen. In A. Munroe (Ed.), *The third mind: American artists contemplate Asia 1960–1989* (pp. 199–215). New York, NY: Guggenheim Foundation.

Nordstrom, L., & Pilgrim, R. (1980). The wayward mysticism of Alan Watts. *Philosophy East and West, 30*(3), 381–401.

Norrman, R. (1999). Creating the world in our image: A new theory of love of symmetry and iconicist desire. In M. Nanny & O. Fischer (Eds.), *Form miming meaning: Iconicity in language and literature* (pp. 59–82). Amsterdam, The Netherlands: Benjamins.

Oldmeadow, H. (2004). *Journeys East: 20th century encounters with Eastern religious traditions.* Bloomington, IN: World Wisdom.

Ostdiek, G. (2015). Signs, science, and religion: A biosemiotic mediation. In D. Evers, M. Fuller, A. Jackelan, & K-W Saether (Eds.), *Issues in science and theology: What is life?* (pp. 169–177). London, UK: Springer.

Patterson, S. (2007). Philosophically informed: Exploring the ethics of help. *Journal of College Admissions, 197,* 4–7.

Peach, R. (2011). *Through the dessert of anxiety into the oasis of love: A collective vision of the pleroma in Watts, Teilhard and Merton.* Essay presented to the annual meeting of the International Thomas Merton Society, Louisville, Kentucky.

Perry, W. N. (1972). Anti-theology and the riddles of Alcyone. *Studies in Comparative Religion, 6*(3), 176–192.

Pickering, A. (2011). Cyborg Spirituality. *Medical History, 55*(3), 349–353.

Ponce, D. E. (1987). The sound of two hands clapping: Zen Buddhism and Christianity in the Philippines. *Buddhist-Christian Studies, 7,* 235–241.

Pope, A. (2012). Contributions and conundrums in the psycho-spiritual transformation of Alan Watts. In P. J. Columbus & D. L. Rice (Eds.), *Alan Watts—here and now: Contributions to psychology, philosophy, and religion* (pp. 183–202). Albany: State University of New York Press.

Prebish, C. (1978). Reflections on the transmission of Buddhism to America. In J. Needleman & G. Baker (Eds.), *Understanding the new religions* (pp. 153–172). New York, NY: Seabury Press.

Pribram, K., Howe, T. C., Money, J., & Watts, A. W. (1963). What is a woman? In S. M Farber & R. H. L. Wilson (Eds.), *The potential of woman* (pp. 86–101). New York, NY: McGraw-Hill.

Puhakka, K. (2012). Buddhist wisdom in the west: A fifty-year perspective on the contributions of Alan Watts. In P. J. Columbus & D. L. Rice (Eds.), *Alan Watts—here and now: Contributions to psychology, philosophy, and religion* (pp. 203–217). Albany: State University of New York Press.

Queen, E. L., Prothero, S. R., & Shattuck, G. H. (2009). Watts, Alan Wilson (1915–1973). *Encyclopedia of American religious history* (3rd ed., p. 1048). New York, NY: Infobase.

Rascke, C. A. (1980). *The interruption of eternity: Modern Gnosticism and the origins of the new religious consciousness.* Chicago, IL: Nelson-Hall.

Recoulley, A. L. (1986). Daemon est deus inversus: The androgynous dialectics of Alan Watts. *USF Language Quarterly, 25*(1–2), 13–21.

Reed, J. H. (2007). Religious language. *Internet encyclopedia of philosophy.* Retrieved from http://www.iep.utm.edu/rel-lang/

Responses to Alan Watts. (1974). In J-D Robinson (Ed.), Word out of silence: A symposium on world spiritualities. *Cross Currents, 23,* 2–3, pp. 377–386.

[Review of the book *In My Own Way*]. (1973). *Commonweal, 98,* 117.

Rice, D. L. (2012). Alan Watts and the neuroscience of transcendence. In P. J. Columbus & D. L. Rice (Eds.), *Alan Watts—here and now: Contributions to psychology, philosophy, and religion* (pp. 123–148). Albany: State University of New York Press.

Richards, W. A. (2003). Entheogens in the study of mystical and archetypal experiences. In R. L. Piedmont & D. O. Moberg (Eds.), *Research in the social scientific study of religion, 13* (pp. 143–155). Leiden, The Netherlands: Brill.

Rigby, A. (2006). *Dimitrije Mitrinovic: A biography* (2nd ed.). York, UK: Sessions.

Robinson, J-D. (1974). Revelation at the drinking party. *Cross Currents, 24*(2–3), 133–147.

Roszak, T. (1995). *The making of a counterculture: Reflections on the technocratic culture and its youthful opposition.* Berkeley: University of California Press. (Original work published 1969)

Ruland, V. (1975). *Horizons of criticism: An assessment of religious-literary options.* Chicago, IL: American Library.

Rutherford, H. (Ed.). (1987). *Certainly, future: Selected writings by Dimitrije Mitrinovoc.* New York, NY: Columbia University Press.

Sadler, A. W. (1974a). The complete Alan Watts. *The Eastern Buddhist* (new series), *7*(2), 121–127.

Sadler, A. W. (1974b). The vintage Alan Watts. *The Eastern Buddhist* (new series), *7*(1), 143–148.

Sadler, A. W. (1976). [Review of the book *Alan Watts*]. *Horizons, 3*(2), 301–304.

Sadler, A. W. (1985, November). Editorial jottings: Alan Watts, Alan Whittemore & others. *Whittemore Newsletter,* 1–4.

Sato, K. J. (2008). D. T. Suzuki and the question of war. (T. Kirchner, Trans.). *Eastern Buddhist, 39*(1), 61–122.

Seager, R (2013). *Buddhism in America.* New York, NY: Columbia University Press.

Seigler, E. (2010). Back to the pristine: Identity formation and legitimation in contemporary America. *Nova Religio: The Journal of Alternative and Emergent Religions, 14*(1), 45–66.

Shibayama, Z. (1974). Ordinary mind is Tao. In *Zen comments on the Mumonkan* (pp. 145–152). New York, NY: Mentor.

Shipley, M. (2012). *"Effing the ineffable:" Alan Watts, purposeless play, and the aporia of language.* Essay presented at the 54th annual convention of the Midwest Modern Language Association, Cincinnati, Ohio.

Shipley, M. (2013). *"One never loves enough:" Psychedelics and spirituality in post-World War Two America.* Unpublished doctoral dissertation, Michigan State University.

Siff, S. (2015). *Acid hype: American news media and the psychedelic experience.* Champaign: University of Illinois Press.

Singer, J., & Roundtree, C. (2005). Modern woman in search of soul: An interview with June Singer, February 12, 1999. *San Francisco Jung Institute Journal, 24*(1), 54–72.

Sjogren, E. (2013). *The sound of rain needs no translation: Alan Watts on society and modern man.* Undergraduate thesis, University of Stockholm, Sweden. Retrieved from http://urn.kb.se / resolve?urn=urn:nbn:se:su:diva-104296

Slattery, (2011). *Communicating the unspeakable: Linguistic phenomena in the psychedelic sphere.* Doctoral dissertation, University of Plymouth, United Kingdom. Retrieved from http://pearl.plymouth.ac.uk / handle / 10026.1 / 549

Smith, D. L. (2010). The authenticity of Alan Watts. In G. Storhoff & J. Whalen-Bridge (Eds.), *American Buddhism as a way of life* (pp. 13–38). Albany: State University of New York Press.

Smith, D. L. (2014). How to be a genuine fake: *Her*, Alan Watts, and the problem of the self. *Journal of Religion and Film, 18*(2), Article 3. Retrieved from http://digitalcommons.unomaha.edu / cgi / viewcontent.cgi?article=1239&context=jrf

Smith, L. (2011). *Zen Buddhism and mid-century American art*. Master's thesis, State University of New York-Stony Brook. Retrieved from https://dspace.sunyconnect. suny.edu/bitstream/handle/1951/56123/Smith_grad.sunysb_0771M_10508.pdf? sequence=1&isAllowed=y

Snelling, J. (1987). Introduction. In J. Snelling, M. Watts, & D. Sibley (Eds.), *The early writings of Alan Watts* (pp. 1–14). Berkeley, CA. Celestial Arts.

Society for Arts, Religion, and Contemporary Culture. (1970). In J. Campbell (Ed.), *Myths, dreams, and religion* (p. 6). New York, NY: Dutton.

Spallier, R. (2012). *A philosophy of pain: Pain and pleasure—The Siamese twin of Da Vinci in the philosophy of the Stoics, Nietzsche, Taoism and Alan Watts*. Unpublished master's thesis, University of Antwerp.

Steere, D. V. (1949). [Review of the book *Behold the Spirit*]. *Journal of Religion, 29*(4), 321–322.

Stirling, I. (2006). *Zen pioneer: The life and works of Ruth Fuller Sasaki*. Emeryville, CA: Shoemaker & Hoard.

Stranger, W. (2012). Introduction: E. Graham Howe's psychology of incarnation. In *The druid of Harley Street: The spiritual psychology of E. Graham Howe* (pp. 1–25). Berkeley, CA: North Atlantic.

Stuart, D. (1983). *Alan Watts*. Briarcliff Manor, NY: Stein & Day. (Original work published 1976)

Study of the mind. (1955). *Manas, 8*(34), 1–2.

Subbiondo, J. L. (2011). CIIS and American higher education. *Integral Review, 7*(1), 11–16.

Suligoj, H. (1975). The mystical philosophy of Alan Watts. *International Philosophical Quarterly, 15*, 439–454.

Sutcliffe, S. (2007). The origins of "New Age" religion between the two world wars. In D. Kemp & J. R. Lewis (Eds.), *Handbook of the new age* (pp. 51–76). Boston, MA: Brill.

Sutich, A. J. (1976). The emergence of the transpersonal perspective: A personal account. *Journal of Transpersonal Psychology, 8*(1), 5–19.

Swearer, D. (1973). Three modes of Zen in America. *Journal of Ecumenical Studies, 10*(2), 290–303.

Taylor, E. (2003). Buddhism and Western psychology: An intellectual memoir. In S. R. Segall (Ed.), *Encountering Buddhism: Western psychology and Buddhist teachings* (pp. 179–196). Albany: State University of New York Press.

Tyson, A. (2013). The mystical debate: Constructivism and the resurgence of perennialism. *Intermountain West Journal of Religious Studies, 4*(1), 78–92. Retrieved from http://digitalcommons.usu.edu/cgi/viewcontent.cgi?article=1022&context=imwjournal

Unger, S. M. (1963). Mescaline, LSD, psilocybin, and personality change. *Psychiatry: Journal for the Study of Interpersonal Processes, 26*(2), 111–125.

Versluis, A. (2014). *American gurus: From transcendentalism to new age religion*. New York, NY: Oxford University Press.

Victoria, B. D. (2003). *Zen war stories*. London, UK: Routledge Curzon.

Victoria, B. D. (2006). *Zen at war* (2nd ed.). Lanham, MD: Rowman & Littlefield.

Wallia, C. S. (1970). Preface. In *Toward century 21: Technology, society, and human values* (p. xiii). New York, NY: Basic Books.

Wang, H. (2009). Life history and cross-cultural thought: Engaging an intercultural curriculum. *Transcultural Curriculum Inquiry, 6*(2), 37–50.

Waterhouse, E. S. (1953). [Review of the book *The Supreme Identity*]. *Philosophy, 28*(107), 273–274.

Watts, A. W. (1936). *The spirit of Zen: A way of life, work, and art in the far east.* London, UK: Murray.

Watts. A. W. (1937). *The legacy of Asia and western man: A study of the middle way.* London, UK: John Murray.

Watts, A. W. (1940). *The Meaning of happiness: The quest for freedom of the spirit in modern psychology and the wisdom of the East.* New York, NY: Harper & Row.

Watts, A. W. (1941). The problem of faith and works in Buddhism. *Review of Religion, 5*(4), 385–402.

Watts, A. W. (1944). *Theologia mystica, being the treatise of Saint Dionysius pseudo-areopagite on mystical theology, together with the first and fifth epistles.* West Park, NY: Holy Cross Press.

Watts, A. W. (1946a). The case for God. *Roodcroft papers.* West Park, NY: Holy Cross Press.

Watts, A. W. (1946b). The Christian doctrine of marriage. *Canterbury Club Tract, 1,* 3–14. Boulder: Episcopal Church at the University of Colorado.

Watts, A. W. (1946c). The meaning of priesthood. *Advent Papers, 7,* 1–24. Boston, MA: Church of the Advent.

Watts, A. W. (1947). *Behold the spirit: A study in the necessity of mystical religion.* New York, NY: Pantheon.

Watts, A. W. (1948). *Zen.* Stanford, CA: James Ladd Delkin.

Watts, A. W. (1950c). *The supreme identity: An essay on Oriental metaphysic and the Christian religion.* New York, NY: Pantheon.

Watts, A. W. (1951a). The negative way. *Vedanta and the West, 14*(4), 97–101.

Watts, A. W. (1951b). *The Wisdom of insecurity: A message for an age of anxiety.* New York, NY: Pantheon.

Watts, A. W. (1953a). Asian psychology and modern psychiatry. *American Journal of Psychoanalysis, 13*(1), 25–30.

Watts, A. W. (1953b). The language of metaphysical experience: The sense of non-sense. *Journal of Religious Thought, 10*(2), 132–143.

Watts, A. W. (1953c). *Myth and ritual in Christianity.* New York, NY: Vanguard.

Watts, A. W. (1953d). On philosophical synthesis. *Philosophy East and West, 3*(2), 99–100.

Watts, A. W. (1954). The works of Deisetz Teitaro Suzuki. *Philosophy East and West, 4*(3), 278–279.

Watts, A. W. (1955). The way of liberation in Zen Buddhism (1955). *Asian Study Monographs,* No. 1. San Francisco, CA: American Academy of Asian Studies.

Watts, A. W. (1956). Convention, conflict, and liberation: Further observations on Asian psychology and modern psychiatry. *American Journal of Psychoanalysis, 16*(1), 63–67.

Watts, A. W. (1957). *The way of Zen.* New York, NY: Pantheon.

Watts, A. W. (1958a). Beat Zen, square Zen, and Zen. *Chicago Review, 12*(2), 3–11.

Watts, A. W. (1958b). *Nature, man and woman.* New York, NY: Pantheon.

Watts, A. W. (1959). Eternity as the unrepressed body [Review of the book *Life against death: The psychoanalytical meaning of history*]. *ETC.: A Review of General Semantics, 16*(4), 486–494.

Watts, A. W. (1960). *This is IT, and other essays on Zen and spiritual experience*. New York, NY: Pantheon.

Watts, A. W. (1961). *Psychotherapy East and West*. New York, NY: Pantheon.

Watts, A. W. (1962a). *The joyous cosmology: Adventures in the chemistry of consciousness*. New York, NY: Pantheon.

Watts, A. W. (1962b). Oriental and Occidental approaches to the nature of man. *Journal of Humanistic Psychology, 2*(2), 107–109.

Watts, A. W. (1962c). Zen and politics. *New Politics: A Journal of Socialist Thought, 1*(2) 170–172.

Watts, A. W. (1963a). The individual as man/world. *Psychedelic Review, 1*(1), 55–65. (Essay presented at the Harvard University Social Relations Colloquium, April 12, 1963, Cambridge, MA)

Watts, A. W. (1963b). Prefatory essay. In D. T. Suzuki, *Outlines of Mahayana Buddhism* (pp. x–xxv). New York, NY: Schocken Books.

Watts, A. W. (1963c). *The two hands of God: The myths of polarity*. New York, NY: Braziller.

Watts, A. W. (1963d). The woman in man. In S. M Farber & R. H. L. Wilson (Eds.), *The potential of woman* (pp. 79–86). New York, NY: McGraw-Hill.

Watts, A. W. (1964a). *Beyond theology: The art of godmanship*. New York, NY: Pantheon.

Watts, A. W. (1964b). A psychedelic experience: Fact or fantasy? In D. Solomon (Ed.), *LSD: The consciousness expanding drug* (pp. 119–131). New York, NY: Putnam & Sons.

Watts, A. W. (1966). *The book: On the taboo against knowing who you are*. New York, NY: Pantheon.

Watts, A. W. (1967). The mind-less scholar. *The Eastern Buddhist, 2*(1), 124–127.

Watts, A. W. (1968). Psychedelics and religious experience. *California Law Review, 56*(1), 74–85.

Watts, A. W. (1970a). The future of religion. In C. S. Wallia (Ed.), *Toward century 21: Technology, society, and human values* (pp. 296–303). New York, NY: Basic Books.

Watts, A. W. (1970b). Western mythology: Its dissolution and transformation. In J. Campbell, (Ed.), *Myths, dreams, and religion* (pp. 9–25). New York, NY: Dutton.

Watts, A. W. (1971a). Ordinary mind is the way. *The Eastern Buddhist* (New Series), 4(2), 134–137.

Watts, A. W. (1971b). Worship in sacrament and silence. In E. H. Odell (Ed.), *A college looks at American values* (Vol. 1, pp. 123–131). Ellensburg: Central Washington State College.

Watts, A. W. (1973a). *In my own way: An autobiography—1915–1965*. New York, NY: Vintage.

Watts, A. W. (1973b). The new alchemy. In *This is IT, and other essays on Zen and spiritual experience* (pp. 125–153). New York, NY: Vintage. (Original work published 1960)

Watts, A. W. (1974a). Psychotherapy and Eastern religion: Metaphysical bases of psychiatry. *Journal of Transpersonal Psychology, 6*(1), 19–31.

Watts, A. W. (1974b). Unity in contemplation. *Cross Currents, 24*(2–3), 367–377.

Watts, A. W. (1975a). Philosophy beyond words. In C. J. Bontempo & S. J. Odell (Eds.), *The owl of Minerva: Philosophers on philosophy* (pp. 191–200). New York, NY: McGraw-Hill.

Watts, A. W. (1975b). *Tao: The watercourse way.* New York, NY: Pantheon.

Watts, A. W. (1979). No more armed clergymen. In L. Richmand & G. Nogura (Eds.), *The new gay liberation book* (pp. 143–146). Palo Alto, CA: Ramparts.

Watts, A. W. (1995). Ultimate authority. In *Myth and religion: A thorn in the flesh* (M. Watts, Ed., pp. 1–17). London, UK: Eden Grove.

Watts, A. W., & Ungerer, P. D. (1969, summer–fall). An interview with Alan Watts. *Existential Psychiatry, 7,* 109–117.

Welwood, J. (2000). *Toward a psychology of Awakening: Buddhism, psychotherapy, and the path of personal and spiritual transformation.* Boston, MA: Shambhala.

White, R. M. (2010). *Talking about God: The concept of analogy and the problem of religious language.* Burlington, VT: Ashgate.

Williams, R. J. (2014). *The Buddha in the machine: Art, technology, and the meeting of East and West.* New Haven, CT: Yale University Press.

Wolter, D. C. (2013). In search of the self: Eastern versus Western perspectives. *Oglethorpe Journal of Undergraduate Research, 1*(1), Article 1. Retrieved from http://digitalcommons.kennesaw.edu/ojur/vol1/iss1/1

Woodhead, L. (2001). The turn to life in contemporary religion and spirituality. In U. King (Ed.), *Spirituality and society in the new millennium* (pp. 110–123). Sussex, UK: Sussex Academic Press.

Yamada, S. (2009). *Shots in the dark: Japan, Zen, and the West* (E. Hartman, Trans.). Chicago, IL: University of Chicago Press.

Zaretsky, E. (2015). From psychoanalysis to cybernetics: The case of *Her. American Imago, 72*(2), 197–210.

PART ONE

Language and Mysticism

CHAPTER ONE

On the Meaning and Relation of Absolute and Relative (1950)

DO YOU EVER WONDER?

How interesting would it be to be able to read the thoughts of others? There they are, walking down the street or sitting idly in a train or bus, and their eyes tell little or nothing of what is going on inside their heads. What do they think about? What schemes, what puzzles, what dreams, what mysteries, are they turning over in their minds? It might not be interesting at all, for it is possible that, whether working or idling, so many of these people are not interested, and who is not interest*ed* is not interest*ing*. Their minds may just be turning over the most humdrum little worries, or odds and ends of gossip, or merely futile fantasies. In this case, the power to read thoughts would be a dubious gift—the mastery of a language with an exceedingly dreary literature.

But surely there must be times when the thoughts of the dullest person are wonderful. Of course, we use the word "wonderful" in two senses: "I have just had a wonderful time," or "This is a most wonderful universe." In the first sense, "wonderful" is just an exaggeration for pleasant or amusing. In the second, it means what it says—full of wonder, of fascination, mystery, and interest. Yet the two senses are not always separate, because a life that has been spent in wondering will almost certainly have been a wonderful life. Most children seem to be having an interesting time, for the world is a new thing in their eyes, and they are always asking questions. The more one asks, and gets answers to, questions, the more are the questions to be asked, for the more we know,

Reprinted from an unpublished work-for-hire (1950, Franklin J. Matchette Foundation) with permission of Nell S. Ernst, President of the the Franklin J. Matchette Foundation.

the more we know we don't know. The size of the mystery always grows in proportion to the increase of knowledge. Discovery is always, to some extent, the finding of new things about which you are ignorant.

A person who has given up asking questions, who has ceased to wonder, has stopped living because he has stopped growing. For life is like a stream in the sense that it must flow on or cease to be a stream. And where the mind of man ceases to flow out in wonder and interest towards the ocean of reality that surrounds him, it turns back upon itself and becomes a stagnant pool. A person who is miserable or bored is one whose mind has turned back upon itself, a person who gets in the way of his own experience, who frets over how he feels and how he would like to feel, and yet always seems to feel the same—frustrated. Yet all this turning back, this self-concern, is like a snake trying to make a good meal off his own tail—a futile procedure that makes him gag, and that boils down to the ultimate absurdity of trying to feed on one's own hunger.

Obviously, then, life is interesting and wonderful to the extent that one has interest in it and wonder for it. It is superficially wonderful if you wonder only at superficial things, and deeply wonderful if you wonder at deep things. To wonder what Mrs. Smith will wear for the party, what would have happened if you had been the son of a millionaire, what the dentist will have to say about your teeth, or whether it will be a fine weekend, is to wonder only at surfaces. It seems astonishing that there can be minds that never go deeper, that never want to know *who* or *what* is the mysterious power of consciousness that looks out through Mrs. Smith's eyes, how it is that I am myself and not someone else, why it is that I love pleasure and hate pain, or how there comes to be a sun that can shine.

It is difficult to imagine many questions more interesting than these. Yet the asking and answering of them is a process called philosophy, which is popularly thought to be one of the drier subjects in a college curriculum as well as one of the most unprofitable professions. If such things are dry and dull, life is then dry and dull at its very core, and one must just as well commit suicide without further ado. This is, perhaps, what our world is doing. Its daily life must be such a round of inane tedium that it can think of nothing better to do with the marvels of atomic fission than make a sensational bang, and blow itself up.

Needless to say, philosophy is not just another course in college, or the wearing out of one's mind with volumes of incomprehensible verbiage. Philosophy, as Aristotle said, begins and ends in wonder—wonder at what lies beneath the surface, not only of the sun, moon, and stars, but also of the most trivial and commonplace events. Every child is born a philosopher. Not only does he take things apart to find out how they work, but also he asks the most profound questions as to who made God, whether space goes on forever, what happened before anything happened, whether *he* would have been born if Mother had married someone else, why this, why that, why anything and everything. It is tragic that this spontaneous venture of wonder and interest in the roots of life bogs down either in parental annoyance, or in university courses where gentlemen expert in chopping logic dismiss all such questions as meaningless.

In a very strict sense it *may* be meaningless to ask why there is a universe, or whether I might have been someone else than me. But if the human mind had never wondered at these things, there would have been no physics, no chemistry, no biology or astronomy. Perhaps a question that has no answer is a meaningless question, but we can never find this out until we are *sure* it has no answer. And the good scientist is never *quite* sure, being the least dogmatic of people.

For many hundreds of years the scientific mind has been trying to find out what things are—what stones and stars and men are made of. Reducing them to simpler elements, it wants to know, in turn, what these are made of. Finding that men and mountains and air are arrangements of such simpler things as carbon, oxygen, sulfur, and hydrogen, and that these are composed of molecules, and these of atoms, and these of electrons, protons, and neutrons, we begin to wonder how much further we can go, how much longer we can ask, "What is it made of?" For we have brought everything down to such a fine point, that the investigation is now rather like trying to stick the point of a needle into the point of a needle. If the mind of man is of the same substance as the universe that it investigates, must there not come a time when the whole inquiry is just a single substance trying to define itself—like a mouth trying to kiss itself or a flame to burn itself?

At present there does seem to be a tendency among scientists to feel that this "main line" of inquiry has reached its limits, as if the mind had reached an impenetrable wall, and must henceforth be content to explore its surface. In a remarkable passage in *The Evolution of Physics* Einstein and Infeld (1938) say:

> In our endeavor to understand reality we are somewhat like a man trying to understand the mechanism of a closed watch. He sees the face and the moving hands, even hears its ticking, but he has no way of opening the case. If he is ingenious he may form some picture of a mechanism which could be responsible for all the things he observes, but he may never be quite sure his picture is the only one which could explain his observations. He will never be able to compare his picture with the real mechanism and he cannot even imagine the possibility or the meaning of such a comparison. (p. 38)

Back at the end of the nineteenth century, Maxwell foresaw the same problem, and explained it with an illustration employing a cabinet instead of a watch. Imagine a cabinet whose doors are forever sealed, but in each door there is a minute hole from which there extends a string. When we pull string A, string B goes up, and conversely. The scientist can but note the regularity of this event. As to what goes on inside the cabinet—whether A and B are two ends of one string, or whether there is some more complex mechanism—he can only speculate; he can never know for certain.

If physics cannot penetrate the watch or the cabinet, or if its method of inquiry has reduced itself to a needle trying to prick the point of a needle, must the whole problem be brought to a close? Must it be said that any further questioning as to *what* reality is, is meaningless? One may *say* so, and yet the human mind will go on wondering, because unsatisfied with the answer. The problem is simply whether it is entirely useless and absurd to do so.

The very analogy employed by Einstein and Infeld (1938) suggests an answer. Strictly speaking, the function of science may be simply to observe, measure, and predict the movements of the watch's hands and the rhythm of its ticking. Beyond this point, no observation is possible, and no measurement. But in fact, the scientist does form theories of what lies inside the watch, and tests them by the degree to which they enable him to predict what the watch will do. In this respect science enters the realm of philosophy and metaphysics, which is the act of wondering about the inside of the watch or the cabinet, about the depths of reality that are beyond the experience of the senses.

The philosopher forms and tests his theories in somewhat the same way as the scientist. He develops an idea of what may be inside the watch and responsible for its external movements from things that he has seen outside the watch. Outside, he has observed the things that make movements and noises similar to those of the watch, as well as the processes that cause them. He then reasons that the movements and noises of the watch must have similar causes, assuming that the relation of cause and effect that exists outside must also exist inside.

To these theories he applies a test not unlike the scientist's test of prediction. He asks whether his theories enable man to make a better adaptation to the world. If they do so, he assumes that his theory is in harmony with, or corresponds to, the unknown reality that causes this world. But this is not all. The problem of adaptation to the future course of events is not the philosopher's only or even chief concern. For he realizes that it is of no use to be able to predict and adjust oneself to the future unless you are also capable of having harmony with life in the present. Lacking this, you are always preparing for a tomorrow that never comes. You predict, but do not fully enjoy the fruits of prediction and planning when they become present.

Therefore the philosopher also loves philosophy for itself. He finds that wondering is perhaps the highest form of enjoyment, because in this act he loses himself in the contemplation of the most fascinating of all things—the reality that lies beyond the senses. All enjoyment, all real happiness involves this loss of self-consciousness through absorption in something wonderful. Can there, then, be any other higher happiness than absorption in the "highest" mystery—the unseen reality that underlies this whole universe? In the words of Goethe, "The highest to which man can attain is wonder; and if the prime phenomenon makes him wonder, let him be content; nothing higher can it give him, and nothing further should he seek for behind it; here is the limit."

OUR INCOMPLETE MAP OF LIFE

We come, then, to the barrier that the scientists say they cannot pass unless they join hands with the philosophers and begin to speculate and wonder. This wondering is no useless reaching into the void, and no mere attempt to satisfy curiosity. The correct solution to many of the problems of living in this everyday world depend upon accurate reasoning about the world beyond the senses. For this other world is in no way remote from the world of practical life; it is really the same world, understood more deeply. It is as if we were traveling across a sheet of ice. The senses can see, as it were, only the surface, and other means must be used to discover where the ice is thick enough to carry our weight, and so to decide what course the journey must take.

We must be prepared, however, for reasoning about the unseen to lead us to some strange conclusions. Already the scientists have found that their own theories of "the world below the surface" are very hard to describe in concrete images. They speak of space being curved, and how can we imagine space with a curve in it, as if it were the film of a soap-bubble without, however, either an inside or an outside? While we shall always use concrete images for purposes of illustration, it must nevertheless be remembered that these are *only* images, and that what we are talking about is not exactly like them. A familiar example of this difficulty may be seen in trying to draw a cube on a flat surface.

To represent a cube on this flat sheet of paper, we draw two squares, and then join their corners with straight lines (see figure 1.1). But this figure is not a cube. For all the angles of a cube are right angles, but in this drawing many of them are not. Yet because we know what a real cube is, we can imagine one from this drawing by using the convention of perspective. Because we are familiar with a world of three dimensions, we can easily understand representations of this solid world upon a flat surface where there are only two dimensions.

Supposing, however, there were people living in a world of two dimensions, people who had never seen, and had no idea of a third. They would find it most difficult to understand this drawing. A line perpendicular to their world would seem to them like a point, a surface like a line, and a solid like a surface. They

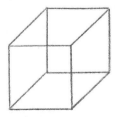

Figure 1.1. A Necker Cube representing a three-dimensional perspective.

would see the drawing here only as two squares with triangles adjoining them. Thus we are somewhat like these inhabitants of "Flatland" in our attempts to understand the world beyond our senses. Indeed, it took many centuries for our own ancestors to understand how this earth could be spherical, because to their limited point of view it seemed so flat. How could anyone walk on the underside of such a globe without falling off?

It is easy enough to see how the inhabitants of "Flatland" could not understand our drawing of a cube. It is fairly easy to put ourselves in their position by doing something else to our drawing. Here is the square. Think of it as made by moving the upright line at the left (one dimension) over to the right (two dimensions) (see figure 1.2). Here we have the two dimensions of length and breadth. Now by moving the whole square through the third dimension of depth, we have once more the cube (see figure 1.3). So far the figure is quite understandable. But now let us suppose that there is still another dimension, at right angles to each one of the three. We move the whole cube through this dimension, and get what is called a tesseract (see figure 1.4).

Now you can feel like the people in "Flatland," for you are looking at a drawing of a four-dimensional cube, which is something you cannot possibly imagine. Thus thinking about a four-dimensional world in terms of three is not unlike thinking about the unseen world in terms of the seen. We can represent it, but not exactly.

Figure 1.2. A square representing a two-dimensional perspective.

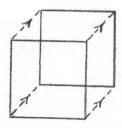

Figure 1.3. A Necker Cube representing acquisition of a three-dimensional perspective.

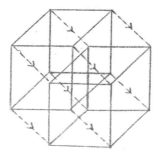

Figure 1.4. A tesseract representing a four-dimensional perspective.

We know, then, that one of the chief characteristics of our ordinary, everyday world is that it has three dimensions. What are some of its other important characteristics? Perhaps the most obvious is that everything is, without exception, in a state of movement and change. Every planet moves around its sun. Every sun and star moves around other suns and stars. Every solid object is in fact a cluster of pulsating electrons. Not only is every form in motion, but at the same time every form is inconstant, changing in shape and substance rapidly (as the smoke) or extremely slowly (as the rocks). In the words of the Greek philosopher Heraclitus, "Everything flows," and even

> The hills are shadows,
> And they flow from form to form,
> And nothing stands.

Hardly less obvious is the fact that all known things exist only in relation to each other. In the first place, they depend on each other. Every thing is an effect, and thus depends upon some cause. There can be no life apart from water, air, and sunlight; no air and water without an earth; no earth without a sun; no sun without a galaxy of stars; no stars without space, time, and energy—and so on to we know not what extent. In the second place, our knowledge of this world depends entirely upon the relation of contrasts or opposites. Light is unimaginable without darkness. Long is meaningless save by contrast with short. Substance is unthinkable without space, motion without relative stillness, heat without cold, fast without slow, hard without soft, sound without silence, pleasure without pain, and life without death. Indeed, it is absolutely impossible to express a meaning without making a contrast, or to think of a thing that is in no way distinguished from something else.

The known world is then a world of change and relativity. Everything changes, and everything is relative to some other thing. We have never come across anything entirely permanent and absolute. Must we therefore conclude that there *is* nothing unchanging, eternal, and absolute?

This is, indeed, the picture of the universe that is presented by many of the most influential thinkers of our time—a world of pure relativity in which there is no single stable element. It is something like an infinitely tall skyscraper where floor stands upon floor, but no floor stands on solid ground. From the height at which we now stand, we can look down (into the past), and see the building disappearing to a "vanishing point" in an immense well of space. But if there is no solid ground on which the whole structure can stand, the floors must descend for ever beyond this vanishing point, standing on each other and on nothing else. Or, to change the illustration, such a universe is not unlike a nation where each individual makes his living, not out of the soil, but by taking in his neighbor's washing. Such a nation would be as economically unstable as the skyscraper would be architecturally unstable. The entire structure would be a process of collapse.

But we need never entertain such fantastic pictures if we look carefully at the idea on which they are based—the notion that "Everything is relative; everything is in a state of change." For in fact these statements do not mean anything at all. They are pure nonsense.

We saw that such ideas as change, motion, and energy had meaning only because of their opposites. "Change" is a meaningful word, an understandable process, only in relation to stillness or permanence. We recognize change by comparing it with something unchanging. If, then, *everything* changes, how do we know that it changes, since there is nothing permanent in relation to which it changes? We might just as well say, "Everything is half," or "Everything is up," or, for that matter, "Everything is blah."

But if such things as change and permanence exist only *in relation* to each other, can we not say that "Everything is relative"? Certainly the same rule must apply. The word "relative" is meaningless when applied to everything. Indeed, there is something fundamentally peculiar about these "Everything is" statements. None of them make sense. And the peculiar thing is this: to say something about everything is to say nothing about everything! It is like painting a picture that is all one color: you have no picture.

We can go further. If it makes no sense to say "Everything is relative," it does not even make sense to say "Everything *is*." To say that everything has existence adds absolutely nothing to one's knowledge of the universe, for one is not actually saying anything about everything. It is merely to say, "Every thing which exists, exists." In other words, "A rose is a rose." So what?

We can begin to see, now, what is the real difficulty with these statements. In making them we have used many words that actually mean something—"thing," "relative," "is," "change," "exists." I can say, "Some things (such as planets and men) exist," and make sense because I am implying that "Some things (such as gryphons and goblins) do not exist." Obviously, then, the difficulty is simply in the word "everything." It cannot mean anything unless it has an opposite. But if it does not have an opposite, it will be impossible for us to form any ideas at all about the world, the universe that we experience as a whole.

So we must ask the question, "Is there anything else besides everything?" It may sound like a silly question, but if the answer is "No," we shall have to take the word "everything" out of the dictionary as a mere meaningless noise. Who, then, are the candidates for the position of the opposite of everything?

The first to be examined is obviously "Nothing." This is a strange candidate who has to be disqualified at once, having the odd defect of not even appearing for the examination. He is not. Furthermore the word "nothing" cannot be used in any sensible statement as the opposite of everything. I can say, "There is nothing in this box," and make sense. But if nothing is the opposite of everything, I should also be able to say, "There is everything in this box," and still make sense. But I can't.

In other words, to oppose everything to nothing is simply not to oppose it to anything. If no other opposite can be found, the idea of everything, of the universe itself, is in a most precarious position. And if the idea is precarious, what about the reality? For surely the two are inseparable. Surely the word "everything" has meaning in that it denotes a reality—the reality of all stars, all galaxies, all bodies in space and time, all processes, all relations, all electrons. Yet apparently these things, all things, are like some princess in a story-book who must find a husband or be beheaded. Nothing, in other words, no husband, simply won't do.

What, then, *could* be the opposite that will make the idea and the reality of everything both meaningful and possible? For if this opposite is to be some thing, as distinct from nothing, will not this something already be included in "everything" and so still be unable to be its opposite?

Indeed, it seems as if the strangeness of reality will have to surpass every flight of fancy that myth, legend, or fairy-tale has ever conceived. For the prince who can save the princess from having her head chopped off must be neither a nothing nor a something, for a nothing is no husband, and a something is the princess herself.

It depends, of course, on what we mean by a *thing*. For to talk about all things is actually to talk about all stars, electrons, etc., that is, about all *relative* things. If the Flatlanders were to talk about all things, they would be meaning all things in their world of two dimensions. But we know of other things, such as cubes, which would be outside their definition of all things.

Let us suppose that the relative world that we know is like a map, but an incomplete map in the sense that it has edges or margins at which roads, rivers, and oceans simply come to an abrupt end. These edges are the limits of our sense-knowledge. Now science gives us theories of what lies beyond these edges, but these theories have a particular limitation. The scientist looks at the map, and sees that on the map itself every road leads to a town and every river to an ocean—except those that run off the edge. He cannot see how these end. But he reasons that roads and rivers running off the map will do the same things as those on the map: they will lead to other towns and other oceans. His theories as to the positions of these other towns and oceans may be most ingenious. He may deduce that two roads that, at the point of leaving the map, have been approaching each other will probably lead to the same town. But this particular kind of reasoning leads only to the idea of more towns, more roads, more rivers, and more oceans.

Yet the philosopher wants to know whether this map is simply one section of a surface that goes on for ever and ever. Is there anything else, he asks, besides indefinite map, indefinite towns, roads, and rivers? Is there anything else besides everything?—"everything" being defined as a surface bearing towns, roads, and rivers.

Now the philosopher knows, from evidence within his experience, that you cannot have unsupported surfaces. He has never seen any object that was simply a surface, much less a surface indefinitely extended. He knows that every surface is finite, and is the outside of a solid. If you travel across a surface, you will go round the solid and return to the same place. He reasons that the same will be true of the map. Follow any road far enough off the map, and you will return to the same place on the map—sometime—whether the shape of the underlying solid be spherical, cubic, ovoid, or pyramidal.

The same process of reasoning suggests, therefore, that the known universe is part of a finite system. It is not galaxies of stars and areas of space extending for ever and ever, still less a series of effects and causes going backwards for ever and ever in a straight line of time—a skyscraper standing on nothing. Underlying the finite surface is a solid; underlying two dimensions is a third; underlying the map is the terrestrial globe. But just as the Flatlanders cannot conceive a third dimension, a cube or sphere, so we have difficulty in conceiving the kind of "Something" that would underlie the "everything" that we know with our finite senses.

Nevertheless, it is reasonable and necessary to suppose that this "Something" exists as the solid, the opposite, supporting and giving meaning to all that we know. It is not in the class of relative things, just as the sphere is not in the class of surfaces, and the earth not in the class of towns, roads, rivers, and oceans.

It is furthermore reasonable to conclude that if all known things are relative and changing, spatial and temporal, the "Something" that supports them and gives them both meaning and existence by *contrast*, will be absolute and permanent, spaceless and timeless. For want of a better name, we shall call it the Absolute.

BEYOND TIME AND SPACE

When you take a voyage into unknown latitudes, you must remember that you cannot remain on course without making corrections for wind and currents. Similar "corrections" must be made, and held constantly in mind, in trying to go beyond time and space into the realm of the Absolute. Remember that you cannot represent a cube on a flat surface without using the convention, the trick, of perspective. You represent the third dimension with lines that are still in two dimensions. Similarly, when you want to show, on a flat map, that the earth is spherical you draw curved lines of longitude, or draw each "side" of the globe within a circular border. This results in distortions and inaccuracies, which will be confusing if it is forgotten that "tricks" have been used.

Representing the globe on a flat map is like trying to talk and think about the Absolute. The two dimensions of the map correspond respectively to time and space, and the human mind cannot think except in terms of time and space. Alternatively, we can think of the two dimensions of the map as corresponding to the fact that we have to think in terms of opposites. Because the mind is part of the relative world, it cannot possibly escape this limitation.

Therefore we can only talk about the Absolute by using a convention. To avoid confusion, we must be clear from the start as to what this convention is, and constantly make "corrections" for it. In brief, the convention is that we must talk about the Absolute *as if* it were another relative thing. Otherwise we should not be able to talk it at all, for we have no language, no ideas, at our disposal other than the relative.

This will be clarified if we rehearse, in another way, the argument that compels us to admit that there is an Absolute. Experience shows us nothing whatsoever that is not dependent on something else. No part of this universe can exist without dependence on, and relation to, other parts. This *is* relativity. But it is simple to understand that if *everything* is dependent, the universe *cannot* exist. For if absolutely everything is dependent, there is nothing on which it depends.

It does not help in the least to try to get out of this dilemma by making the dependent universe infinite, for you do not get an independent thing by adding many dependent things together. A hat hangs on a peg attached to a hat that hangs on a peg attached to a hat. . . . However large this hat-chain may be, it collapses unless it finally arrives at some fixed and independent peg. Hanging all by itself, it is absurd, like the grin of the Cheshire Cat in *Alice in Wonderland*, which hung in the air when the cat had vanished. To make the chain infinite is only to make it infinitely absurd. This is not a solution of the problem. It is merely the indefinite postponement of a solution. Nor does it help to hang the last hat on a peg attached to the first, making the process of dependence circular. It still collapses.

But we know that there *are* things, and that all known things are dependent. We are thus forced to the conclusion that there must be some unknown thing that is independent—that does not hang on anything because it does not need to. If there is not, then there cannot be any dependent things. But there are!

In our known world there are only relatively independent things. That is to say, there are only things that are independent of some things. For instance, hat No. 4 on the chain will be independent of 3, 2, and 1, but dependent on 5 and all those above. For us, then, the terms dependent and independent are relative. They have meaning only by contrast with each other. We cannot really think or conceive a thing independent of all other things, because every known thing is dependent.

To put it in another way: we describe and know things by their relations with each other. We know light by contrast with darkness. Light without darkness, or darkness without light, are alike inconceivable. Similarly, a relative, or dependent, world is meaningless save by contrast with an absolute or independent. But it should follow, logically, that an absolute is inconceivable without the relative. If so, we shall only be saying that the independent must depend on the dependent, or that the absolute can exist only in relation to the relative. But this will amount to saying that it is neither absolute nor independent!

This is the inescapable limitation of our two-dimensional way of thinking. We are compelled to think of the Absolute as the opposite of the relative, because we can only think in opposites—in relativities. This is the convention that we must use if we are to think of the Absolute at all; we have to represent it as something relative, as, on the surface, the solid must be represented by something flat. Therefore we have to remember this correction: the Absolute is the opposite of the relative, without which the relative could have neither meaning nor existence. But it is not opposed to the relative in the same way that relative things, such as light and darkness, are opposed to each other. The difference is this: whereas the relative cannot exist without the Absolute, the Absolute *can* exist without the relative. If it could not, it would not *be* the Absolute because it would depend on the relative.

This proposition is only illogical in the same sense that the angles of a cube drawn on a flat surface are not all right angles. Logic is simply the law of relativity. It corresponds to the fact that on a flat surface—in the world of relativity—you can only have length and breadth. You may draw a third line to represent depth, but in fact it will still lie in the dimensions of length and breadth, and your statement that it forms right angles with the other two lines will seem absurd—i.e., illogical. But it is only illogical *if* there are no other dimensions than length and breadth.

Similarly, it is only illogical to speak of the Absolute *if* "everything is relative." But logic itself is enough to show that the statement, "Everything is relative," is meaningless. Thought, in other words, requires something beyond itself that it cannot define, just as the existence of a surface requires an underlying solid that cannot, however, be actually represented in terms of surface.

Now we can never arrive at the Absolute by indefinite extension of the relative, just as we shall never get the idea of the solid from the indefinite increase of the surface—unless, perhaps, the surface bends back on itself and we return to our starting-point. This was the weakness of the old arguments for the Absolute that tried to prove that events must run back to a First Cause in time. Beyond every time you can always imagine an earlier time, beyond every hat you can always conceive another hat. Logically, you need *never* arrive at the first time, or the fixed hat-peg. But because you need never do so, logic itself is indicating that the *direction* of your search is futile.

We ask, "On what does this dependent universe depend?" We look back and back into time, or out and out into space, to find only more and more dependent things. In this direction we never arrive at anything final. The only gain from this quest is an increasing sense of the absurdity of a purely relative cosmos.

Our thinking must, therefore, take a new departure—a jump into a new dimension, not following time and space for ever, but, as it were, turning off at right angles to them. This will give us a very different picture of the First Cause than the old picture of the Original Push that, aeons ago, started the universe off. The universal process is not, so to speak, a row of bricks falling down because God pushed the first brick (see figure 1.5). We shall find the First Cause not so much at the temporal beginning of everything as at the present root of everything. Picture time as a sphere, like the astronomers' curved space. The Origin of this sphere, the First Cause, the Absolute, will not be anywhere on the sphere, but "inside" it (see figure 1.6). This shows us all the events in time, and for that matter in space too, radiating from the First Cause. Only we must be careful to remember that this is a "conventional" picture, and that there is not actually any space or time between the center and any point on the outside.

Around the outside of this sphere all events depend on one another in a complex network that has no observable beginning or end. But while each

Figure 1.5. "The First Cause."

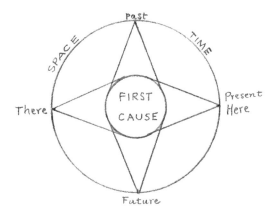

Figure 1.6. Events in time radiating from the First Cause.

depends on the others, all depend on the center—that does not depend on anything at all.

Something analogous to this idea of the Absolute as the "center" of all things is found in modern physics. For in asking, "What makes the universe tick?" physics has found that the most profitable line of inquiry has not been the investigation of an unobservable past, nor even the plumbing of fathomless space. The most fruitful results have come from looking into the heart of things, asking not "What made them as they are?" but "What *makes* them as they are?" In such a way we seek the First Cause neither in an immeasurably distant past, nor in a heaven beyond the uttermost nebulae. We seek it within the electrons that constitute our being at this moment.

The clue, then, to an understanding of the Absolute is that the relative world requires an opposite in order to exist, since by itself relativity is meaningless. But this opposite is not within the scheme of relativity, for which reason, *it* does not require the relative. Between relative things, opposition is mutual and reciprocal. But in the Major Dyad of Absolute and Relative, the opposition is "one way only."

Keeping this peculiar relationship in mind, we can understand certain properties of the Absolute simply by contrasting it with properties of the relative. Other properties of the Absolute can be suggested by asking what kind of reality would be sufficient to cause all various qualities and relations of the known universe.

We saw that among the chief characteristics of the relative world were time, space, and change. By contrast, these imply that the Absolute is eternal, infinite, and immutable. But in using these words, we must be careful not to confuse them with certain popular and incorrect senses that custom has attached to them.

To the average man *eternal* means everlasting, eternal life being a life that goes on through endless time without ceasing. But this somewhat nightmarish idea has nothing to do with eternity in its true sense. For eternity is not time—much less unending time. Time is perhaps not easy to define. When asked what time was, St. Augustine replied, "I know, but when you ask me I don't!" Yet if we consider what we mean by time, it is easy to see that it means at least this—the experience, or occurrence, of events in a one-way stream of succession. Time is really change—a process in which events come one after another in an irreversible order. In our basic diagram of the Absolute and the Relative, time is motion round the outer circle, so that B is *after* A and *before* C. A, B, and C stand in *successive* order (see figure 1.7).

But from the standpoint of the center, from which the whole surface "radiates," A, B, and C are all equally present, for we saw that there is neither time nor space between the center and any point on the circumference. Eternity is, then, a standpoint from which all events are not successive but *simultaneous*.

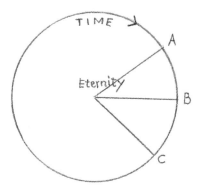

Figure 1.7. Relations of time and eternity.

When you look at your hand, you can see all five fingers at once, even though they are distant from each other in space. Supposing, however, that the five fingers are five distant points of time—the years 1900, 1905, 1910, 1915, and 1920. Eternity is a point of reference to which these five points of time are as present as your fingers are present to you.

Or again: if you walk into a dark room with a flashlight that casts a thin beam, you will only be able to know what is in the room by shining the bean upon one small section after another, successively. This is like the viewpoint of time. But if you turn on the main light in the ceiling, you will see the whole room at once, having a view somewhat like that of eternity. Eternity is therefore a sort of permanent moment, in which all times are now.

Somewhat the same principles underlie the true meaning of infinity. To say that the Absolute is infinite is not to say that it is indefinitely immense, like a space going outward for ever and ever. As eternity is a point of reference to which all times are now, infinity is a point of reference to which all places are *here*. This is why it is possible to say that the Absolute is everywhere, or omnipresent, not like a gas that is diffused, but as something that is present at every point of space in its entirety. Infinity in the "immense" meaning, would not be true infinity at all: it would be ordinary, relative space.

Likewise, to say that the Absolute is immutable is not to say that it is static—i.e., that it remains without change or movement for an interminable period of time. This is merely relative stillness—the stillness of a rock as compared with the stillness of a river. A static stillness of this kind could hardly be responsible for all the motions of this universe. The Absolute is immutable because it does not change, and it does not change because its whole action and existence is simultaneous—not successive. The "action" by which it causes the relative world requires no effort, that is, no crossing of space or perpetuation through time. The action by which it caused the lighting of the first suns is the same identical action by which it now causes the vibration of a mosquito's wing. There has been no change, for it does all things at once.

Although, to this point, we have said several things about the Absolute, we have not actually said *what* it is. We have said *that* it is, because a purely relative world requires it as its necessary opposite. We have said what it is *not*, because, by opposition to the relative world, we find it to be nontemporal, nonspatial, and nonchangeable. But we are never going to be able to say *what* it is, because human thought and language can only answer the question "What?" by standing outside the object to be described, and comparing it with other things. But we cannot stand outside the Absolute without immediately ceasing to exist. Every point from which one might look at it is a point "inside" it, and the very ability to look is a power that the Absolute supplies. Now if our eyes cannot look at themselves, if the knower cannot know himself, how much less can we see and know the Origin of sight and knowledge.

In the act of knowing, the knower knows *that* he is. He also knows that he is *not* the things that he knows, as the eyes are not the things that they see. Our knowledge of the Absolute is, then, similar to this obscure knowledge of ourselves, since we know that we are and what we are not, rather than what we are. We cannot stand outside ourselves to see what we are. This kind of knowledge of the Absolute may make it seem something peculiarly vague and negative.

But still another kind of knowledge is possible, knowledge based on the fact that, because everything in the relative world depends on the Absolute and is caused by it, the nature of the Absolute must be *adequate* to produce this world. Let us suppose for a moment that the Absolute is some kind of blind force, like electricity—a force essentially blind and unconscious and mechanical. Would a force of this kind be able to produce the everyday world that we know? To many people, this seems possible enough, for if a blind force were to go on shaping and re-shaping itself long enough, the chances are that it would eventually shape itself into *this* form—this form that we call life, knowledge, beauty, order, and so forth.

The idea may seem plausible, but it has a fatal flaw. If I assert that the Absolute, the basic force of the universe, is unconscious and unintelligent, I must also assert that I myself, and my conscious mind, are parts and products of this force. The idea that this is so will also have to be part of it, because it is part of my mind. But if myself, my mind, and my idea, are nothing but special forms of unintelligent force, how can I assert that this idea is intelligent? For I am really saying this: "My idea that the basic force of the universe is unintelligent is itself a form of this unintelligence!" If so, it is not an intelligent idea.

If I am to claim that my own mind is in any sense conscious or intelligent, I am bound to admit that the force that shapes it is *at least* conscious and intelligent. To say that consciousness is a special form of unconsciousness, and intelligence a special form of unintelligence, is to say that the presence of a certain power is a special form of its absence. This comes perilously close to saying that something is a special form of nothing.

Nonsense of this kind is the inevitable result of denying to the First Cause *at least* the properties and faculties that we ourselves enjoy. This is not to say, however, that the Absolute is conscious and intelligent in the *same way* that we are. It is saying that if it can cause intelligence, it must not only be at least intelligent, but, indeed, something *more* than intelligent.

The reason for this "more" is that the less is always the result of the greater, never the greater of the less. Take, for example, the power of heat. Something that is merely warm does not, all by itself, become hot. More heat is not simply the result of less heat. The increase of heat must be derived from something most hot—such as fire. Similarly, more life (or more intelligence) does not just "evolve" all by itself from less life, or no life—for this would imply again the nonsense that the presence of a power is the result of its absence. What we call evolution is the progressive derivation of life from something that is *most* alive—as water gets hotter and hotter, and finally turns into steam, by deriving heat progressively from the fire beneath it.

We can see, then, that the evolution of consciousness and mind from the relatively blind world of vegetable and mineral nature is progressive sharing in the life and power of the Absolute. This implies that the more we are able to share in the life of the Absolute, the more conscious, the more intelligent, we can become. For this reason, knowledge of the Absolute is no mere philosophical pastime, but a matter of the highest possible importance. It can carry us yet further in the course of evolution, and lead to possibilities of life and knowledge beyond our dreams.

This, indeed, is what is implied in the truth that the Absolute is not only our "origin," but also our "goal." In the traditional language of philosophy, the Absolute is known both as the First Cause and as the Final Cause—that is, the end toward which the universal process moves, as well as the point from which it begins.

To understand this point, we must remember again that as the world-process does not start from the Absolute *in time*, neither does it disappear into it in time. Our diagram of the Absolute-Relative relationship is seen in figure 1.8:

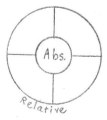

Figure 1.8. The absolute-relative relationship.

Not this (figure 1.9):

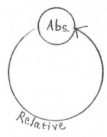

Figure 1.9. An incorrect view of the absolute-relative relationship.

This is only to say that the relative world never was, and never will become, the *same thing* as the Absolute. By its nature, the Absolute is *not* relative, and could not become relative without ceasing to be Absolute. The same is true in reverse. The relative is not the Absolute, and could not become the Absolute without ceasing to exist.

The process of becoming lies only around the circle. There is no becoming as between the circle and its center, for becoming requires time, and between circle and center there is no time. When water boils over the fire, it does not become fire, even though fire is the cause of its boiling. It becomes hot water, and eventually steam. In other words, it becomes as *like* fire as water can become. In the same way, the relative world "surrounding" the unchanging fire of the Absolute will, in time, become as like the Absolute as relative things can become.

To know, then, what the Absolute is like in terms of relative things and relative knowledge, to represent the Absolute in the form of the relative, is to move toward the goal and perfection of relative existence. Thus the task of philosophy is to show man where he is going—the end toward which all his activities must be directed if they are not to be in vain.

REFERENCE

Einstein, A., & Infeld, L. (1938). *The evolution of physics. The growth of ideas from early concepts to relativity and quanta.* Cambridge, UK: Cambridge University Press.

CHAPTER TWO

The Negative Way (1951)

To the Western mind, one of the most disconcerting things about Oriental teachings as found in the Vedanta and Buddhism is their negative language. We receive the impression that they think of God, the ultimate reality, as a void, and of man's final destiny as an absorption in this void with the consequent loss of his unique personality. In the Vedanta, Brahman is almost always described by negations—the nondual, the nonfinite, the formless, the nonparticular. At the same time, the finite world of forms and individual beings is described as the unreal, the *maya*, which must disappear from the awakened consciousness.

In Buddhism, the highest reality is called *sunyata*, the empty, which is neither being nor nonbeing, which is so ineffable that every statement about it must be false. It appears that the way to a realization of the ultimate involves the strict denial of one's own and every other form of existence. Most Western people think that "variety is the spice of life," and therefore do not take at all kindly to a view of the highest good that seems to require the obliteration of all finite experiences. A state of "consciousness," which is neither "conscious nor unconscious," in which all particular things seem to vanish into a luminous haze, does not appeal to them as anything but extremely boring. Furthermore, they cannot see that such ideas of the highest reality have any philosophical cogency. For how can the basis, the ground, of these very solid, concrete, and particular finite experiences be so much of a nothing? How can something so startling, so real-seeming, so simultaneously wonderful and tragic as the everyday world, emerge from so impalpable a void?

From *Vedanta and the West*, 1951, 4(4), 97–101. Copyright © 1951 by Vedanta Society of Southern California. Reprinted with permission of Vedanta Press.

The problem here is almost entirely one of language, for it has never been clear to the Western mind in what *sense* these negations are intended. By contrast, the Christian, Jewish, and Islamic religions appear to be very positive, for their statements about the highest reality are affirmations rather than denials. Instead of speaking coldly about the "nondual infinite" they speak warmly of the Righteous Father, who is a living, personal Being, whose nature is unbounded justice and love. So long as it is imagined that, say, the Vedanta and Christianity are speaking the same kind of language, their ideas must seem to be utterly opposed.

If we do not know the ultimate reality, we stand in somewhat the same relation to it as blind men to color. If I am to describe color to a blind man, I can do it in one of two ways. I can tell him what color is *like*, or I can say what it is *not*. I cannot possibly tell him what it *is*. I can compare it to variations in temperature, speaking of red as "warm" and blue as "cold," though this will perhaps mislead the blind man into thinking that red *is* warm. On the other hand, I can say that color is *not* hard or soft, round or square, liquid or solid. The danger here is that the blind man may easily suppose that I am talking about nothing, for I have denied to color every positive quality that he knows.

To some extent, this is the difference between the religious doctrines of the West and the metaphysical doctrines of Asia. The former wants to say what reality is *like*, and the latter what it is not, but the average mind supposes that both are trying to say what it *is*. Hence the confusion.

But the negative mode of approach to the ultimate reality involves rather more than this, and to understand it properly we must try to see exactly what is being negated. Another principle that both the Vedanta and Buddhism hold in common is that, in reality, "all this"—the whole world of experience, including myself and others—is in essence identical with *sunyata* or Brahman. In other words, there is no reality but the absolute, nondual, and ultimate reality. This is taken to be a radical denial of the everyday world, as if distinct people and things had no value or meaning whatsoever.

It is therefore tremendously important to realize that the negative way is not making a negation about reality—about the real "something" that is the basis of everyday experience. The denial applies strictly to the ideas, the concepts, the theories, and the fixed categories of thought whereby we try to understand and grasp what we experience. The metaphysical doctrines of the Orient are saying that you cannot grasp reality in any fixed form of thought or feeling; you cannot nail it down and possess it. We try to do this because almost all of us feel insecure. We have identified our consciousness with a seemingly fixed form—a structure of memories called "I." We discover that this structure is impermanent, and are therefore afraid. We therefore cling all the more tenaciously to life, to "I," and become still more afraid, involving ourselves in a vicious circle of clinging that is called *samsara*—the "round" of existence.

But the real world, which is the basis of everyday experience, cannot be "fixed"—and every attempt to do so results in frustration and vicious circles.

Yet this world, this reality that we experience at every moment is Brahman. For example, I point to a tree and say, "This is a tree." Obviously *this* and *tree* are not actually the same thing. *Tree* is a word, a noise. It is not this experienced reality to which I am pointing. To be accurate, I should have said, "This (pointing to a tree) is symbolized by the noise *tree*."

If, then, the real tree is not the word or the idea *tree*, what is it? If I say that it is an impression on my senses, a vegetable structure, or a complex of electrons, I am merely putting new sets of words and symbols in place of the original noise *tree*. I have not said *what* it is at all. I have also raised other questions: "What are my senses?" "What is a structure?" "What are electrons?"

We can never say *what* these things are. We can symbolize them by sundry noises and patterns of thought. We can, in turn, symbolize these noises by other noises—"*Tree* is a *word*," or "A pattern of thought is an *idea*"—but this does not really explain anything. We still do not know *what* a tree, a word, a noise, or an idea actually is. And yet we have experienced mysterious "somethings," which we have arbitrarily paired off with each other—the sight of the tree with the noise *tree*, the process of thinking with the noise *idea*, and the noises *tree* and *idea* with the noise *words*.

Human beings are very much bewitched by words and ideas. They forget that they are mere symbols. They tend to confuse them seriously with the real world that they only represent. The reason for this confusion is that the world of words and ideas seems to be relatively fixed and rational, whereas the real world is not fixed at all. Thus the world of words and ideas seems to be so much safer, so much more comprehensible than the real world. The word and idea *tree* has remained fixed currency for many centuries, but real trees have behaved in a very odd way. I can try to describe their behavior by saying that they have appeared and disappeared, that they have been in a constant state of change, and that they flow in and out of their surroundings.

But this does not really say what they have done, because *disappear*, *change*, *flow*, and *surroundings* are still noises representing something utterly mysterious.

Our problem, then, is that so long as we try to fit the real world into the "nice little, tight little" world of definitions, ideas, and words (*nama-rupa*), we shall never succeed in doing so, save in the most approximate and impermanent way. On the other hand, to know Brahman, to see God, is to be aware of the real world in its undefined (i.e., infinite) state. This is to know life without trying to capture it in the fixed forms of conventional words and ideas. It is only by convention that the aspect of reality called *man* is separated off from all other aspects—the earth, the air, the sun, moon and stars. It is convenient to do this (which is what "convention" means), but it does not fully correspond to the facts, which are that man is a process continuous with every other process, and that the boundaries between these processes are fixed arbitrarily by the human mind. For example, who is to say whether a man begins and ends with birth and death, or with conception and the final decay of his corpse? Is he limited in space by his skin, or does he extend out to the distance to which he can hear, smell, and see? All these boundaries are as conventional and arbitrary as the length of an inch or the weight of a pound: you can put them anywhere you like, so long as you agree about them with others.

At root, then, to cling to oneself is as absurd as cleaving passionately to an inch. It just cannot be done, and the attempt is pure frustration. To say, then, that reality is not any particular thing, and that individuals are unreal, is in principle exactly the same thing as pointing out that two yards have no existence apart from a real piece of cloth or wood. You cannot make a dress out of two, or two million, abstract yards.

We have to learn, then, to take all conventional distinctions and definitions for what they are—purely arbitrary and unreal conveniences—and to be keenly aware of life *as it is* (*yatha bhutam*) apart from all definitions, measurements, and arbitrary boundaries. To see the world in this way is to see Brahman, the undefinable. In this sense, every one of us has already an obscure and neglected knowledge of Brahman—but it is not knowledge in the ordinary meaning of the word. Ordinarily, we mean that to know something is to be able to define it. In fact, however, we know a whole world that we cannot define at all, but we do not make friends with it. We are afraid of it, and are always trying to tie it up safely in watertight packages.

When St. Augustine was asked what time was, he replied, "I know, but when you ask me I don't." The same is true of reality. We know it all the time, but when we begin to think about it, it vanishes. Thus it is said in Zen Buddhism, "If you want to see into it, see into it directly. When you begin to think about it, it is altogether missed." For the same reason the *Kena Upanishad* says, "He who thinks that Brahman is not comprehended, by him Brahman is comprehended; but he who thinks that Brahman is comprehended knows It not. Brahman is unknown to those who know It, and it is known to those who do not know It at all."

Brahman, then, is the real world as it is in itself, before we begin to describe or define it in any way, before we split it asunder into millions of arbitrary distinctions called feet, inches, stars, trees, men, ounces, pounds, and mountains. A Chinese poem expresses it thus:

> Plucking chrysanthemums along the east fence;
> Gazing in silence at the southern hills;
> The birds flying home in pairs
> Through the soft mountain air of dusk—
> In these things there is a deep meaning,
> But when we are about to express it,
> We suddenly forget the words.

I know, but when you ask me I don't. If you want me to show you God, I will point to the ash can in your back yard. But if you ask, "Then you mean that this ash can is God?"—you will have missed the point altogether.

CHAPTER THREE

The Language of Metaphysical Experience

The Sense of Non-Sense (1953)

There is an area of human experience for which we do not have any really suitable name in our Western languages, for while it is basic to such matters as religion, metaphysics, and mysticism, it is not identical with any one of them. I refer to the perennial type of experience that is described as a more or less immediate knowledge of God, or of the ultimate reality, ground or essence of the universe, by whatever name it may be represented.[1]

According to the ancient spiritual traditions of both Europe and Asia, which include ways of life and thought as widely different as Buddhism and Catholicism, this experience is the supreme fulfillment of human life—the goal, the final end, toward which human existence is ordered.

According, however, to modern logical philosophy—scientific empiricism, logical positivism, and the like—statements of this kind are simply meaningless. While it is admitted that there may be interesting and delightful experiences of the "mystical" type, logical philosophy finds it altogether illegitimate to regard them as containing any knowledge of a metaphysical character, as constituting an experience of "ultimate reality" or the Absolute.

This critique is based not so much upon a psychological analysis of the experience itself as upon purely logical analysis of such universal concepts as God, Ultimate Reality, Absolute Being, and the like—all of which are shown to be terms without meaning. It is not the purpose of this paper to describe the steps of this critique in any detail, since it should be familiar enough to every student of modern philosophy, and since there seems no need to take issue with the logical argument itself. The starting point of this paper is one which,

From the *Journal of Religious Thought*, 1953, *10*(2), 132–143. Copyright © 1953 by Howard University. Reprinted with permission of Howard University.

perversely it may seem, regards the basic argument of modern logical philosophy as a highly important contribution to metaphysical thought—enabling us to evaluate the true character and function of metaphysical terms and symbols far less confusedly than has hitherto been possible.

This evaluation, however, is not the sort of devaluation that the individual exponents of logical philosophy, such as Russell, Ayer, and Reichenbach, propose. For the positive contribution of logical philosophy to metaphysics and religion has been obscured by the fact that such exponents were not content to be logicians. Because of a certain emotional bias against religious or metaphysical points of view, this logical critique has been used as an instrument in a polemic, even a propaganda, with emotional rather than logical motivations.

It is one thing to demonstrate that the concept of Being is without logical meaning. It is quite another to go on to say that this, and similar metaphysical concepts, are not philosophy but poetry, where the term "poetry" carries a very strongly implied pooh-pooh. The implication is that the "poetry" of religious and metaphysical symbols may be cause or effect of very exquisite and inspiring emotional experiences, but these, like "the arts" in wartime, are among the nonessentials of life. The serious philosopher regards them as charming toys—as means of decorating life, not of understanding it—in somewhat the same way as a physician might adorn his office with a medicine mask from the South Seas. All this is merely damning with faint praise.

While the exponents of logical philosophy have, on their side, sought to devalue the insights of metaphysics and religion, the would-be defenders of Faith have for the most part looked around somewhat ineffectually for means of defeating logical philosophy at its own game. On the whole, the more successful counterattack has seemed to be returning one pooh-pooh for another; as, for instance, the quip that Ayer, Reichenbach, and company have exchanged philosophy for grammar.

Yet in the context of Western philosophy and religion this situation is not at all surprising, for we have always been under the impression that religio-metaphysical statements are of the same order as scientific and historical statements. We have generally taken it for granted that the proposition, "There is a God," is a statement of the same kind as, "There are stars in the sky." The assertion that "all things have being" has always seemed to convey information in the same way as the assertion that "all men are mortal." Furthermore, "The universe was made by God" has seemed as much a statement of historical type as that "the telephone was invented by Thomas Edison."

Dr. F. S. C. Northrop is thus perfectly correct in pointing to the essential similarity between science, on the one hand, and the Hebrew-Christian religious tradition, on the other, in so far as both are concerned with "truth" as a structure of objective reality, whose nature is determinate even if unseen. Indeed, the scientific spirit has its historical origins in the type of mentality that is concerned to know the supernatural and the unseen in terms of positive propositions, which wants to know *what facts* lie beneath the surface of events. Thus Christian theology and science stand in somewhat the same historical relation as astrology and astronomy, alchemy and chemistry, both constituting a body of theory to explain the past and predict the future.[2]

But Christianity did not disappear with the alchemists. Since the rise of modern science, theology has played a most problematic role. It has taken many different attitudes to science, ranging from denouncing it as a rival doctrine, through conciliation and adaptation, to a sort of withdrawal in which it is felt that theology speaks of a realm of being inaccessible to scientific inquiry. Throughout, there has been the general assumption on the part of both theologians and scientists that the two disciplines were employing the same kind of language, and were interested in the same order of objective, determinate truths. Indeed, when some theologians speak of God as having "an objective, supernatural reality, independent of our minds and of the sensible world," it is impossible to see how their language differs from that of science. For it appears that God is some specific thing or fact—an objective existence—supernatural in the sense that he or it is imperceptible within the "wave band" of our sense organs and scientific instruments.

Where this confusion between the nature of religious or metaphysical statements, on the one hand, and scientific or historical statements, on the other, remains unclarified, it will, of course, be difficult indeed to see how modern logical philosophy can make any positive contribution to metaphysics. In a theological system where God plays the part of a scientific hypothesis, that is, a means of explaining and predicting the course of events, it is easy enough to show that the hypothesis adds nothing to our knowledge. One does not explain what happens by saying that God wills it. For if everything that happens is by divine intention or permission, the will of God becomes merely another name for "everything that happens." Upon logical analysis, the statement, "Everything is the will of God," turns out to be the tautology, "Everything is everything."

To cut a long story short, thus far the contribution of logical philosophy to metaphysics has been entirely negative. The verdict seems to be that, under logical scrutiny, the entire body of metaphysical doctrine consists either of tautology or nonsense. But this amounts to a total "debunking" of metaphysics only as it has been understood in the West—as consisting of meaningful statements conveying information about "transcendental objects." Oriental philosophy has never been of the serious opinion that metaphysical statements convey information of a positive character. Their function is not to denote "Reality" as an object of knowledge, but to "cure" a psychological process by which man frustrates and tortures himself with all kinds of unreal problems. To the Oriental mind, "Reality" cannot be expressed; it can only be known intuitively by getting rid of unreality, of contradictory and absurd ways of thinking and feeling.

The primary contribution of logical philosophy in this sphere is simply the confirmation of a point that has long been clear to both Hindus and Buddhists, though perhaps less widely realized in the Christian tradition. The point is that the attempt to talk about, think about, or know about the ultimate Reality constitutes an impossible task. If epistemology is the attempt to know what knows, and ontology the attempt to define "is-ness," they are clearly circular and futile procedures, like trying to bite one's own teeth. In a commentary on the *Kena Upanishad*, Shankara says:

> Now a distinct and definite knowledge is possible in respect of everything capable of becoming an object of knowledge; but it is not possible in the case of That which cannot become such an object. That is *Brahman*, for It is the Knower, and the Knower can know other things, but cannot make Itself the object of Its own knowledge, in the same way that fire can burn other things but cannot burn itself.

In the same way the *Brihadaranyaka Upanishad* says:

> Thou couldst not see the seer of sight, thou couldst not hear the hearer of hearing, nor perceive the perceiver of perception, nor know the knower of knowledge (iii, 4. 2).

Or in the words of a Chinese Buddhist poem:

> It is like a sword that wounds, but cannot wound itself;
> Like an eye that sees, but cannot see itself.[3]

A similar difficulty exists for physics in any attempt to investigate the nature of energy. For there is a point at which physics, as much as metaphysics, enters the realm of tautology and nonsense because of the circular character of the task that it attempts—to study electrons with instruments that are, after all, electrons themselves. At the risk of quoting a source that is somewhat *passé*, the classical statement of this problem is in Eddington's (1935) *Nature of the Physical World*:

> We have perhaps forgotten that there was a time when we wanted to be told what an electron is. The question was never answered. . . . *Something unknown is doing we don't know what*—that is what our theory amounts to. It does not sound a particularly illuminating theory. I have read something like it elsewhere:
>
> > The slithy toves
> > Did gyre and gimble in the wabe.
>
> There is the same suggestion of activity. There is the same indefiniteness as to the nature of the activity and of what it is that is acting. (p. 280)

Eddington (1935) goes on to point out that, despite this indefiniteness, physics can "get results" because the electrons, the unknowns within the atom, are countable.

> Eight slithy toves gyre and gimble in the oxygen wabe; seven in nitrogen. By admitting a few numbers even "Jabberwocky" may become scientific. We can now venture on a prediction: if one of its toves escapes, oxygen will be masquerading in a garb properly belonging to nitrogen. . . . It would not be a bad reminder of the essential unknownness of the fundamental entities of physics to translate it into "Jabberwocky"; provided all numbers—all metrical attributes—are unchanged, it does not suffer in the least. (p. 281)

The point that emerges is that what we are counting or measuring in physics, and that what we are experiencing in everyday life as sense data, is at root unknown and probably unknowable.

At this point modern logical philosophy dismisses the problem, and turns its attention to something else on the assumption that the unknowable need not and cannot concern us further. It asserts that questions that have neither the physical nor the logical possibility of an answer are no real questions. But this assertion does not get rid of the common human *feeling* that such unknowns or unknowables as electrons, energy, existence, consciousness, or "Reality" are in some way *queer*. The very fact of not being able to know them makes them all the queerer. Only a rather dry kind of mind turns away from them—a mind interested in nothing but logical structures. The more complete kind of mind, which can feel as well as think, remains to "indulge" the odd sense of mystery that comes from contemplating the fact that everything is at base something that cannot be known. Every statement that you make about this "something" turns out to be nonsense. And what is specially queer is that this unknowable something is also the basis of that which otherwise I know so intimately—myself.

Western man has a peculiar passion for order and logic, such that, for him, the entire significance of life consists in putting experience into orders. What is ordered is predictable, and thus a basis for "safe bets." We tend to show a psychological resistance to areas of life and experience where logic, definition, and order—i.e., "knowledge" in our sense—are inapplicable. For this type of mind the realm of indeterminacy and Brownian movements is frankly embarrassing, and the contemplation of the fact that everything is reducible to something we cannot think about is even disquieting. There is no real "reason" why it should be disquieting, because our inability to know what electrons are does not seem to interfere with our capacity to predict their behavior in our own macroscopic world.

The resistance is not based on some fear of an unpredictable action, which the unknown may produce, although I suspect that even the most hardened logical positivist would have to admit to some odd feelings in face of an unknown called death. The resistance is rather the fundamental unwillingness of this type of mind to contemplate the limits of its power to succeed, order, and control. It feels that if there are areas of life that it cannot order, it is surely reasonable (i.e., orderly) to forget them and turn to areas of life that *can* be ordered—so that the sense of success, of the mind's own competence, can be maintained. The contemplation of these intellectual limitations is, for the pure intellectual, a humiliation. But for the man who is something more than a calculator, the baffling is also the wonderful. In the face of the unknowable he feels with Goethe that

> the highest to which man can attain is wonder; and if the prime phenomenon makes him wonder, let him be content; nothing higher can it give him, and nothing further should he seek for behind it; here is the limit.

In the type of metaphysical or mystical experience that we are discussing, this feeling of wonder—which has all kinds of depths and subtleties—is one of two major components. The other is a feeling of liberation (the Hindu *moksha*), which attends the realization that an immense amount of human activity is directed to the solution of unreal and purely fantastic problems—to the attainment of goals that we do not actually desire.

Speculative metaphysics—ontology and epistemology—are the intellectual aspects of fantastic problems that are basically psychological, and by no means confined to persons of a philosophical or even religious turn of mind. As already indicated, the essential nature of this kind of problem is circular—the attempt to know the knower, to make fire burn fire. This is why Buddhism speaks of release—*nirvana*—as deliverance from the Wheel, and of seeking Reality as "like looking for an ox when you are riding on one."

The psychological basis of these circular problems becomes clear when we look into the assumptions upon which, for example, the problems of ontology are based. What premises of thought and feeling underlie men's efforts to know "being," "existence," or "energy" as objects? Clearly, one assumption is that these names refer to objects—an assumption that could not have been made if there were not beneath it the further assumption that "I," the knowing subject, am somehow different from "being," the supposed object. If it were perfectly clear that the question, "What is being?" is, in the final analysis, the same question as "What am I?" the circular and futile character of the question would have been obvious from the beginning. But that it was far from clear is shown by the fact that metaphysical epistemology could ask that question, "What am I?" or "What is that which is conscious?" without recognizing a still more obvious circle. Obviously, questions of this order could be taken seriously only because of some nonlogical feeling of the need for an answer.

This feeling, common, perhaps, to most human beings, is surely the sense that "I," the subject, am a unique, isolated entity. There would be no need whatsoever to wonder *what* I am unless in some way I felt strange to myself. But so long as my consciousness feels strange to, cut off, and separate from its own roots, I can *feel* meaning in an epistemological question that has no logical sense. For I feel that consciousness is a function of "I"—not recognizing that "I," the ego, is just another name for consciousness. The statement "I am conscious" is, then, a concealed tautology saying only that consciousness is a function of consciousness. It can escape from this circularity upon the sole condition that "I" is taken to mean very much more than consciousness or its contents. But, in the West, this is not a usual use of the word. We identify "I" with the conscious will, and do not admit moral authority or responsibility for what we do unconsciously and unintentionally—the implication being that such acts are not our deeds but merely events that "happen" within us. When "I" is identified with "consciousness," man feels himself to be a detached, separate, and uprooted entity acting "freely" in a void.

This uprooted feeling is doubtless responsible for the psychological insecurity of Western man, and his passion for imposing the values of order and logic upon the whole of his experience. Yet while it is obviously absurd to say that consciousness is a function of consciousness, there seem to be no means of knowing that of which consciousness *is* a function. That which knows—and which psychologists call somewhat paradoxically the unconscious—is never the object of its own knowledge.

Now consciousness, the ego, feels uprooted so long as it avoids and refuses to accept the fact that it does not and cannot know its own base or ground. But when this is recognized, the consciousness *feels* connected, rooted, even though it does not know *to what* it is connected, *in what* it is rooted. So long as it retains delusions of self-sufficiency, omni-competence, and individual free will, it ignores the unknown on which it rests. By the familiar "law of reversed effort," this refusal of the unknown brings the feeling of insecurity, and in its train all the frustrating and impossible problems, all the vicious circles of human life, from the exalted nonsense of ontology down to the vulgar realms of power politics, where individuals play at being God. The hideous contrivances of the police (the 100 percent safe and ordered) state for planning the planners and guarding the guards and investigating the investigators are simply the political and social equivalents of the quests of speculative metaphysics. Both alike have their psychological origin in the reluctance of consciousness, of the ego, to face its own limits, and to admit that the ground and essence of the known is the unknown.

It does not matter very much whether you call this unknown Brahman or Blah, though the latter term usually indicates the intention to forget it, and the former to keep it in mind. Keeping it in mind, the law of reversed effort works in the other direction. I realize that my very substance, that which I am, is altogether beyond grasping or knowing. It is not "I"—a word that suggests that it means something; it is non-sense and no-thing, which is why Mahayana Buddhism calls it *Tathata*, of which a good translation might be "da-da," and *Sunyata*, the "void" or indeterminate. Similarly the Vedantists say, *"Tat tvam asi"*—*"That* art thou"—without ever giving a positive designation of what *that* is. The man who tries to know, to grasp himself, becomes insecure, just as one suffocates by holding one's breath. Conversely, the man who really knows that he cannot grasp himself gives up, relaxes, and is at ease. But he never really knows if he simply dismisses the problem, and does not pause to wonder, to feel, and to become vividly aware of the real impossibility of self-knowledge.

To the religious mentality of the modern West, this entirely negative approach to Reality is almost incomprehensible, for it suggests only that the world is based on the shifting sands of nonsense and caprice. For those who equate sanity with order this is a doctrine of pure despair. Yet little more than five hundred years ago a Catholic mystic was saying of God, "By love He may be gotten and holden, but by thought never," and that God must be known through "unknowing," through "mystical ignorance" (McCann, 1943).[4] And the love of which he spoke was not emotion. It was the general state of mind that exists when a man, through the realization of its impossibility, is no longer trying to grasp himself, to order everything and be dictator of the universe.

In our own day logical philosophy provides the same technique of negation, telling us that in every statement in which we think we have grasped or defined or merely designated Reality, we have uttered only nonsense. When the tongue tries to put *itself* into words, the most that may be expected is a tongue twister. For this reason, the procedures of logical philosophy will only be disquieting to those theologians and metaphysicians who imagine that their definitions of the Absolute actually define anything. But it was always perfectly clear to the philosophers of Hinduism and Buddhism, and to some fewer Catholic mystics, that words such as "Brahman," "Tathata," and "God" meant not something but no-thing. They indicated a void in knowledge, somewhat as a window is outlined by the frame.

Yet logical philosophy pursues its criticism further, and says that nonsense statements and exclamations of this order do not constitute philosophy because they contribute nothing to knowledge—by which they mean that they do not assist us to predict anything, and offer no directions for human conduct. That is, in part, true, though it misses the very obvious point that philosophy—wisdom—consists as much in its spaces as in its lines, in recognizing what is not and cannot be known as in the contrary. But we must go farther than this truism. Knowledge is more than know-how, and wisdom is more than predicting and ordering. Human life becomes a fantastic vicious circle when man tries to order and control the world and himself beyond certain limits, and these "negative metaphysics" at least convey the positive injunction to relax this excess of effort.

But beyond this they have a positive consequence that is still more important. They "integrate" logic and conscious thought with the indeterminate matrix, the non-sense, which we find at the root of all things. The assumption that the task of philosophy, as of human life, is fulfilled only in predicting and ordering, and that the "nonsensical" has no value, rests upon a sort of philosophical "schizophrenia." If man's work is entirely to go to war on chaos with logic, to determine the indeterminate; if the "good" is the logical and the "evil" the whimsical; then logic, consciousness, and the human brain is in conflict with the source of its own life and ability. We must never forget that the processes that form this brain are unconscious, and that beneath all the perceptible orders of the macroscopic world lies the indeterminate nonsense of the microscopic, the "gyring and gimbling" of a "tove" called energy—about which we know nothing. *Ex nihilo omnia fiunt.* But this nothing is a very strange thing.

Logical philosophy does not seem to have faced the fact that "non-sense" terms, so far from being valueless, are essential to every system of thought. It would be quite impossible to construct a philosophy or a science that is a "closed system" rigorously defining every term that it employs. Gödel has given us a clear mathematico-logical proof of the fact that no system can define its own axioms without self-contradiction, and, since Hilbert, modern mathematics employs the point as an entirely undefined concept. Just as the knife cuts other things, but not itself, so thought uses tools that define but cannot be defined; logical philosophy itself by no means escapes from this limitation.

For example, when logical philosophy asserts that "true meaning is a verifiable hypothesis" it must recognize that this very statement is meaningless if unverifiable. Similarly, when it insists that the only realities are those "facts" that are elicited in "scientific observation," it must recognize that it cannot, and does not, answer the question "What is a fact?" If we say that "facts" or "things" are the segments of experience symbolized by nouns, we are merely shifting the irreducible element of non-sense in our definition from "fact" to "experience." Some basic non-sense is entirely unavoidable, and the attempt to construct a completely self-defining system of thought is a vicious circle of tautology. Language can hardly dispense with the word "is," and yet the dictionary can only inform us that "what is" is "what exists," and that "what exists" is "what is."

If, then, it must be admitted that even one non-sense, meaningless, or undefined term is necessary to all thought, we have already admitted the metaphysical principle that the basis or ground of all "things" is an indefinable (or infinite) no-thing beyond sense—always escaping our comprehension and control. This is the supernatural, in the proper sense of what cannot be "natured" or classified, and the immaterial in the sense of what cannot be measured, metered, or "mattered." In all its fullness, this admission is precisely *faith*—the recognition that one must ultimately "give in" to a life-source, a Self beyond the ego, which lies beyond the definition of thought and the control of action.

Belief, in the *popular* Christian sense, falls short of this faith, since its object is a God conceived as having a determinate nature. But to the extent that God can be a known object of definite nature, he is an idol, and belief in such a God is idolatry. Thus in the very act of demolishing the concept of the Absolute as a "what" or "fact" about which meaningful statements and determinations can be made, logical philosophy has made its most vital contribution to religious faith—at the cost of its antithesis, religious "belief." While the logical positivists unwittingly join forces with the Hebrew prophets in their denunciation of idolatry, the prophets are found to be in line with that grand metaphysical tradition that, in Hinduism and Buddhism, has taken the disuse of idols to its proper conclusion.

In sum, then, the function of metaphysical "statements" in Hinduism and Buddhism is neither to convey positive information about an Absolute, nor to indicate an experience in which this Absolute becomes an object of knowledge. In the words of the *Kena Upanishad*: "Brahman is unknown to those who know It, and is known to those who do not know It at all." This knowing of Reality by un-knowing is the psychological state of the man whose ego is no longer split or dissociated from its experiences, who no longer feels himself as an isolated embodiment of logic and consciousness, separate from the gyring and gimbling of the unknown. He is thus delivered from *samsara*, the Wheel, the squirrel cage psychology of all those human beings who everlastingly frustrate themselves with impossible tasks of knowing the knower, controlling the controller, and organizing the organizer, like Ouroboros, the mixed-up snake, who dines off his own tail.

NOTES

1. I have not simply equated this experience with "mysticism" since the latter frequently contains symbolic and affective elements that are by no means essential to the order of experience I am discussing.

2. Of course, there are other interpretations of the proper functions of alchemy and astrology, representing their aims as utterly different from those of science. Deeply understood, neither alchemy nor astrology have to do with the prediction and control of *future* events, but are rather a symbolism of *eternal* "events" and the process of their realization in the *present*.

3. *Zenrin Kushu*—an anthology of Chinese poetry employed in the study and practice of Zen Buddhism.

4. *The Cloud of Unknowing*. The doctrine of "knowing God by unknowing (*agnosia*)" derives from the sixth century Syrian metaphysician writing under the name of Dionysius the Areopagite, and in particular from his *Theologia Mystica*, in Migne's *Patrologia Graeca*, Vol. 3. A translation of the latter work is included in Fr. McCanns's (1943) edition of the former.

REFERENCES

Eddington, A. S. (1935). *Nature of the physical world*. London, UK: Dent.

McCann, J. (Ed.). (1943). *The Cloud of Unknowing, and other treatises by an English mystic of the fourteenth century*. London, UK: Burns, Oats, & Washbourne.

CHAPTER FOUR

On Philosophical Synthesis (1953)

In many respects the formal, academic philosophy of the West has come to a dead end, having confined itself to a method of inquiry that compels it to move in a vicious circle. This is especially true in epistemology, which, because it involves the whole work of self-knowledge, is really the central problem of philosophy. As the West understands it, epistemology is really the task of trying to "think thought"—to construct words about words about words—since philosophical thinking is, for us, not a changing but a verbalization of experience.

The inquiring mind is perennially fascinated with the problem of the mind's own nature and origins—not only to know just by way of information *what* knowing is, but also to employ such information for the greater control of the knower, for is it not frequently said that *the* problem of modern man is to be able to control himself as effectively as he can control his environment?

But there is a basic contradiction in the attempt of reason to transcend itself. To know the knower, to control the controller, and to think thought implies a circular and impossible situation, like the effort to bite one's own teeth. It is for this reason that modern logical philosophy tends to dismiss such inquiries as "metaphysical and meaningless" and to confine philosophy to the investigation of relatively pedestrian problems of logic and ethics. This situation has arisen in the West because, for us, "to know" really means "to control"; that is, to see how events may be fitted to consistent orders of words and symbols so that we may predict and govern their course. But this mania for control leads ultimately to a barren confusion, because we ourselves are by

From *Philosophy East and West*, 1953, 3(2), 99–100. Copyright © 1953 by University of Hawaii Press. Reprinted with permission of University of Hawaii Press.

no means separated from the environment we are trying to control. Western man has been able to pursue this mania only so far because of his acute feeling of individual isolation, of the separation of his "I" from all else. Thus, in philosophy, in technology, and in the whole ordering of our society, we run into the ancient problem of *Quis custodiet custodies?*—who guards the guard, polices the policeman, plans the planner, and controls the controller? The logical end of all this is the totalitarian state of George Orwell's *Nineteen Eighty-Four*, the nightmare of mutual espionage.

On the other hand, such major Oriental philosophies as the Vedanta, Buddhism, and Taoism arise in cultures far less concerned with controlling the world, and in which the whole notion of the dominance of the universe by man (the conscious ego) seems palpably absurd. For all these philosophies it is a first principle that the seeming separateness of the ego from the world, so that it could be its controller, is an illusion. Individual consciousness did not contrive itself and, not being *sui generis* (un-born, *anutpanna*), can never be the directive source of life.

Thus, for Oriental philosophy, knowledge is not control. It is rather the "sensation"—the vivid realization—that "I" am not this individualized consciousness alone, but the matrix from which it arises. This knowledge consists, not in a verbal proposition, but in a psychological change, similar to that which occurs in the cure of a psychosis. One in whom this change has come to pass does not attempt to control the world, or himself, by the efforts of his own will. He learns the art of "letting things happen," which is no mere passivity but, on the contrary, a creative technique familiar to the activity of many artists, musicians, and inventers in our own culture, whereby skill and insight are found to be the fruits of a certain "dynamic relaxation."

It is obvious that a philosophy, a wisdom, which offers deliverance from the vicious circle of "controlling the controller" is of immense value to cultures, like our own, which are hopelessly confused by their schemes to organize themselves. However, it will be extraordinarily difficult for a wisdom of this kind to come within the scope of Western philosophy unless the latter can admit that philosophy is more than logic, more than verbalization, to the point where philosophy can include the transformation of the very processes of the mind, and not simply of the words and symbols that the mind employs.

CHAPTER FIVE

Philosophy beyond Words (1975)

"Of that whereof one cannot speak, thereof one should remain silent." With these words, published in 1921, Ludwig Wittgenstein concluded his *Tractatus Logico-Philosophicus* and brought Western philosophy, as it had been known, to an end. Thereafter all schools of philosophy should have become centers of silent contemplation, as in Yoga or Buddhist meditation. But, on the principle of "publish or perish," even Wittgenstein had to keep on talking and writing, for if the philosopher remains silent we cannot tell whether he is really working or simply goofing off. But with Wittgenstein intellectually respectable and academic Western philosophy became trivial. He showed that it could not discuss metaphysics—that the exciting questions of ontology and epistemology were meaningless, and that thereafter the philosopher must content himself with being simply a sophisticated grammarian or specialist in mathematical logic. William Earle (1960) in his witty essay "Notes on the Death of a Culture" described the new academic philosopher as a pragmatic nine-to-five businessman, going to his office with a briefcase to "do philosophy" in the same spirit as an accountant or research chemist. He would not dream of wandering out at night to contemplate the stars or to ponder such matters as the destiny of man and the final significance of the universe. If he thought he could get away with it, he would go about campus in the scientist's white coat.

As an adolescent I used to frequent an area in London, near the British Museum, where certain shops advertised themselves as purveyors of "philosophical instruments." Imagining that philosophers confined themselves to abstract

From *The Owl of Minerva: Philosophers on Philosophy*, edited by C. J. Bontempo & S. J. Odell, 1975, New York: McGraw-Hill. Copyright © 1975 by C. J. Bontempo & S. J. Odell. Reprinted with permission of the C. J. Bontempo estate and S. Jack Odell.

thinking and required no other instruments than pen and paper, I was surprised to find that these shops sold slide rules, chronometers, microscopes, telescopes, and other scientific appliances, and that they were old-fashioned and venerable shops surviving from an age when science was called "natural philosophy." Thinking it over, this made sense. For philosophy, as Aristotle had said, begins with wonder—so that the true philosopher is a person who is naturally curious, who finds that existence is a marvelous puzzle, and who would like to find out (in Clerk Maxwell's childhood phrase) "the particular go of it." Thus if philosophy is an attempt to describe and explain the world, to discover the order of nature, it must obviously go on into physics and chemistry, astronomy and biology, not to mention mathematics and metamathematics.

But what is the sense of wonder? On the one hand, it is a sort of aesthetic or mystical thrill, like being in love, or as Whitman felt of the planets and stars that "the drift of them is grand." On the other hand, it is an attempt to solve the puzzle of translating the pattern of the world into the linear orders of words and numbers that can be scanned and controlled by the faculty of conscious attention. For there are many of us who do not feel that we know anything, or are humanly competent, unless we can make this translation. The difficulty is that, from the standpoint of linear thinking and scanning, the natural world comprises innumerable variables. Using conscious attention, most people cannot keep track of more than three variables at once without using a pencil. A skilled organist, using both hands and feet, could manage a six-part fugue. But the practical problems of life—of politics, law, ethics, economics, and ecology—involve hundreds of thousands of variables with which the scanning pace of conscious attention simply cannot keep up, even when aided by computers. What scholar, except perhaps an authority on the manufacture of Japanese swords in the sixteenth century, can really keep abreast of the literature in his field? How can the President of the United States possibly be informed of all that he needs to know? There simply isn't time to pass one's eyes along the miles of letters and figures required, much less to absorb and make sense of them.

This is likewise the problem of philosophy, considered as a verbal and conceptual discipline. As natural philosophy, as a discipline that must always keep in mind the findings of the sciences, it cannot keep track of ever more complex descriptions of the world's pattern. It cannot give us a *Weltanschauung*, a total and orderly view of the world, based on masses of intellectually indigestible information. As an attempt to describe or define the nature of being, of consciousness, of knowledge, or even of energy or electricity, we find that this can no more be done in language than one can obtain an answer by spelling out theological questions on the dial of a telephone. Whether spoken or written the word W-A-T-E-R neither quenches thirst nor floats a boat, and, in a somewhat similar way, verbal efforts to describe existence give no understanding of it because you can't say anything about everything. It would be absurd to say that the universe, as a whole, is moving in a certain direction, for this would require some external point of reference, which would, by definition, have to be included in the idea of universe. In fact, we cannot even imagine what kind of verbal or mathematical answer would satisfy such a question as "What is reality?"

But does all this mean that philosophy, or basic wondering, has come to a dead end? A philosopher, a wondering individual, retains an urgent interest in, say, problems of ethics and aesthetics and is not going to stop thinking about them. And a metaphysician, even though he knows that he cannot even formulate his ontological and epistemological questions, will not easily abandon his amazement at being and knowing. He feels incomplete, intellectually and emotionally hungry, unless he has somehow made sense of being an "is" in imminently painful transition to being an "isn't," of experiencing himself as a complex system of vibrations, as a multiplicity of sensitive tubes, tissues, and nerves inevitably doomed to dissolve with the greatest reluctance. He asks, "How and why am I in this delectable-horrible situation?" Above all, he wants to penetrate whatever it is that is the substantial referent of the word "I." No amount of sophistry will persuade him to set aside these questions of feeling and devote himself exclusively to symbolic logic or collecting postage stamps.

I have said that in the West the preoccupations of most academic philosophers have become trivial. In the university, departments of philosophy are usually underpopulated and removed to obscure offices, and the coveted degree *Philosophiae Doctor* is awarded to people who experiment with rats, devise computers, or concoct new drugs. This is not without reason, for I am suggesting that, in the West, *real* philosophy turned into science. To answer the question "What is reality?" we had to go beyond talking and thinking to empirical experiment, to the use of "philosophical instruments." But marvelous as the development of science has been, those almost ineffable questions are still unanswered, and the technologies based on science are seriously threatening the continuance of life on this planet. They have amplified—turned up the volume on—human behavior, and we are not at all sure that we like ourselves.

For this reason alone there is still an important place for the philosopher as a sort of ombudsman or critic of the applied sciences, and in this sense people like Arthur Koestler, Lewis Mumford, Jacques Ellul, Noam Chomsky, and Buckminster Fuller must be considered more relevant philosophers than Carnap, Ayer, Reichenbach, and Anscombe—to mention but a few of the hard-core academicians. But to any *young* reader (as of 1972) who has the philosophical spirit, the wonder at being, all these names are in the past. I don't want to say obsolete or *passé*, for they are in the same eternal past as Voltaire and Hegel. But today young and philosophically enthusiastic people are reading Herman Hesse, Krishnamurti, D. T. Suzuki, Theodore Roszak, Spencer Brown, Fritz Perls, Gurdjieff, Thomas Merton, and Baba Ram Dass, or, to go back a long way, Meister Eckhart, Lao-Tzu, the *I Ching*, the *Tibetan Book of the Dead*, the *Upanishads*, Patanjali, and the *Bhagavad Gita*. (This is just a sample. For verification, consult your local paperback bookstore or *The Last Whole Earth Catalog*.)

This odd miscellany of names and titles indicates that the trend of serious philosophy in the West is going in the direction of contemplative mysticism, that is, to an interior empiricism, which may require such "philosophical instruments" as LSD-25, the control of breath (*pranayama*), or the practice of Zen meditation for the direct exploration of consciousness and its varying states. The problem is that if man, as amplified by technology, is a self-contradictory, suicidal, and nonviable organism, some way must be found of changing or getting beyond whatever it is that we mean by the word "I." It is already clear from the sciences of biology and ecology that every living organism is a single process or field with its environment. But this situation is not ordinarily reflected or experienced in our normal self-consciousness or sense of identity, wherein we still seem to be isolated centers of sensitivity and activity inside bags of skin. But if one were to feel one's existence as the organism-environment process, which the biologists and ecologists describe, one would be having an experience of "cosmic consciousness" or of identity with the total energy of the universe as described by the mystics. The "peak experiences" of an Eckhart, Ramakrishna, Hakuin, or (interestingly enough) Schrödinger (1964) and all the accounts of these changes of consciousness given by James (1936), Bucke (1959), and Johnson (1959) would seem to be vividly sensuous apprehensions of our existence as the biologists and ecologists describe it in their theoretical languages. The mystic is therefore *feeling* himself-and-the-world as it is accurately *described* by scientists, in somewhat the same way as, by informed use of a telescope, one can get the feel of one's place in the solar system and the galaxy, or as by frequent air travel one really knows that the earth is a globe.

Now the mystic tells us things that really do not make sense when put into words: that what we do and what happens to us are actually the same process, as are also something and nothing, solid and space; that as the stars shine out of space the world emerges immediately from the Void in an eternal now of which the past is merely the wake or echo, not the cause; that this Void is in fact one's basic self, but is felt as emptiness in the same way as the head is a blank to the eyes; that each one of us is therefore an aperture through which the universe knows itself, but not all of itself, from a particular point of view; that death is the same total blankness (i.e., our self) from which we emerged at birth, and that what happened once can always happen again. And so on. All this means nothing to a literate intellectual of a Western industrial culture in the same way that descriptions of color, light, and darkness are meaningless to the congenitally blind, or that the most ingenious comments of a music critic give no impression of the sound of a concert.

But this literate intellectual is "blind" only because of the *idée fixe* that the intelligible is only what can be said. Surely I *know* how to breathe even if I cannot describe the full physiology of the process. Furthermore, I learned how to swim not by reading about it in a book but by getting into the water and following certain instructions. Thus, as Spencer Brown (1969) has pointed out, one may go beyond Wittgenstein's limit by analogy with music and mathematics. We cannot say (describe in words) the sounds of music, but by a convenient notation we can instruct a person what to do with a certain instrument—instruction of the same kind as "drop a perpendicular" or "describe a circle" in geometry (pp. 77–79).

Thus in the pursuit of philosophy as a purely verbal discipline Wittgenstein made it clear that because there is no way of answering such questions as "What is reality?" one must regard them as false problems and consign them to silence. But he did not follow his own advice. By "silence" he seemed to mean ignoring or dismissing, and changing the subject of discourse. But if the philosopher, still agog in his heart with the metaphysical question that he cannot formulate in meaningful words, were to follow Wittgenstein's instruction more literally, what then? He would actually *be* silent. He would not only (at least for a time) stop talking, but also stop thinking, by which I mean talking and figuring to oneself *sub voce*. He would hear, see, touch, taste, and smell without comment or judgment, without any attempt to translate the experience into words. If words came into his mind automatically and compulsively, he would listen to them as mere noise, or get rid of them by humming the meaningless sound "Ah!" He would then be in a state to know reality directly so that he would no longer need to ask *what* it is—i.e., into what verbally labeled class it should be put.

Remaining in this state, he might marvel at how many things there are that aren't so. He would have no sensation of himself as an ego or observer separate from the whole field of his experience. He would have no perception of anything that is past or future—only of a vibrant eternal now, which, when felt with the ears alone, would be heard as emerging immediately from silence and nothingness. Discussing it later with colleagues who had made the same experiment, he might agree that our normal view of life is backward: that the present does not follow from the past, but the past from the present, streaming away like a contrail. Having really felt what it is to breathe, he might realize that the distinction between the voluntary and the involuntary is arbitrary—to the evaporation of the problems of free will and determinism. But he would genuinely have had to come to the state where verbal thinking has stopped, and consciousness remains bright and clear. He would then be practicing what is Sanskrit is called *dhyana*, in Chinese *ch'an*, and in Japanese *zen*, and which may approximately be translated "idealess contemplation."

Characteristically, when the professional philosopher hears about this he begins to think up objections without trying the experiment. For he may be sure that not-thinking is a vacuous, anti-intellectual mindlessness from which no good can come, not realizing that if one thinks all the time, there is nothing to think about except thoughts—which is rather like incessant talking without listening. The health of the intellectual life requires precisely that there be pauses in it, and not merely such diversions as sleep, physical exercise, or carousal. Academic philosophers tend to be scholastics like the theologians who refused to look through Galileo's telescope. As natural philosophy developed instruments to explore the external world, theoretical philosophy needs instruments, or at least experiments, to explore and feel the nonverbal world—if for nothing else than to stop confusing the world as it *is* with the world as it is *represented* in common language. W. Pagel (1935, p. 97) and Joseph Needham (1956, pp. 89–98) have documented the collaboration of natural philosophers (scientists) and mystics in the sixteenth and seventeenth centuries in their common opposition to scholastic rationalism and their common interest in the empirical approach, for the mystic wants to go beyond doctrine and dogma, beyond belief, to the actual experience of the Ground of Being—to use Paul Tillich's decontaminated phrase for God.

This means, then, that philosophy in and of the schools must turn (and in some places is turning) to what have been called spiritual disciplines, though (and I think properly) without commitment to any doctrinal system. In fact, beliefs are obstacles to *dhyana* because consciousness must be clear of thoughts. American and British philosophers, with characteristic pragmatism, will of course ask what good this will do, and whether it will provide directives for behavior. But the apparent paradox of *dhyana* is that if one is doing it for a result, one is not doing it, since its essential attitude is to be aware of what is, not what should or might be. In the same way, a musical performer becomes self-conscious and awkward if he worries about what effect he is having on his audience, and thus the results of *dhyana*, are always unintentional. Egocentricity, for example, diminishes without any self-frustrating egocentric intention to get rid of it. Furthermore, the temporary suspension of conscious thought acts in somewhat the same way as "sleeping on" a problem, for it frees the brain as a whole to analyze it, replacing the linear scanning of conscious attention. As is well known, the brain, below the level of consciousness, regulates the myriad variables of our organic processes without thinking. Brain operation, unhindered by conscious effort, is obviously the source of the astonishing performances of lighting calculators, and there seems no reason why such subliminal cogitation should not be effective in being addressed to highly complex social, ethical, and legal questions. After all, it is well recognized in the legal profession that a good judge must not only know the law as written; he must also have a sense of equity—that is, a mysterious sense of fair play that no one has ever been able to define, although we recognize it at once when we see it. Such a judge cannot *teach* equity because, like even the greatest neurologists, he does not understand his own brain, for the order of the brain is so much more complex than what Northrop Frye has called the order of words.[1]

But I think it must be understood that the order of the brain is complicated because, and only because, we are trying to translate it into words. If I may invent a verb, the more we try to "precise" the world, to discern its clearly cut structure, the more precise we compel ourselves to be. The world retreats into ever greater complexity by analogy with the whirlings of a dog chasing its own tail, and, as Spencer Brown (1969) has put it, "In this sense, in respect of its own information, the universe *must* expand to escape the telescopes through which we, who are it, are trying to capture it, which is us" (p. 106). In this game of trying to control the controller and guard the guards, the philosophers and scientists, the lawyers and generals, are compulsively locked. Make almost any statement to a logical positivist or scientific empiricist, and he will say, of the first word or phrase in your statement, that he does not know what you mean. He forces you to define it more precisely, and then pulls the same stunt on whatever definition you give him . . . *ad infinitum*. In the same way, the law complicates itself out of manageability by trying to define itself, and security systems become hopelessly paranoid in trying to secure themselves. To the degree that you make an object of the subject, the subject becomes objectionable. The end is suicide.

To the extent, then, that professional philosophers have locked themselves into a word game, to define definition, they cannot be said to be lovers of wisdom. They will reason, endlessly, about reasoning; calculate about calculating; talk about talking until no one can keep track of it. This does not mean that no more philosophical books can be written or discussions held. There must simply be something to write and talk about, other than writing and talking, and we can write and talk meaningfully only of shared experiences. Thus to have anything to discuss among themselves philosophers must become contemplatives, and mystics in the strict sense (Greek *muein*) of those who, at least sometimes, keep silent—not only vocally but also in their heads. Every so often the philosopher must become again as a child, and contemplate the world as if he knew nothing about it, had no names for it and no idea of what is happening. This is an essential cathartic for the intellectual: to listen directly to the universe as one listens to classical music, without asking what it means. This is Yoga (Sanskrit *yuj* = Latin *jungere*) in the sense of being joined to or one with what is going on. Patanjali's definition, *yogas chitta vrtti nirodha*, means approximately that Yoga is silence of the mind, and this is the way that Western philosophy must go if we are to take Wittgenstein's aphorism as a positive direction.

NOTE

1. Put simply—by Young (1960) and in a highly sophisticated way by Pribram (1971)—it is amazing to see how what really amounts to subjective idealism can be stated in neurophysical terms. The structure of the nervous system (which we do not really understand) determines our view of the world and yet is itself, presumably, something in that world. Which comes the first, egg or hen? And what do I mean by "I" in saying "I do not understand my nervous system," which is presumably what I really and truly am? The limitation of philosophy is that you can't kiss your own lips, which is another way of saying, with the *Upanishads*, TAT TVAM ASI, or "You're IT."

REFERENCES

Brown, G. S. (1969). *Laws of form*. London, UK: George Allen & Unwin.

Bucke, R. M. (1959). *Cosmic consciousness*. New York, NY: Dutton.

Earle, W. (1960). Notes on the death of a culture. In M. R. Stein (Ed.), *Identity and anxiety: Survival of the person in mass society*. New York, NY: Free Press of Glencoe.

James, W. (1936). *Varieties of religious experience*. New York, NY: Modern Library.

Johnson, R. C. (1959). *Watcher on the hills*, New York, NY: Harper & Row.

Needham, J. (1956). *Science and civilization in China*, Vol. 2. New York, NY: Cambridge University Press.

Pagel, W. (1935). Religious motives in the medical biology of the seventeenth century. *Bulletin of the [Johns Hopkins] Institute of the History of Medicine, 3*, 97.

Pribram, K. (1971). *Languages of the brain*. Englewood Cliffs, NJ: Prentice-Hall.

Schrodinger, E. (1964). *My view of the world*. New York, NY: Cambridge University Press.

Wittgenstein, L. (1921). *Tractatus logico-philosophicus*. London, UK: Kegan Paul.

Young, J. Z. (1960). *Doubt and certainty in science*. New York, NY: Oxford University Press.

PART TWO

Buddhism and Zen

CHAPTER SIX

The Problem of Faith and Works
in Buddhism (1941)

It is generally assumed that philosophic Buddhism, and especially that form of it expressed in the Pali Canon, is par excellence the way to salvation or illumination by self-help. For in the philosophy attributed to Gautama by the earliest records no place is given to a God or gods who can assist man in the development of spiritual life; the existence of such divine beings is not denied—it is ignored on the ground that no power on earth or in heaven can interfere with another's *karma*. And *karma* (Pali, *Kamma*) is a very inclusive term, for primarily it means "action" or "doing," though in a secondary sense it has come to mean the law of cause and effect—a sense that has been much overemphasized by Western theosophical interpretations. But it would seem that original Buddhism does not only set aside the possibility of interference with *karma* for the reason that it is impossible to separate a cause from its effect (in the Christian sense of absolution). It also rejects the possibility of divine intervention at the causal end of the process, having no parallel to the Christian concept of Grace. In Christianity there is no human power which can, of its own resources, make for righteousness and salvation, for by reason of original sin it is impossible for man to move upward without the gift of divine Grace. Buddhism, however, would appear to be a method of lifting oneself up by one's own belt, for according to a famous passage in the *Maha-parinibbana Sutta* (v. ii, 27–35), we are advised, "Be ye lamps unto yourselves. Be ye a refuge unto your selves. Take to yourselves no other refuge."[1]

Both Hinayana and Mahayana Buddhism in the historical development of their philosophy and practice have, for the most part, kept to this principle of

Reprinted from *The Review of Religion*, 1941, 5(4), 385–402. Copyright 1941 by Columbia University Press. Copyright not renewed.

absolute self-reliance. If any faith was involved, it was faith in one's own capacity to *work* out one's own salvation, and faith in the ability of Buddhism to supply the necessary method. In the Hinayana system the method was to exhaust the process of *karma* by perceiving the fundamental unreality of the individual (*atta*) who sets *karma* in motion. The Mahayana followed a variation of the same method, but, under the influence of Brahmanic thought, supplemented the idea of individual unreality with the concept of a universal, nondual Reality similar to the Vedantist idea of Brahman. In one sense this Reality, called by such names as *Tathata, Sunyata,* and *Dharmakaya,* was beyond *karma (akarma),* and thus the realization that it alone existed involved deliverance from the toils of *karma,* even though one might continue to live in the "world of birth-and-death." But the radical nondualism of, say, the *Lankavatara Sutra* (Suzuki, 1932) refused even to make any absolute distinction between *karma* and *akarma,* the world of illusion and the principle of Reality, the transient, separate individual and the eternal, undifferentiated "Suchness" (*Tathata*):

> There is no Nirvana except where is Samsara; there is no Samsara except where is Nirvana; for the condition of existence is not of a mutually-exclusive character. Therefore, it is said that all things are non-dual as are Nirvana and Samsara. (p. 67)

The problem of faith and works in Buddhism, as we shall discuss it, will be entirely in terms of the Mahayana school. To understand its doctrinal and psychological background we must pay particular attention to the Mahayanist doctrine of nonduality, bearing also in mind that only in Mahayana has a way of salvation by faith arisen. Our attention will be directed, however, to doctrinal and psychological aspects of the problem rather than historical, for we cannot say precisely whether the historical development of the way of faith came as a logical result of certain philosophic trends or as an answer to a natural human need. Furthermore, the historical aspect of the problem is complicated by our uncertainty as to the exact age of many of the important sutras involved. But we do know that the way of faith developed quite early in Mahayana history, playing an important role in the works of such early patriarchs of the school as Nagarjuna, Asvaghosa, and Vasubandhu.

Mahayana philosophy is centered upon two closely related ideas. The first, descended from Vedanta, is that Enlightenment (the Buddhist life-goal) consists in an inner realization of nonduality. All those things upon which unenlightened man depends for his happiness are dual, and thus conditioned by their opposites. Life cannot be had without death, pleasure without pain, joy without sorrow, youth without age, or good without evil. We cannot, therefore, depend for our ultimate salvation and security upon any one aspect of a given pair of opposites (*dvandva*), for the two are as essential to each other as back and front are essential to the totality of any object. Thus, while we look to such limited states for our salvation, we are involved in a world of ups and downs that goes under the general name of Samsara, the wheel of birth and death.

From the beginning, the purpose of Buddhism was to find deliverance from this wheel, to discover the state of Nirvana, differing from these limited states by being eternal, unchanging, and subject to no ups and downs. In the Pali Canon there is no special emphasis upon the nonduality of Nirvana. It is here something quite outside and different from Samsara—an escape. But the Mahayanist Nirvana is described in much the same language as the Upanishads describe Brahman, the "One-without-a-second." Here Nirvana is the experience that differs from all these limited experiences by *having no opposite.* The Mahayana sutras are at such pains to stress the nonduality of Nirvana and Enlightenment (*bodhi*) that they do not even allow Nirvana to be opposed to Samsara, or Enlightenment to be opposed to Ignorance (*avidya*). To the fully enlightened man Samsara *is* Nirvana; ordinary, everyday experience of the world of opposites is for him transformed into the supreme spiritual experience of deliverance or freedom.

The second important principle of Mahayana is the Bodhisattva-ideal. In one sense the Bodhisattva is a lesser Buddha. In another, he is one who, by patient striving throughout countless incarnations, has attained the right to Nirvana, but who postpones final entry into its eternal rest in order to come back into the world and work for the liberation of "all sentient beings." But this rather picturesque view of the Bodhisattva is actually taken from the Hinayana standpoint. Nirvana is still an *escape* from Samsara, even though the Bodhisattva has temporarily renounced it. But from the thoroughgoing Mahayana standpoint, the Bodhisattva-ideal is the necessary consequence of a philosophy denying the duality of Nirvana and Samsara. The Bodhisattva has no need to escape from Samsara because he realizes that it is Nirvana. Thus, to quote the *Lankavatara Sutra* again,

> those who, afraid of sufferings rising from the discrimination of birth-and-death, seek for Nirvana, do not know that birth-and-death and Nirvana are not to be separated the one from the other; and, seeing that all things subject to discrimination have no reality, imagine that Nirvana consists in the future annihilation of the senses and their fields. They are not aware . . . of the fact that Nirvana is the Alayavijnana (universal mind). . . . (Suzuki, 1932, p. 55)

But whatever the view of Nirvana, the Bodhisattva is the savior, the one who makes vows (*pranidhana*) to postpone any final withdrawal from the world until he has seen all living things liberated and raised to the level of his own understanding. Thus, in a number of Buddhist sects, the monk repeats daily the following vows to identify himself with the Bodhisattva-ideal:

How innumerable sentient beings are, I vow to save them all;
How inexhaustible our evil passions are, I vow to exterminate them;
How immeasurable the holy doctrines are, I vow to study them;
How inaccessible the path of Buddhas is, I vow to attain it. (Suzuki,
    1927, p. 323)

But it will be noted that, although the monk vows to save all sentient beings, he does not seem to expect anyone to save him. The remainder of his vows are firm affirmations of self-help, and this is in line with the main trend of Mahayana philosophy and practice in all but the popular sects, which have put the Bodhisattvas in the position of saviors to be worshipped and relied upon almost exactly as the Christian relies upon the saving power of the Christ. Thus there would seem here to be a huge inconsistency between popular and philosophic Buddhism in the Mahayana school. The purpose of this study, however, is to show that this inconsistency is more apparent than real.

In modern China and Japan, by far the most popular form of Buddhism is a way of salvation by faith. It has attained its most radical and interesting development in Japan, but, as we have seen, its origins are in India, far back in the early days of Mahayana history. Most students of Buddhism are at a loss to find any true similarity of purpose between these popular cults and the highly self-reliant Buddhism of Gautama and philosophic Mahayana. They are generally regarded as a mere degeneration of the creed, a pure concession to unregenerate human nature, which demands supernatural beings to achieve what men are too lazy and too frightened to achieve for themselves. There is no doubt whatever that there are plenty of lazy and frightened human beings and that an easy method of salvation by faith would naturally appeal to them, especially in the more extreme forms which altogether discount the efficacy of works. But there are other considerations, and from a certain point of view these very extreme forms become full of the deepest interest. Here let it be said that I owe this point of view to Dr. D. T. Suzuki (1939), who has recently made a particularly suggestive study of the philosophy and psychology underlying the Buddhism of faith. But as yet he has made no thorough study of the psychological relations of the way of faith and the way of works.[2] This seems to me a very necessary line of inquiry, because I believe that Western students of Christian background can never really understand the Buddhism of works unless they approach it through the Buddhism of faith, itself so close to Christian belief.

Generally speaking, the Buddhism of faith is founded upon the *Sukhavativyuha Sutra* which, so far as we know, was compiled some three hundred years after Gautama's death. The *Sukhavativyuha* tells of one Dharmakara, who, in some immeasurably distant age, made forty-eight vows concerning the liberation of sentient beings. Before making these vows he had devoted himself, for an equally incomprehensible span of time, to innumerable good works, thus acquiring for himself a store of merit sufficient to give abundant aid to the whole world. But he renounced the reward of Highest Attainment due to him for these works, in order that he might preside over the Buddha-land (*Buddha-kshetra*) of Sukhavati, the Western Paradise, and there watch over the world until all living beings had been born into his Pure Land and thus assured of final illumination. From then on he was known as the Buddha Amitabha (Boundless Light) or Amitayus (Eternal Life). The Chinese form of the name is O-mi-to-fo, and the Japanese is Amida, by which he is most generally known. In the second part of the sutra it is declared that those who, in complete faith, turn towards Amida and repeat his name will be born after death into his Pure Land.

But it is hard to find in the sutra itself sufficient ground for some of the later interpretations put upon it, and it was not until the time of the Japanese Amidist, Shinran Shonin, that there evolved a real philosophy of salvation by pure faith. In the sutra, Amida is able to transfer his merit to others because, according to the philosophy represented by the *Avatamsaka Sutra*, each single atom contains in itself the whole universe. Therefore, what is done by one individual effects all others; if one man raises himself, he raises at the same time the whole universe. But here Amida is not the sole source of merit as the Christian God is the sole source of goodness. In early Mahayana the transference of merit (*parinamana*) is a process that may operate mutually between all beings, and, though the individual is helped by sharing Amida's merit, he is yet able to acquire merit by his own unaided efforts, thus adding his own contribution to a universal store. Thus, in the *Sukhavativyuha* the possibility of self-help is by no means excluded, and Amida remains one among many Buddhas; he is not yet raised to the position of sole source of light and life and made the personification par excellence of the final, supreme Reality. His distinction is just that he has made a particularly large contribution to the store of merit in which all may share, and has put his *buddha-kshetra* at the disposal of all who seek it in faith. There is still the difference between *in* faith and *by* faith.

The growth of a cult around Amida was supported by a prevalent view that in this dark cycle (*kali yuga*) of history it is impossible for anyone to attain Enlightenment here on earth, although some progress might be made toward it. Hence the advantage of being born after death into a realm unencumbered by the snares and impurities of earthly life in its dark cycle. And here we are able to note either a rationalization of pure laziness or else the growth of what Christianity calls the conviction of sin, the realization of man's impotence apart from God. There is, moreover, a remarkable parallel to this gradual break from the legalistic, ethical self-reliance of Buddhism in St. Paul's revolt against the Jewish law—and for similar psychological reasons. Thus, in the seventh chapter of his *Epistle to the Romans* St. Paul writes, "Nay, I had not known sin, but by the law: for I had not known lust, except the law had said, Thou shalt not covet. But sin, taking occasion by the commandment, wrought in me all manner of concupiscence."

In just the same way there were Buddhists who found that the rigid morality of monkhood, with its insistence on the negative precept, served only to aggravate the inner desire for vice. They found themselves in a spiritual impasse, unable to change themselves because the self that had to be changed was also the self that had to do the changing—a feat as impossible as kissing one's own lips. Certainly a deep insight into the psychology of the *Lankavatara* and the *Avatamsaka* would have shown a way out of the impasse, a way that many of the self-help school discovered (as will be shown) but that many more missed. The trouble was not in the peculiar difficulties of that psychology, but in the obstacles to be overcome before one could get a glimpse of it. It lay hidden under a vast metaphysical structure, which those unendowed with considerable powers of intellect could not penetrate, sifting the grain from the chaff. And even then they might be left with a grain that mere intellect could not appreciate.

It was, therefore, not surprising that Far Eastern Buddhism revolted in two quite distinct ways from a combination of metaphysics and self-discipline that might have been endurable separately, but hardly together. The first revolution was against the metaphysics, and this gave birth to the Chinese school of Ch'an (Japanese, Zen) whose profound intuitive grasp of the essentials of Mahayana made its ponderous intellectualism unnecessary. Zen discovered a way of communicating the meaning without the words, and for once the Mahayana became, in practice, a psychology and a religion as distinct from a philosophy. But in doctrine and discipline Zen remained essentially a way of self-help. The real revolution against absolute reliance on works and self-discipline came last of all, in Japan. Its leader was Shinran Shonin (1173–1262), a disciple of the great Pure Land (Jodo) teacher, Honen Shonin.

Prior to Shinran, the Pure Land school had been only partially a way of salvation by faith, and even today there are two distinct forms of Pure Land Buddhism in Japan—Jodo-shu and Shin-shu, the former still placing a considerable emphasis on the efficacy of works. Thus Japanese Buddhism is divided into the two great divisions of *jiriki* (self-power) and *tariki* (other-power), the way to Enlightenment by self-reliance and the way by reliance on the Original Vow (*purvapranidhana*) of Amida. Under *jiriki* we include the Zen, Shingon, Tendai, Kegon, and Nichiren schools, under *tariki* the Shin, while Jodo comes more or less in between, though with a list to *tariki*.[3]

Shinran began his Buddhist studies at the famous community of Mount Hiyei, near Kyoto, where he attained a rank of some importance. But, in spite of such attainments, he was overwhelmed by the moral problem, recognizing that in his heart he was no better than the merest novice. He was deeply conscious of his humanity and keenly aware that mere self-discipline was wholly inadequate to deliver him from the bondage of *karma*. Trying to work out *karma* with self-discipline was like trying to pick up soap with wet fingers; the harder you grasp, the faster the soap slips away. (The analogy is mine, not

Shinran's.) More than any of his predecessors, he felt conscious of the over-whelming bondage of earthly life in its present cycle, and, as a man of feeling rather than intellect, he was finally attracted to the *bhakti-marga* of Pure Land in the person of Honen Shonin (1133–1212). To Honen he unburdened his mind, and was advised to put his trust in Amida and to abandon the monkish life by marrying. Subsequently, Shin priests have never vowed celibacy. Shinran did not remain in the Pure Land school to which Honen belonged; he founded his own school to preserve the purity of a faith which he felt that ordinary Jodo priests did not fully understand.

There are two principle features of Shinran's religion. The first is his conception of *parinamana*, or merit transference. For him, Amida was the sole and original source of merit. Birth in the Pure Land was no longer a question of directing one's own store of merit toward Amida—as a strictly accurate reading of the *Sukhavativyuha* would indicate. Shinran turned the sense of the words, making birth in the Pure Land dependent on Amida's turning his store of merit towards the individual. The second feature arises from the first, and is the doctrine of pure faith. According to Shinran, no possible human merit could ever earn the tremendous right of birth in the Pure Land, and to imagine that so great a blessing could ever be claimed as the just reward for human effort was to him the height of spiritual pride. In the light of Amida's infinite compassion (*karuna*), all beings, whether worms, demons, saints or sinners, were equally deserving of love, as if Amida would say, "I have the same feeling for the high as for the low, for the just as for the unjust, for the virtuous as for the depraved, for those holding sectarian views and false opinions as for those whose beliefs are good and true." Those who would put faith in Amida must therefore offer themselves to him just as they are, not imagining that the Pure Land can ever be a reward for human virtue. Amida's love is not to be earned; it is as much universal property as the sun, moon, and stars—something to be accepted with humility and gratitude, but never measured against human merit. Thus Shinran said:

> You are not to imagine that you would not be greeted by Amida in his Land because of your sinfulness. As ordinary beings you are endowed with all kinds of evil passions and destined to be sinful. Nor are you to imagine that you are assured of birth in the Pure Land because of your goodness. As long as your jiriki sense is holding you, you would never be welcomed to Amida's true Land of Recompense. (Suzuki, 1939, p. 253)

All that is necessary is to give up forever any idea of attaining merit by one's own power, and then to have faith that one is accepted by the compas-sion of Amida from the very beginning, no matter what one's moral condition. One must even give up the idea that faith itself is achieved by self-power, for faith, too, is Amida's gift. Thus man as man becomes spiritually passive and, by Amida's grace, lets the eternal love flow into him and save him just as he is, symbolizing his faith by repeating the *nembutsu*, the formula *Namu Admida Butsu* (Hail, Amida the Buddha!). According to the *Anjin-ketsujo-sho*,

> To understand the Vow means to understand the Name, and to understand the Name is to understand that when Amida, by bringing to maturity his Vow and Virtue (or Deed) in the stead of all beings, effected their rebirth *even prior to their actual attainment.* (Suzuki, 1939, p. 249, italics added)[4]

The fact that Amida himself is the sole source of grace is further stressed in this passage quoted from Shinran in the *Tannisho* (Ch. VIII):

> The Nembutsu is non-practice and non-goodness for its devotees. It is non-practice because he does not practice it at his own discretion, and it is non-goodness because he does not create it at his own discretion. All is through Amida's power alone, not through our own power, which is in vain. (Fujimoto, 1932, p. 10)

At first sight it would seem that the efficacy of Shin depends upon certain supernatural sanctions of a kind that ordinary *jiriki* Buddhists would have great difficulty in believing. Such difficulties will always be experienced while Shin is studied in terms of its theology, for to anyone but a Christian it would seem the merest wishful thinking. For it amounts to this: that it is possible to become virtually a Buddha by pure faith. According to Suzuki (1939),

> being born in Amida's Land means no more than attaining enlightenment—the two terms are entirely synonymous. The ultimate end of the Shin life is enlightenment and not salvation. (p. 264)[5]

Thus Shin devotees refer to their dead as *Mi hotoke*, or "Honorable Buddhas." But as soon as we examine the *psychology* of Shin as distinct from its *theology*, it becomes possible to relate it to the deepest experiences of Mahayana as expressed, for instance, in the *Lankavatara* and in some of the writings of Zen teachers, notably the *Lin-chi-lu* (Japanese, *Rinzai-roku*). For we have to ask not what Shin believes, but what are the causes and results of that belief in terms of inner feeling, of those inner spiritual experiences which words alone can never fully communicate.

For example, let us take the case of any person acutely aware of his shortcomings, his fears, desires and passions, his lack of insight, and of any sense of union or harmony with the life of the universe—in fact, just such a man as Shinran. Then someone tells him that, if only he will open his eyes and see it, he is a Buddha (is saved by Amida) just as he is, and that any attempt to make himself into a Buddha by his own ingenuity is rank spiritual pride. By adopting *jiriki* he is ignoring what is offered to him from the very beginning by the laws of the universe, and is trying to manufacture it for himself, so that he can take the credit for having earned it. When we say that a man is a Buddha just as he is, what does this mean in terms of psychology? It means that he is divine or *fundamentally acceptable* just as he is, whether saint or sinner, sage or fool. In Amidist language we would say that he is accepted for birth in the Pure Land by Amida's compassion, which is "no respecter of persons"—in other words, that man is given the sense of freedom to be what he is at this and any moment, free to be both the highest and the lowest that is in him. This results at once in a great relaxation of psychic tension. All self-powered striving and contriving (*hakarai*) is set aside in the realization that Buddhahood can neither be attained nor gotten rid of because it alone *is*. For, in Mahayanist nondualism, the Buddha principle, *Tathata*, has no opposite and is the only Reality. And while the *Anjin* says that Amida effected our rebirth into the Pure Land "even prior to actual attainment," the *Lankavatara* says that, if they realized it, all beings are in Nirvana from the very beginning. Here are two doctrines, but one psychological experience.

In practical terms this experience is one of exhilarating spiritual freedom, amounting almost to the sanctification of ordinary, everyday life. For, when man feels free to be all of himself, there is a magic in every littlest act and thought. Thus the Zen poet, Hokoji, says:

> How wondrous strange and how miraculous, this—
> I draw water and I carry fuel.

One cannot resist quoting Herbert from the Christian standpoint:

> All things of Thee partake;
> Nothing can be so mean
> But with this tincture "For Thy Sake"
> Shall not grow bright and clean.
>
> A servant with this clause
> Makes drudgery divine;
> Who sweeps a room as for Thy laws
> Makes that and the action fine. . . .
>
> This is the famous stone
> That turneth all to gold,
> For that which God doth touch and own
> Can not for less be told.

This experience may be clarified and related more closely to the *jiriki* way by further consideration of the *Lankavatara* and the writings of certain Zen teachers. It will now be clear that Shinran's faith has a right to be considered as philosophic Mahayana expressed in rather colorful, symbolic imagery, even though it appears to be quite dualistic in conception. Philosophic Mahayana would not allow the dualism of self and other, man and Amida; but, if it is followed far enough, Shin arrives in experience at what Mahayana states in philosophy—although complete nonduality is actually beyond philosophic description. Furthermore, the *Lankavatara* insists that Samsara, the world of life and death, *is* Nirvana, and Samsara just as it is, with all its pain and suffering. So, too, Shinran insists that we are saved by Amida just as we are, with all our imperfections. In other words, ordinary men are Buddhas just as they are, and, according to Hui-neng, of the Zen school, those whom we call Buddhas are simply those who understand this truth. Thus it is often remarked in Zen literature that one's "ordinary thoughts" or "everyday mind" is Enlightenment (*satori*). I quote a peculiarly suggestive passage from the *Rinzai-roku*:

> You must not be artful. Be your ordinary self. . . . *You yourself as you are—that is Buddha Dharma.* I stand or sit; I array myself or I eat; I sleep when I am fatigued. The ignoramus will deride me but the wise man will understand.[6]

And further on the text states,

> Wherefore it is said that the everyday mind is the true law.

Suzuki (1933) translates another passage from this text to the same effect; here Rinzai says:

> The truly religious man has nothing to do but go on with his life as he finds it in the various circumstances of this worldly existence. He rises quietly in the morning, puts on his dress and goes out to his work. When he wants to walk, he walks; when he wants to sit, he sits; He has no hankering after Buddhahood, not the remotest thought of it. How is this possible? A wise man of old days says, If you strive after Buddhahood by any conscious contrivances, your Buddha is indeed the source of eternal transmigration. (p. 260)

This kind of writing is very easily misunderstood, for one would naturally ask, "If ordinary life is Nirvana and ordinary thoughts are Enlightenment, whatever is Buddhism about, and what can it possibly teach us, other than to go on living exactly as we have lived before?" Before trying to answer this, we must quote two *mondo*, or Zen dialogues. The first is from the *Mu-mon-kwan* (xix):

Joshu asked Nansen, "What is the Tao?" "Usual life," answered Nansen, "is the very Tao." "How can we accord with it?" "If you *try* to accord with it, you will get away from it."[7]

This looks very much like pure *tariki* psychology. Then Suzuki (1927) gives the following from Bokuju (Mu-chou):

A monk asked him, "We have to dress and eat every day, and how can we escape from all that?" Bokuju replied, "We dress, we eat." "I do not understand." "If you don't understand, put on your dress and eat your food." (p. 12)

Clearly the monk's question involves much more than mere dressing and eating, which stands for life in Samsara as a whole—"the trivial round, the common task."

Applying philosophy to this more direct language, we find that the Zen teachers are demonstrating that Samsara, just as it is, is Nirvana, and that man, just as he is, is Buddha. Zen does not say so as a rule, because the terms, Nirvana and Buddha, are concepts which do not move the soul deeply and lead easily to mere intellectualism. Zen wants us to *feel* nonduality, not just to think it, and therefore when we say, "Nirvana is Samsara," we are joining two things together that were never in need of being joined. For both Zen and Shin aim, in different ways, to effect a psychological or spiritual state that moves the whole being, not the head alone. They are trying to set us free within ourselves, and to make us at home with ourselves and with the universe in which we live. This freedom is known when we give up "contriving" and accept ourselves as we are, but it does not seem to me that the experience can be effective unless there has first been a state of contriving and struggle. In Zen this is self-discipline; in Shin it is coming to an acute awareness of one's insufficiency through a previous attempt at self-discipline. It is difficult to see how the Shin experience could be fully appreciated unless, like Shinran, one had first tried the *jiriki* way. The danger of continuing in the *jiriki* way is that one may so easily become a victim of spiritual pride, expecting to *make* oneself into a Buddha; the danger of the *tariki* way is that the experience may come so easily that its true meaning is unseen and its force unfelt.

Spiritual freedom, however, involves much more than "go on living exactly as you have lived before." It involves a particular kind of joyousness, or what the Buddhists term bliss (*ananda*). It is the discovery that to accord with the universe, to express the Tao, one has but to live, and when this is fully understood it becomes possible to live one's life with a peculiar zest and abandon. There are no longer any obstacles to thinking and feeling; you may let your mind go in whatever direction it pleases, for all possible directions are acceptable, and you can feel free to abandon yourself to any of them. Nowhere is there any possibility of escape from the principle of nonduality, for "you yourself as you are—that is Buddha Dharma." In this state there can be no spiritual pride, for union or identity with the Buddha principle is not something achieved by man; it is achieved for him from the beginning of time, just as the sun has been set on high to give him light and life.

Yet, in the life of the spirit, it is much harder to receive than to give; it is often such a blow to human pride to have to accept from Amida, God, or life what it would be so much more distinctive to achieve for oneself. In Shin terms, we should say that the meaning of freedom is that you can think any kind of thought, be any kind of person, and do any kind of thing without ever being able to depart from Amida's all-embracing love and generosity. You are free to do as you like, and also as you don't like, to be free and to be bound, to be a sage and to be a fool. Nowhere are there any obstructions to spiritual activity. At the same time, there is an intense awareness of the joy of that activity; one feels impelled to exercise it and feel the ecstasy of its abandon, much as we imagine a bird must feel high up in space, free to soar up, to swoop down, to fly north, south, east, or west, to circle, climb, tumble, or hover. For "the wind bloweth where it listeth, and thou hearest the sound thereof, but canst not tell whence it cometh nor whither it goeth. Even so is everyone that is born of the spirit." Or, in the more matter-of-fact language of a Zen teacher,

> There are no by-roads, no cross-roads here. All year round the hills are fresh and green; east or west, in whichever direction, you may have a fine walk. (Yeh-hsien, as cited in Suzuki, 1934, p. 83)

There remains the moral problem. To a superficial understanding the freedom of nonduality seems to be an invitation to libertinism of the most flagrant kind. In terms of philosophy, the Mahayana sutras state very frankly that the principle of nonduality is beyond good and evil, and that its attainment has no essential connection with morality. And morality here includes all kinds of works, both social and spiritual. Certainly the sutras speak of *sila*, or morality, as one of the necessary stages, but sometimes it seems as if *sila* were advocated simply as a safeguard against misuse of the enormous, amoral power of supreme knowledge. Thus the *Lankavatara* says:

> In ultimate reality there is neither gradation nor continuous succession; [only] the truth of absolute solitude (*viviktadharma*) is taught here in which the discrimination of all the images is quieted. . . . But [from the absolute point of view] the tenth stage is the first, and the first is the eighth; and the ninth is the seventh, and the seventh is the eighth . . . what gradation is there where imagelessness prevails? (Suzuki, 1932, p. 186)

In yet another passage we read,

Some day each and every one will be influenced by the wisdom and love of the Tathagatas of Transformation to lay up a stock of merit and ascend the stages. But, if they only realized it, they are already in the Tathagata's Nirvana for, in Noble Wisdom, all things are in Nirvana from the beginning. (p. 186)

An even stronger statement of the philosophy will be found in the *Saptasatikaprajnaparamita Sutra*:

O Sariputra, to commit the offences is to achieve the inconceivables, to achieve the inconceivables is to produce Reality. And Reality is nondual. Those beings endowed with the inconceivables can go neither to the heavens, nor to the evil paths, nor to Nirvana. Those who commit the offences are not bound for the hells. Both the offences and the inconceivables are of Reality, and Reality is by nature non-dual. . . . In the real Dharmadhatu (realm of the Law) there is nothing good or bad, nothing high or low, nothing prior or posterior. . . . Bodhi (Enlightenment) is the five offences and the five offences are Bodhi. . . . If there is one who regards Bodhi as something attainable, something in which discipline is possible, that one commits self-arrogance. (as cited in Suzuki, 1933, pp. 251–252)

Here, besides an unequivocal statement of nonduality, there is again an example of *tariki* psychology, speaking of the arrogance of striving to attain Bodhi by discipline.

Mahayana does not disguise the fact that its wisdom is dangerous and we know that monks of the *jiriki* schools are subjected to rigid disciplines just to pre-condition them against abuse of knowledge, which is unfortunately a fairly frequent occurrence. But it would seem that such abuse is only possible when the experience of freedom is feebly appreciated or improperly understood. Oddly enough, although the experience itself and the thing experienced (*Tathata*) is nondual and beyond good and evil, the result of a truly deep inexperience is morality. Shinran speaks very strongly against those who make use of Amida's vow and then go on behaving as immorally as ever. He likens them to those who, because they have found an antidote to a poison, just go on taking it. But this is rather a negative way of looking at the problem. From the positive standpoint, Shin would say that Amida's compassion for us and all other beings, when realized, calls out a corresponding compassion in ourselves. In terms of philosophic Mahayana we should say that, having understood that we and all creatures are Buddhas, we therefore treat them with the reverence due to the Buddha principle.

A second factor that makes for morality is the gratitude felt for the freedom to be all of oneself, a gratitude so deep that men will often renounce some of that freedom as a thank-offering. Obviously there is more opportunity for this feeling of gratitude to grow when the ultimate Reality is personalized in the form of Amida. From the philosophic standpoint there is no real ground for gratitude, because in nonduality there is neither giver nor receiver. Hence the danger of a merely philosophic understanding. But from the emotional standpoint there appears to be every reason for gratitude. In discovering freedom to be all of oneself one has a similar experience to the Christian forgiveness of sins; however black your soul, it is not outside the love of God which is as omnipresent as God Himself, and in this connection it is worth citing a remarkable passage from the work of a Catholic theologian:

> For we are never really outside God nor He outside of us. He is more with us than we are with ourselves. The soul is less intimately with the body, than He is both in our bodies and souls. He as it were flows into us, or we are in Him as the fish in the sea. We use God, if we may dare to say so, whenever we make an act of our will, and when we proceed to execute a purpose. He has not merely given us clearness of head, tenderness of heart, and strength of limb, as gifts which we may use independently of Him when once He has conferred them upon us. *But He distinctly permits and actually concurs with every use of them* in thinking, loving or acting. This influx and concourse of God as theologians style it, ought to give us all our lives long the sensation of being in an awful sanctuary, where every sight and sound is one of worship. *It gives a peculiar and terrific character to acts of sin.* . . . Everything is penetrated with God, while His inexpressible purity is all untainted, and His adorable simplicity unmingled with that which He so intimately pervades, enlightens, animates and sustains. Our commonest actions, our lightest recreations, the freedoms in which we most unbend—all these things take place and are transacted, not so much on the earth and in the air, as in the bosom of the omnipresent God. (Faber, 1853, p. 65, italics added)

There are important points in which Faber's (1853) words diverge from Mahayana philosophy, for, in Christianity, God is essentially Other. But, in so far as doctrine is a symbol of our inner experience, I can see no important difference between the inner feeling suggested by Faber's words and the inner feeling of Mahayana Buddhism, especially in the Amidist cults. Thus the experience of freedom or Enlightenment is like discovering an immeasurably precious jewel in one's littlest acts and lowest thoughts. One discovers it where all jewels are first found—in the depths of the earth, or lying in the mud. Those who appreciate jewels do not leave them there; they lift them up from the depths, polish them, place them on velvet or set them in gold. This polishing and adornment is our symbol of morality, the expression of our joy and gratitude in realizing that

> This very earth is the Lotus Land of Purity,
> And this very body is the body of Buddha.[8]

It is here interesting to note that considerable importance is given to worship in the Zen school which, philosophically, is the most iconoclastic form of Buddhism. Perhaps there is a clue to the apparent inconsistency of worship and nonduality in the following incident from the *Hekigan-shu*:

> Hwang-pa (Japanese, Obaku) stated, "I simply worship Buddha. I ask Buddha for nothing. I ask Dharma for nothing. I ask Sangha for nothing." Someone then said, "You ask Buddha for nothing. You ask Dharma for nothing. You ask Sangha for nothing. What then, is the use of your worship?" At which remark, Hwang-pa gave him a slap on the face![9]

The Buddhist feeling of worship and gratitude is most notably expressed, however, in the Bodhisattva-ideal, based on a profound intuition of the basic unity of all creatures and things. Those who, having attained Enlightenment, do not become Bodhisattvas, helpers of the world, are termed *pratyeka-buddhas*, which, in Mahayana philosophy, is almost a term of abuse. They are not willing to share their experience of freedom with their other selves, and, strictly speaking, Enlightenment is no Enlightenment unless it is shared and circulated. It is no one's property, and those who try to possess it for themselves do not understand it. Service, morality, and gratitude are our response *as men* for a gift to which we cannot respond *as Buddhas*. The Buddha-principle is beyond morality, but not so the human principle. From the standpoint of nonduality, these two principles are one; yet what is so often overlooked in the study of Mahayana is that from the *same* standpoint they are two. For nonduality excludes nothing; it contains both unity and diversity, one and the many, identity and separation. Japanese Buddhism expresses this in the formula *byodo soku shabetsu, shabetsu soku byodo*—unity in diversity and diversity in unity. For this reason, philosophically, morally and spiritually, Buddhism is called the middle way.

NOTES

1. An interestingly different train of thought is suggested by this passage if we follow Mrs. C. A. F. Rhys Davids' translation of "yourselves" as "the Self," in the Upanishadic sense of *atman*.

2. With the one exception of an essay on the Koan exercise and Nembutsu (Suzuki, 1933, p. 115). This, however, does not relate to our present theme.

3. Actually, the full name of the Shin sect is Jodo-Shinshu, but I use Shin alone to avoid confusion with Jodo.

4. The *Anjin* is a work by an unknown author, see Suzuki (1939, p. 248n).

5. By "salvation" Suzuki means simply birth into Amida's Paradise after death, using the word in its eschatological rather than mystical sense. In the latter sense, salvation would be almost synonymous with enlightenment.

6. I am much indebted to the Rev. Sokei-an Sasaki, Vice-Abbot of Mamman-ji, for allowing me to consult his unfinished translation of the *Rinzai-roku*, which is otherwise unavailable in English.

7. I follow Sohaku Ogata's (1934) translation.

8. From the *Song of Meditation* by Hakuin (1683–1768), one of the most famous Japanese Zen teachers.

9. I follow the version of Kaiten Nukariya (1913, p. 96). Buddha, Dharma and Sangha (the Buddha, the Law and the Order of the monks) are the three refuges (*tri-sarana*) taken by all Buddhists.

REFERENCES

Faber, F. W. (1853). *The Creator and the creature.* Baltimore, MD: Murphy.

Fujimoto, R. (Trans.). (1932). *The Tannisho: A religion beyond good and evil.* Kyoto, Japan: Hompa-Hongwanji.

Nukariya, K. (1913). *Religion of the Samurai.* London, UK: Luzac.

Ogata, S. (1934). *A guide to Zen practice.* Kyoto, Japan: Bukkasha.

Suzuki, D. T. (1927). *Essays in Zen Buddhism.* Vol. 1. London, UK: Luzac.

Suzuki, D. T. (1933). *Essays in Zen Buddhism.* Vol. 2. London, UK: Luzac.

Suzuki, D. T. (1934). *The training of the Zen Buddhist monk.* Kyoto, Japan: Eastern Buddhist Society.

Suzuki, D. T. (1939). The Shin Sect of Buddhism. *Eastern Buddhist, 7*(3–4), 227–284.

Suzuki, D. T. (Trans.). (1932). *The Lankavatara Sutra: A Mahayana text.* London, UK: Routledge.

CHAPTER SEVEN

Zen (1948)

INTRODUCTION

There is nothing that men desire more than life—the fullness of life, Reality itself. In one form or another they try to possess it by every possible means, as happiness, as power, as joy, as wealth, as spiritual insight, and even as simple existence to which they cling with all their might for fear that it will be taken away. But one thing is certain: the harder you try to possess life, the faster it slips away from you, and the less you understand of its mystery. For life itself, whatever it may be, cannot be grasped in any form, whether of matter, of emotion, or of thought. The moment you try to hold it in a fixed form, you miss it. Water drawn from the stream is no longer living water, for it ceases to flow. This is what the Buddha meant in saying that the cause of all human misery was *trishna* or selfish craving, because *trishna* is the attempt to grasp life in some form, more especially in the form of one's own personal existence. Man can only become alive in the fullest sense when he no longer tries to grasp life, when he releases his own life from the strangle-hold of possessiveness so that it can go free and be itself.

In practice, almost all religions are attempts to grasp the mystery of life in either an intellectual formula or an emotional experience. Wherever it may be found, higher religion involves the discovery that this cannot be done, and that therefore man must relax his fearful grip upon life or God and permit it to possess him as, in fact, it does all the time whether he knows it or not. Zen Buddhism is a unique example of this kind of higher religion, and because the word "Zen" (see figure 7.1) indicates this very spiritual state of full liveliness and nongrasping, it is really impossible to define Zen. Nevertheless, Zen has a philosophical and religious history by means of which we can arrive at some suggestion of its meaning.

As a specific form of Buddhism, Zen is first found in China, being the peculiarly Chinese version of the kind of Buddhism which, according to tradition, was brought from India by the sage Bodhidharma (see figure 7.2) in or about the year A.D. 527. Bodhidharma's Buddhism was a variety of the Mahayana School, the Buddhism of Northern India, which is to be distinguished from the Hinayana or Southern School of Buddhism now prevalent in Ceylon, Burma and Siam. The latter is founded on the Buddha's teaching as preserved in the scriptures of the Pali language, whereas the former recognizes, in addition to these, certain Sanskrit scriptures of supposedly later date that are of a deeply metaphysical character.

Bodhidharma's variety of the Mahayana was known as Dhyana Buddhism, pronounced Ch'an in Chinese and Zen in Japanese, and though the nearest English equivalent of Dhyana is "contemplation" this term has acquired a static and even dreamy connotation quite foreign to Dhyana. Dhyana, Ch'an or Zen

Figure 7.1. The Chinese character for "Zen."

Figure 7.2. Drawing of Bodhidharma, based on painting by Soga Josaku, Japanese (15th cent.).

means immediate insight into the nature of Reality or life. In China, Dhyana Buddhism was strongly influenced by Taoism and Confucianism, and, under the guidance of the practical mentality of the Chinese, emerged as the Zen we know today in the seventh century A.D. The development of this distinctively Chinese form of Dhyana was largely the work of Hui-neng (or Wei-lang), whose *Tan-ching* or *Platform Sutra* is one of its most authoritative texts. From 713, when Hui-neng died, until the close of the thirteenth century, Zen flourished widely in China and exercised a profound effect on all branches of art and culture. Ei-sai brought it to Japan in 1191, where it may be found to this day in its most vital form and where, too, it has had an extremely far-reaching effect upon the national culture.[1]

In brief, Zen accounts for itself in the following way. Gautama Siddhartha became the Buddha, the Enlightened One, as the result of a profound spiritual experience, an immediate knowledge of Reality, which he realized while meditating under the famous Bodhi Tree near Gaya in Northern India. This knowledge, being ineffable, could never be put into words, and all the Buddha's verbal teaching was simply an indication or suggestion of its nature, a mere device (*upaya*) for awakening men to real insight. The knowledge itself was, however, directly and mysteriously passed on to Mahakasyapa, the Buddha's chief disciple, on an occasion when, instead of preaching a sermon, the Buddha silently held up a flower before his disciples. All stood nonplussed save Mahakasyapa, whose understanding smile brought this recognition from his master: "I have the most precious treasure, spiritual and transcendental, which this moment I hand over to you, O venerable Mahakasyapa!" Tradition asserts that this knowledge was handed down from Mahakasyapa through a line of patriarchs to Bodhidharma, who brought it to China, where it continued to be passed from teacher to teacher. Because this knowledge can never be written down Zen does not rely on scriptures, even though it may use them as devices. Words cannot convey it, just as they cannot describe colors to a blind man. Thus Zen is summed up as:

> A special transmission (of insight) outside the scriptures;
> No dependence upon words and letters;
> Direct pointing to the soul of man;
> Seeing into one's own nature.

To understand Zen adequately, however, we must realize that it is the fruit and synthesis of the most important trends in both Indian and Chinese religion.

THE BACKGROUND IN INDIAN RELIGION

Indian religion has ever been characterized by the quest for "that One thing, knowing which we shall know all." In the *Upanishads* this "One thing" is termed Brahman, the absolute Reality of the universe beyond all opposites. All ordinary things and experiences have opposites; life is opposed to death, pleasure to pain, joy to sorrow, light to darkness. These opposites are necessary to one another, so that life is always limited by death, and joy by sorrow. But Reality itself has no opposite; it is *advaita*, nondual, and the soul of man is only delivered from death and sorrow by realizing its identity with Reality. For the *Upanishads* taught that Brahman is the true nature of ourselves and of all things. Not to realize this is ignorance (*avidya*) and unhappiness, but to know it is true knowledge (*vidya*) and a transcendental happiness which is eternal because, strange to say, it too has no opposite. Thus the religion of the *Upanishads* was more or less monistic, believing that all forms and objects were in fact manifestations of the One Absolute (see figure 7.3).

Primitive Indian Buddhism also sought this Reality, but its way of approach was purely psychological. The Buddha felt that philosophical speculation about Reality was a waste of time and even a positive hindrance. Reality or Nirvana lay beyond all definition, and nothing was of importance but an immediate and intimate experience of it, and this could only be had by getting rid of *trishna*. Reality is here and now, but it is concealed by attempts to grasp it in this form or that.

Later Indian Buddhism, which is to say Mahayana, linked both the psychological approach of primitive Buddhism and the metaphysical tradition of the *Upanishads*. But whereas the *Upanishads* described the nondual Reality as the One, Mahayana felt this term misleading. One is opposed to Many and None, for which reason Reality must transcend even oneness. Mahayana went beyond monism, and certainly beyond any trace of that Spinozist pantheism so often, and, it may be said, erroneously, attributed to the *Upanishads*. To say that all things are one is to reduce everything to something which is still short of nonduality, since, as we have seen, one-ness has an opposite and so cannot be the Absolute. Furthermore, the very statement, "All things are Reality," contains an *implied* opposition between "all things" and "Reality." In making such a statement we are uniting two things which are in no need of union. They are already united, and to try to *create* the union in thought or in feeling is to

Figure 7.3. The word AUM or OM, written in Sanskrit. This word is employed both in Hinduism and Mahayana Buddhism to denote ultimate Reality.

imply to oneself that it does not already exist. Nirvana (the sense of Reality) IS Samsara (the state of ordinary life) and the very act of trying to realize that they are one implies that they are not. In any case, Reality is not one; it is nondual, having no opposite at all.

Therefore Mahayana spoke of Reality as Tathata, or Thusness, and as Sunyata, or the Void, considered not as mere emptiness but as "solid emptiness." Sunyata resembles a crystal ball, which is visible to our eyes only because of what it reflects. Hold it up before a crowded street, and there within it is a crowded street. Hold it up before the empty sky, and there seems to be nothing in it, but only because it is reflecting the emptiness of the sky. Its true nature remains unknown. As the crystal ball reflects images, the manifold universe appears spontaneously within Sunyata. There is nothing in it, but everything comes out of it. Sunyata is the all-inclusive; having no opposite, there is nothing which it excludes or opposes. This was a philosophical theory expressing a spiritual and psychological state—the state of nongrasping or freedom from *trishna*. To thought and sense and feeling Reality is a void, for they cannot lay hold on it or keep it in any fixed form. But it is a living void, because all forms come out of it, and whoever realizes it is filled with life and power and the Bodhisattva's love (*karuna*)[2] for all beings.

From a somewhat more psychological standpoint, Sunyata is also regarded as the ground of human consciousness—the "essence of Mind," the supraindividual Self, in which all our varying states of consciousness, our thoughts, emotions and sensations have their being, like images produced spontaneously in a mirror. This production of images is held to be playful rather than purposive, as if in the act of "creation" Reality were simply enjoying itself—an idea resembling the Hindu view of the universe as the *lila*, the playful dance, of God. Thus Mahayana considers Reality under three aspects, which, somewhat in the manner of the Persons of the Christian Trinity, are in essence one: Dharmakaya, which is the pure and undifferentiated Sunyata, Sambhogakaya, which is the creative principle of enjoyment, the *lila*, and Nirmanakaya, which is the resultant manifested universe

THE BACKGROUND IN CHINESE RELIGION

While Zen derived its highly practical approach to religion from Confucianism, it was actually more deeply influenced by Taoism as taught by Lao-Tzu (sixth century B.C.) and Chuang-Tzu (third century B.C.). In Taoism Reality is termed Tao (see figure 7.4), another untranslatable word, which has, however, a rather more dynamic connotation than Brahman, Tathata or Sunyata. Tao is life considered as a *flowing* power, like the wind, or a stream, or the present moment. It is sometimes rendered as "the Way of things," or as the Logos. A person who has realized union with Tao is said to be in a state of Te, or "grace," while the method of realization is called Wu-wei (no-assertion), which is highly

Figure 7.4. Chinese character for "TAO."

similar to the Buddhist idea of giving up *trishna*. As in Buddhism, all evils are attributed to man's self-assertiveness, his itch to possess life in fixed forms. But if he can realize that he is one with Tao, the fullness of life, he will cease to want to possess things and will therefore be free from evil. If man ceases from self-assertion and lets go of life, the Tao will have a chance to operate freely within him. His life will be lived not by his own ego, but by Tao.

While Indian religion made its object the realization of man's identity with Brahman or Tathata, of the inherent unity of appearance and Reality, Samsara and Nirvana, Chinese religion made its object harmony with the Tao. To Indian religion, the result of this realization was that man was delivered from the realm of opposites, that is, from life and death as we know them. His consciousness passed from the state of manifestation into the state of absolute Reality. Chinese religion was not in quite so much of a hurry to separate consciousness from everyday life. Man was in harmony with Tao here and now, fully in possession of his ordinary everyday consciousness of people and things. In principle, Mahayana Buddhism was at one with Taoism in this respect, for in insisting that there was no real difference between Nirvana and Samsara it could not allow the idea of *passing* from one to the other. Mahayana was, however, somewhat infected with the characteristically Indian desire to escape from the world of form, but in China it lost this desire almost entirely. It became a world-transforming instead of a world-escaping religion.

Despite superficial differences, it will be seen that these two trends of Indian and Chinese religion have a common essence. Hindu-Buddhist religion discovered the essential Reality of life through detachment from its particular forms, assisted by the practice of meditation. Taoism discovered the essential harmony of everyday life with Tao by letting go of that life so that it could be free to be itself.

Both procedures are grounded in a common faith or trust, namely, that this everyday life IS Reality, that all things ARE in harmony with Tao, and that therefore this will be clear to you if you simply let go of the possessive itch. To try to *attain* union with Reality by action or by inaction (which is simply an indirect form of action) is to imply that you do not already have that union.

There is nothing to be attained. The union simply IS; Samsara IS Nirvana. The effort to attain something is just another form of that acquisitive desire which springs from lack of trust in the one supreme fact. In the words of Hsi-yun:

> By their very seeking for it they produce the contrary effect of losing it, for that is using the Buddha to seek for the Buddha and using mind to grasp mind. Even though they do their utmost for a full kalpa (aeon), they will not be able to attain to it. . . . If it is held that there is something to be attained apart from mind and, thereupon, mind is used to seek it, (that implies) failure to understand that mind and the object of its search are one.[3] (Chu, 1947, pp. 16, 24)

THE MOMENTOUS HARMONY

Historically, Zen is the embodiment of the common truth contained in the Hindu-Buddhist tradition and the Taoist tradition, the synthesis of the contemplative insight of Indian religion, the dynamic liveliness of Taoism, and the down-to-earthness of Confucianism. Zen is grounded precisely in this faith or trust that ordinary life is Tao, and is to be accepted or loved as such. The Zen master Chao-chu was asked, "What is the Tao?" He replied, "Everyday life is the Tao." "How," pursued the enquirer, "does one get into harmony with it?" "If you *try* to get into harmony with it, you will get away from it." The attempt suggests the absence of the reality, and proceeds from lack of faith in the truth that harmony already is. Lack of faith in this harmony creates the sense of inadequacy and insecurity which underlies all our aggressive and evil actions (see figure 7.5).

But Zen is more than a synthesis of these various trends in Indian and Chinese religion. The unique contribution of Zen to higher religion is its method of presenting the truth, a method involving "No dependence on words and letters, and direct pointing to the soul of man"—that is, to the Tao, Buddha-nature, or Reality itself.

Figure 7.5. The Chinese yin-yang symbol, denoting the manifestation of the Tao in the pairs of opposites—light and dark, life and death, male and female, positive and negative.

It is all too easy for ideas and concepts to conceal rather than reveal Reality. Thus the Zen masters say that ideas are fingers pointing at the moon of Reality, but that most people mistake the finger for the moon. Furthermore, we have already seen that it is quite impossible for ideas to describe or convey the deepest truth of life, since ideas are forms and Reality is too living to be held in any form. Zen, therefore, does not consist in acquiring new ideas about Reality and our relation to it; it consists in getting rid of ideas and feelings *about* life in order that we may get to life itself. The statement that ordinary life is Tao, or that we are one with Reality just as we are, here and now, is still an idea, and while it remains an idea it is still an attempt to capture the living truth in a fixed formula. Really to understand Zen we have to get away from this abstract and dead realm of concepts and come face-to-face with Reality as it stands quite clearly before us here and now.

There is only one place where we are truly alive, where we come into immediate contact with Reality, and that is *now*—this present moment. The past was only real when it was the present moment, and the future will only be real when it becomes it. The past continues to be real to the extent that it lives on effectually in the present. But real life is always now. In fact, we have no knowledge of any other reality than the present moment, and, strictly speaking, nothing has any existence save at this moment. Yet what we call the present moment is strangely elusive. As soon as we try to catch hold of it, it seems to run away. We cannot delay or hold it in any of the forms that it assumes or contains. We have moments of pleasure and moments of pain, but when we try to grab hold of the moment of pleasure, the moment, the movement, the life leaves the pleasure and it turns to dust in our hands. So, too, when we try to examine the moment, we cannot discover it, for it is too small to see. The more we look for it, the tinier it becomes, until we realize that it is infinitesimal and thus infinite.

Yet however much we may try to delay or grasp the moment, the fact remains that while, from one point of view, it eludes us, from another, we cannot get away from it. We may try to lag behind in the past or to hurry on into the future, but inevitably we do our lagging or hurrying in the present moment. As soon as we realize that the moment is in reality inescapable, we shall no longer try to grasp it; for whether we know it or not, it grasps us. For the now, this present moment, is Reality. All things proceed from it and exist in it, and yet when we look at it directly it seems nothing. Now is Tao, and Tao is now, and even though we do our damnedest to possess it, we are still unable to get out of it. Our union with Reality is the truth whether we realize it or not, whether we strive to attain it or not.

But to say that the now is Tao, or is Reality, at once introduces a concept, which, useful though it may be for a time, instantly distracts our attention from the real now. At once our religion becomes dead and removed from life, for although this now, this eternal moment, looks so void and so uninteresting to sense and thought, in fact it is the mysterious source of all liveliness and power. The genius of Zen lies in its way of pointing to the real now without distracting the attention with concepts. But the human mind, because of its inherently possessive nature, lets go of concepts with extreme reluctance, for which reason Zen has sometimes to attack and smash them quite violently. Thus its technique has often the appearance of spiritual shock-tactics.

DIRECT POINTING

The Zen way of teaching is to demonstrate Reality rather than to talk about it, or, if words are used at all, to avoid formally religious terminology and conceptual statements. When Zen speaks it expresses Reality, not with logical explanations and doctrines but with everyday conversation, or with statements that upset the normal conceptual mode of thinking so violently that they appear as utter nonsense. Because Zen desires to get rid of concepts, to shatter the rigid frames in which we try to possess life, it employs a thorough-going iconoclasm (see figure 7.6). At the same time, Zen as a formal religious cult reads the scriptures, uses images and ceremonies, and sometimes breaks down far enough to include sermons and explanations. But it is just the preservation of this formal aspect of religion that makes the informal and iconoclastic such a puzzling and effective contrast, a truth that Western reformers and iconoclasts have never appreciated.

The greater part of Zen literature consists of *mondo*, of brief dialogues between masters and pupils, which illustrate its peculiar method of instruction, pointing to the real now without interposing ideas and notions about it. Here, for example, is the way in which Zen deals with the problem of nonduality, concerning which Indian Buddhism has composed so many volumes of intricate explanation:

Figure 7.6. Line drawing of bamboo, based on painting by Chu Lu (1553–1632), Chinese. Many references to bamboo appear in Zen literature, and it is a favorite subject of Zen painters. A verse that describes Zen life says: "The bamboo shadows are sweeping the stairs, but no dust is stirred."

A monk asked Dosan, "How do we escape the heat when summer comes and the cold when winter is here?"

The master said, "Why not go where there is no summer, no winter?"

"Where is such a place?"

"When the cold season comes, one is thoroughly chilled; when the hot summer is here, one swelters."

As to escaping from Samsara, the world of opposites and everyday consciousness, to Nirvana, the realm of absolute unity and peace, Zen has this to say:

Bokuju was once asked, "We have to dress and eat every day, and how can we escape from all that?"

The master replied, "We dress, we eat."

"I don't understand."

"If you do not understand, put on your dress and eat your food."

Or again:

"Pray show me the way to deliverance."

"Who has ever put you in bondage?"

"Nobody."

"If so, why should you ask for deliverance?"

Another master deals with this question rather more explicitly, but we must be careful that he does not fool us:

Hui-hai was asked, "How can one attain the Great Nirvana?"

"Have no karma that works for transmigration."[4]

"What is the karma of transmigration?"

"To seek after the Great Nirvana, to abandon the defiled and take to the undefiled, to assert that there is something attainable and something realizable, not to be free from the teaching of opposites—this is the karma that works for transmigration."

"How can one be emancipated?"

"No bondage from the very first, and what is the use of seeking emancipation? Act as you will, go on as you feel—without second thought. This is the incomparable way."

Hui-hai's final remark must not, however, give the impression that Zen is just living lazily and fatuously in the present and taking life as it comes. If this be used as a formula for grasping the reality of Zen, the whole point is missed. A master was asked, "What is the Tao?" "Walk on!" he shouted. Thus whenever you think you have the right idea of Zen, drop it and walk on.

More and more we shall see that the essence of Zen is simply the giving up of any attempt to grasp life in ideational or emotional forms. It involves a thoroughgoing acceptance of life and experience just as it is at any given moment, which, whether we know it or not, is precisely what our basic, mirror-like consciousness is doing all the time. Passion, anger, elation, depression, ideas of good and evil, mine and yours—these are varying forms taken by our feelings and thoughts, whereas the essence of Mind, the essential consciousness, is ever formless, free and pure. "The perfect man," said Chuang-Tzu, "employs his mind as a mirror; it grasps nothing, it refuses nothing, it receives, but does not keep." At the same time, this must not lead us to form the *concept* of a pure and unchanging consciousness separate and apart from the changing forms of thoughts and things. The point is not at all to reject phenomena and cling to the Absolute, because the very nature of the Absolute, of the essential Mind, is nonclinging. As soon as we conceive a formless Self or mind-essence underlying and distinct from the changing contents of experience, we are denying the very nature of that Self. For its nature is not to separate itself from anything, not to stand apart from experience but to accept and identify itself with it. Its very life and power consist in a perpetual self-abandonment to its varied experiences, an identification of itself with its changing forms, which in Christian language would be called the divine love. Nor must it be thought that we have to *make* the pure Mind perform this act of self-abandonment; it does it by itself all the time, in us and through us, whether we wish it or not.

This, then, is why Hui-neng constantly insisted that the only difference between an ordinary man and a Buddha, an enlightened one, is that the latter knows he is a Buddha whereas the former does not. When asked, "What is enlightenment?" a master replied, "Your everyday mind." "When a thought moves," wrote Kaku-an, "another follows, and then another—an endless train of thoughts is thus awakened. Through enlightenment all this turns into truth." In reality the enlightened consciousness is not different from our ordinary everyday consciousness; to seek it as something over and above our mind as it is at this moment is immediately to set up a dualism. We thrust realization from us in the very act of regarding it as something to be attained. This seeming paradox is aptly expressed by Ma-tsu:

> In the Tao there is nothing to discipline oneself in. If there is any discipline in it, the completion of such discipline means the destruction of the Tao. But if there is no discipline whatever in the Tao, one remains an ignoramus.

It is only through seeking enlightenment that we find there is no need to seek. He goes on:

> One thought follows another without interruption; the preceding one does not wait for the succeeding; each one is self-contained and quiescent. This is called the "Meditation of the Ocean-stamp," in which are included all things, like the ocean where all the rivers however different in size empty themselves. (Suzuki, 1935, pp. 126–127)

Whether we know it or not, the "ocean" of pure consciousness perfectly accepts the stream of our thoughts and impressions all the time. At every instant we are in complete harmony with the Tao, but an apparent discord arises when, through a wrong use of memory and anticipation, we allow past and future experiences to conflict with the present. In the words of Emerson:

> These roses under my window make no reference to former roses or to better ones; they are for what they are; they exist with God today. There is no time to them. There is simply the rose; it is perfect in every moment of its existence . . . But man postpones or remembers; he does not live in the present, but with reverted eye laments the past, or, heedless of the riches that surround him, stands on tiptoe to foresee the future. He cannot be happy and strong until he too lives with nature in the present, above time.[5]

But between the unconscious harmony of the rose and the conscious harmony of the perfect man lies the illusion of self-consciousness, separation and discord, wherein we strive blindly for what in truth we have never lost. Yet this itself is no more an *actual* loss of the Tao than the disappearance of the rose in winter is a violation of its natural and proper life. The bloom is forgotten and the seed goes underground. "Unless a grain of corn falls into the earth and dies," said Jesus, "it remains alone; but if it dies, it bears much fruit." In spiritual development there must always be the middle stage wherein by apparent loss, by seeking and striving, we become conscious of the harmony that is our unconscious possession all long.

> Before a man studies Zen, to him mountains are mountains and waters are waters; after he gets an insight into the truth of Zen through instruction of a good master, mountains to him are not mountains and waters are not waters; but after this when he really attains to the abode of rest, mountains are once more mountains and waters are waters. (Ch'ing-yuan, as cited in Suzuki, 1927, p. 12)

The ignoramus, the primitive "simple" man, accepts life for what it is, just as it comes. The "seeker," however, looks for the God, the Reality, the absolute and eternal consciousness behind life, regarding the images of ordinary experience as a distracting illusion. But the perfect man, consciously one with the Tao, again accepts life for just for what it is.

T'an asked a student, "What were you before you became a monk?"

"I used to be a cowherd."

"How do you look after the cattle?"

"I go out with them early in the morning and come home when it grows dark."

"Splendid is your ignorance!"

Zen is spiritual freedom or spiritual poverty, that is, the liberation of our true nature (Buddha-nature or essence of Mind) from the burden of those fixed ideas and feelings about Reality which we accumulate through fear—the fear that life will run away from us. "Scholars," said Lao-Tzu, "gain every day; but Taoists lose every day." Or in the words of Jesus, "Blessed are the poor in spirit, for theirs is the kingdom of heaven. . . . Blessed are the pure (i.e., naked and free) in heart, for they shall see God." Such poverty and freedom are expressed in this poem from the *Mumon-kan*:[6]

> Hundreds of spring-flowers; the autumn moon;
> A fresh summer breeze; winter snow:
> Free your mind from idle thoughts,
> And for you any season is a good season.

But again, we must "walk on" even from spiritual poverty if this be used as a means to *grasp* the truth of Zen. Chao-chu was asked, "What would you say to one who comes to you with nothing?" "Throw it away!"

These *mondo* may seem puzzling to the uninitiated, but in fact there is nothing obscure or hidden about them. The truth which they indicate is, however, of such radical simplicity and self-evidence that our complex and burdened minds find it hard to see.

> It is so clear that it takes long to see.
> You must know that the fire which you are seeking
> Is the fire in your own lantern,
> And that your rice has been cooked from the very beginning.[7]

Or, as Pai-chang said when asked how to find Reality, "It is very much like looking for an ox when you are riding on one."

Kozankoku, a Confucian, came to Kwaido to ask about the hidden teaching of Zen. Kwaido said, "There is a passage in the text you are so thoroughly familiar with, which fitly describes the teaching of Zen. Did not Confucius declare, 'Do you think I am holding something back from you, O my disciples? Indeed, I have held nothing back from you.'"

Kozankoku could not understand this, and vainly pressed the master for a further explanation. But later, when they were walking together in the mountains, they passed a bush of wild laurel.

"Do you smell it?" asked Kwaido.

"Yes."

"There, I have kept nothing back from you!"

It would be fatal, however, to interpret this in a sentimentally pantheistic sense, as if Kwaido were saying that the smell of the wild laurel is the Tao.

No such conceptualism enters here. Pantheism, deism, theism, monism, dual-ism—all these are intellectual forms that must fail to grasp the living Reality. But when this has been thoroughly understood, intellectual forms may be used again without captivating the mind.

Strictly speaking, Zen does not have a method for awakening our minds to Reality, unless it may be called a "method of no-method." A method, a technique for discovering Reality implies an attempt to grasp it, and this, according to Zen, is as misleading and unnecessary as "putting legs on a snake" or "adding frost over snow." In the words of Lin-chi:

> The true man who has an insight into Reality . . . gives himself up to all manners of situations in which he finds himself in obedience to his past karma. He appears in whatever garments are ready for him to put on. As it is desired of him either to move or to sit quietly, he moves or sits. He has not a thought of running after Buddhahood. He is free from such pinings. Why is it so with him? Says an ancient sage, "When the Buddha is sought after, he is the cause of transmigration." (Suzuki, 1934a, pp. 32–33).[8]

ZEN MEDITATION

While, from one point of view, Zen has no method, from another it has a definite technique of meditation. It is against this background of definite technique that the "method of no-method" has its value as a surprising contrast. The success of Zen lies in its freedom both to use technique and to dispense with it; it is not bound to any one-sided procedure. The Zen way of meditation, known as za-zen, is the result of a long process of development.

Zen has always been a semi-monastic religion, though Zen monks do not take life vows, because many of them remain in the monastery only for a period of training before going back into the world as secular priests or lay-men. In some ways these institutions resemble our theological seminaries rather than monasteries in the strict sense. Originally Zen "monasteries" were small groups of monks gathered around an approved roshi or master, whose way of handling them was relatively informal and spontaneous. The early mondo are simply records of the daily life and teaching of these primitive communities. Before long, however, these mondo were collected and some of them were used as formal koan, or subjects for meditation. Monks devoted part of their time to meditation, and part to manual work in support of the community, a way of life somewhat like the rule of St. Benedict.

In meditation the monk sits cross-legged in the "lotus-posture" (padmasana), and by slow, rhythmic breathing brings his mind to a state of calm and freedom from ideas. He then takes up his koan and drops it into his mind like a stone into a still pool, whereafter he simply watches its effect. Some of the famous *koan* are these: "Before father and mother, what is your true nature?" or, as we might word it, "Beyond time and space, what is Reality?" "What is the sound of your hand?" "Stop the booming of the distant bell"—how can this be done? "When asked, 'What is Buddha?' Ummon answered, 'Dried dung!' "—what does this mean?[9] Sometimes the *koan* seem to contradict each other. When asked, "What is Buddha?" Ba-so answered, "This mind is Buddha," but on another occasion he said, "This mind is not Buddha."

At regular intervals the monk goes to the *roshi* for an interview (*sanzen*) when he is expected to demonstrate his view of the *koan* assigned to him. This is not to be done by wordy explanation, but by some kind of direct action or direct pointing to Reality in the true Zen style. The *roshi* responds in the same way, sometimes with a laconic comment, sometimes with silence, sometimes with a bang on the head from the big stick which lies before him—for all these measures are parts of his spiritual shock-tactics. Usually the monk sees into the meaning of his *koan* suddenly, experiencing a flash of insight termed *satori*, and this may occur during meditation, during *sanzen*, or while he is going about his ordinary work. For we see into Reality suddenly just because there is no real method or succession of stages for approaching it (see figure 7.7).

There are some 1,700 *koan*, and approximately 50 are needed for a full Zen training. It would seem that the various types of *koan* are used for getting rid of different types of conceptualism and mental fixation, and thus for revealing different "aspects" of the full understanding of Zen. More advanced *koan* have to do with the way in which Reality manifests itself in life and action. But it is almost impossible to discuss this subject with profit, since experiment alone can make sense of it. In the course of centuries *koan* meditation has become an art of the deepest subtlety, though much may be learned from the general attitude of Zen quite apart from work with *za-zen*.

Figure 7.7. The Chinese characters for "wu hsin" (Japanese "mushin"), literally, "no-mind." This is a special term for the Zen consciousness that is impossible to render in any one English phrase. It might be said that the whole art of Zen is in learning to understand the difference between *wu hsin* and mere empty-mindedness or unconsciousness. *Wu hsin* is the psychological equivalent of Sunyata, the "solid" or creative void that effortlessly produces and embraces the universe.

THE CULTURAL EFFECTS OF ZEN

Zen has entered into many aspects of the life of the Far East—painting, architecture, gardening, chivalry, tea-ceremony, etiquette, poetry and ethics. Zen affects every sphere of daily life from the statecraft of the ruler to the menial work of the labourer. As a Zen poet says:

> How wondrous, how miraculous, this—
> I draw water and I carry fuel!

Its moral effects are profound but not obvious, for the oriental idea of goodness is not so self-conscious and self-assertive as the occidental. As Lao-Tzu said, the wise man hides his virtue and appears on the surface like a fool, for "true grace (Te) does not appear as grace, and thus is grace; false grace is so aware of itself as grace that it is not grace." Zen produces thousands of Bodhisattvas who do not advertise themselves (see figure 7.8).

The most obvious effects of Zen are in the realm of aesthetics, for Chinese art of the T'ang, Sung and Yuan periods, the Japanese painting of Sesshu and the Sumiye school, the gardening art of Kobori Enshiu, the *haiku* poetry of Basho and others—all these have had direct inspiration from Zen, or from a Zen-flavored Taoism. Three major characteristics of Far Eastern art exemplify aspects of the Zen life:

1. Absence of symmetry. The phenomena of nature are rarely symmetrical in form; at most there is only an approximation to absolute symmetry, and Zen perceives in this fact the lively and dynamic quality of nature. For symmetry is a state of such perfect balance that movement is no longer possible; a form so balanced is dead, and thus the symmetrical form is analogous to that mental and emotional fixation, which in Zen is ever broken down. It is for this reason that Chinese and Japanese paintings are so seldom architectural and wooden. There is no feeling at all of stuffing and the glass case in their drawings of birds, and the very rocks and mountains seem to flow. As a Western poet has said:

Figure 7.8. The Bamboo Cutter, supposed to represent Hui-neng, the Sixth Patriarch. Based on the painting by Liang K'ai, Chinese (13th cent.).

The hills are shadows, and they flow
From form to form, and nothing stands.

2. The use of emptiness. As Zen perceives the forms of life within Sunyata, the all-inclusive mystery of the Void, Chinese painting makes the greatest use of the empty background, of large expanses of mist, to suggest depth. For the empty spaces of Chinese painting are no *mere* emptiness; they are creative and suggestive, exciting the imagination and giving a startling clarity and vividness to the objects drawn against and within them. Zen taste deplores the cluttering of a picture or of a room with many objects. It likes to take an empty space, and, within it, concentrate attention on one point—like the *koan* thrown into the still pool of the mind, like the one point of the living moment within the emptiness of past and future.

3. The instantaneous quality. This might be called, too, the momentary quality, for Chinese and Japanese art love to portray moments of life, as if the painter had just glimpsed his subject for a second. A duck is painted just in the act of alighting, or a spray of bamboos caught in a sudden gust of wind. The very media of the art—brush, ink and silk or absorbent paper—require a swift, evenly flowing technique. As in life itself, a stroke once made can never be retouched. Zen, as Suzuki (1936) points out,

> permits no ossification as it were of each moment. It takes hold of each moment as it is born from Sunyata, that is, Emptiness, according to Buddhist philosophy. Momentariness is therefore characteristic of this philosophy. Each moment is absolute, alive, and significant. The frog leaps, the cricket sings . . . a breeze passes through the pine branches . . . Buddhism is quick to catch each movement of nature and expresses its impressions in a seventeen syllable poem or in a few strokes of the brush. (p. 26)

CONCLUSION

The occidental reader must not gather from the foregoing that Zen is an easy-going aestheticism, a philosophy of idling along with the stream of events. Zen has also been the religion of warriors who applied it on the battlefield in the very moment of danger:

Under the sword raised high
Is hell, making you tremble.
But walk on!—
And there is the Land of Bliss.

The momentariness of Zen lies above and beyond the two wrong extremes of idling and hurrying, in an amazing poise, not of rigidity, but of balance in motion,

Figure 7.9. Autograph by Abbot Kozuki of Empukuji, Kyoto. Within the circle of the Void (Sunyata) is written: "Not one thing inside."

not of the statue but of the dancer. For this is the balance of living Reality itself, of the unmoved Mover, of the whirlwind with peace at the heart (see figure 7.9).

In essence, Zen involves no doctrine. It is an experience of Reality beyond doctrine, for which reason Zen may be of use to people of any religion. It is to be doubted, however, whether one can ground one's life in pure, essential Zen alone, for even as a specific religious cult Zen employs forms and symbols, and the normal *structure* of the Buddhist religion. For pure life expresses itself within and through structure. Life without structure is unseen; it is the unmanifested Absolute. But structure without life is dead, and religion has altogether too much of this death.

For the ordinary religious consciousness grasps too much, and has too little faith in the actual present fact of the Life of life as the most all-absorbing and self-evident reality of our existence.

> Like unto space it knows no boundaries;
> Yet it is right here with us, ever retaining its serenity and fullness;
> It is only when you seek it that you lose it.
> You cannot take hold of it, nor can you get rid of it;
> While you can do neither, it goes on its own way;
> You remain silent and it speaks; you speak and it is silent;
> The great gate of charity is wide open with no obstructions whatever
>   before it.
> (Hsuan-chiao, *Cheng-tao Ke*, 34, as cited in Suzuki, 1935, p. 115)

NOTES

1. A somewhat different account of the history of Zen in China is given by Hu Shih (1932). He traces its origins back to Tao-seng (d. 434), a disciple of a school of Taoist interpreters of Yoga represented by Hui-yuan (d. 416) and Tao-an (d. 385). According to Hu Shih, Bodhidharma arrived in Canton as early as 470, but, even so, found Tao-seng's

Dhyana school already in existence. The account given above follows Suzuki (1927), but at present there is insufficient material at hand to enable the occidental student to decide between Suzuki and Hu Shih. Suzuki's account follows the official version of the Zen school.

2. *Karuna* is the moral equivalent of all-inclusiveness.

3. The term "mind" as used here signifies that ground of consciousness or mind-essence which, as explained above, is identical with Sunyata.

4. Karma (literally, action) is the law of causality, and thus the phrase "karma that works for transmigration" means the kind of action which has the effect of binding the agent to Samsara, where, according to general Buddhist belief, man is born again and again into the world until he realizes Nirvana.

5. *Essays*, First Series. "Self-Reliance."

6. The *Mumon-kan* (Chinese, *Wu-men Kwan*) or "No Gate barrier" is a standard collection of *mondo* with brief comments and poems about each. In the verse quoted here "idle thoughts" are fixed concepts.

7. *Mumon-kan*, vii. I am indebted for this translation to the Ven. Sokei-an Sasaki, late abbot of Jofuku-in.

8. Trans. D. T. Suzuki, *Essays in Zen Buddhism*, Vol. III, pp. 32–33. A free rendering of the original Chinese. Buddhahood is the state of Enlightenment or Awakening, or the immediate knowledge of Reality. Buddha is often used as a synonym for Reality.

9. Ummon's answer is sometimes translated, "The dried-up dirt scraper."

REFERENCES

[Note that Watts included in the reference section a list of bibliographic materials extending beyond those cited in the essay itself—Eds.]

Anesaki, M. (1930). *History of Japanese religion*. London, UK: Kegan Paul, Trench, Trubner.

Cat's yawn. (1947). New York, NY. First Zen Institute of America.

Chu, C. (Trans.). (1947). *The Huang Po Doctrine of universal mind*. London, UK: Buddhist Society.

Eliot, C. (1935). *Japanese Buddhism*. London, UK: Routledge & Kegan Paul.

Gatenby, E. V. (1929). *The cloud men of Yamato*. London, UK: John Murray.

Grosse, E. (1923). *Die Ostasiatische Tuschmalerei*. Berlin, Germany: Cassirer.

Hu, S. (1932). The development of Zen Buddhism in China. *Chinese Political and Social Review, 15*(4), 486–489.

Nukariya, K. (1913). *The religion of the Samurai*. London, UK: Luzac.

Ohasama, S., & Faust, A. (1925). *Zen: der lebendige Buddhismus in Japan*. [Zen: The living Buddhism in Japan] Gotha, Germany: Perthes.

Okakura, K. (1926). *The book of tea*. New York, NY: Duffield.

Senzaki, N., & Reps, P. (1939). *101 Zen stories*. Philadelphia, PA: David McKay.

Senzaki, N., & Reps, P. (Trans.). (1934). *The gateless gate*. Los Angeles, CA: Murray.

Shaku, S. (1906). *Sermons of a Buddhist Abbot*. Chicago, IL: Open Court.

Steinilber-Oberlin, E., & Matsuo, K. (1930). *Les Sectes bouddhiques japonaises*. [Buddhist sects of Japan]. Paris, France: Les Editions G. Cres.

Suzuki, B. L. (1938). *Mahayana Buddhism*. London, UK: The Buddhist Lodge.

Suzuki, D. T. (1927). *Essays in Zen Buddhism* (Vol. 1). London, UK: Luzac.

Suzuki, D. T. (1933). *Essays in Zen Buddhism* (Vol. 2). London, UK: Luzac.

Suzuki, D. T. (1934a). *Essays in Zen Buddhism* (Vol. 3). London, UK: Luzac.

Suzuki, D. T. (1934b). *An introduction to Zen Buddhism*. Kyoto, Japan: Eastern Buddhist Society. (German translation, *Die Grosse Befreiung*, with an introduction by C. G. Jung published 1939)

Suzuki, D. T. (1934c). *The training of the Zen Buddhist monk*. Kyoto, Japan: Eastern Buddhist Society.

Suzuki, D. T. (1935). *Manual of Zen Buddhism*. Kyoto, Japan: Eastern Buddhist Society.

Suzuki, D. T. (1936). *Buddhist philosophy and its effects on the life and thought of the Japanese people*. Tokyo, Japan: Kokusai Bunka Shinkokai.

Suzuki, D. T. (1938). *Zen Buddhism and its influence on Japanese culture*. Kyoto, Japan: Eastern Buddhist Society.

Watts, A. W. (1948). *The spirit of Zen*. London, UK: Murray.

Wong M-L. (Trans.). (1944). *The sutra of Wei Lang* (or *Hui-neng*), (New edition, C. Humphreys, Ed.). London, UK: Luzac.

CHAPTER EIGHT

The Way of Liberation in Zen Buddhism (1955)[α]

Words can express no more than a tiny fragment of human knowledge, for what we can say and think is always immeasurably less than what we experience. This is not only because there are no limits to the exhaustive description of an event, as there are no limits to the possible divisions of an inch; it is also because there are experiences that defy the very structure of our language, as water cannot be carried in a sieve. But the intellectual, the man who has a great skill with words, is always in danger of restricting what can be known to what can be described. He is therefore apt to be puzzled and suspicious when anyone tries to use ordinary language to convey an experience which shatters its logic, an experience that words can express only at the cost of losing their meaning. He is suspicious of fuzzy and ill-conceived thinking, and concludes that there is no experience that can correspond to such apparently nonsensical forms of words.

This is particularly true of an idea that crops up repeatedly in the history of philosophy and religion—the idea that the seeming multiplicity of facts, things, and events is in reality One, or, more correctly, beyond duality. This idea is usually intended to convey more than a speculative theory; it is intended to convey the actual experience of unity, which may also be described as the sense that everything that happens or can happen is right and natural in so positive a way that it can even be called divine. To put it in the words of the *Shinjinmei*:

Reprinted from *Asian Study Monographs*, No. 1, by the permission of HSG Agency as agent for the author. The Way of Liberation in Zen Buddhism. Copyright © 1955 by A. W. Watts.

One is all;
All is one.
If only it can be thus,
Why trouble about being imperfect?[1]

To the logician such an utterance is meaningless, and to the moralist it is plainly subversive. Even the psychologist may wonder whether there can be a state of mind or feeling that such words can faithfully represent. For he may insist that sensations or feelings are recognizable only by their mutual differences, as we know white by contrast with black, and that therefore a sensation of nondifference, of absolute oneness, could never be realized. At most it would be like putting on rose-tinted spectacles. One would at first be aware of rosy clouds by contrast with the memory of white clouds, but in time the contrast would fade, and the all-pervasive hue would vanish from consciousness. Yet the literature of Zen Buddhism does not suggest that the experience of unity or nonduality is recognized only temporarily, by contrast with the former experience of multiplicity. It suggests that it is an abiding experience that by no means fades with familiarity. Our best way of understanding it will be to follow, as best we can, the inner process through which the experience is realized. This will mean, in the first place, treating it from the psychological point of view, to find out whether the words express any psychological reality, let alone any logical sense or moral propriety.

It may be assumed that the starting-point is the ordinary man's feeling of conflict between himself and his environment, between his desires and the hard facts of nature, between his own will and the jarring wills of other people. The ordinary man's desire to replace this sense of conflict by a sense of harmony has its parallel in the age-old concern of philosophers and scientists to understand nature in terms of unity—in the human mind's perennial discontent with dualism. We shall see that this is in many ways a rather unsatisfactory starting-point. The problem of telling anyone how to proceed from this point to the experience of unity reminds one of the yokel who was asked the way to an obscure village. He scratched his head for a while and then answered, "Well, sir, I know where it is, but if I were you I wouldn't start from here." But unfortunately this is just where we are.

Let us, then, consider some of the ways in which the Zen masters have handled this problem. There are four ways in particular which seem to deserve special attention, and these may be listed briefly as follows:

1. To answer that all things are in reality One.
2. To answer that all things are in reality Nothing, Void.
3. To answer that all things are perfectly all right and natural just as they are.
4. To say that the answer is the question, or the questioner.

The question itself may assume many different forms, but essentially it is the problem of liberation from conflict, from dualism, from what Buddhism calls the *samsara* or vicious circle of birth-and-death.

1. As an example of the first type of answer, the assertion that all things are in reality One, consider the words of Eka:

> The profound truth is the principle of ultimate identity.
> Under delusion the *mani* gem may be called a broken tile,
> But when you enter truly into self-awakening it is a real pearl.
> Ignorance and wisdom are alike without difference,
> For you should know that the ten thousand things are all Suchness
>   (*tathata*).
> It is out of pity for those disciples who hold a dualistic view
> That I put words in writing and send this letter.
> Regarding this body and the Buddha as neither differing nor separate,
> Why, then, should we seek for something which does not need to be
>   added to us?[2]

The implication of this answer is that liberation from the conflict of dualism does not require any effort to change anything. One has only to realize that every experience is identical with the One, the Buddha-nature, or the Tao, and then the problem will simply vanish. Similarly, when Joshu asked Nansen, "What is the Tao?" Nansen replied, "Your ordinary mind is the Tao." "How," asked Joshu, "can one return into accord with it?" Nansen answered, "By intending to accord you immediately deviate."[3]

The psychological response to answers of this kind will be an attempt to feel that every experience, every thought, sensation, or feeling is the Tao—that somehow the good is the same as the bad, the pleasant the same as the painful. This may take the form of trying to attach the symbol-thought "this is the Tao" to each experience as it arises, though obviously it will be hard to realize much content, much meaning, in a symbol which applies equally to every possible experience. Yet as the frustration of not realizing any content arises, it is asserted that this, too, is the Tao—so that any grasp of what the nature of this One that is All may be becomes more and more elusive.

2. Thus another, and perhaps better, way of answering the original question is to assert that all things are in reality No-thing or Void (*sunyata*), following the doctrine of the *Prajnaparamita-hrdaya Sutra*, "Form is precisely the void; the void is precisely form."[4] This answer provokes no attempt to find content or meaning in the term used to represent the One reality. In Buddhism the word *sunya* or Void implies inconceivability rather than mere nothingness. The psychological response to the assertion that all is One might be described as an attempt to say "Yes" to every experience as it arises, as an attempt to achieve a total acceptance or affirmation of life in all its aspects. Contrariwise, the psychological response suggested by the assertion that all is Void would be an attempt to say "No" to each experience.

This is found also in the Vedanta, where the formula *neti-neti*, "no, no," is used to support the understanding that *no* experience is the One reality. In

Zen, the word *mu*[5]—no, not, or nothing—is used in a similar way, and is often employed as a *koan*[6] or initiatory problem in meditation for beginners in such a way that at all times and under all circumstances one persists in saying the word "No" to everything that happens—including saying the word "No." Hence the reply of Joshu to the question, "How will it be when I come to you without a single thing?" "Throw it down!"[7]

3. Then there are the answers which seem to imply that nothing has to be done at all, neither saying "Yes" to everything nor "No" to everything. The point here is rather to leave one's experience and one's own mind alone and allow them to be just as they are. Consider the following from Rinzai:

> One can only resolve past karma as the circumstances arise. When it's time to dress, put your clothes on. When you have to walk, then walk. When you have to sit, then sit. Don't have a single thought in your mind about seeking for Buddhahood. How can this be? The ancients say, "If you desire deliberately to seek the Buddha, your Buddha is just *Samsara*." . . . Followers of the Tao, there is no place in Buddhism for using effort. Just be ordinary, without anything special. Relieve your bowels, pass water, put on your clothes, and eat your food. When you're tired, go and lie down. Ignorant people may laugh at me, but the wise will understand. . . . The ancients say, "To happen to meet a man of Tao upon the road, you must first not be facing the Tao." Thus it is said that if a person practices the Tao, the Tao will not work.[8]

Similarly, a monk asked Bokuju, "We dress and eat every day, and how do we escape from having to put on clothes and eat food?"[9] The master answered, "We dress, we eat." "I don't understand." "If you don't understand," said the master, "put on your clothes and eat your food." In other incidents the state of nonduality is sometimes represented as beyond the opposites of "heat" and "cold," but when asked to describe this state Zen will say:

> When cold, we gather round the hearth before the blazing fire;
> When hot, we sit on the bank of the mountain stream in the bamboo
>   grove.[10]

The psychological response here seems to be one of letting one's mind respond to circumstances as it feels inclined, not to quarrel with feeling hot in summer or cold in winter, and—it must also be added—not to quarrel with the feeling that there is some feeling you want to quarrel with! It is as if to say that the way you are actually feeling is the right way to feel, and that the basic conflict with life and oneself arises from trying to change or get rid of one's present feeling. Yet this very desire to feel differently may also be the present feeling that is not to be changed.

4. There is finally the fourth type of answer that turns the question back on itself, or on the questioner himself. Eka asked Bodhidharma, "I have no peace of mind. Please pacify my mind." Bodhidharma replied, "Bring out your mind here before me, and I will pacify it!" "But when I seek my own mind," said Eka, "I cannot find it." "There!" concluded Bodhidharma, "I have pacified your mind!"[11]

Doshin asked Sosan, "What is the method of liberation?" The master replied, "Who binds you?" "No one binds me." "Why then," said the master, "should you seek liberation?"[12] There are other instances where the answer is simply the repetition of the question, or some such reply as "Your question is perfectly clear. Why ask me?"

Replies of this type seem to throw attention back upon the state of mind from which the question arises, as if to say, "If your feelings are troubling you, find out who or what it is that is being troubled." The psychological response is therefore to try to feel what feels and to know what knows—to make an object of the subject. Yet, as Obaku says, "To make the Buddha seek after himself, or to make the mind take hold of itself—this is an impossibility to the end of eternity." According to Hyakujo, "It is much like looking for an ox when you are riding on it"—or, as one of the poems in the *Zenrin-kushu* puts it, it is

> Like a sword that wounds, but cannot wound itself;
> Like an eye that sees, but cannot see itself.[14]

In the words of an old Chinese popular saying, "A single hand cannot make a clap."[15] Yet Hakuin always introduced his students to Zen by asking them to hear the sound of one hand!

It is not difficult to see that there is a common pattern underlying all these four types of answer, since all the answers are circular. If all things are the One, then my feeling of conflict between dualities is also the One, as well as my objection to this feeling. If all things are Void, then the thought that this is so is also Void, and I feel as if I am being asked to fall into a hole and pull the hole in after me. If everything that happens is perfectly right and natural just as it is, then the wrong and unnatural is also natural. If I am just to let things happen, what happens when one of these things is precisely my desire to interfere with the course of events? And finally, if the root of the conflict is a lack of self-understanding, how can I understand the self which is trying to understand itself? In short, the root of the problem is the question. If you do not ask the question the problem will not arise. To put it another way, the problem of how to escape from conflict is the very conflict one is trying to escape.

If all these answers are not particularly helpful, this is only to say that the human situation is one for which there is no help. Every remedy for suffering is after all like changing one's position on a hard bed, and every advance in the control of our environment makes the environment harder to control.

Nevertheless, all this mental circulation does at least seem to produce two rather definite conclusions. The first is that if we do not try to help ourselves, we shall never realize how helpless we are. Only by ceaseless questioning can we begin to realize the limits, and thus the very form, of the human mind. The second is that when we do at last realize the depths of our helplessness, we are at peace. We have given ourselves up for lost, and this is what is meant by losing oneself, or by self-surrender, or self-sacrifice.

Perhaps this will throw some light on the Buddhist doctrine of the Void, on the saying that all is in reality empty or in vain. For if the deepest impulse of my being is to escape from a conflict which is substantially identical with my desire to escape from conflict; if, in other words, the entire structure of myself, my ego, is an attempt to do the impossible, then I am in vain or void to the very core. I am simply an itch that has nothing upon which to scratch itself. Trying to scratch makes the itch worse, but an itch is, by definition, what wants to be scratched.

Zen is therefore trying to communicate a vivid realization of the vicious circularity, the helplessness, and the plain impossibility of the human situation, of that desire for harmony which is precisely conflict, that desire which is our core, our very will-to-live. This would be a masochistic discipline of pure self-frustration, were it not for very curious and seemingly paradoxical consequences. When it is clear beyond all doubt that the itch cannot be scratched, it stops itching by itself. When it is realized that our basic desire is a vicious circle, it stops circling of its own accord. But this happens only when it has become utterly clear and certain that there is no way of *making* it stop.

The attempt to *make* oneself do or not do something implies, of course, an inner, subjective duality—a splitting asunder of the mind's integrity, which brings about a paralysis of action. To some extent, then, the statement that all is One and One is all is actually expressing the end of this inner split, and the discovery of the mind's original unity and autonomy. It is not unlike learning the use of a new muscle—when suddenly you move it from inside, or rather, it moves itself, after all efforts to force it from without have been unavailing. This type of experience is vivid enough, but, as we all know, practically impossible to communicate.

It is important to remember that the state of mind out of which this new experience of unity arises is one of total futility. In Zen it is likened to the predicament of a mosquito biting an iron bull, or, as another poem in the *Zenrin-kushu* expresses it:

> To trample upon the Great Void
> The Iron Bull must sweat.[16]

But how will an iron bull sweat? It is the same question as "How can I escape from conflict?" or "How can I catch hold of myself, or of my own hand?"

Now in the intensity of this complete impasse, in which the radical impotence of the ego is vividly understood, it is suddenly realized that—nevertheless—there is a great process of life still going on. "I stand and I sit; I clothe myself and I eat. . . . The water flows blue, and the mountain towers green. . . . The wind blows in the trees, and cars honk in the distance." With my ordinary self reduced to nothing but a completely useless straining I suddenly realize that all this is my real activity—that the activity of my ego has been displaced by the total activity of life, in such a way that the rigid boundary between myself and everything else has completely disappeared. All events whatsoever, whether the raising of my own hand or the chattering of a bird outside, are seen to be happening *shizen*,[17] "by themselves" or "automatically," in the spontaneous as distinct from the mechanical sense of the word.

> The blue mountains are of themselves blue mountains;
> The white clouds are of themselves white clouds.[18]

And the raising of a hand, the thinking of a thought, or the making of a decision happen in just the same way. It becomes clear that this is, in fact, the way things have always been happening, and that therefore all my efforts to move myself or to control myself have been irrelevant—having had the sole value of proving that it cannot be done. The whole concept of self-control has been misconstrued, since it is as impossible to *make* oneself relax, or *make* oneself do anything, as to open one's mouth by the exclusively mental act of willing it to open. No matter how much the will is strained and thought is concentrated on the idea of opening, the mouth will remain unmoved until it opens itself. It was out of this sense of all events happening "by themselves" that the poet Hokoji wrote:

> Miraculous power and marvelous activity—
> Drawing water and hewing wood![19]

This state of consciousness is by no means a psychological impossibility, even as a more or less continuous feeling. Throughout the course of their lives most people seem to feel more or less continuously the rigid distinction between the ego and its environment. Release from this feeling is like release from a chronic illness, and is followed by a sense of lightness and ease comparable to being relieved of the burden of a huge plaster cast. Naturally the immediate sense of euphoria or ecstasy wears off in the course of time, but the permanent absence of the rigid ego-environment boundary remains as a significant change in the structure or our experience. It is of no consequence that the ecstasy wears off, for the compulsive craving for ecstasy disappears, having formerly existed by way of compensation for the chronic frustration of living in a vicious circle.

To some extent the rigid distinction between ego and environment is equivalent to that between mind and body, or between the voluntary and involuntary
neural systems. This is probably the reason why Zen and yoga disciplines pay
so much attention to breathing, to watching over the breath (*anapranasmrti*),
since it is in this organic function that we can see most easily the essential
identity of voluntary and involuntary action. We cannot help breathing, and yet
it seems that breath is under our control; we both breathe and are breathed.
For the distinction of the voluntary and the involuntary is valid only within a
somewhat limited perspective. Strictly speaking, I will or decide involuntarily.
Were it not so, it would always be necessary for me to decide to decide and to
decide to decide to decide in an infinite regress. Now the involuntary processes
of the body, such as the beating of the heart, do not seem to differ very much
in principle from other involuntary actions going on outside the body. Both are,
as it were, environmental. When, therefore, the distinction of voluntary and
involuntary is transcended within the body, it is also transcended with respect
to events outside the body.

When, therefore, it is understood that these ego-environment and voluntary-
involuntary distinctions are conventional, and valid only within limited and
somewhat arbitrary perspectives, we find ourselves in a kind of experiencing
to which such expressions as "One is All and All is One" are quite appropriate.
For this one-ness represents the disappearance of a fixed barrier, or a rigid dualism. But it is in no sense a "one-thing-ness"—a type of pantheism or monism
asserting that all so-called things are the illusory forms of one homogeneous
"stuff." The experience of release from dualism is not to be understood as
the sudden disappearance of mountains and trees, houses and people, into a
uniform mass of light or transparent voidness.

For this reason the Zen masters have always recognized that "the One" is
a somewhat misleading term. In the words of the *Shinjinmei*:

> There are two because there is One,
> Yet cling not to this One . . .
> In the dharma-world of true Suchness
> There is neither "other" nor "self,"
> If you want an immediate answer,
> We can only say "Not two."[20]

Hence the koan question, "When the many are reduced to the One, to what
shall the One be reduced?" To this Joshu replied, "When I was in Seiju Province,
I made a linen robe weighing nine pounds."[21] Strange as it may sound, it is in
this type of language that Zen expresses itself most plainly, for this is a direct
language without the least element of symbolism or conceptualism. After all,
it is so easy to forget that what is being expressed here is not an idea or an
opinion, but an experience. For Zen does not speak from the external standpoint
of one who stands outside life and comments upon it. This is a standpoint from

which effective understanding is impossible, just as it is impossible to move a muscle by nothing more than verbal commands, however strenuously spoken.

There is, of course, a permanent value in being able, as it were, to stand aside from life and reflect upon it, in being aware of one's own existence, in having what communications engineers would call a psychological feedback system that enables us to criticize and correct our actions. But systems of this kind have their limitations, and a moment's consideration of the analogy of feedback will show where they lie. Probably the most familiar example of feedback is the electrical thermostat which regulates the heating of a house. By setting an upper and lower limit of desired temperature, a thermometer is so connected that it will switch the heat on when the lower limit is reached, and off when the upper limit is reached. The temperature of the rooms is thus kept within the desired limits. We might say, then, that the thermostat is a kind of sensitive organ which the furnace acquires in order to regulate its own conduct, and that this is a very rudimentary analogy of human self-consciousness.

But having thus constructed a self-regulating furnace, how about constructing a self-regulating thermostat? We are all familiar enough with the vagaries of thermostats, and it might be a fine idea to install a second feedback system to control the first. But then there arises the problem of how far can this go. Followed logically to its limits, it implies an indefinite series of feedbacks controlling feedbacks, which, beyond a certain point, would paralyze the whole system with the confusion of complexity. If it is to be avoided, there must, somewhere at the end of the line, be a thermostat or a source of intelligence whose information and authority is to be trusted, and not subjected to further checks and controls. For to this the only alternative is an infinite series of controls, which is absurd, since a point would arrive when the information would never reach the furnace. It might seem that another alternative would be a circular system of control, as when the civilian is controlled by the policeman, who is controlled by the mayor, who is controlled by the civilian. But this works only when each member trusts the one above it, or, to put it in another way, when the system trusts itself—and does not keep on trying to stand outside itself to correct itself.

This gives us rather a vivid picture of the human predicament. Our life consists essentially in action, but we have the power to check action by reflection. Too much reflection inhibits and paralyzes action, but because action is a matter of life or death, how much reflection is necessary? In so far as Zen describes its fundamental attitude as *mushin* or *munen*,[22] "no-mind" or "no-thought" it seems to stand for action as against reflection.

> In walking, just walk. In sitting, just sit.
> Above all, don't wobble.[23]

Joshu's answer to the question about the many and the One was simply unreflective action, unpremeditated speech. "When I was in Seiju Province I made a linen robe weighing nine pounds."

But reflection is also action, and Zen might equally well say: "In acting, just act. In thinking, just think. Above all, don't wobble." In other words, if you are going to reflect, to think, just reflect, but do not reflect about reflecting. And Zen would also agree that reflection about reflection is action, provided that in doing it we do just that, and have no tendency to drift off into the infinite regression of trying always to stand above or outside the level upon which we are acting. In short, Zen is also a liberation from the dualism of thought versus action, for it thinks as it acts—with the same quality of abandon, commitment, or faith. Thus the attitude of *mushin* is by no means an anti-intellectualist exclusion of thinking. It is action upon any level whatsoever, physical or psychic, without trying *at the same moment* to observe and check the action from outside, that is, without wobbling or anxiety.

Needless to say, what is true of the relationship of thinking to action is also true of feeling, since our feelings or emotions about life are as much a type of feedback as our thoughts. Feeling blocks action, and blocks itself as a form of action, when it gets caught in this same tendency to observe or feel itself indefinitely—as for example, when, in the midst of enjoying myself thoroughly, I examine myself to see if I am getting the utmost out of the occasion. Not content with tasting the food, I am trying also to taste my tongue. Not content with feeling happy, I want to feel myself feeling happy—so as to be sure not to miss anything.

Obviously there is no fixed way of determining the exact point where reflection must turn into action in any given situation, of knowing that we have given the matter enough thought to act without regret. This is always a problem of sensibility, of nice judgment. But the fact remains that however skillfully and carefully our reflecting is done, its conclusions are always a long way short of certainty. Ultimately, every action is a leap into the dark. The only real certainty that we have about the future is that unknown quantity called death, standing as the final symbol of the fact that our lives are not in our own control. In other words, human life is founded upon an irreducible element of the unknown and the uncontrolled, which is the Buddhist *sunya* or Void and which is the *mushin* or "no-mind" of Zen. But Zen is—beyond this— the realization that I do not merely stand on this unknown, or float upon it in the frail barque of my body: it is the realization that this unknown is myself.

From the standpoint of vision, my own head is an empty space in the midst of experience—an invisible and inconceivable void which is neither dark nor light. This same voidness stands behind each one of our senses—both the external or exteroceptive and the internal or proprioceptive senses. It stands, too, beyond the beginnings of my life, beyond my conception in my mother's womb. It stands at the center of the very nuclear structure of my organism. For when the physicist tries to penetrate this structure he finds that the very act of looking into it obscures what he wants to see. This is an example of the same principle that we have encountered all along—that in trying to look into themselves, the eyes turn away from themselves. This is why it is usual to begin training in Zen with one of the many forms of the koan, "Who are you?" "Before father and mother, what is your original nature?" "Who is it that carries this corpse around?"

By such means it is discovered that our "self-nature" (*svabhava*) is "no-nature," that our real mind (*shin*) is "no-mind" (*mushin*). To the extent, then, that we realize that the unknown and the inconceivable is our own original nature, it no longer stands over against us as a threatening object. It is not so much the abyss into which we are falling; it is rather that out of which we act and live, think and feel.

Again, we can see the appropriateness of the language of unity. There is no longer a fixed dualism between reflection and action. More important still, there is no longer a separation of the knower on the one hand and the unknown on the other. Reflection is action, and the knower is the unknown. We can see, too, the appropriateness of such remarks as Hui Hai's "Act as you will; go on as you feel, without second thought. This is the incomparable Way." For sayings of this kind are not intended to discourage ordinary reflection, judgment, and restraint. Their application is not superficial but profound. That is to say, in the final analysis we have to act and think, live and die, from a source beyond all our knowledge and control. If this is unfortunate, no amount of care and hesitancy, no amount of introspection and searching of our motives, can make any ultimate difference to it. We are therefore compelled to choose between a shuddering paralysis or a leap into action regardless of the ultimate consequences. Superficially speaking, our actions may be right or wrong with respect to relative standards. But our decisions upon this superficial level must be supported by the underlying conviction that whatever we do and whatever happens to us is ultimately "right"—which is a way of saying that we must enter into it without "second thought," without the *arrière pensée* of regret, hesitancy, doubt, or self-recrimination. Thus when Ummon was asked, "What is the Tao?" he answered simply, "Walk on!"[24] But to act without second thought is not by any means a mere precept for our imitation. It is actually impossible to realize this kind of action until we have understood that we have no other alternative, until we have realized that we ourselves are the unknown and the uncontrolled.

So far as Zen is concerned, this realization is little more than the first step in a long course of study. For it must be remembered that Zen is a form of Mahayana Buddhism, in which Nirvana—liberation from the vicious circle of Samsara—is not so much the final goal as the beginning of the life of the Bodhisattva. The concern of the Bodhisattva is *upaya* or *hoben*,[25] the application of this realization to every aspect of life for the "liberation of all sentient beings," not only human and animal, but also trees, grass, and the very dust.[β] It might be said, then, that the real discipline of Zen begins only at the point where the individual has altogether stopped trying to improve himself. This appears to be a contradiction because we are almost completely unaccustomed to the idea of effortless-effort, of tension without conflict and concentration without strain.

But it is fundamental to Zen that a person who is trying to improve himself, to become something more than he is, is incapable of creative action. In the words of Rinzai, "If you seek deliberately to become a Buddha, your Buddha is just Samsara." Or again, "If a person seeks the Tao, that person loses the Tao."[26] The reason is simply that the attempt to improve or act upon oneself is a way of locking action in a vicious circle, like trying to bite one's own teeth. Release from this ridiculous predicament is achieved, at the very beginning of Zen discipline, by understanding that "you yourself as you are, are the Buddha." For the object of Zen is not so much to become a Buddha as to act like one. Therefore no progress can be made in the life of the Bodhisattva so long as there is the least anxiety or striving to become more than what one is. Similarly, a person who tries to concentrate upon a certain task with a result in mind will forget the task in thinking about its result.

The irrelevance of self-improvement is expressed in two poems of the *Zenrin Kushu*:

> A long thing is the long body of Buddha;
> A short thing is the short body of Buddha.[27]
> In the landscape of spring there is no measure of worth or value;
> The flowering branches are naturally short and long.[28]

Or the following from Goso:

> If you look for the Buddha, you will not see the Buddha;
> If you seek the Patriarch, you will not see the Patriarch.
> The sweet melon is sweet even through the stem;
> The bitter gourd is bitter even to the roots.[29]

Some Buddhas are short and some are long; some students are beginners, and others are far advanced, but each is "right" just exactly as he is. For if he strives to make *himself* better, he falls into the vicious circle of egoism. It is perhaps difficult for the Western mind to appreciate that man develops by growth rather than self-improvement, and that neither the body nor the mind grows by stretching itself. As the seed becomes the tree, the short Buddha becomes the long Buddha. It is not a question of improvement, for a tree is not an improved seed, and it is even in perfect accord with nature or Tao that many seeds never become trees. Seeds lead to plants, and plants lead to seeds. There is no question of higher or lower, better or worse, for the process is fulfilled in each moment of its activity.

A philosophy of nonstriving or *mui*[30] always raises the problem of incentive, for if people are "right" or Buddhas just as they are, does not this self-acceptance destroy the creative urge? The answer is that there is nothing truly creative about actions which spring from incentives, for these are not so much free or creative actions as conditioned reactions. True creation is always purposeless, without ulterior motive, which is why it is said that the true artist copies nature in the manner of her operation and understands the real meaning of "art for art's sake." As Kojisei wrote in his *Saikontan*:

If your true nature has the creative force of Nature itself, wherever you may go, you will see (all things as) fishes leaping and geese flying.[31]

ENGLISH NOTES

[a]"I wish to take this opportunity of expressing my gratitude to my assistant, Miss Lois Thille, for many hours of secretarial help, and also to Mr. Wing Hoh, for transcribing my atrocious Chinese characters into a legible and elegant form.

[b]In Zen, however, the idea of Samsara as a process of cyclic reincarnation is not taken literally, and thus Zen has its own special meaning for the Bodhisattva's task of delivering all things from the course of endless birth and death. In one sense, the cycle of birth and death is from moment to moment, and a person may be said to be involved in Samsara to the extent that he identifies himself with an ego continuing through time.

CHINESE NOTES

1 一即一切．
一切即一．
但能如是．
何慮不畢．(信心銘)

2 與真幽理竟不殊．
本迷摩尼謂瓦礫．
豁然自覺是真珠．
無明智慧等無異．
當知萬法即皆如．
愍此二見徒措身與佛不彼無餘．
觀身何須更覓作斯差別．
泉云平常心是道趙州云還可趣向否．
泉云擬向即乖．(無門關十九)

4 色即是空空即是色．

5 無．

6 公案．

7 嚴陽尊者問趙州一物不將來時如何．
州云放下著。(葛籐集)

8. 即緣生事，笑莫向我。要行即行，要坐即坐，無一念心希求佛果。緣何如此？古人云：若欲作業求佛，佛是生死大兆。著衣喫飯，屙屎送尿，困來即臥。愚人笑我，智乃知焉。佛法無用功處，祇是平常無事。但能隨緣消舊業，任運著衣裳。逢道人修道，達道不行。古人云：若欲知道，屙屎送尿乃所知道。（臨濟錄　示眾）

9. 問師：終日著衣喫飯，如何免得著衣喫飯？師云：著衣喫飯。進云：不會。師云：不會。著衣喫飯即……（睦州錄）

10. 向猛火坐，寒即圍爐，熱即竹林溪畔。（禪林類聚第二）

11. 將云……磨云：將心來與汝安。二祖云：弟子心未安，乞師安心。祖云：覓心了不可得。磨云：與汝安心竟。（無門關第四十一）

12. 僧問：願和尚慈悲，乞與解脫法門。師曰：誰縛汝？曰：無人縛。師曰：既無人縛，何更求解脫。來為汝師脫，禮曰縛汝。（傳燈錄卷三）

14. 如刀能割不自割。如眼能看不自看。（禪林句集）

15. 孤掌難鳴。

16. 蹈破虛空，鐵牛也汗出。（禪林句集）

17. 自然。

18. 青山自青山，白雲自白雲。（禪林句集）

19. 神通並妙用，運水及搬柴。（傳燈錄第八）

20. 有界自應二，一即一切，一切即一。二由一有，一亦莫守。真如法界，無他無自。要急相應，唯言不二。（信心銘）

21. 問師：萬法歸一，一歸何所？師云：我在青州作一領布衫，重七斤。（趙州真際禪師語錄）

22. 無心無念。

23. 行但行，坐但坐，總不得動著。（雲門錄）

24 去. (雲門錄)

25 方便.

26 若欲作業求佛佛是生死.
若人求道是人失道. (臨濟錄)

27 長者長法身.
短者短法身. (禪林句集)

28 春色無高下
花枝自短長. (禪林句集)

29 覓佛不見佛
討祖不見祖
甜瓜徹蒂甜
苦瓠連根苦. (五祖錄)

30 無為.

31 性天中有化育觸處見魚躍鳶飛.
(洪自誠)

CHAPTER NINE

Beat Zen, Square Zen, and Zen (1958)

It is as difficult for Anglo-Saxons as for the Japanese to absorb anything quite so Chinese as Zen. For though the word "Zen" is Japanese and though Japan is now its home, Zen Buddhism is the creation of T'ang dynasty China. I do not say this as a prelude to harping upon the incommunicable subtleties of alien cultures. The point is simply that people who feel a profound need to justify themselves have difficulty in understanding the viewpoints of those who do not, and the Chinese who created Zen were the same kind of people as Lao-Tzu, who, centuries before, had said, "Those who justify themselves do not convince." For the urge to make or prove oneself right has always jiggled the Chinese sense of the ludicrous, since as both Confucians and Taoists—however different these philosophies in other ways—they have invariably appreciated the man who can "come off it." To Confucius it seemed much better to be human-hearted than righteous, and to the great Taoists, Lao-Tzu and Chuang-Tzu, it was obvious that one could not be right without also being wrong, because the two were as inseparable as back and front. As Chuang-Tzu said, "Those who would have good government without its correlative misrule, and right without its correlative wrong, do not understand the principles of the universe."

To Western ears such words may sound cynical, and the Confucian admiration of "reasonableness" and compromise may appear to be a weak-kneed lack of commitment to principle. Actually they reflect a marvelous understanding and respect for what we call the balance of nature, human and otherwise—a universal vision of life as the Tao or way of nature in which the good and the

From *Chicago Review*, 1958, 12(2), 3–11. Copyright © 1958 by *Chicago Review*. Reprinted with permission of *Chicago Review*.

evil, the creative and the destructive, the wise and the foolish are the inseparable polarities of existence. "Tao," said the *Chung-yung,* "is that from which one cannot depart. That from which one can depart is not the Tao." Therefore wisdom did not consist in trying to wrest the good from the evil but in learning to "ride" them as a cork adapts itself to the crests and troughs of the waves. At the roots of Chinese life there is a trust in the good-and-evil of one's own nature which is peculiarly foreign to those brought up with the chronic uneasy conscience of the Hebrew-Christian cultures. Yet it was always obvious to the Chinese that a man who mistrusts himself cannot even trust his mistrust, and must therefore be hopelessly confused.

For rather different reasons, Japanese people tend to be as uneasy in themselves as Westerners, having a sense of social shame quite as acute as our more metaphysical sense of sin. This was especially true of the class most attracted to Zen, the *samurai.* Ruth Benedict, in that very uneven work *Chrysanthemum and Sword,* was, I think, perfectly correct in saying that the attraction of Zen to the *samurai* class was its power to get rid of an extremely awkward self-consciousness induced in the education of the young. Part-and-parcel of this self-consciousness is the Japanese compulsion to compete with oneself—a compulsion that turns every craft and skill into a marathon of self-discipline. Although the attraction of Zen lay in the possibility of liberation from self-consciousness, the Japanese version of Zen fought fire with fire, overcoming the "self observing the self" by bringing it to an intensity in which it exploded. How remote from the regimen of the Japanese Zen Monastery are the words of the great T'ang master Lin-chi:

> In Buddhism there is no place for using effort. Just be ordinary and nothing special. Eat your food, move your bowels, pass water, and when you're tired go and lie down. The ignorant will laugh at me, but the wise will understand.

Yet the spirit of these words is just as remote from a kind of Western Zen that would employ this philosophy to justify a very self-defensive Bohemianism.

There is no single reason for the extraordinary growth of Western interest in Zen during the last twenty years. The appeal of Zen arts to the "modern" spirit in the West, the work of Suzuki, the war with Japan, the itchy fascination of "Zen-stories," and the attraction of a nonconceptual, experiential philosophy in the climate of scientific relativism—all these are involved. One might mention, too, the affinities between Zen and such purely Western trends as the philosophy of Wittgenstein, Existentialism, General Semantics, the metalinguistics of B. L. Whorf, and certain movements in the philosophy of science and in psychotherapy. Always in the background there is our vague disquiet with the artificiality or "anti-naturalness" of both Christianity, with its politically ordered cosmology, and technology, with its imperialistic mechanization of a natural world from which man himself feels strangely alien. For both reflect a psychology in which man is identified with a conscious intelligence and will standing apart from nature to control it, like the architect-God in whose image this version of man is conceived. The disquiet arises from the suspicion that our attempt to master the world from outside is a vicious circle in which we shall be condemned to the perpetual insomnia of controlling controls and supervising supervision *ad infinitum*.

To the Westerner in search of the reintegration of man and nature there is an appeal far beyond the merely sentimental in the naturalism of Zen—in the landscapes of Ma-yuan and Sesshu, in an art that is simultaneously spiritual and secular, which conveys the mystical in terms of the natural, and that, indeed, never even imagined a break between them. Here is a view of the world imparting a profoundly refreshing sense of wholeness to a culture in which the spiritual and the material, the conscious and the unconscious, have been cataclysmically split. For this reason the Chinese humanism and naturalism of Zen intrigue us much more strongly than Indian Buddhism or Vedanta. These, too, have their students in the West, but their followers seem for the most part to be displaced Christians—people in search of a more plausible philosophy than Christian supernaturalism to carry on the essentially Christian search for the miraculous. The ideal man of Indian Buddhism is clearly a superman, a *yogi* with absolute mastery of his own nature, according perfectly with the science-fiction ideal of "men beyond mankind." But the Buddha or awakened man of Chinese Zen is "ordinary and nothing special"; he is humorously human like the Zen tramps portrayed by Mu-chi and Liang-k'ai. We like this because here, for the first time, is a conception of the holy man and sage who is not impossibly remote, not superhuman but fully human, and, above all, not a solemn and sexless ascetic. Furthermore, in Zen the *satori* experience of awakening to our "original inseparability" with the universe seems, however elusive, always just around the corner. One has even met people to whom it has happened, and they are no longer mysterious occultists in the Himalayas nor skinny *yogis* in cloistered *ashrams*. They are just like us, and yet much more at home in the world, floating much more easily upon the ocean of transience and insecurity.

But the Westerner who is attracted by Zen and who would understand it deeply must have one indispensable qualification: he must understand his own culture so thoroughly that he is no longer swayed by its premises unconsciously. He must really have come to terms with the Lord God Jehovah and with his Hebrew-Christian conscience so that he can take it or leave it without fear or rebellion. He must be free of the itch to justify himself. Lacking this, his Zen will be either "beat" or "square," either a revolt from the culture and social order or a new form of stuffiness and respectability. For Zen is above all the liberation of the mind from conventional thought, and this is something utterly different from rebellion against convention, on the one hand, or adopting foreign conventions, on the other.

Conventional thought is, in brief, the confusion of the concrete universe of nature with the conceptual things, events, and values of linguistic and cultural symbolism. For in Taoism and Zen the world is seen as an inseparably inter-related field or continuum, no part of which can actually be separated from the rest or valued above or below the rest. It was in this sense that Hui-neng, the Sixth Patriarch, meant that "fundamentally not one thing exists," for he realized that things are *terms*, not entities. They exists in the abstract world of thought, but not in the concrete world of nature. Thus one who actually perceives or feels this to be so no longer feels that he is an ego, except by definition. He sees that his ego is his *persona* or social role, a somewhat arbitrary selection of experiences with which he has been taught to identify himself. (Why, for example, do we say "I think" but not "I am beating my heart"?) Having seen this, he continues to play his social role without being taken in by it. He does not precipitately adopt a new role or play the role of having no role at all. He plays it cool.

The "beat" mentality as I am thinking of it is something much more extensive and vague than the hipster life of New York and San Francisco. It is a younger generation's nonparticipation in "the American Way of Life," a revolt that does not seek to change the existing order but simply turns away from it to find the significance of life in subjective experience rather than objective achievement. It contrasts with the "square" and other-directed mentality of beguilement by social convention, unaware of the correlativity of right and wrong, of the mutual necessity of capitalism and communism to each other's existence, of the inner identity of puritanism and lechery, or of, say, the alliance of church lobbies and organized crime to maintain the laws against gambling.

Beat Zen is a complex phenomenon. It ranges from a use of Zen for jus-tifying sheer caprice in art, literature, and life to a very forceful social criticism and "digging of the universe" such as one may find in the poetry of Ginsberg and Snyder, and, rather unevenly, in Kerouac. But, as I know it, it is always a shade too self-conscious, too subjective, and too strident to have the flavor of Zen. It is all very well for the philosopher, but when the poet (Ginsberg) says—

> live
> in the physical world
> moment to moment
>
> I must write down
> every recurring thought—
> stop every beating second

This is too indirect and didactic for Zen, which would rather hand you *the thing itself* without comment.

The sea darkens;
The voices of the wild ducks
Are faintly white.

Furthermore, when Kerouac gives his philosophical final statement, "I don't know. I don't care. And it doesn't make any difference"—the cat is out of the bag, for there is a hostility in these words that clangs with self-defense. But just because Zen truly surpasses convention and its values, it has no need to say "To hell with it," nor to underline with violence the fact that anything goes.

Now the underlying protestant lawlessness of beat Zen disturbs the square Zennists very seriously. For square Zen is the Zen of established tradition in Japan with its clearly defined hierarchy, its rigid discipline, and its specific tests of *satori*. More particularly, it is the kind of Zen adopted by Westerners studying in Japan, who will before long be bringing it back home. But there is an obvious difference between square Zen and the common-or-garden squareness of the Rotary Club or the Presbyterian Church. It is infinitely more imaginative, sensitive and interesting. But it is still square because it is a quest for the *right* spiritual experience, for a *satori*, which will receive the stamp (*inka*) of approval and established authority. There will even be certificates to hang on the wall.

I see no real quarrel with either extreme. There was never a spiritual movement without its excesses and distortions. The experience of awakening which truly constitutes Zen is too timeless and universal to be injured. The extremes of beat Zen need alarm no one since, as Blake said, "the fool who persists in his folly will become wise." As for square Zen, "authoritative" spiritual experiences have always had a way of wearing thin, and thus of generating the demand for something genuine and unique that needs no stamp.

I have known followers of both extremes to come up with perfectly clear *satori* experiences, for since there is no real "way" to *satori* the way you are following makes very little difference.

But the quarrel *between* the extremes is of great philosophical interest, being a contemporary form of the ancient dispute between salvation by works and salvation by faith, or between what the Hindus called the ways of the monkey and the cat. The cat—appropriately enough—follows the effortless way, since the mother cat carries her kittens. The monkey follows the hard way, since the baby monkey has to hang on to its mother's hair. Thus for beat Zen there must be no effort, no discipline, no artificial striving to attain *satori* or to be anything but what one is. But for square Zen there can be no true *satori* without years of meditation-practice under the stern supervision of a qualified master. In seventeenth-century Japan these two attitudes were *approximately* typified by the great masters Bankei and Hakuin, and it so happens that the followers of the latter "won out" and determined the present-day character of Rinzai Zen.[1]

Satori can lie along both roads. It is the concomitant of a "nongrasping" attitude of the senses to experience, and grasping can be exhausted by the discipline of directing its utmost intensity to single, ever-elusive objective. But what makes the way of effort and will-power suspect to many Westerners is not so much an inherent laziness as a thorough familiarity with the wisdom of our own culture. The square Western Zennists are often quite naive when it comes to an understanding of Christian theology or of all that has been discovered in modern psychiatry, for both have long been concerned with the fallibility and unconscious ambivalence of the will. Both have posed problems as to the vicious circle of seeking self-surrender or of "free-associating on purpose" or of accepting one's conflicts to escape from them, and to anyone who knows anything about either Christianity or psychotherapy these are very real problems. The interest of Chinese Zen and of people like Bankei is that they deal with these problems in a most direct and stimulating way, and begin to suggest some answers. But when Herrigel's Japanese archery master was asked, "How can I give up purpose on purpose?" he replied that no one had ever asked him that before. He had no answer except to go on trying blindly, or five years.

Foreign religions can be immensely attractive and highly overrated by those who know little of their own, and especially by those who have not worked through or grown out of their own. This is why the displaced or unconscious Christian can so easily use either beat or square Zen to justify himself. The one wants a philosophy to justify him in doing what he pleases. The other wants a more plausible authoritative salvation than the Church or the psychiatrists seem to be able to provide. Furthermore the atmosphere of Japanese Zen is free from all one's unpleasant childhood associations with God the Father and Jesus Christ—though I know many young Japanese who feel just the same way about their early training in Buddhism. But the true character of Zen remains almost incomprehensible to those who have not surpassed the immaturity of needing to be justified, whether before the Lord God or before a paternalistic society.

The old Chinese Zen masters were steeped in Taoism. They saw nature in its total interrelatedness, and saw that every creature and every experience is in accord with the Tao of nature just as it is. This enabled them to accept themselves as they were, moment by moment, without the least need to justify anything. They didn't do it to defend themselves or to find an excuse for getting away with murder. They didn't brag about it and set themselves apart as rather special. On the contrary, their Zen was *wu-shih*, which means approximately "nothing special" or "no fuss." But Zen is "fuss" when it is mixed up with Bohemian affectations, and "fuss" when it is imagined that the only proper way to find it is to run off to a monastery in Japan or to do special exercises in the lotus posture or five hours a day. And I will admit that the very hullaba-loo about Zen, even in such an article as this, is also fuss—but a little less so.

Having said that, I would like to say something for all Zen fussers, beat or square. Fuss is all right, too. If you are hung on Zen, there's no need to try and pretend that you are not. If you really want to spend some years in a Japanese monastery, there is no earthly reason why you shouldn't. Or if you want to spend your time hopping freight cars and digging Charlie parker, it's a free country.

> In the landscape of Spring there is neither better
> nor worse;
> The flowering branches grow naturally, some long,
> some short.

NOTE

1. Rinzai Zen is the form most widely known in the West. There is also Soto Zen, which differs somewhat in technique, but still closer to Hakuin than to Bankei. However, Bankei should not exactly be identified with beat Zen as I have described it, for he was certainly no advocate of the life of undisciplined whimsy despite all that he said about the importance of the uncalculated life and folly of seeking *satori*.

CHAPTER TEN

Zen and Politics (1962)

The title of Mr. Braun's (1961) article "The Politics of Zen" in itself contains the whole fallacy upon which his diatribe is based, for it is almost as if one were to speak of "the politics of physics" or of "the ethical implications of sight." It is perhaps natural for us to think of Zen as a religion, and thus as a way of life having the same function in the cultures of the Far East as Christianity and Judaism in our own. Though the political records of the latter are none to clean, these religions have an avowedly ethical function: they believe alike that salvation comes by virtue of membership in a loving community—the Church, or the people of God. By deliberate intention, then, such religions are politically and morally normative.

But this is not the function of such disciplines as physics or even medicine. Perfectly sound physical or medical knowledge may be used for good or evil ends. Western physics made possible the unimaginable tortures of Hiroshima, and the healing of a lame man may enable him to kick his children. Would Mr. Braun suggest, then, that physics and medicine be abandoned? Or would he suggest that clear eyesight is a menace because it enables us to aim rifles?

Now Zen is somewhat like a science and somewhat like a highly sensitized faculty of perception, the combination of a certain kind of knowledge and skill. As knowledge, it is the direct (almost sensory) state of affairs which some scientists describe theoretically as the reciprocal or "transactional" behavior of an organism and its environment. It enables one to not only think but also to feel that organism/environment or man/universe is a unified field of behavior—as is, indeed, known to be the case in such sciences as ecology and biology. I have

From *New Politics: A Journal of Socialist Thought,* 1962, *1*(2), 170–172. Reprinted with permission of *New Politics.*

sometimes called Zen the immediate perception of relativity, or of the inseparable relatedness of all things and events. As skill, Zen comprises an art of freeing thought and action from what psychologists call "blocking" or from being non-plussed by certain types of dilemma. These dilemmas are approximately what some modern philosophers would term pseudo-problems or pseudo-alternatives. For example, "Where was your fist before you closed your hand?" is analogous to the Zen *koan* "Who were you before your mother and father conceived you?"

It is perfectly obvious that knowledge and skill of these kinds can be used in any form of action, and that they are as ethically neutral as electronics. Just as it is quite proper for us to question the political and ethical principles of men who employ the sciences, not the ethics of physics but of physicists, so it would have been quite proper for Mr. Braun to question the political inten-tions of various individuals who employ Zen. He would then have to direct his criticism to the philosophies or ideologies which do in fact provide the moral and political values of Far Eastern cultures—e.g., Confucianism and Shinto, and their derivatives.

Zen is concerned with the basic characteristics of life and the universe, but, unlike Christianity (which is similarly concerned), it does not seek in this realm for ethical directives. Christianity does so because of its belief in a per-sonal God who is the guarantor of a supernatural and absolute moral order, but I doubt Mr. Braun would want to invoke this type of sanction for political ethics, for in its own way it is as dangerous as none at all. It is not subject to critical analysis, experiment, and change. As I see it and, as I am sure, many Zen Buddhists see it, the foundation for ethics is not to be found in science, metaphysics, or mysticism, but in mutual agreement between human beings as to how they want to behave. Ethically, we are not so much trains in search of rails as pilots in search of agreement as to schedules and air-lanes.

Mr. Braun, in common with many others, has of course been influenced by Arthur Koestler's (1960) astonishingly poor piece of reporting, *The Lotus and the Robot*, especially the incident in the book where a Zen abbot refuses "to pass ethical judgment on Hitler's murder of the Jews." Readers of Koestler will remember that on this occasion the abbot characterized Hitler's behavior as "foolish" rather than "sinful." I do not know what sort of interpreter was present at this interview, so I can only guess that the abbot attributed Hitler's action, as would any Buddhist, to *mu-myo*, which is roughly translatable as "ignorance" or "unconsciousness." The abbot would have had no word for "sin" because he had no theology in which sin is the transgression of a supernatural moral order. Perhaps Koestler was offended because the abbot expressed no human horror. But I would suggest that a surgeon who gives way to human horror before a cancer operation may cut with an unsteady hand. The legitimate moral charge is that the Japanese did not act as surgeons in identifying Nazism and their own militarism as diseases, and this was the defect not of their Zen-vision, but of their value-judgments and the ethical systems underlying them. If all this made

Koestler lose his interest in Oriental art, did it, I wonder, destroy his interest in Goethe and Schiller, Rilke and Bach?

In short, Mr. Braun has directed a very proper criticism of Japanese political ethics to the wrong address. His mistake, which I do not believe he would have made if he had read my own work carefully, was to identify Zen as a religious phenomenon from which one would expect judgments of value. This is simply not its sphere, just as it is not the sphere of medicine or logic as such. These deplorable cruelties and injustices are the faults neither of Zen in the East nor of nuclear physics in the West, but of our human cultures as wholes. It is, of course, quite understandable that Zen should be confused with a religion, that is, something of the same order as Christianity or Judaism. After all, it is a form of Buddhism, which is normally treated as a religion by many of its students and interpreters, inappropriately in my own view. (Shared by such other scholars as A. K. Coomaraswamy and Rene Guenon.) But Buddhism is a phenomenon with many levels and departments, reaching out with many different lines of inquiry. Zen is but one of these, and it happens to be concerned with the nature of man and the universe at a level which lies beyond good and evil. I see no way of denying the existence or validity of this level without absolutizing the standards of good and evil in some such form as the person of God.

To conclude with three points of detail: (1) Dr. Fujisawa's book, *Zen and Shinto* (1959), is about as representative of Zen as Edgar Guest of American poetry. (2) My own social philosophy has changed considerably since I wrote *The Supreme Identity* in 1949 [and published in 1950], and I have tried to express some part of it in the final chapter of *Psychotherapy East and West*, written in 1960 [and published in 1961]. (3) Mr. Braun (1961) says that I have written "reams of pure unmitigated nonsense on the healthy sexual attitudes. . . . in the rustic paradise of the Asiatic village" (p. 180). I do not remember having written a single line, let alone reams, on the sexual life of the Asian village. In so far as I have discussed Asian sexual practices at all, I have been concerned with the rarely used and even quite esoteric sexual disciplines of Hindu and Buddhist Tantra. I wonder if Mr. Braun is *really* concerned with ethics.[1]

NOTE

1. [See Braun (1962) for a reply to Watts—Eds.]

REFERENCES

Braun, H. (1961). The politics of Zen. *New Politics: A Journal of Socialist Thought, 1*(1), 177–189.

Braun, H. (1962). Mr. Braun replies. *New Politics: A Journal of Socialist Thought, 1*(2), 172–173.

Fujisawa, C. (1959). *Zen and Shinto: The story of Japanese philosophy*. New York, NY: Philosophical Library.

Koestler, A. (1960). *The lotus and the robot*. New York, NY: Macmillan.

Watts, A. W. (1950). *The supreme identity*. New York, NY: Pantheon.

Watts, A. W. (1961). *Psychotherapy East and West*. New York, NY: Pantheon.

CHAPTER ELEVEN

Prefatory Essay to Suzuki's
Outlines of Mahayana Buddhism (1963)

Several years ago, an eminent British scientist was discussing his theories with a friend in a London restaurant. A fascinated eavesdropper at a nearby table, no longer able to contain herself, at last went over and said, "Excuse me, but I just couldn't help listening to your conversation, because the ideas you were discussing sounded exactly like Mahayana Buddhism!" The scientist avowed almost total ignorance of this subject and asked for the names of some books that would enlighten him. The lady gave him titles which included works by both Dr. Suzuki and myself, and thus it was that, in the course of the marvelous interconnectedness of all things, this scientist and I became friends. Oddly enough, one of his special interests is the problem of simultaneous discovery—as when two or more investigators working quite independently in different parts of the world, hit upon that same scientific invention. For something of the same kind happens when, in modern times, we unknowingly rediscover the ideas of ancient India and China.

Indeed, there is an almost uncanny affinity between some of the major trends of modern Western thought and Buddhist philosophy. Bergson, Whitehead, Wittgenstein, Schrodinger, Dewey, Korzybski, Heidegger, Whyte, Tillich—all in some quite significant respects think like Buddhists. But why stress the point? Few of them, if any, began their work with a serious study of Eastern thought, even though the book in your hands [Suzuki's *Outlines*] was first published in 1907. Moreover, there is no sense in using this affinity as a pawn in the game of sectarian one-upmanship, as if to say, "See how up-to-date and scientific the Buddhists were in contrast to those superstitious Christians!" There is, perhaps,

Reprinted from *Outlines of Mahayana Buddhism* (pp. ix–xxv) by D. T. Suzuki, 1963, New York: Schocken Books. Work in public doman, per Schocken Books, February 11, 2016.

a trace of such one-upmanship in this book, but it is understandable enough considering that Dr. Suzuki wrote it at a time when Eastern philosophy commanded little of the intellectual respect which it enjoys today—thanks, in no small measure, to his own work. The importance of the parallels between Mahayana Buddhism and various trends in modern thought lies in a wholly constructive direction, which has nothing to do with any sort of sectarian propaganda for Buddhism. Indeed, a really serious student of the disciplines which Mahayana Buddhism involves would be simply dismayed by the propagation of Buddhism in the West as an organized religion.

Although Dr. Suzuki speaks here of Buddhism as a religion, this is only in the most vague and general sense of the term. For the study of its disciplines has nothing to resemble the considerations which would influence one to be a Roman Catholic rather than a Baptist, or vice versa. The real concerns of Buddhism are closer to psychotherapy, or even to something such as ophthalmology, than to the choice between differing systems of belief which we recognize in the West as adopting a religion. A convert to Buddhism is as unimaginable as a convert to cookery, unless the conversion means simply that one has become a cook instead of a cobbler, or that one has become interested in cooking well. For Buddhism, whether Hinayana or Mahayana, is not a system of doctrines and commandments requiring our belief and obedience. It is a method (one of the exact meanings of *dharma*) for the correction of our perceptions and for the transformation of consciousness. It is so thoroughly experimental and empirical that the actual subject-matter of Buddhism must be said to be an immediate, nonverbal experience rather than a set of beliefs or ideas or rules of behavior.

In sum, Buddhism is a method for changing one's sense of identity, that is, of the way in which one experiences the fact of being alive. For it seems that, East and West, today as in 600 B.C., most people experience themselves as lonely and isolated selves or souls, minds or egos, confined within bags of skin. Both the external world of material events and the internal world of thought and feeling are realms which the self *confronts* as alien to and other than itself. The individual therefore experiences himself as something *in*, but not truly *of*, a universe which cares nothing for him, and in which he is a very impermanent fluke. Buddhism—in common with Vedanta and Yoga in India, and with Taoism in China—considers this sensation of separate identity a hallucination.

The hallucination is an unhappy by-product of the high degree to which man has developed the power of conscious attention—the power of concentrating awareness upon figures to the exclusion of their backgrounds, upon things and events to the exclusion of their environmental contexts. The penalty for this brilliant but circumscribed form of awareness is ignore-ance (*avidya*) of the ground that goes inseparably with the figure, of the context that goes with the event, and of the cosmic environment that goes with the individual organism. In short, an over-specialization in this mode of highly selective and exclusive consciousness gives man the illusion that he himself—his identity—is confined within his skin. But a proper correction of perception would show that "he" is as much the universe outside the skin as the system of organs within it. The behavior of the one is the behavior of the other, and the existence of the two is as interdependent, mutual, reciprocal, or correlative as that of front and back.

Normal commonsense is almost a conspiracy to prevent people from seeing that this is true. Our languages, our habitual but learned modes of thought and perception, and our social conventions as a whole make it amazingly difficult to see and to feel the individual and the universe as one field, one system, and one process of activity—in short, as one Self. Man therefore regards the birth and death of individual organisms as the beginning and end of selves, not realizing that they come and go like leaves upon a tree, and that the tree—so to say—is the actual self. But this realization requires an expansion and deepening of consciousness so that the narrow spotlight of normal attention discovers the origin from which it shines.

The real content and work of Buddhism is, then, this very expansion of consciousness. And just this, rather than any set of concepts, is what it has to contribute to the development of modern thought. For, as we shall shortly see, Western philosophy and science have arrived at theoretical points of view remarkably close to those of Mahayana Buddhism. But for the most part those viewpoints remain theoretical: there is no actual and corresponding change in the state of consciousness, and, as a result, the individual knows things without feeling them. In other words, the scientist of the twentieth century knows in theory, from his study of ecology and biology, that he is an organism-environment field. But in practice he feels subjectively as if he were still in the sixteenth or second century, sensing himself as an organism merely in and confronting its environment. He has never felt the new identity which his theory suggests, and may even fear such an experience as some form of pathological and "regressive" mysticism.

I want to review the main respects in which I feel that philosophical and scientific thought in this twentieth century runs parallel to Mahayana Buddhism. But it may, as a preliminary, be worth asking whether there has been any historical influence of the latter upon the former. The question is peculiarly difficult to decide, for, although reliable information about Buddhist philosophy has been available at least from the beginning of this century, it has not—until recently—been something in which the academic philosopher or scientist would admit a serious interest, unless, of course, he were an orientalist or philologist. His interest would then be purely formal, concentrating, as a rule, upon the literary and antiquarian aspects of Buddhism as distinct from its philosophical and experimental content. Nevertheless, there is evidence that a number of Western scholars have had a practical interest in these materials, which they were cautious in admitting to their colleagues.

On the one hand, there was the traditional association of Buddhism with heathenish idolatry and with cultures which it was convenient for Western colonialism to define as backward and primitive. On the other hand, around the turn of the century Eastern philosophy was widely associated with various forms of Theosophy, and thus with the stress of the latter upon occult or psychic phenomena, which in no way commended it to the temper of scientific thought at that time. Yet from shortly before 1900 there has appeared a slowly increasing volume of work on Mahayana Buddhism, and other types of Eastern philosophy, that is both scholarly and sympathetic to the practical and experimental aspect of this philosophy. The present work [Suzuki's *Outlines*] is one of the earliest examples of this trend, and, in comparison both with its author's later works and with the general progress of Buddhist scholarship, the present-day reader may not at once appreciate what a remarkable achievement it is.

So far as I can see, Dr. Suzuki was the first Asian, Buddhist or Hindu, to combine a fine mastery of English with a scholarly knowledge of his own philosophical tradition that was at once sound by Western standards and sympathetic to the subject, and then to write a systematic account of an Asian philosophy, the *Outlines of Mahayana Buddhism*. Searching the bibliographies, I find nothing comparable from an Asian hand at any earlier date.[1] Suzuki was, then, the first great scholar-interpreter of the East to the West to come out of Asia, and it is marvelous to reflect that as I write this, in the summer of 1963, he is still alive and vigorous, approaching the age of 94. His best known work did not appear until twenty years after the *Outlines*, for it was in 1927 that he published the first volume of *Essays in Zen Buddhism*. It was shortly after this that James Bissett Pratt made the celebrated remark that there two kinds of cultured people: those who have read Suzuki and those who have not. It would have been pointless to say this unless a great many people of culture had indeed read him. Perhaps some literary detective will one day trace out the actual channels of Suzuki's influence. It cannot have been negligible, but at the same time ideas have a way of being "in the air," so that we catch them without knowing their source.

What are, then, some of the dominant trends in Western scientific thought which are so closely akin to Mahayana Buddhism? First of all, there is relativity in its most general sense—the recognition that there is no universal truth that can be stated in any meaningful proposition. Everything that is so, is so for a particular observer or in relation to a particular situation. It is obviously impossible to speak simultaneously from or for all possible points of view. (The last two sentences may appear to be universal propositions, though actually they are no more than statements about observation and description.) There is thus no way of making any valid proposition about Reality, Being, or the nature of all things. This is the general consensus of modern analytical philosophy—logical positivism, scientific empiricism, or whatever it may be called. So far as it goes, this is also the Mahayanist doctrine of *sunyata* or "voidness," which is not, as some have believed, the assertion that the universe does not really exist, but that all propositions or concepts about the universe are void and invalid.

But unlike, say, logical positivism, the Mahayana does not rest its enquiry here and busy itself with logical trivia. It goes on to concern itself with a knowledge of the universal, of Reality, which is nonverbal. *Sunyata* has, as it were, a positive aspect that is experienceable but unmentionable. This must be approached through a further meaning of the term, which is that in the real, nonverbal world there are neither things nor events. This is a point of view, which, in the modern West, is associated with various forms of semantics, and especially with the work of Korzybski, Sapir, Whorf, and, to some extent, the earlier Wittgenstein. For this work has made it clear that things and events are units, not of nature, but thought. Basically the thing or event is any area of space or span of time upon which attention may be focused. Thus to assimilate the world to our thinking we have to break it down into these manageable units. This is the way we apply the calculus to the measurement of curves, and also the way in which we ingest our food. Food has to be reduced to gulps or to bite-sized units. But as cows do not grow ready sliced, the natural universe does not exist ready thinged. This does not mean that the real world is a formless and unvaried mush. It exists just as we perceive it, but not necessarily as we conceive it.

Therefore to conceive the world as a multiplicity of separate things is to ignore the basic unity that exists between widely distant bodies in space, just as it exists between the proportionately distant molecules of one's own body. Our clumsy attempts to account for one event by others through the mysterious connections of causality, is simply a failure to see that the events so connected actually constitute a single event, and that this in turn (looking at it one way) makes up, or (looking at it another) expresses The Event, which Mahayanists call the Dharmakaya, the Body of Being.

Part of the discipline of Buddhism is therefore the cultivation of intellectual silence, for certain periods of time. This is to be aware of whatever happens to be, without thinking about it, without forming words and symbols in the mind. The world is then seen in its fundamental state of *tathata*, for which English has only the awkward equivalent of "thusness" or "suchness." But it represents what Korzybski called the "unspeakable," that is, the nonverbal level of reality. The point of the Buddhist discipline is to see that life is, in itself, quite unproblematic. There are such specific problems as how to build a bridge or put out a fire, but there is no Problem of Being unless one creates it for oneself out of nothing. For, as Wittgenstein saw, we manufacture the Problem of Life by asking questions or making demands upon ourselves or others which are meaningless or self-contradictory. We make a complex game out of the world by setting values upon nature's chips, and then confuse the game with the world itself. In Wittgenstein's (1922/1960) own words:

> The sense of the world must lie outside the world. In the world everything is as it is and happens as it does. *In* it there is no value—and if there were, it would be of no value.

If there is a value which is of value, it must lie outside all happening and being-so. For all happening and being-so is accidental. (6:41)[2]

The Mahayanist would go on to point out that realizing that there is no value in the world does not mean that it is valueless, for this word, as we use it, implies the negative value-judgment that the world is chaotic, absurd, meaningless, and so forth. *Tathata*, suchness, is simply the world as beyond valuation, whether positive or negative. At this level, the world is also accidental in the sense of such terms as *svayambhu* (self-existent, becoming so of itself) or the Chinese *Tzu-jan* (spontaneous, of itself so, nature, natural). The English "accidental" has the misleading sense of something happening at random in a world that is supposed to be orderly.

Sunyata and *tathata* are therefore basic and complementary terms. *Sunyata* means that all such terms as eternal or temporal, one or many, real or unreal, being or nonbeing, good or bad, are inapplicable to the world as a whole. Each of these words has meaning only in terms of its opposite, or of some contrast. But there is nothing outside the whole with which to contrast it. Thought is really a system of classification, of sorting experiences into intellectual boxes. Every class, every box must have both inside and outside, but the world as a whole has no outside and therefore no inside: it is in no class. *Sunyata* means, further, that the world is not actually divided into, or composed of, separate things and events. For very division is also a union, an interdependence. The figure stands out sharply against the background, but without the background the figure is not manifest. *Sunyata* is the exhaustion of thought in its attempt to grasp existence. But when thought relaxes its hold, the world is, not conceived but experienced, as *tathata*. That is to say, all that happens seems to be self-explanatory, self-sufficient, and complete just by happening. Yet in such a way that one doesn't say, "So what?" but, "My God!" Or, "Well, I'll be damned!"

One of the profoundest insights of Mahayana Buddhism has its modern counterpart in the transactionalism of John Dewey, and in the organismic philosophy of Whitehead, and of the biologists von Bertelannfy, Goldstein, and Woodger.[3] Suzuki wrote his *Outlines* before he had begun his exhaustive study of a text known as the *Avatamsaka Sutra*, a text that represents the high point of Mahayanist philosophy. The central theme of the *Avatamsaka* is what is known as the *dharmadhatu* theory of the mutual interpenetration of all things and events. Dr. Takakusu (1947) expressed it as follows:

Buddhism holds that nothing was created singly or individually. All things in the universe—matter and mind—arose simultaneously, all things in it depending upon one another, the influence of each mutually permeating and thereby making a universal symphony of harmonious totality. If one item were lacking, the universe would not be complete; without the rest, one item cannot be. (p. 40)

The word "simultaneously" in the above passage is perhaps not quite happily chosen. Everything in the universe has not come into being at the same time. The idea is rather that all events, past, present, and future, here and elsewhere, are mutually interdependent. The earlier event A does not occur unless the latter event B is assured, just as an electric current does not depart from the positive terminal until the negative terminal is connected. A departure requires a point of arrival. Furthermore, although event A may be defined as having ceased before event B begins, the occurrence of B will depend upon A having happened. It is in this way that all depends upon each, and continues to do so even when the individual event has vanished. A universe in which, say, Socrates did not, or could not, exist would not be this kind of universe.

The *Avatamsaka* likens the cosmos to a many-dimensioned network of gems, in which each contains the reflection of all the others—*ad infinitum*. Any one implies all the rest, because all project themselves into each. Many people have some intellectual difficulty in grasping this kind of reciprocal or polar relationship, even though the principle is as simple as two sticks supporting each other in the form of an inverted V: the one does not stand without the other. This is in some respects remarkably close to Dewey's theory (Dewey & Bentley, 1954) of the transactional nature of the relationship between the individual and the world. The term transaction is chosen in preference to interaction or reaction because of its stress upon the mutuality of the relationship. In the transaction of buying and selling, the two operations go to together: there is no buying without selling, or selling without buying.

Thus a living, individual organism is not only part of the world, but it goes with a world of just this nature, as apples go only with apple trees. But, conversely, this kind of a world—a world of light and sound, weight and texture—is what it is in terms of our organic structure. Only eyes can evoke light from the sun. It appears, then, that as the organism is something in the world, the world is at the same time something in the organism, since light and sound, shape and substance, are states of the organism.

This is further clarified by the biologists and ecologists who see, no longer organisms *in* environments, but organism-environments which are unified fields of behavior. In describing the behavior of any organism, the biologist soon finds that he is also describing the behavior of the environment. He realizes, then, that he must talk in terms of a new entity—the organism-environment. This has the interesting consequence that attributes which have formerly been ascribed to the organism alone—intelligence in particular—must also be ascribed to the environment. It is for this reason that biologists now speak of the evolution of environments as well as that of organisms, for a given organism will arise only in an environment that is sufficiently developed to maintain it.

This sort of thing was difficult to see so long as science was set on explaining things by a purely analytical method—that is, by trying to account for the larger units of the world by studying the structure of the smaller units that "compose" them. (Note the transitive verb.) This approach had the indispensable merit of giving us a clear picture of the whole structure, but it led to the illusion that the smaller units, such as cells or molecules, were in some way responsible or causative of the larger, of organisms. But, as von Bertelannfy (1960) showed so clearly, *what* a cell is and does depends upon the kind of system or context in which it is found. Blood in a test-tube is not the same thing as blood in the veins, because, for one thing, it is behaving differently.

Insights of these kinds have been enormously helped by the recognition that in science one speaks, not so much of what things are as of what they do. The world is described as behavior or process, so that what was formerly "thing" is now simply "event." One no longer asks *what* (thing) is behaving in such-and-such a way; one simply describes the behavior and says where it is happening. In other words, action does not have to be ascribed to an agent defined as something quite different from action. The agent, too, can be sufficiently described *as* action. This is precisely the Buddhist *anatman* doctrine that deeds (*karma*) exist but no doers, that human behavior is not propelled by a subjective soul or ego.

Thus as Western science approaches a view of the world as a unified field of behavior, it approaches an idea of the Dharmakaya, the Universal Body (Organism), or of the Dharmadhatu, the Universal Field. But only the idea. The empirical approach of Western science should be sympathetic to the principle that hypothesis must be followed by experiment and observation. If, therefore, the hypothesis that man is organism-environment, individual-universe, is to be translated into experience, what is to be done? Obviously, the individual must find out how or what he is prior to and behind all ideas and images of himself. He must somehow strip off his masks, his identification of himself with stereotypes and roles, and find out what he is existentially, or, as Buddhists would say, what he is in the domain of "suchness."

When Buddhism is called the *dharma*, the word has the meaning of method rather than doctrine. For, speaking very strictly, there are no Buddhist doctrines. The method is essentially a dialogue between a Buddha, a person who is awakened to his real identity, and an ordinary individual, who experiences himself as a separate being. The dialogue begins when the latter raises a question, which may be as radical and simple as how to escape from suffering. What happens then is that the teacher (though the Asian idea of a *guru* is not really what we mean by a teacher) proposes an experiment. He does not give an answer, but rather suggests something that the enquirer might do to test the grounds upon which he bases his problem. He may suggest that since suffering is the consequence of desire, the solution is to eliminate desire, and then send the enquirer away to *try* that. Thus what appear to be the doctrines of Buddhism, as that the origin of suffering is desire or craving, are in fact only the opening stages of a dialogue (involving also a series of experiments)—a dialogue that may conclude in a way that is hardly foreshadowed at the beginning.

The essential principle of the dialogue is the application of *sunyata*—that is, to let the enquirer find out that nothing that he can do, or refrain from doing, think, or refrain from thinking, will answer his question. For his question is based upon the false assumption that "he" is something separate from all that he experiences, something *to* which the universe happens, something that confronts, but is not, everything else in the world. The aim of the teacher is to show that this separate "experiencer" of the world is fictitious; that it can neither do nor not do, and that all stratagems of thought designed to grasp the world to the satisfaction of the experiencer are futile. In short, the dialogue, and the experiments in meditation and thought-control that go along with it, is constructed to bring the enquirer to a complete impasse. He comes to the point of finding all his philosophical and metaphysical notions absurd, all his motivations the wrong ones, and of being in a situation where he has nothing left to grasp for spiritual or psychological security.

At this point he has no alternative but to let go, or rather, a letting go comes about through the whole of his being, since it is an action no longer attributed to the ego as agent. He is, as it were, thrown into *sunyata* like a person falling, for the first time, into water, into the ocean of relativity. Because, in water, there is nothing to be grasped, the rule of floating is to let go—and then the water bears one up.

Analogously, at this moment *sunyata* is experienced in a peculiarly positive way, for which Mahayana philosophy supplies no clear theoretical basis, no real explanation of why it happens. Almost invariably, with this full letting go, the individual finds himself deeply in love with the world. As the *sutras* say, there is aroused within him a great compassionate heart. It turns out that although the Dharmakaya is always described in negative terms that make it sound entirely abstract and arid, the real experiential Dharmakaya is quite otherwise. Whatever it may be in itself, when realized in human experience it becomes the force of *karuna*—the compassion of one who knows that, in some way, all suffering is his own suffering, and all "sentient beings" the disguises of his own inmost nature. It is in these final steps that Mahayana Buddhism may have some contribution for Western culture.

NOTES

1. I am, of course, speaking of interpretive studies, not translations. Suzuki's only competitor for this honor would be Swami Vivekananda, but his approach was avowedly that of preacher and popularizer rather than scholar. Bunyu Nanjio and Junjiro Takakusu, both eminent scholars, published work in English before 1900, but in the form of catalogues and articles on minutiae. The next work by an Asian, comparable to Suzuki's, seems to be Sogen Yamakami's (1912) *Systems of Buddhistic Thought*.

2. "Outside the world" would seem to mean: in terms of some symbolic system, e.g., thought or language, which represents the world.

3. Joseph Needham (1956, pp. 291–303), also a biologist of the organismic school, has produced ingenious, if not wholly convincing, reasons for the idea that Whitehead's philosophy of organism may be traced back to the Taoist Chuang-Tzu—through Leibniz's monadology, deriving from Leibniz's study of the first Latin translation of Taoist literature.

REFERENCES

Dewey, J., & Bentley, A. F. (1954). *Knowing and the known*. Boston, MA: Beacon Press.

Needham, J. (1956). *Science and civilization in China* (Vol. 2). Cambridge, UK: Cambridge University Press.

Takakusu, J. (1947). *Essentials of Buddhist philosophy*. Honolulu: University of Hawaii Press.

von Bertelannfy, L. (1960). *Problems of life*. New York, NY: Harper.

Wittgenstein, L. (1960). *Tractatus logico-philosophicus*. London, UK: Routledge.

Yamakami, S. (1912). *Systems of Buddhistic thought*. Calcutta, India: Calcutta University Press.

PART THREE

Christianity

CHAPTER TWELVE

Theologia Mystica

Being the Treatise of Saint Dionysius Pseudo-Areopagite on Mystical Theology, Together with the First and Fifth Epistles (1944)

INTRODUCTION[1]

The relation of God to the world must be considered in two ways. On the one hand, God is revealed in the world—in the divine humanity of Jesus Christ, in the faculties and virtues of the human soul and mind, in the beauty and power of the natural universe. On the other hand, God is infinitely greater than the world, and so differs from it in kind and degree that no creaturely image or form can possibly give any true idea of His greatness, His holiness and His essential Self. God reveals Himself to us, and yet remains infinitely mysterious. He is something like things that we know, like a Father, like the humanity of Jesus, and yet, in Himself, He is quite other than the things we know and experience. He is as different, much more different, from the world as color is different from shape. A circle is different from a square, a beautiful shape from an ugly shape, only in degree; but the color red is different from the shape circle in kind, and as no color can be described in terms of shape, the essential Being of God cannot be described in terms of any created thing. We can form rather less of a true idea of God's essence than a man born blind can form a true picture of a radiant sunrise.

By itself this truth might lead us to wrong conclusions, for it is equally true that we are given a correct idea of God's nature in Jesus Christ. Yet this is as if someone tried to reveal the beauty of color to a blind man by means of beautiful sound. Jesus is, as it were, the glorious sound of God's light; for the sound and the light (or color) have in common the quality of beauty. God and the humanity of Jesus have in common the qualities of perfect goodness, holiness and love, and as we might represent the beauty of the sunrise to the blind man by beautiful music, so God represents to us the beauty of His transcendent nature by the beauty of His Incarnate Word. Though the blind man cannot realize what the sunrise actually looks like, he can know positively and surely that it is incomparably beautiful.

These two truths underlie the mystical theology of St. Dionysius the pseudo-Areopagite, which is at the root of the whole Catholic tradition of contemplative prayer.[2] He teaches that there are two ways of knowing God, one according to the way He reveals Himself in the world, and the other according to the way in which He is infinitely other than the world. The first is the subject of his book *The Divine Names*, and the second of his *Mystical Theology*. Obviously the second way is much more difficult, but he maintains that in the end it leads to a truer understanding than the first because it is the way of contemplative prayer in which the soul rises above all creatures to the pure knowledge of God. But we must begin the spiritual life by the first way, for we require revelation, positive knowledge of God's nature and will, mediated to us in terms of human life. Such revelation is neither false nor misleading, but necessarily incomplete, for which reason the deepest knowledge of God that may be granted us in this life must be in other than creaturely terms.

His *Mystical Theology* is therefore based on the principle of God's transcendence. God as the Maker of all things, all virtues, all ideas, is preeminently greater and other than what He has made, and to know God one must seek Him ultimately in a realm beyond all kinds of ordinary knowledge, whether it be knowledge of the senses, of the mind, or of the feelings. For God who is the Author of sense, mind and feeling can neither be touched, known nor felt. Whatever may be touched, known or felt is a creature and not God. God and His creation are absolutely incommensurable, in somewhat the same way as shape and color.

At first sight this might seem to be saying that between God as He is in Himself and His creation there is an impassable gulf, and that to know God as He is one must not only look for no information from ordinary knowledge but even get rid of ordinary knowledge. Some have tried to understand Dionysius in this way, as if he advised us to seek God through violent extermination of the activity of the senses and the intellect, as if God and the world were not only incommensurable but radically incompatible. According to this view, knowledge of God and knowledge of the world cannot exist together; to know God one must blot out all consciousness of creatures.

But this is an entirely false interpretation of his theology. Nowhere does he teach the Gnostic heresy that God and His creation are incompatible; for the whole theme of the *Divine Names* is the compatibility of the two. The analogy of color and shape will again help us to clarify his ideas, for color and shape are certainly not compatible, save in the sense that an ugly shape is incompatible with a beautiful color. Thus the world is incompatible with God only as disfigured by sin. But just because shape and color are incommensurable they can be perfectly united. We cannot unite perfectly a square and a circle, and in the same way there could be no perfect union of God and man if God belonged to the same order of being as man, if He were greater than man only in degree. But as there can be perfect union between the color red and a circle, God and the world can be united without conflict while remaining essentially different. Therefore God's transcendence, so far from removing Him from the world, is just what makes it possible for Him to be intimately present in it without any loss of His absolute supremacy and holiness. For God can be present in the world yet never limited or contaminated by it, much as the purity and intensity of a color can never be lessened by its presence in an ugly shape. The shape could writhe and contort itself for ever, and yet have not the slightest power over its color.

Our first knowledge of God is through earthly and creaturely things that are something like Him, but those who are called to the mystical life are never content with this kind of knowledge. They want God Himself, not some creature like God. At first, therefore, they try to capture Him in some form. Such a form may be an idea about God, for we find that we are assured of His presence by thinking of the various doctrines of the Church concerning His nature. For a time this satisfies, but after a while we find that we are using the doctrine to catch hold of God and make Him as it were our own property. And, then, because He wants us to know Him more deeply, He makes this way of knowing His presence not untrue but inadequate. He slips from our grasp. Or again, the form in which we try to possess Him may be some state of mind or feeling. We may have some minor order of mystical experience and try to work ourselves up into the same experience again and again, imagining that we can possess a sense of God by pressing the right psychological button.

But as we persevere in these attempts to hold God in some form, whether a sensible image or state of mind, we learn that in truth we cannot possess God at all. "What," asked von Hugel, "is a sense of God worth which would be at your disposal, capable of being comfortably elicited when and where you please? It is far, far more God who must hold us, than we who must hold Him. And we get trained in these darknesses into that sense of our impotence without which the very presence of God becomes a snare." Such attempts to capture the sense of God in some form are much like trying to catch the wind in a bag; what can be caught is not the wind but only stagnant air, for the God who is a Spirit can never be held. It is He that must hold us, bearing us up in His Spirit like leaves upon the wind.

All men seek God, even though they may not know it. They seek Him blindly as wealth, power or material happiness; going higher than this, they seek Him in the strict performance of a moral law, in some feeling of spiritual elation, or some sensation of a mighty Presence. But all these things Dionysius shows to be creatures of God and not God Himself. Those called to the higher stages of the spiritual life must pass beyond them, resolutely setting aside everything that can be known or felt, saying, "This is not yet God." But this does not mean that the contemplative must utterly cease to know and feel in the ordinary way; it means that he must cease to identify anything that he knows or feels with God. He goes on with his daily work and with his normal Christian duties, but he tries to maintain at all times a loving faith in the immediate presence of the God whom he can neither feel, see nor know. He walks through a darkness so far as his comprehension of God is concerned, knowing God as That which he does not know—as a glorious mystery.

This is no mere agnosticism, for the Unknowable Reality of the agnostic is not an object of faith and love. Mystery for the agnostic is mere absence of knowledge, but for the contemplative it has a tremendous attractive power. It draws him into itself like a vacuum, and he reaches out into this void in the simple faith that it is a void only to his human faculties, and in reality is filled with the living God. In one way this is a hard, arid and costly task, for he has to devote his whole life and being to the love of what seems to be a void, though by faith he knows that it is the hiding-place of the Most High.

But there are compensations, and at the last a great reward. For he understands that the presence of God does not depend on his willing, knowing or feeling it. He sees that God's presence is given quite apart from any effort he may make to feel it. To try to feel this given presence is to ignore the truth that God is here and now in all His fullness. It is like a bird flying in search of the air. But as a bird can fly up or down, left or right, because it is in the air and has no need to find it, so we can give ourselves entirely and joyfully to the work of each moment, whether it be chopping wood or praising God, because we and all that we do are in God. For it is through rejoicing in His possession of us, and not in trying to possess Him, that we come to a true knowledge of God.

Thus the contemplative begins to have a true awareness of God not by seeking Him as yet another form of experience, but by accepting His presence as given like an invisible color in every shape of experience. He can thus devote himself wholeheartedly to his work in the simple faith that God is as much with him when he is not specifically thinking about God as when he is. God, he finds, is as present with him as the present moment; he may be thinking of past or future events but he can never escape from the present moment, which seems to carry him along with itself even when his thoughts are not immediately concerned with it. God is with us and carries us forward through our lives in rather the same way, for as it is said in Psalm 139:

Whither shall I go from Thy Spirit? Or whither shall I flee from Thy presence? If I ascend up into heaven, Thou art there: if I make my bed in hell, behold, Thou art there. If I take the wings of the morning, and dwell in the uttermost parts of the sea; even there shall Thy hand lead me, and Thy right hand shall hold me. If I say, Surely the darkness shall cover me, even the night shall be light about me. Yea, the darkness hideth not from Thee; but the night shineth as the day: the darkness and the light are both alike to Thee.

"The night shineth as the day." This is the seeming paradox upon which Dionysius loves to dwell, for he speaks of the contemplative state as the "divine darkness," a darkness of the spirit that Christian mystics have always associated with that mysterious cry from the Cross, "My God, my God, why hast Thou forsaken me?" This darkness is the climax of the Purgative Way, which is less a preliminary stage of the mystical life to be passed and left behind than the constant and primary condition of mystical prayer. We are always in the Purgative Way, and in this life never outgrow the need either for the forgiveness of sins or for the purification of our knowledge of God. In purifying our knowledge of God we come to the point where He seems, to all knowledge and sense, to have forsaken us utterly. For we have purified that knowledge of every attempt to grasp God in sensible and intellectual forms, so that there is nothing left to know in any ordinary sense of the word, save what may be known by simple faith in the truths that God has revealed about Himself. This darkness is as far as Dionysius takes us, for words can go no further except to say with him that the divine darkness "overfills our unseeing minds with splendors of transcendent beauty." After purgation comes illumination, for God takes possession of the soul when all its faculties are surrendered to Him, and no longer strive to make Him their own property.

The apparent paradox of a night that shines as the day is unthinkable without belief in a living God who acts and exists independently of our knowledge of Him. People of timid faith feel subconsciously that apart from some image of God in their minds there might be no God at all. Their God tends to be subjective and even idolatrous for they are putting faith in a mental or emotional image of their own making. They dare not reach out into the void beyond such images and feelings, fearing that God might not after all be there. Some such fear haunts almost all of us, for which reason, while it may sound simple, the complete abandonment of ourselves to this divine darkness is no easy matter. It means the abandonment of ultimate faith in all creatures whatsoever, whether they are objective people and things or subjective thoughts and feelings.

Some people regard this quest for knowledge of God in the divine darkness as a "tragic accident of Christian thought," a way of pure negation that denies all interest in creative life, fitted only for hermits who have a dismal delight in contemplating mere emptiness. But Dionysius's mysticism is negative only in the sense that the Cross and sacrificial death is negative. For this negative way of prayer is based on implicit trust in the existence of a positively excellent and glorious God who is only negative in so far as His glory cannot be described directly in any human terms. The divine darkness is a spiritual death out of which comes a resplendent life, because through dying to himself the individual is taken over and lived by God. He returns to the creative work of living and attends to it with the power of God in his body and soul, for "I live; yet no longer I, but Christ liveth in me."

The divine darkness can seem a negative and dismal goal only when there is lack of faith in the objective though invisible reality of a God who will mysteriously emerge from that darkness and fire the mystic with His own creative life. To the doubting mind it may seem incredible that the glory of God can come out of such emptiness. But it can for the simple reason that this glory is not of our own making, and that God will give it to those who do not try to substitute for it the visions of their own imaginations. Truly, "the desert shall rejoice and blossom as the rose." This negative way of Dionysian mysticism is, then, the central Christian mystery of "as dying, and, behold, we live." It is like the chrysalis tomb, passing through which the grub becomes gloriously winged. For the mystical life follows the primal Christian pattern of Him who was crucified, dead and buried, yet rose again in a transfigured body, full of the glory of God.

According to St. Dionysius, contemplation is that high order of prayer in which the soul draws near to the very essence of God in a divine darkness, which neither sense, thought nor feeling can penetrate. The power so to outdistance our own faculties of perception in the approach to God is only given to those whom God calls. While the possession of such a vocation is not necessarily a sign of great holiness, the very nature of the contemplative work demands that complete dedication of the self to God in which holiness consists. Others who have not this vocation and know little or nothing of mystical prayer may arrive at a holiness as great as that of the mystic in a purely active life of service and charity. We cannot say how many souls are called to the contemplative work; but not all souls are called, for which reason those who are able to use this order of prayer must not despise or belittle the other and more ordinary ways of prayer, or consider themselves more holy than those who cannot use it. For the ways to God are as many as the lives of men.

No infallible rules can be laid down for determining whether or not a soul is called to this prayer, but those who feel drawn to it would do well to consult an experienced director and watch out for certain temptations. Contemplatives are sometimes accused of being lazy people who like to sit and think about nothing, and a false idea of the contemplative work may indeed attract those who simply cannot be bothered with the more formal disciplines of prayer and meditation. The work of contemplation may also attract those who wish to pride themselves upon their spiritual superiority, since mystical writers are accustomed to speak of it as a "high" and "sublime" type of prayer. Such a

motive simply nullifies the work. Yet only rarely is a soul free from this kind
of pride, for which reason those drawn to contemplation must, of all people,
constantly search for it in themselves and lay it before God for His forgiveness.

Contemplation is advisedly called a work, for it is no mere basking in the
light of vague aspirations and "lofty" sentiments; it is rather a journey through
a desert, bereft of most of the emotional and intellectual consolations of other
kinds of prayer. It is a work because it requires a much greater degree of
concentration, for the will has to leave behind the convenient props of verbal
prayer and discursive meditation, and direct itself into the divine darkness with
a single act of love and faith. Thus it should not be undertaken unless the soul
feels positively and genuinely unable to use these other forms of prayer with
spiritual benefit.

Strictly speaking, contemplative prayer is prayer of the will. For if we
say that the human soul has the four faculties of sensation, intellect, feeling
and will, vocal prayer, in which we use the sensible forms of definite words
or such external aids as the rosary, is prayer through the faculty of sensation.
This is usually the easiest form of prayer for the beginner. Next we rise to
mental prayer, or discursive meditation, which is prayer through the faculty
of the intellect, in which we ponder various divine truths or images in the
thinking mind. Following this, the faculty of feeling comes into play as affective prayer, in which we feel about those truths rather than think about them.
Instead of thinking love toward God, we feel love toward Him, and this feeling
may express itself in short ejaculatory sentences or phrases of adoration and
praise. But at last the diverse sensations of vocal prayer, the diverse thoughts
of mental prayer, and the diverse feelings of affective prayer become a single
and simplified act of the will, as if many shapes and colors were merged into
a pure white light. For the will is the central and all-determining faculty of
the soul, and in contemplative prayer we simply will toward God. For God is
no longer conceived in the form of an image arousing sensations, thoughts or
feelings; God is now known as One who can neither be sensed, thought nor
felt; He is a mystery, a divine darkness, to be loved in faith by a pure act of
will. Only the will can approach a God who is no longer to be conceived in
some creaturely form about which we can have sensations, thoughts and feelings. All these lesser faculties find the divine darkness a total void that renders
them impotent. But the will can reach out into that darkness, moved by the
simple faith that the transcendent, infinitely loveable God is there by virtue of
His own power, which is wholly independent of our thinking and knowing.

Thus contemplative prayer begins with what is sometimes called the
"prayer of quiet" or the "prayer of simple regard," the latter term qualifying
the former and showing us that contemplation is not a state of pure quiescence.
The term "prayer of quiet" refers to the quiescence of the sensations, thoughts
and feelings, but the term "simple regard" refers to an intense activity in that

center of consciousness, which underlies these three faculties. But this activity is not diversified. In sensing, thinking and feeling our psychological activity is relatively complex, embracing a diversity of objects, impressions or ideas. The light-beam of consciousness is diffused and moves from one object, or part of an object, to another. In the pure willing of contemplation the beam is less diffused, more intensified, and is brought to rest upon a single point. Activity ceases only in regard to the movement of the beam, but not in regard to the intensity of light.

It is particularly important to remember this principle because one of the great dangers attending this work is the temptation to pure quietism and a wholly negative and abstract view of God. Quietism may take one or both of two forms. It may be the notion that in prayer the soul should be completely inactive, abandoning even the direction of the will to God in love and faith. It may also be the notion that the contemplative should refrain as far as possible from every kind of active work, even the fulfillment of charitable duties and the active disciplines of the religious life. Now there are times when contemplation seems to involve a complete passivity of will, but this passivity is apparent only. The will has been utterly taken over by the will of God and experiences a great peace. Yet the sense of ease and peace is the result, not of complete inaction, but of acting with the will of God that bears up the soul like a mighty stream. As to the avoidance of charitable and religious duties, it must never be forgotten that God gives us His power, grace and love to be used both bodily and spiritually. We are to worship Him in act as well as in thought, and to love our brethren in both act and thought, for "if we love one another, God dwelleth in us, and His love is perfected in us" (I John 4:12).

Quietism, which makes peace an end in itself, is generally associated with a passive and negative conception of God, sometimes fostered by thinking of Him too much in philosophical and abstract terms. The philosophical theologians speak of God as pure Being or as the unmoved Mover, but this should not give us the impression that God is in a state of blissful inertia, passively awaiting our discovery. God is unmoved in the sense that no other person or principle moves Him; He is absolutely self-moved. Nor does He rest inertly and merely await discovery like so much buried treasure. He reveals Himself; He acts; He gives Himself to us; ourselves and all the universe are a part of His activity, for we are something that God is doing. The faith that God acts quite independently of us is essential for the spiritual life, for it is by this faith that we are able to recognize His presence as given, quite apart from our efforts to become aware of it. By this faith also we are able to know that the power and love of god bears us up in spite of ourselves, even before we begin to abandon ourselves to Him. It is this faith that prevents the conceit that in contemplation, in seeking union with God, we are doing all the work, for in fact we are really giving the entire assent of our wills to something that God has already done.

We give ourselves to God, not forgetting, however, that we already belong to Him entirely and that in this sense our selves are not ours to give Him. The realization of our absolute dependence upon God is perhaps the most helpful factor in abandoning our lives to His will, for it tells us that we have nothing to lose save a purely imaginary self-sufficiency. To try to be self-sufficient apart from God is like pretending that we are held to the earth by our own strength and not by the force of gravity.

This is not the place to discuss the more technical details of contemplative prayer, which must always be treated at some length because they will vary according to different people. It will therefore be necessary to consult such works of the masters of contemplative prayer in the Dionysian tradition as the *Cloud of Unknowing*, Fr. Augustine Baker's *Holy Wisdom*, Walter Hilton's *Scale of Perfection*, and St. John of the Cross's *Dark Night of the Soul* and *Ascent of Mount Carmel*.[3] Even in these works the technical suggestions are not of so precise a nature as would be expected, for instance, in a textbook of music or even in a manual of ascetic theology. For the art of contemplative prayer cannot be compressed into formulae or communicated in exact prescriptions, which when fulfilled will lead inevitably to the desired result. Generally speaking, the instructions to be given are of extreme simplicity, but there is the greatest variation of their application to individual souls, while the work itself is naturally almost as difficult as the instructions are simple.

The reader will find that most of these works have a deceptive somberness, for the authors approach their subject with gravity and caution, and give frequent warnings of the crosses that the contemplative must bear. They are wise, for they do not want to encourage souls to enter the work foolhardily. It should be said, however, that this apparent somberness conceals a divine gaiety of spirit such as one will find in the lives of St. Teresa and St. Francis, for their faith penetrates beyond the darkness to the music, the love and the laughter of heaven whither "the Lord is gone up with a merry noise." "If," said Coventry Patmore, "we may credit certain hints contained in the lives of the saints, love raises the spirit above the sphere of reverence and worship into one of laughter and dalliance: a sphere in which the soul says:—Shall I, a gnat which dances in Thy ray, *dare* to be reverent?" (cited in Underhill, 1930, p. 438).

Here is all the holy frivolity of those who have ceased to be burdened with the seriousness of themselves. In the knowledge of their entire and inescapable dependence upon God, they abandon themselves to Him without reserve, finding that herein is the only true security and freedom. And loosed from the anxieties and cares of the world, their inward spirit is as jubilant as a bird soaring and circling in the vastness of the sky. But their sky is not far above them in space, nor does the solid earth give it any downward limit, for those who have faith in the omnipresent, inescapable God find heaven upon earth, and, in the soul's dark night and death to self, perpetual light and everlasting life.

ON MYSTICAL THEOLOGY:
THE TREATISE OF ST. DIONYSIUS TO TIMOTHY[4]

I. OF THE DIVINE DARKNESS.

1. Thou Trinity beyond being,[5] thou Godhead and most perfect Guardian of the divine wisdom of Christians, direct us to the height of mystical revelation, sublime beyond all thought and light; wherein the simple, absolute and immutable mysteries of Divine Truth are hidden in the translucent darkness of that silence that revealeth in secret. For this darkness, though of deepest obscurity, is yet radiantly clear, and, though beyond touch and sight, it overfills our unseeing minds with splendors of transcendent beauty.

This is my prayer. As for you, beloved Timothy, exerting yourself sincerely in mystical contemplation, quit the senses, the workings of the intellect, and all that may be sensed and known, and all that is not and is.[6] For by this you may unknowingly[7] attain, in as far as it is possible, to the one-ness of Him who is beyond all being and knowledge. Thus through indomitable, absolute and pure detachment of yourself from all things, you will be lifted up to that radiance of the divine darkness that is beyond being, surpassing all and free from all.

2. But take heed lest the profane hear—those, I say, who cling to creatures, and imagine in themselves that nothing is beyond being, beyond existences, but suppose themselves to *know* Him "who maketh darkness His hiding-place."[8] If, then, the divine mysteries are beyond such, what shall be said of those yet more profane who conceive the underlying Cause of all in terms of the outward forms of things,[9] and assert that He exceeds not these impious and manifold conceits of their own making? In so far as He is the Cause of all things, we must needs impute and affirm of Him all their attributes; but in so far as He is beyond and above all, we must needs deny those attributes to Him entirely, yet not suppose that this affirmation and denial are contradictory, but that He Himself is before and above all denials, and beyond all negating and imputing.[10]

3. After this manner, then, the blessed Bartholomew says that Divine Truth is both much and very little, and the Gospel both wide and great, and yet brief. This seems to me a marvelous insight, for the excellent Cause of all things may be revealed with many words, with few words, and with even no words, inasmuch as He is both unutterable and unknowable, because beyond being He stands above all nature. He is truly revealed without coverings only to those who pass above all things impure and pure, who go beyond all climbing of sacred heights, and leave behind all heavenly lights and sounds, and supernal discourses,[11] and are taken up into that darkness where, as the Scripture says, He truly is who is beyond all things. For not unmeaningly was the blessed Moses himself first bidden to be purified; and after entire purification he heard the many-voiced trumpets, and beheld a multitude of lights, giving forth pure and manifold beams. After he was set aside from the manyfolk, he went before the elect priests to the uttermost peak of sacred heights.[12]

But thus far he had not yet converse with God Himself, nor beheld Him, for He is without aspect, but saw only the place where He dwells.[13] This I take to mean that the most heavenly and lofty of things, which may be seen and known are no more than certain images of things subordinate to Him who transcends all. Through them is shown His presence, exceeding all comprehension, standing on those heights of His holy places, which may be known of the mind. And at times he who is set free of things seen and of things seeing, enters into the truly mystical darkness of unknowing, wherefrom he puts out all intellectual knowledge, and cleaves to that which is quite beyond touch and sight—the entire essence of Him who is beyond all. Thus through the voiding of all knowledge, he is joined in the better part of himself not with any creature, nor with himself, nor with another, but with Him who is inwardly unknowable; and in knowing nothing, he knows beyond the mind.

II. IN WHAT MANNER WE MUST NEEDS BE UNITED WITH GOD, AND OF THE PRAISE OF THE MAKER OF ALL THINGS, WHO IS ABOVE ALL.

We long exceedingly to dwell in this translucent darkness, and through not seeing and not knowing to see and to know Him who is beyond both vision and knowledge—by the very fact of neither seeing Him nor knowing Him. For this is truly to see and to know, and, through the abandonment of all things, to praise Him who is beyond and above all. For this is not unlike the art of those who hew out a life-like image (from stone), removing from around it all that impedes clear vision of the latent form, showing its true hidden beauty solely by taking away. For it is, as I believe, more fitting to praise Him by taking away than by ascription, for we ascribe attributes to Him when we start from universals, and come down through the intermediate to particulars.[14] But here we take away all things from Him, going up from particulars to universals, that we may know openly the unknowable, which is hidden in and under all things that may be known. And we behold that darkness beyond being, concealed under all natural light.

III. WHAT MAY BE AFFIRMED OF DIVINE TRUTH, AND WHAT DENIED.

In the *Theological Outlines*[15] we have praised those things that fitly pertain to the theology of affirmation; how the divine and excellent Nature may be spoken of as One, and how as Three; how in accord therewith the Fatherhood of God may be explained, how the Sonship, and in what manner the truth of the Spirit may be revealed; how out of the incorporeal and undivided Excellence they put forth these three interior lights of goodness, and how in Himself and in Themselves, and in Their mutual and co-eternal propagation They remain together, nowhere going apart; how Jesus, while above all creation, may be in very truth of the substance of human nature; and whatsoever else that is set forth in Scripture we have explained in the *Theological Outlines*. And in the book *Of the Divine Names* we have told how He may be called Good, Being, Life, Wisdom, and Power, and whatsoever else concerns the spiritual naming of God. In the *Symbolic Theology*[16] we have told what divine names may be taken from things of sense, as well as what divine forms, figures, members, instruments, heavenly places and realms (may be spoken of in terms of sensible images). We have also explained such other terms as are used as symbolic forms and sacred figures of the image of God (e.g., in the *Old Testament*), to wit the divine anger, sorrow, hatred, the inebriation and abandon, the swearing, cursing, sleeping and waking.

I think, too, that you have understood how the discussion of particulars is more lengthy than of universals; for it was fitting that the *Theological Outlines* and the treatise *Of the Divine Names* be less wordy than the *Symbolic Theology*. For the more we aspire to higher things, the more our discourse upon things of the intellect is cut short, even as, when we enter that darkness that passes understanding, we shall find not brevity of speech but perfect silence and unknowing. Herein speech descends from the universal to the particular, and as it descends it is increased in proportion to the multiplicity of things. But now, in truth, it ascends from the particular to the universal, and going up is withdrawn as it rises, and after the whole ascent it becomes inwardly silent, entirely united with the ineffable. But for what reason, you ask, do we ascribe as the divine attributes things universal, and begin our negations (concerning the Divinity) from things particular? Because in ascribing, to That which is beyond all, attributes that are more fitting to Him, it is proper to ascribe things abstract. But in taking away attributes from Him who is beyond all privation we take away what is truly most remote from Him. For is He not more truly Life and Goodness than air and stone? And, on the other hand, is He not more truly remote from dissipation and anger than He is unspoken and unthought?

IV. That He partakes not of sensible things who is
preeminently their Maker.

We say, therefore, that the transcendent Maker of all things lacks neither being, nor life, nor reason, nor mind, yet He has no body; neither has he form, nor image, nor quality, nor quantity, nor bulk; He is in no place, nor is He seen, nor has He sensible touch; nor does He feel, nor is He felt, nor has He confusion and tumult, nor disturbance of material passions; neither is He without power, succumbing to the contingencies of sensible things; neither is His light in any deficiency, nor change, nor corruption, nor division, nor lack, nor flux, nor is He nor has He any other sensible thing.

V. That He partakes not of intelligible things who is
preeminently their Maker.[17]

Going yet higher, we say that He is neither a soul, nor a mind, nor an object of knowledge; neither has He opinion, nor reason, nor intellect; neither is He reason, nor thought, nor is He utterable or knowable; neither is He number, order, greatness, littleness, equality, inequality, likeness, nor unlikeness; neither does He stand nor move, nor is He quiescent; neither has He power, nor is power, nor light; neither does He live, nor is life; neither is He being, nor eternity, nor time, nor is His touch knowable; neither is He knowledge, nor truth, nor kingship, nor wisdom, nor one, nor one-ness, nor divinity, nor goodness; neither is He Spirit, as we can understand it, nor Sonship, nor Fatherhood, nor any other thing known to us or to any other creature; neither is He of things that are not, nor of things that are; neither do the things that are understand Him, as He is in Himself, nor does He Himself understand them as existing in themselves; neither is there utterance of Him, nor name, nor knowledge; neither is He darkness, nor light, nor falsehood, nor truth; neither is there any entire affirmation or negation that may be made concerning Him.[18] But on the other hand we make affirmations and denials of those things that are less than Him (and follow from Him); but of Himself we neither affirm nor deny anything, since He who is beyond all attributes is perfect and alone the Cause of all—beyond all negation the height of that which is entirely free from all and beyond all.

FROM THE EPISTLES

Epistle I, To Gaius Therapeutes

The divine darkness becomes invisible with light, and especially with much light. Knowledge[19] obscures unknowing, and especially much knowledge. Take these sayings in a sublime and not in a negative sense, and understand this loss (of light and knowledge) as in relation to that Truth that is transcendent.[20] For that unknowing that is of God eludes those who possess light and knowledge (of God) in terms of creatures;[21] and His transcendent darkness is concealed by every light and hidden to all knowing. And if anyone, seeing God, were to understand what he saw, he would not have seen God, but some one of His creatures that exist and may be known. But He that is set on high above mind and being, exists beyond being and is known beyond mind by the very fact that He is wholly unknowable and does not belong to the realm of being. And that perfect unknowing of the highest order is knowable of Him who is above all things known.

Epistle V, To Dorotheus Liturgus

The divine darkness is the inaccessible light, wherein God is said to dwell.[22] And this darkness is indeed invisible because of supernal light, and inaccessible because of light too great in transcendent intensity, whereinto each one is born that is worthy to see and know God. Such a one, by the very fact of not seeing and not knowing, truly enters into Him who is beyond sight and knowledge, knowing this, too, that He is in all things that are felt and known. At this he says with the prophet, "Such knowledge is too wonderful for me; it is high, I cannot attain unto it,"[23]—even as the blessed Paul is said to have known God in knowing Him as beyond all thought and knowledge. For which reason he says that His ways are past finding out, His judgments unsearchable, His gifts indescribable, and His peace passing all understanding.[24] This he says as one who has found Him who is beyond all, and has known this that is beyond thought—that He, being the Cause of all, is beyond all.

NOTES

1. I should like here to express my thanks to Father Whittemore, Superior of the Order of the Holy Cross, for a number of valuable suggestions in the preparation of the introduction; and to Mr. Adolph Teichert, III, for his generous assistance in the publication of the text.

2. Originally supposed to be St. Paul's Athenian convert, St. Dionysius was probably a Syrian monk of the late fifth or early sixth century. His works were widely quoted and deeply respected by mystical and theological writers of the middle ages, and notably by St. Thomas Aquinas, who regarded them as of the highest authority.

3. There are also a number of excellent modern works upon the subject. A standard but somewhat ponderous work is Poulain's (1910) *Graces of Interior Prayer*. Saudreau's (1924) *Mystical State* is a particularly sound and valuable discussion of the various phases of mystical union. One of the best works for introductory purposes is Hughson's (1935) *Contemplative Prayer* to which should be added the various works of Fr. Bede Frost (e.g., 1931, 1939). An extremely full and profitable discussion is in Evelyn Underhill's (1930) *Mysticism*.

4. While the purpose of this translation of the *Theologia Mystica* and of the first and fifth Epistles of St. Dionysius the pseudo-Areopagite is devotional rather than academic, it should be said here that with a few exceptions it follows the text given in Migne's *Patrologiae Graecae*, vol. 3. This text has been compared with the earliest Latin version, by John Scotus Erigena, in Migne's *Patrologiae Latinae*, vol. 122. The translation comprises all his strictly mystical writings. I should like here to express my thanks to the Reverend E. J. Templeton, S. T. M, Instructor in Greek and Hebrew at Seabury-Western Theological Seminary, for his careful checking of the translation.

5. "Beyond being" (*hyperousios*). A more literal translation of the Greek would be "super-essential," a word of common recurrence in the Dionysian writings. It is not likely that St. Dionysious used the term *ousia* (*substantia*) in the sense of the Nicene-Constantinopolitan Creed, where God's essence or substance is understood as His very nature. It would be sheer nonsense to say that God is beyond His own essence. Nor are we to understand God as beyond being in the Thomist sense of the word *ens*. The thought is rather that God is beyond all objective and derived essence and existence, which is to say every kind of being that the human mind can conceive. God *is*, but not in the same manner that anything else is.

6. The meaning is obviously to quit the senses, etc., in so far as the quest for knowledge of God is concerned. The would-be contemplative is not advised to become

as unintelligent and unfeeling as a lump of stone, taking complete and final leave of his senses.

7. Unkowningly. The term unknowing (*agnosia*) is one of the Dionysian keywords, meaning much more than mere ignorance or absence of knowledge. To know God by unknowing is to surrender the mind entirely to God instead of trying to possess God as a concept of the mind or an object of knowledge. The mind knows God by unknowing in the same way that the soul is saved by losing itself. To abandon the mind to the Void of the "divine darkness" in the loving faith that God is there, is the equivalent of abandoning the body to a sacrificial death in the full faith that God is beyond the darkness of the grave. In either case the very act is accompanied by a mysterious sense of the peace and joy of God, which is why the darkness of unknowing is described as full of light.

8. *Psalm* 18:11.

9. Lit: "in terms of those things last in being (*ta eschata*)." The "last things in being" are those most removed, functionally but not morally, from God—i.e., particular, material objects. The strong Neoplatonic influence in Dionysian thought is apparent here.

10. To negate and impute, affirm and deny, ascribe and take away,—these terms denote the two ways of knowing God, according to His immanence and according to His transcendence. To know God through His immanent self-revelation in creatures is, in Dionysian terminology, kataphatic knowledge; to know Him as beyond creatures, to approach Him negatively in the understanding that He is neither this creature nor that, is apophatic knowledge.

11. Dionysian mysticism has no connection with the so-called mysticism of visions and "psychic experiences," preoccupation with which can be one of the most misleading false trails that cross the mystic's path. This is not to say, however, that all such visions are inherently false. On the contrary, God does on occasion vouchsafe distinct visions of supernatural things for purposes of conversion or encouragement. But these are not the true end of the mystical quest, which lies in the realm of essence and not appearance.

12. *Exodus* 19.

13. *Exodus* 33:18–23.

14. Here again, the text is treating of the two ways of knowing God, for, according to Neoplatonic ideas, the creative, self-revelatory process begins from universals and works downward and outwards to particulars. This is God's decent to man, but man's ascent to God works up from particulars, through universals, which are the highest created things, and beyond to the essence of God Himself.

15. One of the supposedly lost works of St. Dionysius. It is possible, however, that the phrase *theologikai hypotyposeis* refers to his treatises in general and not to a particular work, although in this chapter he clearly refers to other treatises by name.

16. Another of the lost works. The reference here is unequivocal.

17. This chapter may easily be misunderstood if it is not remembered that when St. Dionysius says that God is not reason, or power, or light, or goodness, he means that He is not these things as we are able to experience them with our created minds and senses. We have only seen and known created light and power, and goodness as it exists in creatures, and these created qualities are not God because He has made them.

18. Created light or truth is the polar opposite of creaturely darkness or falsehood, but God does not stand in relation to darkness and falsehood as its polar opposite, for

this would degrade Him to equality with them. The goodness of God is therefore in no dualistic or mutually interdependent relationship with evil, as is purely human goodness. Our created minds cannot grasp the mystery of evil because they cannot rise above dualism and conceive an order of goodness, which is definitively *not* evil and yet is not the equal and opposite of evil. Because purely human goodness is the equal and opposite of evil it can have no final victory over it. But God has final victory over evil because He is not in a dualistic relation to it. Evil is creaturely, and the dualistic relation can be between one creature and another, but not between Creator and creature. The absolute and essential goodness of God has no opposite which can limit and condition it so far as He Himself is concerned. *Deo nihil opponitur.*

19. This is a special sense of the word knowledge, the original term being *gnoses* (in the plural). Here again, it is not meant that God is obscured by ordinary work-a-day knowledge of people and things, but that (a) *gnoses* in the sense of so-called objective knowledge or visions of God obscure the genuine mystical knowledge (*agnosia*); or (b) that the mystical union is impeded by gnoses in the sense of conceptual notions of God adhered to as final and ultimate truth.

20. The latter part of this sentence is a free rendering of the Greek *apopheson hyperalethos*, or "apophatize super-truly," which is impossible English.

21. The text as in Migne does not make sense here, and the translation given follows the text of the *Codex Dionysianus* and the Latin version of Erigena.

22. 1 *Timothy* 6:6.

23. *Psalm* 139:6.

24. *Romans* 11:33; 2 *Corinthians* 9:15; *Philippians* 4:7.

REFERENCES

Frost, B. (1931). *The art of mental prayer.* Milwaukee, WI: Morehouse.

Frost, B. (1939). *Priesthood and prayer.* London, UK: Mowbray.

Hughson, S. C. (1935). *Contemplative prayer.* West Park, NY: Holy Cross Press.

Poulain, A. F. (1910). *Graces of interior prayer: A treatise on mystical theology.* St. Louis, MO: Herder.

Saudreau, A. (1924). *The mystical state: Its nature and phases.* London, UK: Burns, Oates, & Washbourne.

Underhill, E. (1930). *Mysticism.* London, UK: Methuen.

CHAPTER THIRTEEN

The Case for God (1946)

The existence of God can be proved, but not demonstrated. It can be proved by the same method that a man is proved guilty of theft in a court of law, when neither judge nor jury have seen the theft committed, and the thief has not been caught in the act of stealing. Under these circumstances the thief is proved guilty by reasoning from evidence gathered at the scene of the crime, or from other sources. His guilt is not demonstrated beyond all possible doubt because his crime was not seen. There is a remote chance that someone else committed it. But the court is assured of his guilt because there is no flaw in the chain of reasoning that concludes his guilt from the evidence.

In the same way the existence of God cannot be demonstrated beyond all possible doubt because he cannot be seen. He is invisible and intangible. But from the evidence of the universe and of our five senses we can prove the existence of God by the same method that would satisfy a court of law in the case of a crime. We can prove it by a chain of reasoned argument in which there is no flaw. The argument can only be contested by doubting the evidence of our senses and the principles of reason, which is to say, by committing intellectual suicide. For once we doubt our own senses and the laws of reason, intelligent thought and discussion about life become impossible. Since modern philosophers have taken this doubt seriously, philosophy has largely degenerated into a profitless and unfruitful wrangling not about life, but about the processes of thought—about whether anything can be known at all.

It is not presumption to attempt to prove the existence of God by reason. It is, on the contrary, the duty of reason and the chief purpose for which this faculty is given to us. Those who can reason have no excuse for doubting the existence of God, for, in the words of St. Paul, "The invisible things of God since the creation of the world are clearly seen, being perceived through the things that are made, even his everlasting power and divinity; that they may be without excuse" (*Romans* 1:20).

THE EVIDENCE OF THE UNIVERSE AND MAN

The evidence upon which the reasoned proof of God's existence is based is provided by our senses. It is the fact of a universe containing man who perceives and thinks about it. But the existence of this universe does not explain itself; it does not show us how it came into existence, nor yet how it is maintained in being. In other words, we do not see its cause. Does the universe cause itself? Obviously not, for the universe is simply the sum total of things, and none of them causes its own being. They are caused, directly and immediately, by other things that come before them, as we are caused by our parents. By scientific research we may trace these direct causes back some considerable distance. Organic life may be traced back to the original protoplasm that lived in primaeval slime. The inorganic matter of mountains, waters and stars is traced to less diversified and complex centers of stellar energy.

But here, without going back any further, we find the chain of direct causes ceasing to explain itself. The evidence now before us contains elements that simple protoplasm and stellar energy do not explain. It contains the complex and (at least relatively) ordered structure of stellar systems, of crystals, and of a thousand electrical and chemical phenomena. It contains the still more complex and ordered structures of organic life, of eyes, ears, hearts and stomachs, and finally of the human mind, which reflects upon itself and upon the impressions of its senses. Can we admit that stellar energy or simple protoplasm are adequate or sufficient causes for such highly complex and organized things?

Every effect must have a sufficient cause. That is to say, something cannot be caused by nothing, because nothing is not sufficient to cause something. In the same way, figs do not grow on thistles because there is nothing in a thistle sufficient to produce a fig. It doesn't have it in it to make a fig, just as a moron doesn't have it in him to become a mathematician. Our problem then is: Do matter and energy, or atoms and electrons, have it in them to produce protoplasm, and through protoplasm to produce man?

Let us admit that they do, and see where this admission takes us. Let us also assume, along with materialists and others who deny the existence of God, that this primal matter-energy is a purely blind and unintelligent substance. (Why do they assume this while confessedly ignorant of what substance is?) Matter-energy must therefore produce its effects, not by intelligence or conscious design, but by untold billions of permutations and combinations that necessarily, if they go on long enough, produce the universe and man. Even monkeys, it is said, typing for long enough on enough typewriters would be bound eventually to write the Bible. This is to say, therefore, that blind and unconscious elements are a sufficient cause for this universe, provided that they are able to combine and re-combine haphazardly for a sufficient length of time. By pure statistical necessity, a human mind will eventually be the result. What, therefore, we term mind, intelligence and personality are in fact peculiar arrangements of atoms produced in course of time by blind necessity. To put it more simply, intelligence is a special form of unintelligence, and consciousness a special form of unconsciousness.

Granting that this position is not already absurd, let us take it a step further. The individual who argues in this way is himself the product of blind necessity; his argument, which is part of himself, is likewise the haphazard result of necessity. Because, then, his argument is part of the universe, he cannot claim for it what he denies to the universe—meaning. He can only claim that the meaning of his argument is a special form of meaninglessness. He is then saying that the presence of a thing (meaning) is a special form of its absence, or indeed that something is a special form of nothing. To deny intelligence to your own sufficient cause is to deny it to yourself. If all sense is in fact a peculiar kind of nonsense, man's intellectual suicide is complete. He might just as well be reciting "Jabberwocky" as propounding philosophical theories.

Furthermore, his entire argument began with a huge begging of the question. Quite arbitrarily he has termed the principle substance of the universe blind and unconscious. This is a mere guess, for he admits he does not know *what* substance is. Why, then, does he make this assumption? Because he wishes to deny his own spiritual and rational responsibility, because he finds it morally inconvenient to admit that he is what he seems to be—a free, rational, and conscious person. By showing that he and all his thoughts and deeds are the results of blind necessity, he can renounce responsibility for himself. But not only does his argument begin with a purely arbitrary assumption; it ends in the denial of its own rationality and meaningfulness.

But the argument for the existence of God begins with an assumption that is not arbitrary, an assumption that we make naturally and are compelled to make in order to live any kind of rational life. It begins with the evidence (or assumption, if you insist) of sense, feeling and intuition that man *is* a conscious, intelligent, responsible, and relatively free person. We have therefore to account for the appearance of this intelligent and self-conscious thing called a person. Personality cannot be explained as a special form of impersonality, any more than the playing of a violin can be explained as the mere scraping of cat's entrails with horsehair. The emergence of human personality from the universe must have a *sufficient* cause, which is to say a cause that itself has the property of personality. The cause of personality must be *at least* personal since the lesser cannot of itself make the greater, the presence of a thing cannot be explained in terms of its absence, and something cannot come out of nothing.

The principle evidence for the existence of God is not just the fact of an objective, organized universe. It is rather the appearance of man in it as a part of it. If the universe is the effect of a cause, consciousness cannot appear in the effect without existing in the cause. The cause must be sufficient to produce the effect, to evolve from substance and protoplasm all the properties of human personality—not only consciousness, intelligence and reason, but also love, goodness, and beauty.

THE FIVE PROOFS OF ST. THOMAS

Having considered the principle evidence, the reduction to absurdity of the contrary position, and the general scope of the reasoned argument for God's existence, we can turn to the details of the proof, following the five different ways of proof proposed by Saint Thomas Aquinas in the *Summa Theologica*.

1. The first proof has to do with the origin of motion. The fact that things are in motion is clearly perceived by our senses, as well as the fact that their motion does not originate in themselves. Everything that is moved is moved, at least originally, by something other than itself. We are forced to one of two conclusions: either motion begins with a "first mover," which, unlike everything else, is absolutely self moved, or that there is no origin of motion, that the series of movers and moved goes back forever to infinity. But if motion is forever derived from something else and *never* originates in anything, motion must be without origin and without cause. But this would lead to one of two absurd conclusions: (1) that it is then its own cause, which, seeing that it is always *derived* from something else, is impossible, or (2) that it is a causeless effect, a something emerging from nothing, which is also impossible. We are compelled, then, to accept the idea of a First Mover, absolutely self moved and the cause of all other motion. And we might add to St. Thomas's argument that since man is the most self-moving of known beings, it is highly probable that the First Mover is a living Being rather than an impersonal force.

2. The second proof is akin to the first, seeking the First Cause instead of the First Mover. We know of nothing that is its own cause, and unless we can arrive at a First Cause we are left with the absurd conclusion that there is simply an infinite series of causes and effects, the whole of which hangs absolutely uncaused in a void, like the Cheshire Cat's grin in *Alice in Wonderland*. For we do not only have to find the first, beginning cause of the series. Even if the universe were eternal and had no beginning in time, it would still have to have a cause beyond itself; otherwise it would be like a country where all made their living by taking in each other's washing. That is to say, if every cause in the series was an effect, the whole would be an effect without a cause. The mere size or duration of such a series, such an uncaused universe, would make no difference to its absurdity. To make it infinitely long or infinitely large is only to

make it infinitely absurd. There must therefore be a First Cause that is not an effect of anything but itself; "and this" concludes St. Thomas, "men call God."

3. There is nothing in the universe that exists in its own right, for of all things that we know it is possible for them both to be and not to be. Obviously a thing that has the possibility of *not* existing does not exist *necessarily*—in its own right; if it existed necessarily it could never cease to exist. If, then, things do not have being in their own right, they must derive being from something else. A series of beings, none of which exist in their own right, all of which derive their existence from one another, is by itself impossible—however enormous it may be. If every being in the series derives its existence from something else, the whole series must also derive its existence from something else. For a being that can at some time not exist is not an eternal being,[1] and no number of temporal beings will add up to an eternal being just as no number of geometric points will add up to a line, and no amount of shapes will make a color. But if there is no eternal being there was a time when things were not, in which case they could never have come into existence. Therefore there must be an eternal being that exists necessarily, in its own right, which does not *have* being (and so can possibly *not* have it) but which *is* being. And this, too, is what men call God.

4. The fourth proof is based on the different grades of perfection to be found in things. There are, for example, varying degrees of warmth and of consciousness. Things are understood to be more or less warm or more or less conscious to the extent they approach that which is most warm and most conscious. Something that is less warm cannot become more warm by itself. The extra warmth must come from somewhere, and that can only be from what is *most* warm, i.e., fire, in one form or another. We are saying, in fact, that there cannot be less or more of a given quality or perfection until there is a most, from which the less and the more can be derived. If there is not a most perfect form that the less and the more perfect can be derived, we are saying that the greater can be explained in terms of the less, that more of a given quality is the result of less of it—which is manifest nonsense. Therefore all perfections in all things must be explained with reference to a most perfect Being that does not receive perfection from another, but that possess the fullness of these perfections in its own right. Man is more conscious than the animal; man, however, is not the most conscious because animals do not derive their consciousness from man. Thus the necessary most conscious and most perfect being will be what we call God.

5. The fifth proof comes from the fact of a certain order in unintelligent things—a type of order that is not simply read into them by the human mind. For example, the eye of a bird is ordered toward seeing. The power of sight is for the good of the bird, yet certainly the bird has neither the intelligence nor power to produce its own eye and order it to the perception of light as distinct

from sound and smell. The fact that unintelligent things are ordered toward ends—eyes to seeing, ears to hearing, nerves to feeling, lungs to breathing—is not to be explained by chance, because to do so would be to commit the old error of explaining order in terms of disorder. Both the idea and the fact of chance presuppose the existence of order and purpose, and even if we say that the notion of order exists only in the human mind we have still to explain its existence *there*. But the ordering of eyes to seeing is in no sense an "imagined" order that the mind of man reads into external events as, perhaps, he reads design and beauty into the patterns of frost upon a window. Yet because eyes and a million other natural phenomena clearly do not order themselves to their ends, there must be an intelligence directing them; and this intelligence we call God.

THE NATURE OF GOD

The five proofs of St. Thomas tell us not only that God exists; they tell us also something of what God is like. From the first, which has to do with motion, we learn that God is power. From the second, dealing with God as the First Cause, we see that God is *creative* power. From the third we learn not just that God has being, but that he is Being itself. The fourth adds to this that God is not mere being; he does not simply exist like a stone, or a man after a heavy dinner. God is the fullness of Being, possessing every perfection of which Being is capable. And finally the fifth tells us that God is the source of all intelligence, order, and design.

Reason, therefore, leads us not only to the fact that God is; it gives us also some knowledge of his nature, though this knowledge is incomplete beside God's own revelation of himself in the prophets and in Jesus Christ. There are, however, three specially important aspects of the divine nature that reason deduces from our experience of the universe, and though implied in the fore-going argument, it will be well to examine them more closely since nothing detracts more from belief in God than absurdly unworthy ideas of his nature.

1. The first is that God is life. The sufficient cause of a universe containing persons must, as we saw, be *at least* personal—that is to say, a living, conscious, intelligent and integrated being. God is the most of qualities that we find in more or less degree in the world, and because created things are more or less alive God is that which is most alive. The higher a form of life, the greater its degree of consciousness and integration, and the greater its independence of physical limitations. We are thus led to the thought of God as one who is absolute consciousness, absolute wholeness and unity, and absolute freedom from other than self-imposed limitation. Therefore to say that God is personal is in no sense to limit or belittle him. It is not to imprison God in a form or shape. On the contrary, it is to say that he is the absolute maximum of life and freedom, bursting, as it were, the bonds of form and finitude not because he is vague and misty but because he is utterly and intensely alive.

The idea of a personal God is so often criticized as idolatry, as making God in man's image. But the alternatives offered by such critics are yet more idolatrous since they conceive God in terms of less living forms than man—as blind and abstract mechanism, force or principle, unlimited only in the inane and vacuous sense of infinite space or aether. The error of idolatry is not that it makes a finite image of the infinitely Vast and Vague, but that it is an attempt to capture the infinitely Alive One in a fixed, dead and petrified form of thought or imagination. Try to capture the wind in a bag and you have only stagnant air. Thus the assertion that God is personal is not to say that God is like man; it is to say that man, in so far as he is personal, is something like God, having in some slight degree the awareness, the selfhood, the unity, the intelligence, and the freedom of absolute and perfect life.

2. The second is that God is being—he who IS, the only one who can truly say, "I am." It is this truth that leads us to the knowledge of God's perfection and goodness. A perfect thing is a complete thing, a thing that lacks nothing and is not frustrated or limited by anything else. As the first cause, as necessary being, and as the source of all possible perfections to be found in creatures, God is obviously quite self-sufficient and lacks nothing. If there were anything that he lacked, he could not be its cause, and if some being or quality existed uncaused by God, he would not be the *first* cause, in which case he would not be God. In general, however, things are limited and frustrated by their opposites—life by death, pleasure by pain, and joy by sorrow. Not only are they limited by their opposites, but they cannot exist without them, as life (*as we know it*) cannot exist without death since it lives on dead plants and animals.

But because God is being he has no opposite. The opposite of being is nothing, which by definition doesn't exist. God, then, is called good because he is the triumphant and unopposed fullness of being, possessing every perfection, every positive and excellent quality of which being is capable. Yet we are used to thinking of evil as the opposite of good, and if God is the purely good, must not evil be his opposite? We are mistaken in calling evil the opposite of good. We should think rather of evil as the *attempt* to oppose good, an attempt that can never succeed since to oppose the good entirely and successfully would be to cease from being. Evil is a parasite upon the good, depending on the good for its existence. For example, an evil handkerchief is one containing a hole—a handkerchief lacking complete being and going in the direction of nonbeing. A purely evil Handkerchief would be one that was all hole. It would not exist at all. Yet whereas the handkerchief can exist without a hole (the good without the evil), the hole cannot exist without the handkerchief (the evil without the good). Evil is thus dependent upon and subordinate to good; it is not its equal and opposite.

All evil is destructive. In whatever form it is a tendency toward nonexistence, for the things we call evil are those that destroy and inhibit life, which makes holes in things otherwise complete and perfect. We praise God as the absolutely good because it is impossible to "make holes in him." One who exists necessarily, who *is* being, cannot be made to cease to be even partially. But from one who only *has* being, being can partially or wholly be taken away.

The fact that God, as being, has no opposite makes him the Supreme Good in the sense of the supremely desirable One, the true, if unacknowledged, object of all human yearning. For the heart of man desires to have life, happiness, love and peace *eternally*. But this desire is frustrated again and again because these various goods, as we ordinarily experience them, have opposites upon which they depend. As created life is opposed to and dependent on death, created happiness is unknown apart from the contrast of sorrow. A life independent of death, and a happiness independent of sorrow can only be the eternal life and happiness of God himself. Hence the only final satisfaction of human desire must be found in a union of man with God so intimate that man becomes a partaker of the divine nature. This will be possible if it is true that to become one life with God is the purpose for which man exists, if man is ordered to union with God as the eye is ordered to the perception of light.

3. The third important aspect of the divine nature is, then, that God is love. Love is the unreserved giving of one's whole being to another person. As the noblest and most positive of all human virtues, it is necessarily derived from God, who must possess it, like all other perfections, in the very highest degree. But God does not simply *have* these perfections just as he does not simply *have* being. In order to be the sufficient cause of a certain quality, he must not only have it; he must *be* it, and thus we may say that God *is* love.

Creation itself is an act of the divine love, because in creating God gives himself to others. A person or a thing can only exist because God has given it a share in his own being. And since he is one and indivisible, God gives his whole being, his whole mind, his whole will, to every single creature that he makes, although each creature receives the gift of God in accordance with its capacity. Man receives the gift more perfectly than a stone, but no creature can receive it with absolute perfection because in so doing it would cease to be a creature and become God. We receive God partially, but he gives himself wholly; the degree to which we can receive him will depend on our likeness to God, who, like the sun, sheds down the entire light of his love upon every place and thing. And as bright objects reflect the sun more perfectly and dark objects less perfectly, so the life and the love of God is received with varying degrees of perfection although it is given to all alike.

The special peculiarity of man is that being a person, an image of God, he can return that love. Under certain circumstances man can give the whole of himself to God as God gives the whole of himself to man. For this reason there can exist between God and man the most intimate of all unions—the union of love, the Spiritual Marriage. Love necessarily desires union with the beloved object, and love turns into the bitterest suffering if that union cannot be had. It would therefore be contrary to every reasonable idea of the divine perfection and justice if man were capable of loving God, but not of union with him.

The good news, the gospel, of the Christian religion is precisely that God has given man the power to receive this union, to become one life with God and to share and enjoy eternally his unopposed goodness, love, peace, and happiness. The realization of this union is what is meant by "going to heaven," and the imagery of wings and harps and halos, of the celestial city whose temple, light and center is God, of the unending song of praise and adoration, is designed to tell us in symbolic form of the joy and illumination of those who have become one with God and transfigured into his radiance like iron plunged into fire.

CONCLUSION

Human reason, just because it is human and not divine, cannot be absolutely perfect, and consequently the reasoned proof of God's existence and the reasoned deduction of what his nature must be cannot have *absolute* certainty. Two things, however, may safely be claimed. First, it is clear that belief in God is more reasonable than any other theory of ultimate Reality that human reason has to offer.[2] To suspend judgment on the bare chance that this reasoning may not be true, is like refusing to go out of the house because of the much stronger chance that you may be hit by an automobile. It is a thousand times easier to prove that you can trust in God than that you can trust yourself to the hazards of a city street. People do the latter every day. That they do not do the former can only be attributed either to inability to reason, or to sheer moral cowardice, or, in some cases, to mere lack of information.

Secondly, it is also clear that a reasoned consideration of God's existence and nature shows that this central doctrine of Christianity, together with its necessary implications, is not at all the crude, naive, and superstitious notion it is currently supposed to be. The Christian Church does not teach that the ultimate Reality is a cosmic superman with white whiskers who sits upon a golden throne above the stars. Nor, however, does it commit the opposite folly of supposing that God is merely the personification of our highest ideals who exists only in the sense of Uncle Sam. It does not even ask us to believe in God as a "gaseous vertebrate," or as a rather large, ubiquitous and beneficent superspook.

On the contrary, it carries human reason to the highest, the most sublime, the most subtle idea that it can form; and, having taken it to that splendid height, makes it bow down in wonder and humility—the philosopher with the child—because on the very topmost peak one thing becomes certain beyond all else: that the Reality so far surpasses the idea in glory that all human knowledge is seen as comparative ignorance, and the curious chatter of thought becomes the loving silence of contemplation.

NOTES

1. A thing that either begins or ends is by definition not eternal. The eternal can neither start not finish, because this would constitute an end to what is by definition endless. A start is an end in the same sense that the "beginning" of a road is one end of the road.

2. The fact that the argument for the existence of God does not *of itself* answer various related problems, such as the existence of evil and suffering, is nothing against it. It is only when its conclusions are seen to be *true* that the problem of evil is raised.

CHAPTER FOURTEEN

The Meaning of Priesthood (1946)

Like all highly developed organisms, the Catholic Church is complicated. It is so complicated that both churchmen and outsiders are apt to lose sight of the forest because of the multitude and the variety of trees, and this danger is most present when we are considering the Church's organic structure—the complex sacramental life of Christ's Mystical Body. Few churchmen understand what Christianity is about, what are its essential and basic principles, and what is its ultimate goal. At the same time there are plenty of churchmen who have a very thorough knowledge of secondary principles. They can tell you what the doctrine of the Holy Trinity is, what the sacraments are, what are the rules and precepts of the moral and spiritual life, but they cannot, or do not, tell you what they mean. They present you with a complex of interesting but unrelated information, all of which has some vague connection with the salvation of one's soul. But if you will inquire carefully, you will find that not one Christian in fifty (a generous estimate) can tell you what salvation means, except perhaps that it has something to do with moral goodness. This ignorance is largely due to the fact that Catholic worship involves so much liturgical and sacramental "know how" that in the few hours available for religious education there is little time left for instruction in basic principles—the nature of God, the destiny of man, the meaning of salvation. The Anglican Communion complicates things still further with a mania for ecclesiastical history so great that the average confirmand knows more about Henry VIII and Matthew Parker than he knows about God—and I am sometimes afraid that the same thing might said of the average student in our theological seminaries.

No discussion, therefore, of one of the functions of Christ's Mystical Body, in this case the priesthood, can be intelligible unless it is related immediately to fundamentals. There are, I believe, three basic principles, which, if understood, will clarify everything in the Catholic religion from contemplative prayer to the blessing of holy water, and these are the three principles in relation to which we are going to consider the organic function of the priesthood. Briefly they are these:

1. That since God is love, and since the goal of love is union with its object, the aim of the Christian religion, that is, salvation, is to realize the eternal union of man with God. By union I do not mean identity but a perfect union of different things, as when color and shape unite to form, say, a red circle.

2. That this union is realized through mutual love between God and man, where love is defined as giving oneself wholly and unreservedly to another. God gives himself wholly to man, and man gives himself wholly, in body, soul and spirit to God.[1]

3. That this union is achieved, in the first instance, by God who initiates the union by giving himself and his own eternal life to sinful men. "Herein," wrote St. John, "is love: not that we loved God, but that he loved us." It follows, therefore, that eternal life is not a prize to be earned but a free gift to be realized, appreciated and used. In other words, Christian sanctity is not what we do to get union with God; it is what we do with it. It follows also that the Catholic Church is not an association formed by men to discover God, but an association formed by God to discover men.

It is significant that the second of these principles, at least in part, is far more widely recognized and understood than either the first or the third. Every Christian, and for that matter every Jew and every Hindu, understands that religion involves the giving, the dedication of himself to God—in a word, sacrifice. The truth that sacrifice is of the essence of religion is a revelation that has penetrated human consciousness from time immemorial. But in practice the other two principles have been minimized and obscured because, for dimly conscious reasons, we cannot quite bear them. A false humility makes us timid in acknowledging the tremendous destiny that God has prepared us—eternal union with his own divine Being—a destiny that popular notions of heaven almost entirely obscure. And the glorious message of the Christian gospel, that in Christ God has freely *given* us this union, is a complete outrage to our pride. For it means that God has put us in an infinite and irrepayable debt, and we are so embarrassed by such unmerited love that we are loath to admit it and adopt almost any means to conceal it. Thus the average Christian of today hears little or nothing of the gift of union with God, of divine sonship; he hears only that Christ came to the world to cancel past debts, to give him a fresh start, to set him an example of righteousness, and to bestow upon him a dose of spiritual power to help him earn his passage to heaven.

Therefore as popularly conceived there is no *essential* difference between Christianity and any other form of ethical theism, between the old law of Moses and the prophets and the new dispensation of Christ. The only difference is one of degree—as if our Lord had come into the world merely to give us a fresh start with a new and improved moral law, a bigger and better Pharisaism, a more rigorous and demanding code of sacrifice. In actual practice popular Christianity is no more than a rarified Judaism, though Catholics are perhaps less prone to this error than liberal Protestants, and the reason is simply that the world does not want to face the implications of the Incarnation. According to the liberals it would seem that the only difference between the old covenant and the new is that the price of redemption is no longer the sacrifice of bulls and goats but the sacrifice of one's very self, with the encouragement of Christ's example. In this case the gospel is not very good news. A more Catholic type of misunderstood Christianity embellishes this story with one rather dubious improvement: that whereas the sacrifice of bulls and goats and obedience to the law of Moses would *not* purchase entry to heaven, the sacrifice of oneself will—because Christ has opened the gates. God, in other words, has agreed to let us in, though now he is talking in terms of a vastly increased entrance fee.

Of course it has been stated very briefly, but in fact that is about as much of the truth of Christianity as manages to reach the mind of the ordinary Christian. In practice the doctrine of the Atonement means to him no more than that Christ has opened the very distant gates of heaven, and because the age of the old covenant, when the gates were closed, is so remote in time the fact that they are now open has lost its impressive novelty. The rest of the truth, wherein lies the full splendor of the gospel, the truth of one "full, perfect and sufficient sacrifice, oblation and satisfaction for the sins of the whole world" is for him a veiled and incomprehensible mystery. In effect, therefore, most Christians are still trying to live under the conditions of the old covenant, wherein each man's own sacrifice, not of bulls and goats but of his whole life, is the only means of finding favor with God.

It follows, then, that the popular conception of the Christian ministry differs only superficially from the priestly and prophetic ministry of the old covenant. The minister is holy, not because he is an ordinary sinner called to a special union with Christ, but because he himself has dedicated his own life to God, and is specially righteous as a vicarious sacrifice for his people or at best as an example of individual goodness and individual sacrifice for them to follow. The people dance and drink, but not the minister. The people laugh and joke and relax, but not the minister, save perhaps in an obviously artificial manner so that we may be sure it isn't real. The Protestant minister is a subtle and up-to-date form of human sacrifice, and what he ministers is not the gift of union with God but "precept upon precept, precept upon precept; line upon line, line upon line." At least, that's what seems to be expected of him, though the grace of

God sometimes makes him more human and lovable. The Catholic priesthood is, on the whole, in a rather better position, despite the fact that a family will offer a son for the priesthood in much the same spirit as an old Hebrew family would offer first-fruits for the altar. And do the people understand him as one who ministers union with God in Christ? On the contrary, he is all too often the mere mediator of individual sacrifices of a crudely commercial character—"sacrifices of masses" to be had at so much cash, remission of sins for so many "Hail Marys," curtailment of Purgatory for so many novenas. But at least his people get the impression that somehow or other he is a source of life and power, however magical and trivial its nature.

But the truth contained in the Old Testament, that sacrifice, and sacrifice involving our own lives, plays some essential part in our relations with God, still remains. Without sacrifice creatures cannot be made holy, which is to say healthy, whole, one with God. The word sacrifice itself has the double meaning of offering a thing to God and making a thing holy. Man is created for union with God in love, and since love consists in giving oneself to another freely, man's love of God is precisely sacrifice, the free surrender of his whole being—physical, mental, and spiritual—to God. To be acceptable to God a sacrifice must be perfect, and in practice this means that it must be offered to God absolutely, without conditions or reservations, because the only way to render a human life without blemish is to put it entirely in the hands of God.

Obviously the priesthood of the old covenant was quite inadequate to achieve such a sacrifice. To begin with, what it offered at the altar was not human life but mere symbolic tokens of that life—portions of the meat and drink whereby that life was sustained. Furthermore, it was a purely human priesthood, and one individual human being can no more sacrifice for another than he can eat another's food for him. How much less could he offer another person's whole life to God, when the essence of such an offering is that it be one's own free action? For individual human persons are mutually exclusive; I am I, and you are you; I cannot see through your eyes; I cannot, unless you permit me, command your will; I cannot surrender your soul to God. Thus the priesthood of the old covenant was only a sign, a type, a figure of what had to be done. The sacrifices that it offered could not effect the forgiveness of sins because they could not effect union with God: the two states are one and the same. God *is* forgiveness; his "nature and property is always to have mercy," and to be one with God is to be one with forgiveness. Under the old covenant each man was in reality his own priest, because the real sacrifice required by God was that every man should offer himself and his all. "Thou shalt love the Lord thy God with all thine heart, and with all thy soul, and with all thy might."

But the gates of heaven were closed in the sense that man simply could not make such a sacrifice. By his own power he is still incapable of it, for try as you may you simply cannot freely and fully abandon your life and being to God. This is that state and effect of original sin, of man's characteristic and

Eternal life is the state wherein God and man are united in mutual life, so that man participates in the love that is between God and Father and God and Son, God the Lover and God the Beloved, sharing in its unutterable joy. "Every soul," wrote Coventry Patmore, "was created to be, if it chose, a participator of this felicity, of 'the glory which the Son had with the Father before the beginning of the world.' . . . He who has not attained, through denial of himself, to some sensible knowledge of this felicity, in reality knows nothing; for all knowledge, worthy of the name, is nuptial knowledge." Our love for God, by means of which we deny ourselves and receive eternal life, is of course the reflection of God's love for us. "This," said St. John, "is love; not that we loved God, but that God first loved us." For God takes the first step in our redemption by giving his very self, in Christ, to each and every member of the human race, for, in our Lord, God is uniting himself to the world. We accept this gift of union with God when we become members of his Church.

This is a truth that cannot receive too much emphasis, not only because no aspect of the Christian Faith is intelligible apart from it, but also because it receives an absolute minimum of attention in modern Church teaching. We talk interminably of how we ought to love God and our neighbors, but say all too little of the infinite love that God has for us. We too easily conceal its immensity and infinity by speaking of it simply as *grace*, which the average layman understands simply as a handout of power from a distant deity, a dose of spiritual gasoline received at the altar on Sunday, sufficient to last until next week. We do not make it sufficiently clear that God's love for us is precisely the gift of himself, that by grace we sinful men, through no merit of our own, are given nothing less than eternal union with the divine essence, the very Godhead. The Christian life, Christian morality, Christian sanctity, must be understood as the uproar of thanksgiving and gratitude for this overwhelming gift—not as the price at which we earn our pie in the sky.

For by the power that the gift involves we can begin to love God in return, as a mirror turned toward the sun has the image of the sun within it and reflects the light back to its source. Our lord used this very symbol of sunlight to describe the Father's love, who, as he said, "maketh his sun to shine upon the evil and the good," for the divine love is like sunlight in that it pours itself out impartially in an act of pure generosity. It gives itself wholly and seeks no gain, for nothing can be added to the glory of God. Thus love, in the Christian sense of the word, means to give oneself wholly and unreservedly to another.

But in common speech the world *love* can mean different things. Greek has two words for our one, and generally uses the term *agape* for the purely generous, self-giving love of God. With the other word, *eros*, it denotes a self-seeking love, loving something because it supplies that which you lack and for which you hunger. Because he lacks nothing, God's love is always *agape*, but since human beings are imperfect and finite, not to say sinful, their love, apart from divine grace, is always *eros*. Man's natural love for God, his thirst for congenital tendency to love himself rather than God. The Chinese have a proverb that aptly describes this condition: "When the wrong man uses the right means, the right means work in the wrong way." If you start, then, by being the wrong man you are in a seemingly hopeless case, for whatever means you take to turn yourself into the right man will surely work in the wrong way. If you are by nature selfish, all your righteousness, all your efforts to love God and give yourself to him will have at their foundation a selfish motive. Like a fly stuck on fly-paper, the more you struggle to get off, the more firmly you will be stuck.

This is a truth that all of us know well from experience. We know, for example, that worry is a sin involving lack of trust in God. We know, too, that it's stupid to worry and that worry will solve nothing. But just try, by sheer will power, to stop worrying about something. Before you know where you are, you are involved in a perfectly horrible vicious circle, for you find not only that you can't stop worrying, but that you are worried because you can't stop, and that makes you doubly upset and nervous, so that you are alarmingly worried at worrying because you can't stop worrying.

Similarly, we know that in order to be possessed by God and to be one with him, we must let go of ourselves. Being fond of ourselves we hang on to them with all our might lest something should take them away, and slowly strangle in the process. So we know we ought to let go. We want to let go. But why? Because we are afraid of strangling ourselves. But you see, we are still afraid *for ourselves*, and in practice all our attempts to let go mean that we just hold on tighter. Thus when psychologists observe human virtue simply as human virtue, they come to the conclusion that altruism is merely indirect selfishness, repressed sexuality, or will-to-power, and thus prove to the hilt all that the Church has taught about original sin. When a human being attains enough self-consciousness to realize this predicament he becomes quite desperate. Some of the Apostles had experienced this despair. St. Paul's epistle to the Romans is for the most part a discussion of this very problem, and according to the *Book of Acts* St. Peter raised it at the First Council of Jerusalem when he observed that it was quite impossible for men to obey the old law. This was the despair that underlay St. Augustine's conversion, and prompted Luther's revolt against the reversion of mediaeval Roman Catholicism to Judaic legalism—a revolt entirely justified however regrettable its excesses.

God's solution to this predicament is the Incarnation, the projection into time, space and history of his eternal disposition and action towards man. Because God is love and with his whole infinite being wills the union of each single creature with himself, man's sin does not alter God's nature but rather, from the relative human standpoint, intensifies the flow of the divine love towards him. In spite of the whole enormity of human sin, in spite of the pride whereby man would usurp God's own throne—the center of the universe, God gives man that which he cannot earn, and performs in man and for man that priestly action that man cannot do for himself. God gives himself to man in an eternal union from which even hell affords no escape, and there offers and sacrifices our human nature to himself to complete and consummate the bond. As an historical event the Incarnation reveals this truth to us in all its tragic and triumphant meaning.

The creeds state plainly that in Christ God became *man*, not *a* man. The humanity of Christ is our own human nature, for as St. John says, coming into the world he enlightens *every* man. The Incarnation is local and historical to make it visible, and then to lead us on to the understanding that it is also cosmic and eternal—that it takes place not only at a distance from us in time and space, but also here and now, always, within us. In short, God is incarnate in *your* human nature; he has made the perfect offering of *your* human nature to the eternal Father on the cross; he has raised *your* human nature from the dead, and finally has carried up *your* human nature into heaven, into the inner life of the Holy Trinity. As St. Paul tells us in his epistle to the Colossians, we are already dead to ourselves, and our life "is hid with Christ in God," for our real life is now Christ himself.

This then is the meaning of the Atonement, the at-one-ment of God and man, the one perfect sacrifice that Christ as our High Priest came to perform. It cannot be stated too strongly. We have eternal union with God as a free gift. We do not have to make any sacrifice; we do not have to give ourselves to God—we have already been given. One thing alone remains for us to do, one power of the soul remains to be exercised that original sin has not destroyed—the power to say "Yes—Amen," to give assent to what has been done for us. For we are carried along in an inescapable union with God as in a mighty torrent. We may swim against it, but we do not move against it; we are carried along just the same, but under protest. All we have to do is to turn around—repent. We can no more escape from union with God than we can escape from the present moment, and not only have we done nothing to deserve such a privi-lege, but almost everything to oppose it. The love of God is incomprehensible.

The force of this truth has been somewhat hushed up by certain timid theologians who at any word of a given union with God are apt to throw up their hands in horror and scream, "Pantheism!" Be it therefore noted in passing that pantheism involves a necessary and automatic union of the creature with God, whereas Christianity involves an entirely *un*necessary union that depends solely on the free and loving will of God. This is a far more exciting kind of union than pantheism can possibly conceive.

From what has been said it should be easy to see what a vast difference lies between the priesthood of the old covenant and the priesthood of the new,—the one offering many individual and ineffective sacrifices, a human priest-hood, and the other embodying, affirming, pleading one cosmic and perfect sacrifice, a priesthood both human and divine. For the new priesthood is simply Christ extended; it is his High Priesthood realized in human persons just as, in a wider sense, the whole Church is the Incarnation realized and extended in human persons. For the Church is the body, the fellowship, of those people who have accepted the gift of union with God that Christ is and that Christ brings. The Church is made up of those who have said "Amen" to the identity of their own humanity with Christ's humanity, so that in a very real sense the Church is Christ's Body.

We saw that the Incarnation is cosmic and eternal as well as local and historical, for since the human mind functions chiefly on the local and histori-cal plane, it has to be approached on that plane. To get an abstract idea across to a child you must make it concrete, illustrate it with a story. Because God's love extends to the whole human race, which is largely made up of very simple and childlike minds, he makes his eternal action concrete, and illustrates it in the story of Jesus. As the extension of the Incarnation, the church is likewise a cosmic and eternal organism as well as a local and historical institution, and herein lies its sacramental character. For a sacrament is a special instance of a cosmic and eternal action, a special instance of the union of God with the world. The ultimate object of the Incarnation and of the Church is to realize the union of the whole universe with God, for as the office hymn says:

> From the holy Body broken,
> Blood and water forth proceed;
> Earth and stars and sky and ocean
> By that flood from stain are freed.

But its imperfect and finite nature makes it impossible for the human mind to grasp such a union all at once, and if we try to look upon everything as holy, it will shortly come about that nothing is holy. To enter into human conscious-ness holiness must be differentiated, localized, set apart.

According to this principle, then, we have an organic series and system of differentiations, of special instances, of God's loving gift of union with himself to the world—the Incarnation, the Church, the sacraments, the orders of the Church. It is by differentiation of function that an organism develops and mani-fests its powers, every function remaining, however, a property of the whole organism lest differentiation become disintegration. By virtue of her union with Christ the Church as a whole exercises the priestly office of Christ—the sacrificing, the offering and making holy, of creation. But for working purposes, that is, for sacramental purposes, this crucial function is differentiated into the sacred order of priests, which stands at the focal point of the Church's life— the altar—and in the sacrifice of the Mass projects again and again into time and space the eternal sacrifice, dispensing also in Holy Communion the gift of union with God that it involves. The work of the priesthood, central in the Church, is the work of the Cross, central in the universe—the realization of union with God through Christ's sacrifice. In short, the difference between the old priesthood and the new is this: that whereas the old stood at the altar to offer his own and our personal sacrifices, the new stands to offer Christ's that is both God's and our own.

The truth that the new sacrifice of the Mass realizes must not be minimized, and the whole work of the priesthood is to reiterate this truth—that in Christ God has offered our lives to himself and bestowed his own eternal life upon us here and now. The bread and wine set on the altar at the offertory is your own life and nature. Christ in and as his priest takes that human nature, makes it his own flesh and blood, and offers it perfectly to the Father. In Holy Communion it returns to you, enters into you, as the gift of union with the divine essence—not just as a dose of spiritual power to help you to be good through the coming week. The sanctity that should follow from this sacrament is an outpouring of appreciation and gratitude for the fact that God has given his eternal life to a wholly unworthy creature.

From the gift of union with God flows the forgiveness of sins, and as the primary function of the priesthood is to minister the gift of union, so its secondary function is to minister forgiveness. For sacramental purposes, that is, for making things distinct, clear and simple to our concrete minds, the gift of absolution from sin is differentiated from the gift of union, Holy Penance is differentiated from Holy Communion, although the two are really one and are administered by one and the same priesthood. As our Lord's exercise of the authority to forgive sins was perhaps his most outstanding claim to divinity, so his bestowal of that authority upon the Church is perhaps the clearest possible sign of the Church's union with God, for God alone can forgive sins committed against him. Although the Sacrament of Penance normally precedes the offering of Mass in time, in the spiritual order it is derived from Mass. The confession of sins and the acceptance of God's forgiveness is a way of appreciating, a way of saying "Amen," to the gift that the Mass brings. A person who receives the Holy Communion without repentance and without accepting God's forgiveness is not really and sincerely accepting Communion. You do not accept union with God unless you accept forgiveness from God, and you do not accept forgiveness unless you accept it concretely and realistically for your specific sins.

The priest can say, "I absolve thee from thy sins" because he can say with Christ, "This is my Body." For we are cleansed, not by our own repentance, but because we have been incorporated into Christ and offered by him to the Father. Repentance is the consequence of this fact; it is our appreciation of it, our response to the revelation of God's unfailing love, apart from which "the continual dew" of his mercy falls off us like water from a duck's back. The Prayer Book points out the essential unity of the two sacraments in the Prayer of Humble Access—"that our sinful bodies may be made clean by his body, and our souls washed through his most precious blood." The priest cleanses us from sin because he offers the sacrifice that effects forgiveness, though in both instances he is the focal point of a function that belongs essentially to God incarnate in the whole Body of Christ.

The third function of the priesthood is the ministry of the Word, and this again proceeds from the priest's union with Christ. Once more, because he can say, "This is my Body" he can say, "This is my Gospel," for in preaching and teaching the priest is to speak as Christ and to convey and explain the truth that inheres in his office. "The Spirit of the Lord is upon me, because he hath anointed me to preach the good tidings to the poor." The Christian priesthood involves also the prophetic ministry, and as there is a radical difference between the old and new priesthood, so there is a radical difference between the old and the new prophecy.

Generally speaking the message of the old prophecy was one of judgment and wrath, and of exhortation to repentance. Sadly enough, the message of the Church must sometimes be the same. But that message will be of no effect unless a very definite primacy is given to the "good tidings," for "God sent not his Son into the world to condemn the world, but that the world through him might be saved." The priest's authority to preach is not, therefore, to be taken primarily as authority to moralize. For so many hundreds of years clergy have moralized Sunday by Sunday, bombinating and fulminating from their pulpits like Amos and Jeremiah, that our people have by and large a thoroughly perverted and unbalanced notion of the Gospel, and that the Church simply stinks in the nostrils of the general and pagan public. If such harangues were adequate to win souls, Amos and Jeremiah would not have been succeeded by Christ.

The priest's ministry of the word involves not only public preaching, but also private teaching—in particular the individual direction of souls in the spiritual life: a task that any parish priest is liable to be called upon to perform, whether he is trained for it or not. How can we expect the Church to have any vitality at all (especially in this state of nervous fidgets called modern civilization) unless we set out definitely and systematically to develop the interior life? Direction in such a matter as this should surely be expected from the spiritual pastor of a community, but this has been so neglected that the interior life, so far as people have any at all, has become the special province of Christian Science practitioners, theosophists, swamis and psychoanalysts. Generally speaking, Roman Catholics relegate such matters to the cloister. Protestants, with the exception of Quakers, heed them not at all, and Anglicans *occasionally* get around to it. There cannot be any vital religion when it consists only of receiving the sacraments and getting some general edification on Sundays. There *must* be the daily life of prayer, and of prayer beyond the "Gimme-gimme-God-bless-Mother" stage. In the Church as constituted today it is an essential of the function of priesthood to be the source of direction and training in that interior life without which we can hardly expect any personal realization of union with God. Yet many, many churchpeople have no idea that the Church *has* any teaching on such matters, and when they begin to experience the first stirrings of inner spirituality find in Unity[2] or Emmet Fox[3] a more sympathetic voice than in their priest, from whom they expect only incomprehension and a few moral platitudes.

The priest is elected to teach because the nature of his office is the central truth of the Gospel. The priest is the minister of Christ, the God-man, of union with God given to our humanity. And union with God he must teach, revealing the length, the breadth, the depth and the height, the full and undiluted implications of God's love. His teaching, as someone has recently said, must emphasize not *ought* but *is*—what God is and has done for man. An ought-message deflects our attention to ourselves and our own discouraging and uninspiring failures. But an is-message lifts up or minds to God. It is the same as when you are trying to read a rather difficult book. If you think, "I must try to concentrate, I ought to get on with it," your attention is deflected from the words on the page to yourself trying to read them.

Therefore in preaching, in the confessional, at the altar, the office of a priest is to lift up our hearts and minds and souls with Christ to the eternal Father, telling us that this lifting up is not a long, hard, agonizing journey to bring us to the verge of despair—but that, on the contrary, whether we know it or not, feel it or not, we are already lifted up because God has come down to earth and has ascended with us into heaven. "For I, if I be lifted up, will draw all men unto me." Therefore, "my yoke is easy and my burden light."

That is why, in the confessional, it does not belong to the office of a priest to scold or to judge the degree of a penitent's sinfulness. He is only to make sure that the person repents sincerely, and then by absolution and by counsel, if necessary, reveal the wonder of God's love so that amendment of life may be inspired, not by shame, guilt or fear, but by gratitude. He is to remember the words of our Lord to the woman taken in adultery, "Neither do I condemn thee; go and sin no more."

So also, in offering Holy Mass at the altar, the priest's whole action is theocentric, for he is to focus the mind of the congregation upon God and upon the gift that descends from him. Therefore the altar, not the minister, is the center of attention, and the priest must efface his own eccentricities of voice and gesture, making his own personal part natural, impersonal and unobtrusive so that he does not constitute a barrier and a distraction between the people and their God.

While it is true that the function of priesthood belongs to the Church as a whole, it must be remembered that the Church is a dispensation of God's love to *all* men both wise and foolish, rich and poor, exalted and lowly. The world's work, the gathering of daily bread, has to be done, and this work has to be made an integral part of Christ's Body since most people in the world are fully and necessarily engaged in it. Hence the vital function of sacramental priesthood cannot be entrusted to all. The stewardship of the mysteries of God must not be entrusted to those who are perforce burdened with the cares of the world, to more than ordinarily foolish human beings, or to those who would serve God much more ably by offering him in Christ some secular work. Furthermore, there are certain spiritual disadvantages in being a priest, for when you have to occupy your mind with formally religious considerations from one day's end to another, it is not at all easy to *be* religious. You may have to talk about and think about religion so much that you have little energy left to practice it, and the practice of an incarnational religion must of necessity go beyond formally religious actions. I sometimes think it is more Christian to plant potatoes to the glory of God than to say so many formal prayers or offices. But the function of the priesthood is vital, because without formal, sacramental and localized religion, we might lose sight of religion altogether. That is a concession to human weakness.

Despite, however, its disadvantages and temptations, and in virtue of its tremendous responsibility, the office of priesthood involves one supreme privilege. For the priesthood is something more than a merely expedient differentiation of one of the whole Church's functions. Holy Order is a sacrament conferring upon its recipient a permanent and peculiar character. In Baptism, Confirmation, Communion, Penance, Matrimony and Unction the soul *receives* union with God in its various modes. But by ordination to the priesthood one becomes, in and as Christ, a *giver* of union with God to others. It is as if the baptized soul were a mirror reflecting the light of God's love back to its source, and as if the ordained soul were also a window admitting the light. Every Christian ministers to others the love that flows from his union with God, but the priest ministers the union itself. This, then, is the meaning of that special union with Christ that the priesthood is said to have. It is not that priests are nearer to our Lord or more loved by him than layfolk; clergy who give themselves special airs as if they were the Lord's elect are a very unattractive breed. The privilege of priesthood is simply to be able to have the joy of giving to others the supreme gift of the Incarnation—union with God and the forgiveness of sins. And if it is true that a priest is a priest for ever and has a special function even in heaven, I believe that function will be to share, not only in the joy of being able to see God, but in God's own joy that the redeemed are able to see him.

In this present time there is an urgent need for the priesthood to be true to its function, because in general the clergy are attempting to fulfill all kinds of functions other than that for which they were ordained, and as a result the glorious meaning of the gospel has been clouded. The primary function of God's priest is not to be chief executive of a huge social-welfare organization, a keeper of public morals, an amateur politician, an adornment of drawing rooms and civic committees, nor yet to purvey an archaeological religion of ecclesiastical history and tradition garnished with unexplained and unthoughtout theological clichés. This kind of thing has reduced the gospel to such a piffling system of ethics with remote and unconvincing eschatological sanctions that it is no wonder that it arouses the barest minimum of enthusiasm. Enthusiasm means to have God in you. Therefore the function of the priest is to minister the love of God to the world, and to proclaim that love not as a mere distant well-wishing but as the gift to each one of us, here and now, of union with God's very self to all eternity. The closing words of our Lord's High Priestly prayer in St. John's Gospel give the essence of that work of priesthood, which is his and ours: "That they all may be one; as thou, Father, art in me, and I in thee. . . . And the glory which thou gavest me I *have given* them; that they may be one, even as we are one: I in them, and thou in me."

NOTES

1. Although God gives himself wholly, creatures do not receive him wholly. The sun sheds its light upon all things, and they reflect it in varying degrees, but none equal to the sun in brilliance.

2. [Watts is referring to the Unity Church founded by Charles and Myrtle Fillmore in 1889, and focused on the practical application of Christian principles in everyday life—Eds.].

3. [Emmet Fox (1886–1951) was a spiritual leader of the Divine Science Church of the Healing Christ in New York City—Eds.].

CHAPTER FIFTEEN

The Christian Doctrine of Marriage (1946)

It is impossible to understand any aspect of the Christian religion unless it is brought into immediate relation with the ultimate goal and purpose of the Faith, which is to say the final end to which human life is ordered. The supreme and all-important goal of our religion is God, for we have been created in order that we may realize an eternal union with our Creator. The aim of the Christian religion is the eternal union of man with God in body, soul, and spirit. The Prayer Book relates Christian marriage directly to this end, for the preamble to the marriage service states that "matrimony is an honorable estate, instituted of God, signifying unto us the mystical union that is betwixt Christ and his Church." In other words, Holy Matrimony is the highest earthly analogy of that creative union of God and man, Christ and Church, which is the end and fulfillment of human life.

It is for this reason that Christian marriage has the dignity of a sacrament, that the *Song of Songs* is admitted to the books of Holy Scripture, and that our Lord constantly employed the symbolism of marriage to explain the meaning of his presence in the world. "Love your wives," wrote St. Paul to the Ephesians, "as Christ also loved the Church, and delivered himself up for it, that he might sanctify it, cleansing it by the laver of the water of life. . . . So also ought men to love their wives as their own bodies. . . . For this cause shall a man leave his father and mother, and shall cleave to his wife, and they shall be two in one flesh. This is a great mystery, but I speak in Christ and the Church." Thus to understand marriage we must study the union of man with God; and to understand union with God we must study the ideals of Christian marriage.

Reprinted from *Canterbury Club Tract*, No. 1, 1946, Episcopal Church at the University of Colorado, Boulder, CO. Copyright 1946 by Alan W. Watts. Copyright not renewed.

divinity, which he has in spite of the fall, is thus also *eros*, and non-Christian religions, to the extent that they are purely natural religions, are religions of *eros*-love. But the true sanctity of supernatural religion is where man loves God with God's own *agape*-love, exclaiming, to adapt the words of Job, "Though he slay me, yet will I love him!" For the Christian's love of God is a sharing in Christ's love for the Father, the self-abandoning and self-emptying love of the cross, which is only possible for the Christian because he is one with Christ.

The distinction between *agape* and *eros* explains, too, the difference between Christian marriage and purely natural marriage, for the natural love of man and woman is *eros*-love. But because a Christian, by virtue of union with God, is capable of *agape*-love, marriage between Christians is a relationship in which the natural love of man and woman is transformed into the supernatural, the self-seeking type of love into the self-giving.

Now this transformation of natural into supernatural love is not just the addition of some extra cream to the cup of marital bliss. On the contrary, it is something without which the relations between man and woman, husband and wife, are problematic, troubled, and fundamentally unworkable. In complete variance with secular opinion, the Christian doctrine of marriage assumes that, because of the fall, the natural relations of man and woman, whether monogamous, polygamous, or wholly promiscuous, are in a thorough mess. This is no arbitrary theological disgruntlement with the joy of life; it is a strictly realistic and scientific observation. Ever since history was written, the relations of man and woman have been problematic through and through. Look at this modern world that ceases not day and night to praise the joys of natural love, and that goes on seeking them so greedily just because it doesn't find them. The true commentary on the modern praise of natural love is the concomitant popularity of easy divorce and that staggered polygamy, which subscribes to the frustrating and perpetually disappointing creed that the grass on the other side of the fence is always greener. If this is not enough evidence, one need only turn to the literature of all ages for immense and reiterated witness to the fact that natural love is at root unhappy and frustrated love. The world's classic love stories—Tristan and Isolde, Heloise and Abelard, Romeo and Juliet, Orpheus and Eurydice, to mention a few from the Western world alone—are essentially stories of frustrated love, for they reflect the experience of the race.

The Christian sacrament of holy matrimony is not given to the world to deny or to trim the joys of natural love to a minimum. The fact that must be drummed into the secular mind is that Christian marriage is the *only* alternative to frustration, the only realistic cure for the diseased condition of natural marriage, the only form of essentially happy love. It is not that Holy Matrimony entirely abolishes the problems of marriage, but rather raises them to a level where they become fruitful and redeeming instead of frustrating and damning, where, like the pains of the cross, they have an undertone of essential and absolute joy.

At root the Christian doctrine of marriage is quite simple. Its essence is that Holy Matrimony is constituted by two baptized persons entering into the marriage contract and living together as man and wife. Because they are baptized they are one with Christ and partakers of the divine nature and the divine love. Thus the love that they have for one another must be a degree of *agape*, God's own love, for which reason their union is analogous to the union of God and the world in Christ. Such is the basic principle upon which the whole structure of the doctrine depends. It has two primary consequences.

The first is that Holy Matrimony is a state in which the man gives himself wholly to the woman, and the woman to the man, for in the Christian *agape* sense love can mean nothing less than this. Christian marriage is therefore monogamous and permanent. It is monogamous because the love of one partner for the other is whole and undivided. Only God, being infinite, can give himself wholly to many objects. It is permanent, "til death do us part," because to give oneself wholly in love means that you give not only what you are now, but also what you will be; you give your whole life, both as it expands in space and in *time*. Furthermore, you give yourself unreservedly. You burn your bridges behind you; you commit yourself irrevocably and leave no way of escape. If this is rash and foolish, it is none other than the foolishness of that love that showed itself on the cross. For unless you are prepared to do this you do not really love, and if you have the divorce-court in the back of your mind as a way of escape your marriage is not likely to work for the simple reason that your love is incomplete. It is not Godlike love. For the marriage vow to live as one flesh "for better for worse, for richer for poorer, in sickness and in health," to stay by your partner come what may, is precisely a reflection of the love wherein God unites his very self with us to all eternity even though we elect to be damned.

The second consequence may sound more simple than it is: namely, the object of one's love in the state of Holy Matrimony is another person. The real reason for the failure of natural love is that its object is not really another person; it is oneself—projected upon another. *Eros* is self-love; it is the love of the sensation, the emotion *within oneself* that another person arouses. In essence natural love is to be in love with the state of being in love. The other person is merely the occasion for this state. "Eros," writes Denis de Rougemont, "treated a fellow-creature as but an illusory excuse and occasion for taking fire." *Agape*, on the other hand, is outgoing and extraverted; its object is that other unique human person, and is more often a reflection of the creative love of God who gives himself entirely to each one of a multitude of unique beings who are quite other than himself.

The keynote of Christian marriage is therefore *wholeness*, which is after all the same word as holiness. It is the product of a love in which the lover gives himself wholly to all of the beloved, not a mind, not a soul, not just a woman in the abstract, but that totality of aspects and qualities that adds up to a unique human being. The result of total love is total union, the becoming of one flesh, analogous to the realization of eternal life, the goal of religion, wherein we are one life with God.

So much for the theoretical considerations that lie at the root of the Christian doctrine of marriage. We turn now to their practical application, as I wish to show that this is the only workable and practical philosophy of marriage, and not just a highly specialized and select vocation for super-mystics. We must therefore consider the application of *agape*-love to the three great aspects of marriage as of man—the three departments that make up the totality of human life: the realm of body, the realm of mind, the realm of spirit. For marriage, like religion, is a bodily, mental, and spiritual union of lover and beloved. Just as a religion without sacraments is like a marriage without physical love, so a marriage without communion of mind and spirit is like a purely ceremonial religion—mere "spikery."

We shall begin, then, with marriage as bodily union. In the popular view this seems to be the all-absorbing phase of marriage, for it regards marriage and sex as some people regard bread and butter . . . mostly butter. Important as the sexual aspect of marriage may be, in reality it occupies a very small fraction of one's married time, and cannot without complete detriment to itself be isolated from or set above the other aspects of marriage. So many marriages fail for the very reason that sexuality is regarded as an end in itself, in ignorance of the fact that, apart from Christian love, sex—like everything else in a fallen world—is a failure.

The Church does not teach, and churchmen should not give the impression, that sex is evil or even a necessary evil. Read your Old Testament. On the contrary, evil is purely spiritual in origin, and sex, like all other material processes and things created by God, is positively good. In common with eating, sleeping, moving and thinking, it is a faculty that becomes evil only when misused. The Church *does* teach that sex becomes a source of evil when separated from *agape*-love, and love in that sense implies a marriage. This is, again, no arbitrary restriction based on the assumption that what is very pleasant is wrong. It is a simple statement of fact, of the fact that without total self-giving love the sexual relation is a failure—even on the purely biological plane.

Contrary to the general belief of mankind, the successful sexual relationship does not come naturally to human beings. So far from being a thing to which any mature person can take "as a duck to water," sexuality is a high art that must be acquired through devotion and discipline like any other art, such as painting or music. Strange to say, many church people find this quite an unfamiliar and sometimes repugnant idea. They are accustomed to thinking of sex as pertaining to the realm of indecency and toiletry, and have no notion at all that it can be supernaturalized. Needless to say, such thinking is wholly vicious and heretical—for if sex is not supernaturalized it becomes at once an occasion of evil, and it makes no difference whether you praise it to the skies, or degrade it to the mud. Both are forms of the same error. Christian marriage alone provides the conditions under which the art of sexuality can be practiced to perfection. However, it is unlike other arts in that almost everyone desires to practice it, and desires it fervently. Failure in the attempt to practice it thus involves serious and wide-spread frustrations, and it is in these that the real evil of misused sex has its origin. This evil consists in the obsessions, fantasies and perverse desires to which sexual failure will so often give rise.

Four conditions, all of which are involved in the Christian concept of marriage, are necessary for the perfection of the art:

1. No art whatever can be called perfect without this first condition, which is that it be done for the glory of God. A Christian is one who tries to do every single daily action for the glory of God, turning his whole life into an act of worship. Sexuality must not be excluded from this worship, for as much as anything else it is done in the eyes of God and will become evil unless dedicated to him. Wherever the danger of evil and temptation lurks, its physical occasion must be offered to God. There is no other escape from sin. But where sex is concerned this is too often the very last thought that will occur, even to the otherwise devout.

2. Self-giving love implies that in the sexual act one must put the pleasure of the *other* partner before your own. Unhappily our American Prayer Book has omitted the phrase that accompanies the giving of the ring in the English Prayer Book, "with my body I thee worship." The natural idea of sexual pleasure is the reverse—"with *thy* body I *me* worship"—and when this is the motive the act will not be sexual communion at all, but simply self-gratification. Generally speaking, this will mean lack of complete satisfaction for the female partner in particular (her reactions being slower than the male) because the man bent purely on self-gratification will approach the act with thoughtless haste and clumsiness. To overcome this he must have a degree of genuine altruism found only in *agape*-love. Similar haste and selfishness on the part of the woman, though more rare, will have the same effect.

3. The sexual life of the married couple must have creative issue. (I say "the Sexual *life*," because this cannot *be said of each sexual act*—quite apart from the question of artificial contraception.) It must have creative result just as the union of man and God, if it is to be realized at all, must have creative result: by their fruits ye shall know them, and every tree that beareth not fruit is cut down and cast into the fire. Save in certain abnormal circumstances, childless marriage denigrates into a selfish "twosome," which, for lack of creative outlet, comes to grief by its own futility. It lacks analogy with God the Creator. Since, too, the sexual act is always liable to produce children, it cannot be entered into with the necessary relaxation and self-abandonment if there is any anxiety as to its results. Only the security of permanent marriage can fully get rid of anxiety and its attendant frustration of pleasure.

4. As in all other arts, the art of prayer or the art of the piano, it is essential that there be constant and regular practice—with the *same* partner. It may take from five to seven years to reach a real degree of perfection, to attain the full adjustment between two unique and highly complex human organisms—an adjustment that can *never* be attained if relations are promiscuous. Like temperance, sexual self-control must not be confused with abstinence. A controlled pianist is not one who plays the piano very seldom; he is one who plays it very often and very well. He will, of course, get tired and stale if he plays too much, but the trouble with so many married couples is not that they have too much intercourse, but too much undisciplined and selfish intercourse. The notion that sexual self-control is merely a matter of longish periods of abstinence proceeds from the same fallacy as sexual promiscuity—that ideal relations are normal and natural. They are not; they are supernormal and supernatural. They necessarily involve the total devotion and self-denying love of the other partner, which is the essence of Christian marriage. For such love and such discipline-in-the-act are only possible for one who has realized some measure of union with the sole source of unselfish love—almighty God.

The absence of any of these four conditions brings in frustration, making the act somewhat disappointing, somewhat below expectations. People can react to such frustration in one of two ways: they can go on practicing and loving until perfection is reached, or they can retire into the realm of fantasy, and simply dream about an easy and readymade perfection. The latter course opens the door to every kind of sexual evil, because these fantasies soon grow to the point where pleasures are imagined that reality can never provide. Attempts may be made to fulfill such dreams in all kinds of promiscuous and perverse relations, but because of the absence of our four conditions these relations will always involve more and more frustration, giving birth to more and more impossible dreams. That way lies sexual obsession that is a hell on earth, destroying character and spiritual life.

Our teaching about sexuality in Christian marriage needs to stress above all that the Church's view, so far from being designed to curtail the joys of physical union is the only really workable approach to the subject. A fully enjoyable sex life may occasionally have been lived but as a rule simply is not found apart from the principles of Christian marriage, because the Church's view is based on the actual facts of nature and the human spirit. Perhaps this is a bold statement, but the evidence is that wherever these principles are not followed, an atmosphere of obsession prevails upon the subject of sex, which is a clear sign of frustration. As St. Thomas insisted over and over again, the principles of the spiritual life do not destroy nature: they perfect it—and it is for lack of this perfection in the realm of sexuality, and consequent lack of real enjoyment, that our modern world, obsessed with the impossible dreams of the frustrated, wallows greedily but unhappily in the sins of the flesh.

But the real problems of marriage do not lie so much in physical union as in mental and spiritual union. It is a truism that one must marry even more for companionship than for physical attraction, but sometimes I think a truism may be defined as a principle that all know and few observe. So few young people seem to realize that the real work of marriage is to learn to live in the same house, in the same room, with another person day after day, year after year, on terms of such great intimacy. Because of this, the adjustment of sexuality is far less difficult than the adjustment, the union, of tastes, interests, minds and characters. As the psychiatrist C. G. Jung once observed, marriage is a task for adults only, and unfortunately there are so few of them.

To approach *this* problem on the merely natural level is surely quite absurd, and it is small wonder that in countries where the Christian religion does not flourish a union on the mental and spiritual plane is seldom even attempted. When the old wife gets boring, put her away in a quiet corner of the harem and get a new one. For heaven's sake don't mix the women up with your social life; make it a tabu to take them out to dinner, and when company comes lock the door to their quarters. And when all else fails, use the big stick. Lacking a supernatural religion all this is very understandable. But our modern problem is this: that 2,000 years of Christianity have abolished this kind of marriage management in the Western world, yet because that world has largely forsaken Christian belief we now have millions of married pagans trying to live in Christian monogamy. No wonder they call it monotony.

I submit that without extraordinary luck or extraordinary grace, it is practically impossible to live on terms of such prolonged intimacy with another person on any other basis than *agape*-love. No amount of mere compromise will effect the necessary adjustment, for compromise assumes that marriage is a 50–50 relationship where I have my rights and you have yours, so let's make a bargain. But there is nothing of the 50–50 compromise about Christian marriage. "The wife," says St. Paul, "hath not power of her own body, but the husband: and likewise also the husband hath not power of his own body, but the wife." In Christian marriage you *give* yourselves 100 percent on both sides, for like all the sacraments of the Church Holy Matrimony is a sacrificial action. Nowhere is sacrifice more necessary in marriage than in the achievement of the union of souls, for outside of a monastery there is surely no more rigorous school for the denial of one's personal pride. How often must you admit, when it comes to a difference of opinion, that you are quite wrong; how often must you eat your most cherished prejudices; or how often must you submit patiently to a black atmosphere when, for conscience's sake, you have had to insist on a point of view? And yet anyone who has consistently done this over the years knows that it leads to a happiness that those who will not sacrifice never can experience.

On the whole, it would seem that in our civilization it is harder for men than for women to let go of themselves and give themselves to the extent required in *agape*-love. We all know, for example, that it is much easier to interest women in religion than men, because a woman is much better adapted psychologically to yielding herself. But Anglo Saxon-American man is afflicted with a certain psychological and spiritual rigidity that makes it most difficult for him to give himself entirely whether in religion or in marriage. In marriage this difficulty is encountered more particularly on the mental and spiritual level. The trouble lies in a certain false masculine pride that causes men to avoid like the plague certain things considered "undignified" and still more things considered "sissy." All too often this is taken to such lengths that men wholly stifle the feminine element in their own nature, and thus destroy all common ground and sympathy with women. In short, the cult of the "strong, silent man" all too easily becomes the neurosis of psychological isolation and the sin of spiritual pride.

First, this attitude is destructive to marital union in the realm of *work*. American men in particular are guilty of becoming so absorbed in business, of making business so much the end-all and the be-all of their lives, that their wives are excluded almost entirely from their husbands' principle interest in life. In a civilization of commuters this is a major gulf between man and wife, and it is not helped a bit when, on coming home to dinner, the man is disposed to be strong and silent about what he has been doing all day.

Second, it is destructive of marital union in the sphere of *recreation*, which might otherwise compensate for inevitable lack of union in work. But what happens? Ousted from a share in her husband's major interest, the wife, in self-defense, goes in for that monstrosity called "Womens' Club Culure," where she is segregated off from the males with her female cronies. American culture is thus a predominantly female culture, whence it is not surprising that men consider the whole cultural and aesthetic side of life "sissy." They avoid it, and once again lose common ground with their women-folk. This recreational segregation of the sexes does not only arise in the realm of the highbrow arts, but also in that of the lowbrow games. It is with his male friends, rather than with his and their wives, that the average man takes his recreation, his golf, his poker, his fishing.

Third, it is most of all destructive of marital union in the realm of *worship*. The average American husband and wife simply do not go to Church together nor have any spiritual life in common in the home. They must face the facts. Either God exists, or he doesn't. If he does, he is the most important reality in life, and a marriage that is not united in God leaves the marriage unconsummated in the major realm of human existence. But, here again, to the ordinary male religion is "sissy." From one standpoint he is right, for since the Reformation both Protestant and Catholic piety have gone on the "mushy" side. But from another standpoint he is quite wrong, since Anglo Saxon-American man could well do with a great deal less toughness and a great deal more suppleness; it would make him much more of a real man, and less of a neuter oaf. It is up to the Church, however, to teach the strength of suppleness and the power of yielding. "Blessed are the meek for they shall inherit the earth." Under the burden of snow, the branches of the willow bend and do not break, whereas the rigid limbs of the pine crack and fall.

This so-called marriage wherein husband and wife neither work together, play together, nor worship together, and very soon cease to sleep together, is an all too common feature of American society. Jiggs and Maggie[1] are very true to life, and I do not doubt that Maggie enjoys herself at the Club, and that Jiggs has a wonderful time with the gang. But such happiness as they have is precisely an escape from marriage, and in real life the insatiable appetite of *eros* will look for satisfaction from all kinds of impossible and harmful sources. And the perpetual frustration of this appetite tells its tale in the steely eyes and tight lips of our hardened clubwomen, and in the early deaths or nervous collapse of men who seek their escape in the squirrel-cage of modern business—which goes faster, to save time, to make money, to go faster, to save more time, to make more money, until something or someone busts. No one can pretend that on this basis, either marriage or the escape from marriage works—or that it makes anyone happy. But people go on doing it, on the supposition that a couple of kids who are more or less congenial at the age of twenty will somehow get along naturally if thrown together in marriage. This, however, is not marriage; it is juxtaposition. Marriage is an action, a work, in which one partner gives his body, mind, and spirit to the other.

In the Christian view, therefore, a marriage simply is not Holy Matrimony unless it is a physical union, a mental union, and a spiritual union, for anything less than this is not a wedding of two entire persons. I believe that before the clergy bless a marriage they should consider whether the couple are actually whole persons, or whether the grace of Matrimony has any chance of making them so. To let a woman of the Church, for example, be married to a man who once received Holy Baptism but has never done anything about it since, is just as disastrous as letting her marry someone with a serious physical deformity such as an undeveloped head. We shall be a thousand times more respected by the world if we have the courage of our convictions and boldly declare that a person with no spiritual life, no interest in *agape*-love, is simply not all there. He is no fit recipient for the sacrament of Holy Matrimony. If the state can refuse a license on the relatively trivial grounds of a positive Wasserman reaction, the church can surely do the same on the grounds of much more serious spiritual diseases.

Doesn't it all boil down to this: do we believe in the Christian religion we talk so much about, or don't we? Do we believe that God exists, that human nature is fallen, that God has given himself to each one of us in Christ, that because of the fall natural marriage is a necessary failure, and that because of Christ, and only because of him, marriage, and all that goes with it can be made healthy, whole and holy? Do we believe it? If we honestly don't we shall help the human race far more by becoming devout Hedonists and making the best of a bad job, of an incurably evil human existence. But if we really do believe that Christ, that this God of love is Reality itself, more actual than these hands, these bones, more concrete than these very walls, more solid than this earth—then we are utterly bound to admit and state plainly that those who live their lives without relation to this Reality are more diseased, more crippled, than the blind, the deaf, and the dumb, more remote from reason than the insane. But God, through us his Church, can heal them, and it for the work of healing that his sacraments are given to the world for all willing to try them and accept their conditions. We need, then, to teach Holy Matrimony not merely as an ideal, a duty, a godly, righteous and sober way of life, but rather as a dispensation of the divine mercy for the healing and transfiguration of what must otherwise be inevitable frustration and bitterness—the passion of human love.

NOTE

1. [Jiggs and Maggie are characters in a cartoon series distributed by King Features Syndicate entitled *Bringing Up Father*, which ran from 1913 to 2000—Eds.].

PART FOUR

Comparative Religion

CHAPTER SIXTEEN

Worship in Sacrament and Silence (1964/1971)

I can't talk to you about worship unless I first give you some idea of my own religious point of view. I want to be quite frank with you so that there shall be no misunderstanding. I do not belong to any standard brand religion. I don't have any religious label because in this day and age, when we know so much about the various religious points of view of the whole world, I consider it to be unintelligent to commit oneself to a particular label. This is prejudice. This is saying I commit myself to a certain point of view in advance of any new discovery, any new knowledge that may turn up. To me the essence of faith is being open-minded. I would say that there is a fundamental contrast between belief on the one hand and faith on the other. Belief comes from an Anglo-Saxon root, *lief*, which means to wish. In my definition, a believer is one who fervently hopes that the nature of the universe is thus and so. He is therefore committed. He is using religion as something to hang on to. And when you use religion as something to hang on to, you are in an attitude that is the exact opposite of faith.

For example, when you are thrown in the water and it is necessary to learn how to swim, the very last thing you must do is to grab hold of the water and try to stay afloat in the water in the same way that you try to support yourself on the dry land. The commitment of faith is very much like being thrown into the water because you suddenly realize that you don't know. You are afloat in a vast universe and you honestly don't know what the nature of life

Presented at the Third Symposium on Human Values, Central Washington State College, 1964. Reprinted from *A College Looks at American Values* (Vol. 1), edited by E. H. Odell, 1971. Copyright © 1971 by Central Washington State College. Used by permission of Central Washington University.

is. Therefore, you have to act as the swimmer, to let go. Take another example. When a cat falls out of a tree, the cat lands safely because it makes an act of faith. If, when the cat let go, it suddenly stuck out its limbs like this and said, "e-e-a-h," the cat would hit the ground and be a bag of broken bones. But all cats have learned from their mothers to relax when they fall, to let go so they land with a soft thud. And that is the act of faith.

Faith I would say is having one's mind open to the facts or the truths, whatever they may turn out to be. Therefore, from my point of view, religion is not a doctrine to be believed in; it is an experience. That is to say, it is an experience in just the same sense that being alive is something that you experience, that falling in love is something that you experience, that being afraid or being happy or whatever is an experience. So for me, religious faith or religious knowledge is that alteration that occurs to one's consciousness, to one's whole being, indeed, as soon as you take an attitude toward life that is fundamentally one of letting go. In Buddhism, for example, the highest state of consciousness is called Nirvana, and a lot of people think that that means nothing at all, annihilation. The word in Sanskrit means "blow out." While the breath is life, if you hold onto your breath you begin to lose it. So, you see, he that would save his life, his breath, shall lose it, but he that loses his life shall find it. Let go. Let the breath go. Let go of God.

In a certain sense—and I don't want you to think I am an irreligious person—there are two kinds of irreligion, the higher and the lower. The lower irreligion we all know about—when one simply doesn't care about these things. The higher irreligion could be called atheism in the name of God. There was once upon a time, though everybody's forgotten it, a technical Christian theological term for this. It was called apophatic theology or the *via negativa*, and its great proponent was a certain saint who goes by the name of Dionysius the Areopagite. The idea was this: that the most dangerous of all idols are not the idols made of wood and stone, but the idols made of imagination and thought. Therefore, all ideas of God, all conceptions of God that are fixed and positive and formal are idols. The truly religious man of faith must be one who smashes his own idols, or if I may put it another way, he scrapes from the window the paintings of the sun and the blue sky that have been put on the glass. He looks as if he were destroying something but actually he's letting the real light in. So, in my philosophy, all conceptions of God to which people cling for spiritual security are their major obstructions to faith and to religious knowledge, and the best thing to do is to get rid of them.

Now this applies particularly to ideas, to concepts, that might very well be mistaken for the reality that they represent. The ideas of God as the "necessary being," or as the "undifferentiated aesthetic continuum" or as the "infinite absolute mind," are far more dangerous idols than say De Lawd of Green Pastures. De Lawd of Green Pastures wears a top hat and smokes a cigar, and this is not a dangerous idol because nobody would dream of taking it seriously. In the same way, the good old-fashioned God who has a beard and sits on a golden throne is not in danger of being taken seriously by any intelligent person. But at the same time, there is something marvelous about these images just because they will not be taken seriously, and because they are also very expressive.

It is very difficult to conceive a being in higher terms than in human terms. Once you have tried to conceive God as something like "necessary being" or "pure spirit," you get a conception of God that is rather more like an infinite sea of tapioca pudding than anything else. Whereas to think of Him in the form of men is to think of Him in the highest form that we know, provided you have this little thought in the back of your mind, what the Germans call *hintergedanke*—a little thought, a little reservation—that this isn't really the way it is. (This is the essence of mythological symbolism. Mythological symbolism is very powerful and very necessary.) So when I speak of God in anthropomorphic human terms I do so with a twinkle in the eye so that you won't take me quite seriously. Nevertheless there is something to be said, there is something to be conveyed by this message.

Now, having abandoned all religious believing, I want to tell you from my own experience what happens. In order that you can understand it, I have to express what happens to you in some sort of mythological terms. They are better, they are clearer than attempting to be aridly philosophical. (I could put it to you in that way too, but I'm not going to tonight.) Now what I come to is this: the fundamental nature of the universe is based on the game of hide-and-seek, or lost-and-found, or peek-a-boo; the universe as we know it physically consists of a sort of now-you-see-it, now-you-don't sort of thing, something like the positive and negative aspects of electricity, the up and down of the wave, the here-we-are and the here-we-aren't of a discontinuous vibration. We know things exist because they just don't stay put; they keep coming and going. For example, if I put my hand on your knee and leave it there, you will soon cease to notice it, but if I keep patting you on the knee you will keep knowing that I am there. In the same way, here in front of me is a hard object, a microphone. The reason it's hard is that it keeps going out of existence and coming back into existence so that my fingers won't go through it just as I can't put my finger through the rapidly evolving blades of an electric fan. This microphone is going much faster than any electric fan. My finger is going pretty fast, too. All of those electrons or whatever they are, waves or wavicles, go b-r-r-r the whole time; and b-r-r-r is here-we-are and here-we-aren't. You can also test this out by playing with a baby. The game that all babies like is when you hide your face and the baby starts to giggle. That's because the baby in its unspoiled state is profoundly in touch with the metaphysical core of the universe. So, that's the fundamental game.

Now, suppose I were God, what would I do? Let me put it to you in a simpler way. Suppose that every night you could dream any dream you wanted to dream, what would you do? I am sure we would all spend many nights having wonderful wish-fulfillment dreams. When we had got through with enormous meals and dancing girls and concerts and great gambols, we would then go into adventures and thrills. But when we had gone through that for several months, we would decide we wanted a surprise dream where we didn't know what we were going to dream. First of all a pleasant surprise, several months of pleasant surprises. Then we'd have the adventure of an unpleasant dream, knowing that we would wake up in the end. In reality, we do that all the time, because when we go to plays, when we read books, we like to know the fundamental plot. Everything starts out O.K.—*status quo*. Then a villain has to come in and upset everything and, although we know it's a play, we still sit a little bit on the edges of our chairs, especially if the play is well acted. We go through the thrill of seeing everything go to pieces and then everything is restored again. So, if you were the Lord God, what would you do?

Well, of course, you would have imaginary things going on. You would imagine a creation, and you would imagine after a while that you weren't in charge of the creation anymore, that you were mixed up in it. That would be like having a surprise dream, or like the perfect technological push-button universe in which everything we desire can be had immediately by pushing a button. Five minutes of that would be enough. We'd have to have a button labeled "surprise." So you might say the Lord is the supreme dramatist who forgets that he is the Lord: he goes through the game of pretending that he's all of us; he becomes involved like a great actor in myriads of parts; and he gets absorbed in them because he's such a good actor that he takes himself in. He has himself sitting on the edge of his throne absolutely spellbound. Is it going to come out all right?

You see, there really are only four great philosophical questions. Oh, I think there may be five. The first one, "Who started it?" The second, "Are we going to make it?" The third, "Where are we going to put it?" The fourth, "Who's going to clean up?" and the fifth one, which I just thought of, "Is it serious?"

Now from the ordinary religious point of view, from what I call the point of view of standard brand religion, it is serious. The Lord is a very serious person as we shall see shortly. But in the view that I have come to the Lord is *not* serious, because the Lord's fundamental function is play. Just as Shakespeare says, "The play is the thing." The whole universe is in this sense dramatic. (I am not trying to preach to you; I'm just telling you what I think.) The whole universe is dramatic. It's a drama that's so good that it takes itself in and looks as if it isn't play. It looks as if it's serious, but it isn't. And the reason it isn't serious is that basically every one of you—although you may not know it, and most of you probably don't—every one of you is really the Lord in disguise, and you are therefore fundamentally "what there is." You're *it*. See the game of hide-and-seek. You're it. So there's really no need to worry; that's the fundamental attitude of faith. You don't need to hang on to God or to cling to God, because the moment you do so you deny the fact that you're *it*. By trying to have faith you don't have faith. By trying to believe, you aren't really religious because the fundamental thing in religion is to realize oneness with or union with God.

Now I don't attempt to say what I mean by God, I'll just give you the idea of the old gentleman on the throne, because the real thing you couldn't think of any more than you can bite your own teeth or look straight into your own eyes without a mirror. In this sense, you see, none of us knows who he is because each one of us is the absolutely fundamental root and ground of being. Now some people will object to this idea. They'll say it's pantheistic. That's a dirty word in theological circles, because it's supposed to disrupt all morals. After all, if I'm God, and you're God and everybody's God it really doesn't matter what happens. And when we say it doesn't matter, that's a way of saying that matter is no matter. It really doesn't amount to anything because it's a game, a good game, a wonderful game. In that sense it matters—a glorious game—but it is only a game.

Here I find a difficulty. The moment you try to root ethics and morals in the nature of God you get into trouble. The Chinese have a proverb: "Don't swat a fly on a friends head with a hatchet." In the same way, if you make good and bad and moral behavior depend on God, it's too much. It overwhelms things. It's saying that the distinctions between good and evil are so eternal that the good people will be happy forever and ever, but the evil people will have to scream in hell forever and ever. And that's really very immoral. There's nothing more immoral than making morality absolute. We know what good grammar is, and we all agree fairly well to speak proper English. But we don't have to say that English is the one, authoritative, true, absolute language. So we get much better agreement on speaking English than about moral behavior just because we don't put such heavy sanctions on it. We don't swat the fly on the friend's head with a hatchet.

I feel that a schizophrenic universe in which there is an infinite gulf between the creator and the creature is an unthinkable and absurd system. It's as if—and many people feel this—it's as if the universe were primarily a whole lot of things, a sort of cosmic flotsam and jetsam that happened to gather together from nowhere. Whereas I like to think of the world the other way around. For example, I like to think of it as a star that radiates from a center, where all the differences in the world are linked in a fundamental unity. Just as petals come out of a flower, as rays from a star, as legs from a spider, as tentacles from an octopus, as spines of a sea-urchin, all of us are the many, many functions and doings of one center. Then I feel I have an integrated universe, a whole universe, and thus a holy universe.

Now, then, if we take this point of view as fundamental, what is the place of worship? You might say in this kind of religious philosophy there is no place for worship because worship as most of us understand it is kowtowing. Historically, most forms of worship in the West—Jewish, Christian, and Islamic—are based on the idea of the behavior of a subject in the courtroom of a monarch. Here the monarch sits on his throne, and everybody who comes in bows or prostrates himself. Why do people prostrate themselves? A monarch is a person who is fundamentally afraid. For if you take the world in hand to govern it by force, you must be frightened since everybody will be trying to take the power from you. So when you come into the presence of an absolute monarch he has his back and his throne against the wall, his guards on either side, and everybody prostrates himself because in that position they can't attack. And so it is with worship in Christianity, as we have known it in the past, whether Catholic or Protestant.

This form of worship is exactly what goes on in the court of a king. Indeed, the great cathedrals are sometimes called basilica because that is the place of the king. There is the throne, very often behind the high altar where the representative of the monarch, the representative of the Lord of Heaven, the bishop, archbishop, or pope or whoever he may be, sits, and the ceremonial is based on the court ceremonials of Roman and Byzantine emperors. In the Protestant churches, the scene is not very different. It's republican rather than monarchical since the protestant church is modeled after a court of justice. The presiding person doesn't wear royal vestments. He wears the black gown of a judge. There are boxes and stall and a pulpit. You get behind a stall to protect you from the people, just in the same way as the judge. But still it's based on a court scene. Both of these forms of worship presuppose that God is something not *in* us but *above* us. Even if in some sense he is within us, he is above us. And, although he may be within us, we have to worship him externally. Actually, we're turning things around to worship that which is *in* us but *not* us—not fundamentally us—but always infinitely other.

This is an attitude suitable to human beings who have been bamboozled into being afraid. Thus, when they hear the thunder they cower a little; they think about their guilty conscience and wonder if the lightning is going to hit them. But this is an attitude suitable to childhood, and perhaps it may not even be very suitable to childhood. But it is a childlike attitude, or rather, a childish attitude, bowing down to authority not realizing that you yourself are the source of that authority. If you say, "I believe in the Bible or the Church because I'm *told* to do so," your belief is an act of obedience. Don't kid yourself. But it was your *choice* to obey, wasn't it? *You* give to whatever you believe such authority as it has for you. So you may say that Protestants interpret the Bible in their own way. Catholics interpret the Bible as they're told to. And therefore they're more obedient. But that's not true because they consented to it in the first place. It was their choice to accept the authority of the Church, which interprets the Bible. So it is fundamentally on your authority that you assent to any kind of religious doctrine and belief.

Now if there could be some form of worship that is relating oneself communally—all worship is fundamentally something we do together—relating ourselves communally to the heart of the universe, something that is concentric with the real heart in every one of us, what would the pattern of such worship be? We're thinking in symbolism. The old pattern of worship was the courtroom, and the thing we all look at is down at the end, whether it is the altar or the preacher. But a worship that represents God in everybody would be radial. I recently went to France and visited many of the great French cathedrals. In almost every one of them they have moved the altar to the middle of the cathedral. Instead of being far up at the East end, it's right at the crossing. And when the mass is celebrated, the congregation now stands the whole way around the altar, and the priest is in the middle. What does this mean? What's happening? Maybe the dear old church is waking up. Perhaps it is.

Now I offer a rather daring proposal that in some places is not accepted. It is the idea that the act of Christian worship, the mass, the Holy Communion, the Lord's Supper, or whatever you want to call it, is not something you go to see like you go to see a movie. It's something in which you participate. It's not something you hear or witness; it's something you *do*. For example, in the Eastern Church, the church of Greece and Russia, they don't say, "to say mass"; they say, "to make the liturgy." To *make* it. *Poiein* in Greek means not only to make, to do, but also is the root word for poetry, the act of creation.

For a moment may we consider the meaning of this fundamental act of worship in Christianity? Its possibilities for an altogether new feeling of worship are very important. I want to consider it from two points of view. First of all, the original action of Jesus in being with his intimate disciples before he was crucified and instituting what was for those people in that time an absolutely outrageous ceremony. He took the bread and broke it and said "This is my body." Then he took the cup and said "This is my blood of the New Testament, which is shed for you and for many for the remission of sins. Drink it." Now you couldn't say anything more startling to a Jew because the one supreme taboo for the Jew was that you mustn't drink blood, for blood is life and the blood belongs to God alone. When an animal is killed, the blood is poured upon the ground as an offering to the Lord. Jesus was saying, so to speak, from now on drinking the blood signifies for each one of you your oneness with God.

From the second point of view, all life is maintained by eating and drinking. Bread is ground wheat. Wine is crushed grapes, fermented. Upon the sacrifice of the wheat and the grapes depends our life. We are killing something, whether it be vegetables, cows, chickens, turkeys or what not. We are all killing something in order to live. Each one of us, deep down in his heart, has probably a profound sense of guilt for living only at the expense of other life. So when Jesus said "This is my blood which is shed for you for the remission (the putting away) of sins," it means this: Don't feel guilty anymore that you have to drink the grapes and eat the crushed wheat, because all that you eat is me, and I'm offering myself to you and it is my pleasure. I am the one you kill when you kill the cow, and I give myself to you because I am before Abraham was. I am the way, the truth, and the life. I am, therefore, that disguised godhead in all beings whose sacrifice is the act of playing that I am not God, but that I am all creatures. I dismember myself in the beginning of the creation, and after a time I remember myself. Hence, do this in remembrance of me. In other words, as the scattered grain is brought together in one loaf, we are made to realize that we are all one body. "I am the vine and you are branches," and the "I am" is the central "I" in every one of us.

Now let's look at that analogy further. First of all, it is no longer the analogy of the creator above and the miserable little creatures like subjects of the king below. Instead, it is the vine, the tree, the central stem and all the branches coming out from it. Secondly, the basic idea of traditional Christian worship is not that it is man talking to God, addressing petitions, and so on, as if one were to present himself in the court of the king and say, "Your majesty, your humble subjects request that you do so-and-so for us." The very idea of the liturgy of the mass of the Holy Communion as being the central act of worship shows something quite different. Actually, Christian worship is based on the notion of God as Trinity, as a cycle of love. In worship, that aspect of God, which is called the Father loves the Son through the Holy Spirit, so that there is a cycle of love going on. Christian worship was originally intended to be man getting caught up in the cycle like you might catch something in a vortex of a whirlpool. So the worship of God is not what man does to God, but what God does to himself through man. Thus, for example, when Benedictine monks recite the psalms in what they call the Divine Office, they have the idea that the words of the song are the words of the Holy Spirit, not their own personal words. When they sing the songs, the Holy Spirit is talking through their mouths. All worship thus originates in God and returns to God.

In the Christian philosophy, therefore, worship would be defined as God's love for himself through man in which man is like the flute, the reed that is played upon by the wind of the spirit. So you can see that already there is, in germ, the idea that worship is radial. It is not something done to something over there out there. It is not the confrontation of I, man, with Thou, God, because where do these things that confront each other come from? Where do these opposites originate? From somewhere way off? No. The secret is that all opposites, all poles are two ends of the same thing. You can't even arrange a meeting between things that are really opposite; you can't even get them together. But in the poles lies the secret of opposites. We don't know black without white; we don't know light without darkness; we don't know long without short; we don't know infinite without finite; we don't know being without nonbeing. That means that there is a secret conspiracy between them—to look different, like Tweedledum and Tweedledee. Before all diversity there is unity. Before all differences there is agreement. We must agree in order to differ. There can't be a battle between the tiger and the shark. They have no common ground, no common field.

What should be the kind of worship that truly expresses the radial view of the cosmos as distinct from the confrontational view? To be frank with you, I was once a clergyman. I gave it up because it didn't suit my temperament. I was a little bit too much of a bohemian, and also I just couldn't preach at people. It went against the grain. But when I was a clergyman, an Episcopalian chaplain at Northwestern University, I used to say to the students: "Now look here, nobody is allowed to come to church here out of a sense of duty. We don't want skeletons at the banquet. If you feel that you *ought* to come to church, stay in bed on Sunday morning. But if you'd *like* to come, please come. For I announce that there will be a celebration of the Holy Communion, and I mean a celebration."

What are we doing here fundamentally, despite all the agony that the crucifixion represents on the surface, what is deep down here is the joy of the celebration. For it is written in the book of Proverbs that God with divine wisdom creates the universe by playing. Wisdom speaks and says, "I was playing before him, playing in the world, and my delight was with the sons of men." Of course, the King James version, which is rather a pompous translation, says "Rejoice." But the correct Hebrew is "play." So the whole notion here is that worship is making celestial whoopee.

In the Christian mythology—and I don't use the word "myth" disrespectfully, but simply as any idea expressed in images rather than abstract terms—in the Christian mythology, what are the angels doing in heaven? What is the end of man? They say it is the Beatific Vision. To behold God. Well, what's the good of that? But, if God is "the Which than which there is no whicher," then when you are there, you're *there*. There's nothing else to do, so all the angels call out, "Alleluia, Alleluia, Alleluia." Alleluia doesn't mean anything. It's just as if you were so crazy with happiness that you went wh-e-e-e-e. All you could do was just shout for joy.

So from this point of view, God is that which is perfectly useless. Not good for anything at all because he is perfection, and there is nothing else that it serves, no greater ends to which it leads, absolutely of no consequence whatsoever. No consequence. That's what a Buddhist means when he says that the highest state is freedom from *karma*. It is of no effect anymore. It isn't a cause-effect scene. It isn't leading to something because it's already there. You've arrived. And so in this way, all profound worship is a celebration of having arrived. It's where we join hands and dance.

For dancing is very profound. When you dance, you are not going anywhere. You are not aiming at a certain spot on the floor. When you play music, you're not trying to reach the final bar, for if that were the point of music, the best musician would be one who played the fastest, gets there first. There would thus be pianists who would specialize in playing only final chords.

If life is anything like music, it has no aim to get anywhere. But we are all hypnotized, especially in western civilization, into the idea that life is supposed to get somewhere. The result is that when we do get where we think we're going, we don't enjoy it, because we are then thinking about getting somewhere else. A person who lives for the future is never living in the present, so he never gets anywhere. It's of no use for him to plan for the future because when he gets there he can't enjoy it.

The idea of centrality, this whole radial idea I'm talking about, is to know how to be "all here." It's a definition of sanity. Nobody can be sane, really sane, unless he preserves a central area in his life for craziness, that is, for perfect uselessness, for "whoopee,"—for absolutely nothing except blub-blub-blub-blub. That's the touchstone of sanity. The difficulty with most people, especially when they make a religious scene, is that they're too rigid.

You know what happens to an absolutely rigid bridge. When the wind blows it breaks. A strong bridge has to have a little bit of give in it. It's like the movement of the hips in dancing—a little bit of swing. And if you don't have that, you're nutty as a fruitcake. You're insane and you'll fall apart; you'll break down. You have no faith; you have no give. So that worship that corresponds to the Sabbath—remember, that's the day on which the Lord didn't do any work, and said, "Holiday!" *Holy* day—which is a day for laying on the law, for rationality, for listening to sermons, and that's just terrible. Instead, a church should be a place where people go out of their minds for a while and have a great celebration. The idea of the bread and wine is that this is the most friendly thing imaginable. Get a little bit drunk—not too much—and have good bread. It's very difficult to get good bread nowadays, because it's all made out of ticky tacky. That's a combination of paper maché, plaster of Paris, and plastic glue; it comes in any flavor. That's a sign of how remote our culture is from fundamental Christian ideals. For in Christianity, material is very important. "God so loved the world. . . ." And that means honest bread and things like that. Good wine had body to it. But we are trying to get everything disembodied. Eventually, we'll just take some pills and that will be that; it's almost that way now.

In this fundamental idea of worship, the spirit and the flesh are together, and the flesh is seen as the rays, the doings, the activity of the spirit. It is a coming-together in a spirit of celebrating the fact that we are all branches of one vine; that the real deep-down inmost self in us all is the dancer of the worlds, as the Hindus think of the Lord as the great juggler with many arms. Imagine the God with ten arms, each hand juggling ten balls and each ball a galaxy. "Is he going to make it"? We watch with terror this act of juggling. Then suddenly he drops one, and everybody covers his eyes and says "Oh-oh." There's an immense explosion. We think it's the end, but we look again, and suddenly we see all the fragments of that broken ball have turned into ten more gods with ten arms juggling ten balls each. "Good old Shiva," we say, "he did it again." This alternation of terror and suspense, suddenly bursting into joy, is the systole and the diastole of being.

CHAPTER SEVENTEEN

Western Mythology

Its Dissolution and Transformation (1970)

When at the service of Morning Prayer a priest of the Church of England addresses himself to the origin and foundation of the Universe, he will usually make the following statement:

> Almighty and Everlasting God, King of Kings, Lord of Lords, the only Ruler of Princes, Who dost from Thy Throne behold all the dwellers upon Earth, most heartily we beseech Thee with Thy favor to behold our sovereign lady Elizabeth the Queen and all the royal family. Endue her plenteously with heavenly gifts, health and wealth, long to live, etc.

This is obviously the language of a professional flatterer in court. For the most basic model or image of the world that has governed Western civilization has been the idea of the universe as a political monarchy, and this is something extremely troublesome to citizens of the United States, a country in which we are supposed to believe that a republic is the best form of government. But an enormous number of our citizens believe that the universe is a monarchy and, obviously, if the universe is a monarchy, monarchy is the best form of government. Thus until quite recently you could not be a conscientious objector to fighting in a war unless you solemnly declared that you believed in a Supreme Being from whom your orders came, and therefore from a higher echelon of command than the President of the United States.

From *Myths, Dreams, and Religion*, edited by J. Campbell, 1970. New York, NY: Dutton. Copyright ©1970 by Society for the Arts, Religion, and Contemporary Culture. Reprinted with permission of the Society for the Arts, Religion, and Contemporary Culture.

This proved to be difficult for people who declared themselves to be Buddhists or Taoists who do not believe in a Supreme Being in that sense, although I did advise many conscientious objectors that when the lawmakers put in words "Supreme Being," they were trying to find a vague phrase rather than to define a kind of theistic belief. In 1928 the British Parliament was called upon to authorize a new prayer book for the Church of England. They didn't authorize it because they found it too "high church." But in the course of the debate, somebody got up and said, "Isn't it sort of ridiculous that this secular legislative body should be asked to rule upon the affairs of the Church because, after all, there are many atheists among us?" And another member got up and said, "Oh, I don't think there are any atheists here. We all believe in some sort of something somewhere." And so, I suppose the phrase "the Supreme Being" means some sort of something somewhere.

The foundation of common sense behind a great many of the laws and social institutions of the United States is a theory of the universe based on the ancient tyrannical monarchies of the Near East. Such titles of God "King of Kings" and "Lord of Lords" were in fact titles of the Persian emperors. The Pharaohs of Egypt and the lawgiver Hammurabi provided a model for thinking about this world. For the fundamental idea that underlies the imagery of the book of Genesis, and therefore of the Jewish, Islamic, and Christian traditions, is that the universe is a system of order that is imposed by spiritual force from above, and to which we therefore owe obedience. In this idea there is a complex of subideas as follows:

(1) That the physical world is an artifact. It is something made or constructed. Furthermore, this involves the idea that it is a ceramic creation. In the book of Genesis, it is said that the Lord God created Adam out of the dust of the earth, and having therefore made a clay figurine, he breathed the breath of life into its nostrils and this clay figurine became the embodiment of a living spirit. This is a basic image that has entered very deeply into the common sense of most people who have lived in the Western world. Thus it's quite natural for a child brought up in Western culture to say to its mother, "How was I made?" We think that that's a very logical thing to ask, "How was I *made?*" But actually this is a question that I don't think would be asked by a Chinese child. It wouldn't occur. The Chinese child might say, "How did I grow?" But certainly not, "How was I made?" In the sense of being constructed, being put together, being formed out of some basic, inert, and therefore essentially stupid substance. For when you take the image of clay you don't expect ever to see clay forming itself into a pot. Clay is passive. Clay is homogenized. It has in itself no particular structure. It's a kind of goo. And therefore if it is to assume an intelligible shape, it must be worked upon by an external force and intelligence. So you have the dichotomy of matter and form, which you find also in Aristotle and therefore later in the whole philosophy of St. Thomas Aquinas. Matter is a kind of basic stuff that becomes formed only through the

intervention of spiritual energy. This has been, of course, a basic problem of all our thinking—the problem of the relationship between mind and matter.

For how can mind exercise influence upon matter? After all, all good ghosts walk straight through walls, and if a ghost in its passage through a wall does not disarrange the bricks how can the ghost in the machine, the ghost in the body, lift an arm or move a head? This has been a fundamental problem for Western thought because we have made this distinction between the unintelligent brute matter and the intelligent active spirit.

In much of our philosophy of art, in the West, we have thought of the work of the artist as that of imposing his will upon an intractable medium. The sculptor beating stones into submission to his will. The painter taking inert oils and pigments and making them conform . . . and so many of our sculptors and painters feel all the time that the media in which they work are intractable, and that they can never quite get it across because the physical, material, and therefore in some way diabolical nature of the media always resists the vision that the spirit wants to represent. Even such a great historian of art as Andre Malraux speaks of this tension between the vision of the artist, his will and his technique, and the base, material intractability of the medium. So, also, in everybody's everyday common sense we think of the world, the material world, as being a sort of amalgam of clay, of matter that is *formed*. We might even be so strangely depraved as to think that trees are made of wood. Or mountains made of rock in the same way as this podium is *made* of wood by a carpenter, and perhaps it is not insignificant that Jesus was the son of a carpenter as well as being the son of the Architect of the universe. Obviously a tree is not made of wood. A tree *is* wood. A mountain is not made of rock. It *is* rock. The whole point of western science to understand the nature of the physical world was originally, of course, a quest to find out what is the basic material and beyond that, what is the plan, the design, in the mind of the maker?

At this time, Western physics has abandoned the question, "What is matter?" because of the realization that you can describe physical processes only in terms of structure, in terms of form, in terms of pattern. You can never say what *stuff* is. Whenever a scientific description comes in the form of an equation, say $a + b = b + a$ or $1 + 2 = 3$ everybody understands what it means. It's a perfectly intelligible statement. Without anyone having to say what "a" signifies, what "b" signifies, or one-what, two-what, or three-what. The pattern itself is sufficient. For it is the understanding of modern physics that what is going on in the world, what we are, is simply pattern. Imagine, for example, a rope in which the first three feet are made of hemp, the second of silk, the third of cotton, and the forth of nylon, and you tie a knot in the rope, a simple granny knot, and you move the knot along the rope. The material of the knot keeps changing but the pattern of the knot remains the same. In just this way, each one of us is recognizable as an individual by virtue of being a consistent pattern of behavior. Anything that could be described as our substance, that is to say, the milk, the water, the beefsteak, etc., that composes us (for we are what we eat) is constantly changing, and anything that could be considered as a kind of component stuff of our bodies is always passing through, but today you know your friend of yesterday, because you recognize a consistent pattern of behavior. So what science studies, what science now describes, is simply patterns. But the average individual has not yet recovered from the superstition that underneath patterns, inside patterns, there is basically some kind of stuff. For when we examine anything we see first of all the pattern, the shape, and then we ask the question, "What is the shape composed of?" So we get out our microscope to look very carefully at what we thought was the substance of, say, a finger. We find that the so-called substance of the finger is a minute and beautiful design of cells. We see a structure, but then when we see these little patterns called individual cells, we ask again, "What are they made of?" and that needs a sharper microscope, a more minute analysis. Turning up the level of magnification again, we find that the cells are molecules but we keep asking, "What is the stuff of the molecules?" What we are in fact discovering through all of this is that what we are calling "stuff" is simply patterns seen out of focus. It's fuzzy, and simply fuzziness is stuff. Whenever we get fuzziness into focus, it becomes patterns. So there isn't any stuff, there is only pattern. This world is dancing energy.

Though this is the point of view of the latest scientific thought of the West, it is not the average person's common sense. This is not yet the image in terms of which individuals make sense of the world, and that is my definition of "myth." Myth, not meaning falsehood, but in a much deeper sense of the word, is an imagery in terms of which we make sense out of life. When somebody is trying to explain electricity to the nonscientific laymen, he uses, say, the imagery of water, of how water flows, and he explains, through water, which the laymen understands, the behavior of electricity that the layman does not understand. Or an astronomer in trying to explain the nature of curved space will liken the construction of space to the surface of a balloon on which there are white dots. As you inflate the balloon, the dots get further and further away from each other, and this is somewhat like the expanding universe. He is using an image; he's not saying, "The world *is* a balloon;" he is saying, "It's *like* a balloon." So in, of course, the same way, no sensible theologian ever said that God is literally the father of the universe—that God is a cosmic male parent—but that God is *like* a father. This is analogy. But the image always has a more powerful influence on our feelings than abstract and sophisticated ideas. Therefore the image of God as the political king, the authority father, has had a vast influence upon the emotions and feelings of Christians, Jews, and Moslems throughout many, many, centuries. But in the course of time it became an embarrassing image that had to be abandoned, for nobody wants to feel that he is watched all the time by a judging authority however beneficent his intentions may be. You well remember when you were children in school,

sitting at your desks writing some sort of composition or performing a mathematical exercise, and the teacher would sometimes wander along behind you
and look over your shoulder to see what you were doing. Nobody likes this.
Even though you respect your teacher very much you don't want to be watched
while you are working. So the idea that we are constantly observed by one
who knows us through and through and judges us is profoundly embarrassing;
we simply had to get rid of it. Thus there came about the "Death of God,"
that is to say, the death of that particular *idea* of God. For it was substituted,
in the course of the development of Western thought in the eighteenth and
nineteenth centuries, a different model of the universe, which had, however,
continuity with the model of the universe handed down to us through the
Holy Scriptures and the Christian tradition.

Let me remind you that the model of the world, the world made by God,
was basically an artifact, a construct, a mechanism, and therefore something
governed by law. All processes in the universe were looked upon as operating
in obedience to the word of God. For as it says in the Bible, "By the word of
the Lord were the heavens made and all the hosts of them by the breath of
his mouth." In the beginning was the Word . . . so

> *There was a young man who said, "damn!"*
> *For it certainly seems that I am*
> *A creature that moves*
> *In determinate grooves:*
> *I am not even a bus, I'm a tram.*

The whole quest for knowledge in the Western world was to ascertain
the laws, the Word, which is laid down in the beginning and which is obeyed
by all living processes. If we could understand the word of God, we could
predict the future. Much, therefore, of the Scriptures, especially of the Old
Testament, consists of books of prophecy written by those who had heard
the word of the Lord and who knew what was going to happen. This is the
foundation of Western science. The idea of prophecy, of prediction, because
if you know the future, you can prepare for it and control it. But at the same
time this also contains within itself a kind of nemesis, because if you know
the future, the one thing the future tells you for certain is "death and taxes."
Especially death . . . you are going to die. You are going to come to an end.
The future can only be successful for a while, but in the end comes the doom,
unless you can project that, by supernatural intervention, beyond the doom,
the inevitable decay of all physical forms, there will be a resurrection of the
body. Death follows from the inherent intractability and stupidity of matter.
The spirit cannot finally conquer matter and all the things that we create out
of our clay will fall apart, because the formlessness and heaviness of matter
will overcome it. But we project beyond this the hope that spirit will in the end

be more powerful and will be able to miraculize matter and make it immortal. The idea of the resurrection of the body involves the transformation of matter into everlasting life.

That is the technological enterprise of the West. That is what we are after. All technology, especially in medicine where we now transplant hearts, is trying to make matter subservient to the will, to spirit, and to immortalize it. But is that what we really want? I think that on entrance to college every student should be obliged to write an essay called "My idea of Heaven," and it would be emphasized that he had to be extremely specific and really spell out in most particular terms what it is that he wants. Blow the expense, forget practicalities, what would you like to have? What would your greatest ideal of pleasure be? It might well be that if we thought that through, we would not want immortality of the individual personality. We might find that, in the end, it would turn out to be a horrible bore. But ordinarily we don't think these things through. I'm fascinated with all the various kinds of imagery of heaven, with what people would expect it to be like. But they only touch on it, they never go into detail. People go into much more detail about the imagery of hell; that's been worked out in very fine detail. All the tortures have been specified. But of the imagery of heaven we just say, "Oh, it'll be great. We'll have streets paved with gold, harps to play," and children get disgusted right away. "Do you mean that after we're dead, we're gonna have to be in church forever?" Well, that's horrible! Look, too, at the religious art of the Western world. I think particularly of the painting by Jan Van Eyck, *The Last Judgment*. Above there is heaven, below there is hell. Heaven is a solid mass of people sitting in pews, a row of heads like cobblestones on a street. They're looking very demure and just sitting there, and below . . . wowee! The squirming mass of writhing bodies all naked and erotic being eaten up by serpents, presided over by a bat-winged skull. Hell is *something* to look at! Heaven isn't. So, somehow or other we don't think through what we think we desire. As the proverb says, "Be careful of what you desire, you may get it."

We had, then, to get rid of this image of God as the autocratic ruler because it was very uncomfortable. But we justified this by making a still more uncomfortable image as a sort of rationalization. We began to feel belief in a universe that cares about us, in a "ground of being" that is personal and interested in us. This is woolly and wishful thinking. It was all right for little old ladies and perhaps as a story for children, but tough-minded people, to borrow a phrase from William James, faced the facts and the facts are that the universe does not give a damn about human beings or any other species. It is a completely mindless mechanical process whose principles are to be explained by analogy with the game of billiards. This was, of course, the model upon which Newton thought about the physical world. In line with Newton, Freud thought about the physical world in terms of hydraulics—psycho-hydraulics is basic to Freud's thinking—the idea of the unconscious as a river that can be damned up and the dam has to be controlled in some way because the river is also mindless. It is also called libido, and that means "blind lust." Likewise Ernst Haeckel thought of the energy of the world as *blind* energy. It was all mechanical, and our second great model of the world, which I shall call the fully automatic model, was a carryover from the Judeo-Christian model; it was an artifact, and thus a machine, but the artificer and the controller, the personal God, had disappeared, and you were simply left with the mechanism.

Now in this scheme of things the human being was regarded as a fluke, a statistical fluke, as when you have a million monkeys working on a million typewriters for a million years, the chances are that at some point they will type the *Encyclopaedia Britannica*. But the human being regarded as a fluke is not really very different from the human being regarded as the product of a divine whim. God is very whimsical in the book of Genesis. Suddenly he created great whales. Like that! He looked at them, and saw that they were good. He didn't know that they were going to be good, but when he saw what he had done he said, "That's okay. I approve of it." There is always that kind of fluky feeling. Thus the belief that you are a fluke in a mindless, mechanical gyration is, as a matter of fact, what most people believe today.

We have very few religious people in the Western world because most people really do not believe in Christianity even though they may be Jehovah's Witnesses. What they feel is what they *ought* to believe, and they feel very guilty because they don't really believe. So they preach at each other and say, "You really ought to have faith," but don't really believe it because if they did they'd be screaming in the streets. They'd be taking enormous full page ads in the *New York Times* every day, and having horrendous television programs about the Last Judgment. But even when the Jehovah's Witnesses call at your door, they're quite courteous. They don't really believe it. It's simply become implausible and what everybody does in fact believe is the image of the fully automatic model, that we are chance gyrations in a universe where we are like bacteria inhabiting a rock ball that revolves about an insignificant star on the outer fringes of a minor galaxy. And, after a while, that will be that. When you're dead, you're dead. It'll be over. In our ordinary, everyday thought and common speech, we use such phrases as, "I came into this world," or we could quote the poet Housman saying,

> I, a stranger and afraid
> In a world I never made.

There is a sense of somehow not belonging. Of course, if you are a fluke, in that sense you *don't* belong. Likewise, if you are an incarcerated spirit from a spiritual world quite other than this material world, you don't belong. There is in most civilized people's common sense the feeling that you look upon this world as something outside you, foreign to you, alien to you, and so we naturally say, "You must *face* the facts. You must *confront* reality." The "Existential Encounter!" The truth of the matter is that you didn't come *into* this world at all. You came *out* of it, in just the same way that a leaf comes out of a tree or a baby from a womb. You are symptomatic of this world.

Thus if you are intelligent (and I guess we just have to assume as a leap of faith that human beings are intelligent) you are symptomatic of an intelligent energy system, just as Jesus said that one doesn't gather figs from thistles or grapes from thorns. So also you don't gather people from a world that isn't peopling. Our world is peopling just as the apple tree apples, and just as the vine grapes. We are symptomatic of an extremely organized and complex environment. You do not find an intelligent organism in an unintelligent environment in exactly the same way that you do not find apples growing on cottonwood trees. Isn't it curious then, that, especially in the nineteenth century, when the prevailing philosophy of science was called scientific naturalism (involving repudiation of the notion that the world was governed by external and supernatural intelligence) that people calling themselves naturalists began to wage an unprecedented war on nature. The naturalists were those who thought nature is stupid, and therefore that if the values and the intelligence of mankind are to persist, we must beat nature into submission to our wills. We thus initiated a form of technology whose basic premise was that man must dominate rather than cooperate with nature. Our technology has been motivated by a hostile spirit whose two great mythological symbols are the space rocket and the bulldozer.

The space rocket is, quite obviously, a phallic symbol, and a hostile phallus. This has something to do, I suppose, with our sexual inadequacies. A phallus in the biological sense is not a weapon at all; it is a caressing instrument. The whole idea of the phallus is to give a woman ecstasy, and perhaps a baby. It's not to pierce her as if it were a sword. Thus the proper conception of a rocket should not be to conquer space . . . but could you possibly imagine the idea of giving pleasure to space, or our going out into space to confer love and delight upon any other beings that may be out there, and to fertilize naked planets? In the same way the symbol of the bulldozer is to make a horrible fulfillment of the biblical prophecy that "every valley shall be exalted and every mountain laid low and the rough places plane," an attitude of pushing the world around. It is therefore absolutely urgent for our survival that we put behind technology a completely new spirit and attitude. This is not an antitechnological attitude. It is not saying that science is a ghastly mistake, but that what we need is not less science but more. We need more and more study and understanding of our complex relationships to and dependence upon plants, insects, bacteria, gases, astronomical processes—and the more we understand how our existence is one process with the existence of all these other creatures and things, the more we can use technology in an intelligent way, regarding the world outside of ourselves as simply an extension or part of our own bodies.

But the transformation of Western mythology must involve yet another step. We have been through the political image of the universe as ruled and dominated by an essentially violent lawgiver. Incidentally, all preaching, the whole organization of our churches, is violent, it's military. In *Paradise Lost* Milton described what was going on in heaven before Lucifer even thought of rebelling. There were armies with banners and all the heraldic emblems of battle and force. Who's looking for trouble? Think of all the imagery that we love in our churches, of how many people have a heartthrob when they sing the hymn "Onward Christian Soldier?" And the "Cross of Jesus, going on before," the military banner. *In hoc signo vinces.* But the military model of imposing order upon the world by violence hasn't worked, and the whole history of religion is the history of the failure of preaching. Preaching only makes hypocrites, people imitate righteousness because they are afraid of the wrath of God, or afraid in a more sophisticated way of being unreal or unauthentic persons, which is the new version of going to hell. It doesn't work. The fully automatic model doesn't work either, because that is simply another form of hostility. It's saying "I'm a real tough guy because I face the facts, and this universe is just a stupid affair, and if you're a realistic fellow, you're going to face it, see? If you want to believe in God, or that something cares, you're just a sentimental old lady. This is a tough thing, see? The more I believe that the universe is horrible, the more it advertises me as a tough personality, facing the facts."

But somehow more in line with twentieth-century science would be an *organic* image of the world, the world as a body, as a vast pattern of intelligent energy that has a new relationship to us. We are not in it as subjects of a king, or as victims of a blind process. We are not *in* it at all. We *are* it! It's you. Every individual in this organic myth of the world must look upon himself as responsible for the world. You can't look back at your parents and say, "You got me mixed up in this, damn you!" In juvenile courts, children who have learned a little about psychoanalysis can say, "It's not my fault I'm a criminal type. It's that I got mixed up by my mother, and I had Oedipus complex." Then the press says, "Well, then, it's not the children who're at fault; we've got to take care of the parents," and the parents say, "We really can't help it that we're neurotic, it was *our* parents got us mixed up." It goes right back to the story in the Garden of Eden: when Adam was asked by the Lord God "Didst thou eat the fruit of the tree whereof I told thee thou shouldst not eat?" Adam replied, "This woman, that thou gavest to me, she tempted me, and I did eat." And when he said to Eve, "Didst thou eat, etc., she said, "The serpent beguiled me . . ." and the Lord God looked at the serpent and the serpent said nothing. He didn't pass the buck. He knew the answer because the serpent and the Lord God had agreed, long before all this happened, behind the scenes before anything started, that they were going to play out this drama because the serpent is the left hand of God and "let not your right hand know what your left hand doeth." So you see, that's the game, the game of hide-and-seek.

I don't see any possibility of, what I would call, a basically healthy attitude to life in which you blame other people for what happens. As it would be said in Buddhism, everything that happens to you is your *karma*; that means your own doing. It may sound a little megalomaniac, as if to say, well I'm responsible for all this, like I'm God. That's megalomania only if you use the monarchical image of God, which is why we cannot say in the West, "I am God." They then put you in the nut-house because you're saying, "I'm the boss, and you owe me divine honors."

But if we have another image of God, an organic image, similar to the human body, who's in charge? The head? The stomach? The heart? You could make an argument for each of them. You could say that the stomach is fundamental, it was there first. It is the organ that distributes vitality through food to all other organs. Therefore the stomach is primary. You can argue that the head, a ganglion of nerves on the top end of the alimentary canal, is an adjunct of the stomach and was evolved in order to scrounge around more intelligently to get some stuff to feed the stomach. Then the head stands up and argues, "No, I came later, and of course, the stomach was there first, but John the Baptist came before Jesus Christ, and I as the head am latest and most evolved product, and the stomach is my servant. The stomach is scrounging around to give me energy so that I can indulge in philosophy, culture, and religion and art." Both arguments are equally valid or equally invalid. The point about an organism is that it's a cooperation, that is, as Lao-Tzu says, "To be or not to be arise mutually. Long and short subtend each other; difficult and easy imply each other." So do subject and object, I and thou. Inside and outside. They all come into being together. So do heart and head, head and stomach. They are mutual and there is a cooperation in which the order does not derive from imposition from above, from an orderer. So Lao-Tzu speaks of the Tao, the course and order of nature, saying, "The great Tao extends everywhere, both to the left and to the right. It loves and nourishes all things but does not lord it over them, and when merits are accomplished, it lays no claim to them." Likewise, "In governing a great state, do it as you cook a small fish," for when you cook a small fish, don't fuss with it; be very gentle. Don't overdo it.

So we can look forward, perhaps, to a day when the President of the United States may be someone as anonymous as chief sanitary engineer of New York City, who is a very valuable individual performing a most useful function. But when the chief sanitary engineer of New York City goes out in the streets, there is no fanfare, there are no huge escorts of police, for who could care about the sanitary engineer? Even in the Christian tradition there is an odd hint of this. In his *Epistle to the Philippians*, St. Paul says: "Let this mind be in you which was also in Christ Jesus, who being in the form of God, did not think equality with God a thing to be clung to, but made himself of no reputation and was found in fashion as a man and became obedient to death, even to the death of the cross." The self-emptying or renunciation of power by the godhead is called in Greek *kenosis*, self-emptying. The idea that God creates the world by giving up power, by instituting a constitutional monarchy instead of a tyrannical one.

For everybody who has really understood power and the power game, like certain great sages and yogis in Asia who have practiced all sorts of psychic powers, realizes that psychic powers are not the answer. All manuals of yoga and Buddhistic practice will tell you that the *siddhi* or supernormal powers ought to be abandoned because power is not the answer. That's not what you want. See, we get back to the question of thinking through what you want. If you get absolute power and you are in perfect control of everything that happens, which would be the final ideal of technology, you realize what would happen? You have a completely predictable future, you're the perfect prophet, you know everything that's going to happen, and the moment you know everything that's going to happen, you've had it. Because the perfectly known future is a past. When in the course of playing games, it becomes quite certain what the outcome of the game will be, we always, of course don't we, abandon the game and begin a new one because what we want is a surprise. And as one very wise man whom I knew once said to me, "*Gnosis*, the perfect wisdom or enlightenment, is to be surprised at everything."

CHAPTER EIGHTEEN

The Future of Religion (1970)

One of the major roots of tension and paranoia in the United States today is the conflict between religion and politics. It has a fascinating history, which is largely a religious history. Most citizens of the United States who claim to be religious are either Christians or Jews, inheriting a form of religion that is based on a monarchical model of the universe. But the nation itself is a republic, ideally and theoretically democratic, having philosophical origins in an outburst of mysticism that occurred in Western Europe in the thirteenth and fourteenth centuries, associated with such individuals as Meister Eckhart, John of Ruysbroek, Angelus Silesius, and Richard Tauler, and with such movements as the Anabaptists, the Brothers of the Free Spirit, the Levellers, and the Quakers, which arose in the three centuries following as a consequence of this mystical outburst.[1]

Mysticism implies democracy because it is the discovery of what George Fox called the Inward Light in the hearts of all men, of God not only above but also within, thus challenging the authority of the state and the divine right of kings with the authority of the individual conscience. It realizes and implements the views that all men are equal in the sight of God, or rather, at the level of their inmost divinity. From such insights and stirrings as these, as well as from economic pressures, hundreds and then thousands left the feudal and monarchical order of Europe, came to this country, and eventually established a republic as their form of government.

From *Toward Century 21: Technology, Society, and Human Values*, edited by C. S. Wallia, Copyright © 1970. Reprinted by permission of Basic Books, a member of the Perseus Books Group.

THE HINDU CONCEPTION OF GOD

How can one believe that a republic is the best form of government if, at the same time, one believes that the universe is a monarchy? For, obviously, if the universe is a monarchy with God himself in charge, then monarchical principles are the best for ruling. Jews, Catholics, and Fundamentalist Protestants believe emphatically that God is the heavenly king and father who must above all be obeyed. However, is it possible to be religious, to have faith in God, without believing that the universe is a monarchy? Does the idea of God necessarily imply the principle of monarchy at the base of the universe? Surely not, for there are, outside the Western world, many traditional and, for want of a better word, religious views of the universe wherein God—or whatever name may be used for the ultimate reality—is not conceived as a monarch. This would generally be true for the Hindu, and most definitely for the Buddhist and Taoist. The Hindu does not see God as ruling the universe as a king imposes order by force on inferior subjects. He sees God, not as ruling, but as acting the world as a drama in which he is the player of all the parts, so that the whole multiplicity of individual beings are not his subjects but his roles and masks (personae). Usually, the actor himself is so absorbed in each part that he forgets he is merely playing, but, in certain individual instances, he wakes up and says, "Well, at last I have discovered that I am God in disguise." In Hindu culture this discovery is considered, not as madness or megalomania, but as a matter for congratulation, since it is not as if the finite individual had suddenly claimed to be everybody's boss.

THE HEBREW-CHRISTIAN MORALITY

But if we, in the context of the Hebrew-Christian culture, wake up and discover that we are God, we are accused of subversive blasphemy or total insanity, since it is understood that one is claiming to be the universal monarch. At the present time this is giving us considerable trouble, especially in the industrial-electronic, democratic-republican style of culture that has been emerging in the modern world. For we are being brought up under the sway of two mutually inconsistent philosophies. On the one hand, we are told that we must be responsible, and that it's up to us, as independent citizens in equality with all others, to assume responsibility for the government of our country. On the other hand, instead of doing just that, we are also looking over our shoulders for support and authority from tradition, law, and monarchical order deriving from the father and the past. Thus when people do something we don't like, our first, naive reaction is to say, "There ought to be a law against it!"

To give a specific illustration, one of our major social problems today, particularly for young people, is our mistrust and dislike of the police. They have a terrible public image because we are asking them to do what we should be doing for ourselves. We have saddled ourselves with an army of armed clergymen charged with compelling us to be moral, with results that are dangerously confusing to both the citizen and the policeman. Let us not forget that the police officer does not necessarily enjoy this role. For the delegation of such authority to officials of the state is both a hoax on oneself and a source of corruption in the state. Moral behavior is significantly and truly moral only when it is voluntary. Morality by compulsion reduces us to a state that is less than human. It results in a perpetual infantilism in which we ask a governmental daddy to force us to behave as we think we ought to behave but do not want to behave, and toward whom we must therefore have ever-growing resentment.

It is almost a platitude to say that a free society cannot exist without mutual trust and without individual assumption of moral responsibility. To ask the government to be responsible for law and order is to ask for a police state. In a free society the function of the police is primarily to give information (for example, as to the conditions and flow of automotive traffic) and assistance (for example, in the event of such disasters as fires and earthquakes). By and large, and in the long run, it becomes more and more apparent that threats of punishment, and the actual penalties of fine or imprisonment or even death, do not significantly promote civilized and rational behavior. On the contrary, they may in fact foster crime as an expression of resentment, and it is well-known that the Mafia-type syndicates that are involved in gambling and prostitution do not want laws against such activities to be repealed. Repeal would lower the price and open up the market. Thus, in lobbying for the maintenance of sumptuary laws against moral crimes without unwilling victims, the criminal syndicates work hand-in-hand with the churches. Never was there more convincing evidence of the implicit identity of prudery and vice, of righteous, boss-type God and malicious Devil. As Lao-Tzu put it:

> The more laws and regulations are given,
> The more robbers and thieves abound.

All this implies, therefore, that a mature religion (or religiousness) must abandon the monarchical image of God. And this is the God of whom many theologians are now saying, "God is dead!" But, as we have seen, if there is to be any image of conception of God at all, this is not the only option. The Bible has, of course, passed down to our present cultures a mythomorphic image (or idol) of God modeled on the tyrant-kings of the ancient Near-East—the Pharaohs of Egypt, the great Chaldean lawgiver Hammurabi, and the Cyruses (Kyrioi) of Persia, in whose likeness God is still venerated when we sing *"Kyrie eleison*—Lord have mercy," and whose titles "Kind of kings and Lord of lords" are still used in the Church of England's prayer for the King's (or Queen's) Majesty:

O Lord our Heavenly Father, high and mighty, King of kings, Lord of lords, the only ruler of princes, who dost from thy throne behold all the dwellers upon earth: most heartily we beseech thee with thy favor to behold our sovereign Lady Elizabeth the Queen . . .

This is obviously the language of court flattery, and the very design of the church in which such words are heard is the royal court, or basilica, where the king sits enthroned upon a dais with his back to the wall, flanked by a semicircle of ministers and guards, and approached by subjects who prostrate themselves or kneel, so as to be in a disadvantageous position for starting a fight.

Yet today a curious transition is taking place in, of all places, the Roman Catholic Church. (Always keep your eye on the Catholic Church: it is a spiritual weathervane. It's the most conservative institution in the Western world, and thus anything changing there is change at a very deep level.) All over the world, Roman Catholic churches are shifting their high altars from the East end to the center of their temples, so that the God-Christ no longer sits with his back to the wall but comes forward to be the center of the congregation—since "the kingdom of heaven is within you." There is, perhaps, no official realization and, certainly, no open statement of what this change implies, for fundamental transformations begin at an unconscious level. But by this gesture the Church is turning itself into a flower, a *mandala*, instead of a militarized court, and this intimates—along the directions of Teilhard de Chardin's theology—a radical alteration in the Church's ideas of man's relation to God, as of the very nature of God.

What we are beginning to see is a new realization—influenced, no doubt, by oriental philosophy—of the relation of the individual to the basic energy of the universe that Tillich called "the Ground of Being"—in an attempt to find some name for "the Which than which there is no whicher" bereft of all the gloomy and pompous associations that stick to the word "God."[2] For this relationship is no longer to be conceived as that between king and subject, commander and soldier, paterfamilias and filially pious child. It is, instead, the stelliform relationship of star to its rays, center to circumference, hub to spokes, or even role to actor. If God remains in any sense king, the universe is then his crown—not something lying abjectly at his feet.

NEW CONCEPTS OF RELIGION

Concurrently, religion as a way of life ceases to put its emphasis on doctrine (teaching), law (commandments), and obedience, and religious "services" become instead celebrations from which words and preachments increasingly disappear. Actually, the very word "religion" means bondage, or submission to a rule of life. Used in its most exact sense, "religion" is the way of life of a monk or nun undertaking the three vows of poverty, chastity, and obedience—the latter virtue ranking (in practice if not theory) higher than divine charity. Catholics will, for example, reprove Protestants for interpreting the Bible according to their personal opinions and not to the authority of the Church, forgetting, however, that the notion of the Church's authority is their own personal opinion. Likewise, supposedly "liberated" people of our own times who put themselves under the authority of a guru fail to see that they themselves confer authority on the guru by choosing him.

The monarchical conception of the universe, implying religion as a way of obedience, perpetuates forms of ritual, worship, and liturgy with a dominant emotion of groveling guiltiness and intensely earnest obsequiousness. Absolutely no laughter is allowed. The Romans had a saying that when priests laugh before the altar, the religion is dead. But how, then, could Dante's vision of hell, purgatory, and paradise be entitled the Divine *Comedy*? How could he have described the singing of the angels as the "laughter of the universe?" The underlying supposition of monarchical religion as that you as an individual are something quite other than God. You are merely a creature, evoked out of total nothingness by a fiat, or whimsy, of the divine will. Contrary to the republican axiom that every man has certain inalienable rights; you have no right to exist whatsoever: you exist solely by the will and at the pleasure of your sovereign Lord, and between you and your divine Author there is an absolute metaphysical and ontological gulf. The very core of your being is not the Ground of Being itself. You exist on probation.

Yet as a result of the philosophical thought and the scientific investigations of the eighteenth, nineteenth, and twentieth centuries, this conception of the order of the universe has become implausible. We simply do not believe in it, although there are many who feel most strongly that they ought to believe, which is why there are so many sermons in the churches on the need for a revived faith. When it is necessary to have billboards proclaiming the "The family which prays together stays together," we realize that both the family and prayer are obsolete.

In fact we believe that the universe is a mindless mechanism; that mankind is a biological fluke on a minute and utterly unimportant planet. That is to say, we still view ourselves as subjects and minions—but without a king; as slaves with no other master than the laws of nature—and there is no lawmaker. This is the image of the universe as a completely computerized bureaucracy with a high percentage of inefficiency. In such circumstances, man's only recourse is to fight nature and beat it into submission, realizing at the same time that his victories are only temporary, and that his role is essentially tragic since

> all which it inherit shall dissolve,
> And, like this insubstantial pageant faded,
> Leave not a rack behind. We are such stuff
> As dreams are made on; and our little life
> Is rounded with a sleep.

We have developed this mechanistic view of the world because we began, historically, with the model of the universe as an artifact made by God. Perhaps it is not insignificant that Jesus was the son of a carpenter.

Looking at things this way, we can preen ourselves as realistic, tough-minded men who face the hard and brutal facts without illusions or wishful thinking. The more lifeless, mindless, and dead our concept of cosmic energy, the more the individual can come on with the role of tragic hero. We put ourselves down, as biological flukes, in order to put ourselves up as hard-fact-facers taking pride in the skill and intensity of our hostility toward our environment. The natural outcome of this attitude is a technology that exploits, erodes, pollutes, and destroys our physical surroundings.

But any biologist can demonstrate that man and his physical environment constitute an inseparable field or pattern of energy. (That this, unless he is the cantankerous, "what-a-realist-I-am" kind of fellow who insists, for example, that birds hate flying.) It is nothing more than a conceptual myth, a hallucination, that the human organism with its ego-ghost-chauffeur (Koestler's *Ghost in the Machine*) is other than or apart from the total process of nature, and that human intelligence functions separately from the marvelously integrated organization of plants, insects, bacteria, animals, gases, and geological formations that constellate its environment. Thus the current commonsensical attitude to nature that sees man as the ruler and conqueror of the world is, in fact, an emotional hangover of the former view of the universe as a mindless chaos put into order by the monarchical power of God the Father, which, as we have seen, has ceased to be plausible.

SPECULATIONS ON "RELIGION" OF THE FUTURE

What, then, is the coming direction of intelligent religious thought and practice? Let me begin with a slightly facetious fantasy. Within 20 years, Asia will be laced with super-highways, littered with hot-dog stands, billboards, and neon-signs, and every coolie will be sporting a business-suit. On the other hand, our own highways will be sprouting grass, and there will be an abundance of stately lamaseries and ashrams. People will be strolling about in easy robes, fingering rosaries and twirling prayer-wheels. There will be enormous schools of philosophical and theological inquiry, as also of meditation-practice celebrated for the superb chanting of Sanskrit and Chinese sutras, and frustrated Tibetans will be coming to Chicago to study Buddhism.

The point is that the direction of our spiritual endeavors will be away from interminable verbiage and laying-down of laws. Hitherto, all our churches have been talking, preaching, and praying places—reverberating with words upon words upon words. The new religious values will be in the domain of experience as distinct from ideation and formulation. As Alfred North Whitehead said back in 1926:

> When you understand all about the sun and all about the atmosphere and all about the rotation of the earth, you may still miss the radiance of the sunset. There is no substitute for the direct perception of the concrete achievement of a thing in actuality. We want concrete fact with a highlight thrown on what is relevant to its preciousness. . . . We are too exclusively bookish in our scholastic routine. . . . In the Garden of Eden Adam saw the animals before he named them; in the traditional system [of education], children named the animals before they saw them. (Whitehead, 1926/1933, pp. 247–248)

We have confused knowledge with what can be expressed in words or numbers as against what can be felt and sensed. Thus Western religions have stressed the overwhelming importance of dogma and belief, that is, of correct ideas even beyond the importance of correct behavior. Salvation comes through faith rather than works, and, in this context, faith has meant not so much trust in life as assent to certain theological propositions. Contrariwise, such oriental "religions" as Hinduism, Buddhism, and Taoism—in stressing the importance of immediate experience rather than intellectual concepts—are, oddly enough, more down-to-earth and (in the best sense) materialistic and empirical than even Western science. For what a man senses and feels in his very bones underlies how he thinks and behaves. The scientists know, theoretically, that organism and environment, man and nature, are all of a piece. But few of them *feel* it. Their theoretical view is not vividly experienced at the level expressed by such terms as "cosmic consciousness," *satori*, or *samadhi*. For these are states of consciousness as total and overwhelming as falling in love; they are not opinions or beliefs, wishes or hopes. They are the direct, immediate, and concrete experience of the individual's identity with the entire energy of the universe, of himself as an expression of the Ground of Being, set and centered in timeless, ultimate reality.

My position is not that of an anti-intellectual for, after all, my profession is the manipulation of words and the pursuit of scholarship in the field of comparative philosophy and religion. However, the intellectual life must, to have any substance, be based upon nonverbal and nonconceptual experience. If I talk all the time, I cannot hear what others have to say. Similarly, if I think (or talk to my self) all the time I have nothing to think about except thoughts. I know the map but not the territory; I have read the menu but not tasted the dinner.

We need to reach this level of experiencing in the sphere of religion, and the current fascination for the empirical religions of Asia, for encounter groups, sensitivity training, and for sundry experiments in the transformation of consciousness by both chemical and psychological methods shows the direction in which younger people are moving. If I may, again, be just slightly frivolous, I am predicting that we have in circulation a new, but actually very ancient religion called *OM*—a sound that Hindus and Buddhists have used to designate the total energy of the universe because it comprises the whole range of sound from the bottom of the throat to the lips, sometimes spelled Aum. This religion has neither members nor nonmembers, no hierarchy, no offices, no buildings, no organization, and, above all, no doctrines. It is strictly "do-it-yourself" religion, consisting entirely of meditation, music, and ritual—but not according to any prescribed formulas. To understand it, you must participate in it; there are no explanations.

In meditation, music, and ritual gesture we become free from the hypnotic tyranny of words and concepts and return to reality. I will not define reality. It cannot be defined, and yet all of you know what it is. It cannot be called material or physical, spiritual or mental, for all these are verbalizations and concepts. Reality is what the Hindus call *nirvikalpa* or "nonconceptual," and it is apprehended in meditation because meditation (*dhyana*) is the silencing of the chatter of thoughts in the mind—an art that is assisted by the nonverbal adjuncts of music and ritual (*mantra* and *mudra*). It brings us into a state of awareness in which the notions of self and other, past and future, knower and known, mind and body, feeler and feeling, thinker and thought have simply disappeared.

Most civilized peoples have lost this awareness. We all had it as babies—in what Freud called the "oceanic" feeling in which the individual and the surrounding world were not distinguished. But the oceanic feeling of a baby is as different from mature *samadhi* as an acorn from an oak tree. The baby has not yet developed a rich intellectual, emotional, and kinesthetic life, and thus has not mastered the technique whereby his oceanic feeling can be expressed or realized. However, in the process of education and civilization, most people lose this original sense of existence and learn to identify themselves with the isolated personality John or Mary by confusion of the symbol with the event. To regain it, we must temporarily suspend the symbolizing process in meditation, even though in meditation itself we have no goal or purpose because we are then living completely in the present. Meditation, as generally practiced in Asia, is not a self-improvement exercise done with an eye to the future; it is being centered in the eternal now, and can be maintained not only while sitting in the lotus-posture but also in going about one's ordinary affairs. To use Frederic Spiegelberg's phrase, one might say that real meditation is "the religion of no-religion," since "religion" ordinarily means symbolic action and such verbalization as prayer and the study of scriptures. But when Zen monks chant the sutras, they concentrate on the sound and pay no attention to the meaning.

If the human race is to continue in operation, such a new direction in religion is essential. It is absolutely urgent that we do not allow our preoccupation with symbols to distract our awareness from the real world. For what on earth is the value of money or status when water is poisonous, air foul, food tasteless, and habitation ugly? It is useless to plan for the future when you cannot live in the present, for you will never be able to enjoy the fulfillment of your plans. Furthermore, all our major quarrels and wars are concerned with such symbolic abstractions as ideologies, creeds, states, nations, races, monetary investments, contracts, and laws. I am not saying that all such abstractions should be abolished forthwith, but—on the principle that the Sabbath is made for man and not man for the Sabbath—they should be seen as strictly subordinate and instrumental to life itself, having only the same degree or reality as inches or lines of longitude. One has but to compare a political map or globe with a physical map (or with the new and glorious photograph of the earth from the moon) to realize that the former is ugly, unnatural, and absurd.

In sum, then, I am suggesting that in times to come the focus and center of religion must not be on a *conceptual* God. We must realize that the confusion of God with theological images is a far more dangerous idolatry than the ritual veneration of crucifixes and buddhas, which no sensible person ever believed to be the actual deity. The word "God," if it is to be retained at all, must simply designate reality—the dimension of inconceivable, unutterable, and ineffable energy in which we not only "live and move and have our being," but that is also the only presence that corresponds to the words "I am." This as experience—not belief—is the only thing that can take us beyond the banality of life considered merely as a trip from the maternity ward to the crematorium.

NOTES

1. You will see these connections clearly by reading Gooch and Laski (1967).

2. It is of interest that the younger generation in Japan use the word *kurai* ("dark," "dank," "gloomy"), in relation to certain forms of Buddhism, even though no conception of a monarchical God is involved. Nevertheless, it is used with reference to Buddhist sects that overstress the patriarchal authority of the priesthood and have strict adherence to traditional proprieties.

REFERENCES

Gooch, G. P., & Laski, H. G. (1967). *English democratic ideas in the seventeenth century* (2nd ed.). Cambridge, UK: Cambridge University Press.

Whitehead, A. N. (1933). *Science and the modern world*. Cambridge, UK: Cambridge University Press. (Original work published 1926.)

CHAPTER NINETEEN

Unity in Contemplation (1974)

Yoga is, of course, the same as the Latin *jungo*, and the English *yoke*, meaning "union"—or "integration," if we want to get a little bit fancier. There are many kinds of yoga, suited to different types of people, but there are three principal types: Jnan Yoga, the way of knowledge; Karma Yoga, the way of action; and Bhakti Yoga, the way of devotion. I imagine that the majority of people in this gathering are Bhaktis. In your contemplation, the method is centrally adoration of the Godhead as manifested in Jesus Christ, and this is Bhakti. I happen temperamentally to be a Jani, and so some of the things that I say may seem rather coldly intellectual and lacking the passion that you would normally expect from a discourse on contemplative meditation. However, even if you go along this Jani way, it is still possible to join in with the Bhakti devotions perfectly easily and with considerable enthusiasm, as I have during this week in this extraordinary and miraculous assembly.

Let us begin with the Bhakti way because it is fundamental for most of us here. "Thou shalt love the Lord thy God"—not just going through the motions, but "with all your heart and with all your soul and with all your strength." This is the first and great Commandment. How can anybody possibly obey it? In the Epistle to the Romans, chapter seven, St. Paul explains that God gave the law through Moses, not in the expectation that it would be obeyed, but in order that man, in attempting to obey it, would find out that he couldn't, and would therefore be, in Paul's language, convicted of sin. Now what is sin? *Amartanein*

Presented at Word Out of Silence: A Symposium on World Spiritualities, Mount Saviour Monastery, 1972. Reprinted from *Cross Currents*, 1974, 24(2–3), 367–377. Copyright © 1975 by Convergence, Inc. Used by permission of John Wiley & Sons, Ltd., publisher of *Cross Currents*.

in Greek, which is the word we translate or mistranslate as "sin," means *to miss the point*. To be on the point is what we call *yoga* or *dhyana*—concentration—centeredness. And a bishop in Greek is an *episcopos*, which not only means an overseer, but the man on the spot. The man who gets the point. Similarly, the way of Christ is to be on the mark, not to miss the point.

Well, you will say, what is the point? How can we get it? We're too big! To enter Heaven you have to go through a pearly gate, and you know that's not a gate all studded with pearls. A gate of heaven is *one pearl*. There are twelve of them, because the writer of the Apocalypse designed Heaven according to the Zodiac. So there are twelve gates representing twelve different kinds of people according to the signs of the Zodiac, or the twelve tribes of Israel, or the twelve Apostles. The entrance to into the pearl is the tiny little hole through which the string goes. The string is the self-thread that joins the pearls of all our different incarnations, but is not any one of them. To go through into Heaven you have to be not-you, because, as Jesus said, "Whither I go you cannot come." You have to leave yourself behind, therefore, in order to get in. How can it possibly be done? How can one give oneself up, and by one's own power completely abandon oneself to the love of God? That's the puzzle. That's what has to be tried. All the disciplines that we undertake, all the devotions that we make, all the meditative exercises that we do are efforts to give ourselves up. Well, you know what it's like. It's like having molasses in one hand and feathers in the other, and you clap them together and then try to pick off the feathers. And the more you do it, the more you're involved; you're *stuck*.

When you realize this, you ask yourself a question: "Why do I want to love God? Do I really love God? What do I mean by loving God? I've never seen God. I've never seen Jesus. I've read about him in the Bible, but I don't really know what kind of a person he was." Then you get one of those manuals of devotion, little black books with pink edges, and you kneel down before the Blessed Sacrament and you say, "Jesus, I love you; Jesus, I give my heart to you; Jesus, I adore you." You try, and you say all this and you know you're a *complete phony*—if you're honest! Why you're saying this is because you think that's what you ought to do and you want to be on the side of the big battalions. If God the Father is the boss of the universe, you'd better get with it and get close to Jesus his Son. Otherwise, you might be going to hell.

If the fear of the Lord is the beginning of wisdom, perfect love casts out fear, but how are we going to get perfect love? Nobody can ever give the answer. I remember Bernard Phillips, who's a great Zen student, going to a Jesuit Father and saying, "Sure, I'll be a Christian, but I want to be a *real* Christian. I don't want just to say I'm a Christian. Tell me how I'm going to be a Christian with absolute devotion and no holds barred." Well, everybody flunks out. When I was a little boy, I was told, "You must do your work." And I said, "Sure, be most happy. Love to have books around me, I love the smell of books, I love everything to do with books." But it was all wrong. They said, "You're not working." They couldn't explain. I even copied the teachers' handwriting, so that I could reflect their personalities somehow, and I became an expert forger!

In the same way, you can become a spiritual forger. You can have all the outward forms of great spirituality. That's why I use them, so that you *know* I'm phony! And they're fun, anyway. But how are we to love God? Well, this puzzled St. Paul. He said, "The law brought about sin in me. I had not known lust except the Law had said, 'Thou shalt not covet.'" Then he says, "Shall we sin that grace may abound? Oh, heaven forbid!" But the point was, he said, that you are told to come up to a certain standard of selfless behavior, like the Sun of Justice itself, to make you see that you *can't*. St. Augustine and Martin Luther saw the same thing, that the reason they were trying to love God was that they were incurably selfish. And what do you do about that? There's a Chinese saying that when the wrong man uses the right means, the right means work in the wrong way. Preaching religion, telling people they *ought* to behave this way, that they *should* have faith, that they *should* love one another, generates nothing but hypocrisy, unless we get to the depths of hypocrisy and realize we are hopeless hypocrites. Then we start asking, "What am I to do? When I come to the end of my tether, I can't do anything about it."

It's the same if you follow another way. Say your idea is not that you should love God or love Jesus Christ, but that you should *let go*. Well, that certainly applies to Jesus, too. "Be not anxious for the morrow, consider the flowers of the field, how they grow. . . ." I've never heard a sermon preached on that text, incidentally—it's completely subversive. It's all very well for Jesus to follow such a way because he was the boss's son and it was no problem to him, but we practical people are responsible, and have to do what is known as keeping the world going, earning livings, and things like that. We say, "*We* can't be not anxious for the morrow." That's one of the troubles about Christianity: Jesus was the boss's son and therefore had a unique advantage over all the rest of us. So you can't follow his example. That's one of the most important things to understand: that you cannot follow the example of Christ. That is the only really good reason for believing that Jesus was the unique incarnation of the Son of God. But this means Christianity becomes an impossible religion, which cannot be practiced by us.

Now what does all this mean? It sounds awfully hopeless. I can't let go of myself because I have a selfish reason for wanting to let go of myself. It would make me feel better, make me feel more protected against suffering. I'd be like a cat; you know, absolutely, that all is God, and there's nothing to be afraid of whatsoever? You'd have no attachments or hang-ups, and you'd be full of delight and joy. Wouldn't you like that? But when we look into ourselves we find a sensitive, quaking mess. And there's nothing *you* can do about it. But this not being able to do anything is a concealed positive. When, for example, God is called infinite, without bounds, this could seem very wishy-washy. Something without bounds isn't there; it would be like meeting an infinitely tall person! But we do not say God is infinite in order to say that God has no effective power. This negative word is affirmative. It's the same in Hinduism, when it says of the Brahman *neti, neti*: Brahman is not this, not that, not anything that one can conceive. This is an affirmation. In the same way, when you find there's absolutely nothing you can do to improve yourself spiritually, to be more loving of God, to be less defensive of self, that there's *nothing* you can do, there's a message there, a very important message.

The reason you can't do anything is that the "you" you think you are doesn't exist. What we call the ego has a particular existence. It exists in the same way as the Equator, or a line of longitude, or an inch. It is a social institution, or a convention, but it is not an effective agent, an effective energy, and *that's* why you can't do anything about it. Let's analyze this ego, therefore, and see what it is. First of all, it arises from a fundamental human confusion between the world of real events and the world as described. The first step is language, and it is typical of all civilized and even many uncivilized peoples that they confuse words with realities, just as we confuse wealth with money, and status with happiness. We are the kind of people who would rather eat the menu than the dinner. You see it going on all the time, and the whole of advertising is based on this confusion, so that the wealthiest among us are not rich. They dress like morticians and drive around in hearses; they don't enjoy themselves at all like we've been enjoying ourselves. We've had an absolute uproar here for a week, and we got away with it because we let the world outside know that we were doing something very specially holy. Of course, we know *how* to enjoy *ourselves*; and I'm sure that's "as being poor but making many rich, as having nothing but possessing all things." But the wealthy of this world, the rich in money, are mostly miserable people. People think, "If only I could get some more money. I've got all these mortgages and bills and dependents. I just want a little more money and then everything would be fine." So you get it. And then you start worrying about whether you're going to get sick; you can worry about that endlessly. Or about whether the tax collector is going to take it away from you, or whether there's going to be a revolution. There's always something to worry about if you're the kind of person who's inclined to worry. We confuse the world as it is with the world as described. That's not a put-down on words, or symbols, or the intellect, but only to say that you cannot use words and the intellect properly unless you know that nothing is what you say it is.

> For the word is not the thing,
> The word is not the thing,
> Hi ho the derry-o,
> The word is not the thing.

And, incidentally, there are no things either, but we'll go into that later. But you definitely can't get wet in the noise-water, nor will that noise quench your thirst. The confusion of ourselves with our ego is the result of confusing reality with a concept.

The reality of ourselves is our organism, but the organism is inseparable from a particular environment—of other people, plants, animals, air, etcetera, forever. And if you fully felt your organism, if you experienced it thoroughly, you would know it was inseparable from the entire universe—that the entire universe is simply your extended body. But the concept of the ego does not include the organism. We say, "I have a body"; we don't say, "I am a body." Now, what information is there in your ego-concept about how you circulate your blood? How you work your nervous system? How you secrete important fluids from your glands? After all, you *do* all that, but your concept of yourself contains no information whatsoever about how it's done. How do you make a decision? You say, "I open my hand." How do you do it? Well, a physiologist might explain something about it to you, but he can't open his hand any better than you can. Because when you do it, you know how to do it and, in a sense, you just do it—out it comes. But how? You can't explain, because your self-image does not contain that information. So your image of yourself is given to you by your parents, your teachers, your relatives, and your peer-group. But don't blame them, because *you* bought it. They tell you who you are.

I remember when I was a little boy I admired another boy who lived up the street, and I sometimes came home and imitated his mannerisms. My mother would look at me in a severe way and say, "Alan, that's not you, that's Peter." She was concerned to give me an identity. And when I did something terrible, she said, "It's not like you to do a thing like that." So, everybody wants you to know who you are. There are a number of personalities you can choose from—there are certain personality types, like psychological types. You can be an introverted intuitive, an extroverted feeling type, and so on. Everybody has to have one. Is you is or is you ain't? Are you a Christian or a Jew, Catholic or Protestant, Republican or Democrat, male or female? (That's a very tricky one—there are twelve sexes not just two.)[1] Everybody's got to be in a compartment of some kind. And we identify ourselves with an image. It's called a personality, the word *persona* meaning mask, that through which the sound comes, the megaphonic mask of Greek or Roman drama. It's an act, and we are increasingly convinced that we *are* that *persona*. But the *persona* is nothing more than a caricature, suggesting something with a few lines and leaving the rest out. All that tremendous complex of human relationships and relationships with nature that we really are is completely ignored.

We say, "I still have a feeling of *I* which is more than my image. I have a feeling of great reality, a me, a particular me. What do you suppose that is?" Well, it took me a long time, but I found out. When you're a child, they put you under a basic double-bind: you are *required* to do things that will be acceptable only if you do them *voluntarily*. So a mother says at night when a baby is restless, "Darling, *try* to go to sleep." "You *mustn't* be constipated. You *have* to have a bowel movement every day after breakfast." "As a good child, you *ought* to love your mother, not because I say so but because you really want to." Imagine what happens later in life, when you get married and you get up in front of an altar because you're itchy, and say—you'll swear anything to get hold of that girl—that you will love that woman till death do you part! Of all things! That is the greatest expression of disrespect for God the Almighty because eventually, as you know, you won't have these excited feelings. It becomes, after all, everyday. Some people have luck in this respect and sometimes it doesn't happen, but most people get bored. And then she says, "Darling, do you really love me?" What answer does she want? "I am trying my best to do so?" That's not what was wanted at all. If the beloved would say, "I love you so much I'm your helpless slave," that would be more like what was wanted.

I sat next to a boy in school who had great difficulty in reading. He wanted to show that he really was trying. He made noises, he made a special effort so the teacher wouldn't get angry and have him beaten. We learn early that concentration is something you do with the muscles in your forehead. What do you do when somebody says to you, "Now take a hard look at this, carefully"? You will immediately find that in ordinary conditioning there is tension around the eyes. "Now listen. Be very attentive to this!" You will find muscles straining around the ears. "This needs grit. You've got to go through with this. It's a painful situation. Tighten your jaws or clench your fists." Or, "Control yourself," and you go tight in the solar plexus or in the rectum. All these muscle strains become chronic habits and they're all perfectly futile because they don't have any effect on the efficiency of the nervous system. They get in the way of it. If you look at something, such as a clock in the distance, and you can't read the time, you start staring. But it will just become blurred. If you want to see a clock in the distance, you should close your eyes and imagine that you're looking at a black velvet curtain on a pitch-black night, then open your eyes and let the light shine through. Then you might by chance see the clock.

In all operations of the nervous system we use the intelligence. The reason why neurologists don't fully understand the nervous system is that it's more intelligent than they are. Therefore, what we call our ego is not only the image of ourselves; it's also a chronic sensation of muscular strain, which in some people is centered in the solar plexus and in others in the region of the heart. In Japanese it's called *kokoro*. And you feel that chronic strain there, and that is "I." The true individual (I'm not saying that the individual is unreal) is a total organism in relation to its environment. That's why the half-baked science (it is at least *half*-baked) of astrology draws a picture of the soul by drawing a picture of the universe as centered on the particular individual organism. Of course, it's a very crude picture of the universe. Many things aren't there, and I don't think most astrologers know how to read the map, but the idea is fundamentally sound.

Now we come to the point where we have discovered that what we call ourselves is a mere symbol, plus vain strainings. So what are you going to do about that? Here's the beginning of the religious life, where "man's extremity is God's opportunity." But what can you do? There you are, stuck with this illusion, and when you say, "What can I do about it?" you're asking what the illusion can do to get rid of itself. It is absolutely important to see that nothing, nothing, nothing can be done about it. So then what? Go out and shoot yourself? Well, it does occur to you that, somehow or other, something *is* going on. You're still breathing. Or are *you* breathing? Or does it breathe you? The vibration that we call existence is still there. What is it?

You may get frightened at this point and begin to ask, "Who's in charge around here? If I'm not in control, if nobody's in control, how will I know that I can speak the English language five minutes from now?" Here I am giving you a talk, and I don't know how this talk is happening. I might lose my nerve at any moment, but somehow it talks and I don't really think ahead what I'm going to say. But it goes on. So I might begin to wonder, "Am I simply the puppet of some god or universal process other than myself?" But where's the puppet? I can't find this puppet. Then am I God? Am I in charge of everything? That's a frightful responsibility—I'm terrified of it. There was once a young man in Los Angeles who got LSD in the wrong way and thought that he was God, and was terrified. He turned himself into the police with a note saying, "Please help me." Signed: Jehovah. But supposing both things are true? Or both untrue? That there is no puppet being pushed around and there is no boss pushing things around. Supposing there is simply a happening, what the Chinese call *Tzu-jan*, their word for nature, which means "what is so of itself." In Thomistic theology it is called aseity, to be so of itself. Aseity is one of the attributes of God you don't hear much about. So there is God—the great Happening, what is, in other words, *on the mark*, or "where it's at."

You realize that you cannot understand the world through concepts. The word is not the thing, so you become silent. There's nothing you can do, so you watch. But there's nobody watching! The idea that there has to be an experiencer of experience is merely a concept. What you call the experiencer is just one of your thoughts. It's rather that the happening, the universe is aware of itself though your eyes. You're an aperture through which the universe is aware of itself, and you realize nobody ever *was* in charge. Things have gone along reasonably well, most of the time. (I can prove from Hindu cosmology that seven parts of life in ten are good, three are bad, but we won't go into that now.) But it muddles through reasonably well, and so you watch and you hear yourself thinking to yourself. All this chatter going on inside your skull. You try to stop it, and there's absolutely nothing you can do. You want peace, you want silence, you want to stop thinking about what you must do tomorrow, what you did wrong yesterday, and all that stuff. You say, "Couldn't we have peace for a while?" but you're trying to get peace because you want to escape reality. Eventually you see that you just can't help thinking. It goes on like the birds outside or the noise of the air-conditioning. So you treat your thinking as just that. Just nonsense and hubbub going on inside your head. "You have to pay the rent, you have to pay the rent." Eventually you see the futility of all that, and your mind of itself becomes still. Left alone, it clears itself of the mud, the waves cease, and you get clarity. Clarity is very important. This is the meaning of "Blessed are the pure in heart, for they shall see God." Pure in heart doesn't mean that you don't tell dirty jokes: it means clear like crystal. "Purity" or "clarity" suggests two things to us. First, it's complete emptiness—the sky, with no clouds. But "clarity" also means absolutely articulate form: you've made it clear. That's why in Buddhism it is said that the form is the same as the void, and the void is the same as the form.

When you realize that you're not your ego, you unaccountably disappear, and become what is absolutely obvious to you from the beginning. What does your head look like from your eyes? Do I experience my head as a black spot in the middle of everything, or a fuzzy place? No—it just isn't there. I'm completely headless. All of you have heads; I apparently don't. Nevertheless, out of this absolutely blank spot, I see. In the same way the stars shine out of space. We think space isn't there, it's nothing, it's not important—until you stop to realize that you can't have stars without space. How could you have a universe without space? How could there be a solid without space? The truth of the matter is that every something comes out of nothing. Listen with your ears—concentrate with that sense as we were listening yesterday morning to all the small sounds in and around the chapel. You hear sounds coming *now* out of silence. They arise spontaneously out of silence, because in this moment you are witnessing the creation of the universe. When you stop thinking (Yoga is the cessation of *vritti* in the mind or *chitta*) with concepts, you suddenly find that there is no past and no future. There is an eternal now, but you don't know what that means, because now has meaning only in relation to then. When there is no *then*, there's no *now*. So you really don't know what to say about it. It says in one of the Zen texts that you're like a dumb man who's had a marvelous dream. Everybody wants to tell everybody else about a marvelous dream, but when he opens his mouth he can't say anything. If I try to tell you what this state is, all I do is weave a pattern of words, which I'm clever at, because the art of the poet and the philosopher is to say what cannot be said—to describe the indescribable, to eff the ineffable, and unscrew the inscrutable. But so long as one talks, he never gets there.

That is why I want to emphasize the value of the contemplative life, of that silence of the mind. But the moment I say it's valuable, that you ought to pursue it, I've said the wrong thing. There is no other reason for it than *doing* it. There is no external or ulterior reason whatsoever to participate in that superessential joy that is called God. It's not your duty, it won't be good for you. If you think, "I'm doing this for a reason, because it will be good for me," you won't see that meditation is the one thing in which you are com-pletely here and now. There's no reason for it; there's nothing in mind as a consequence. You must treat all that chatter ("I'm meditating, I ought to be doing this or that") as gobbledygook. See? That's all it is. Then you're centered in the only place there is; you're on the mark; you're not sinning. I feel this has to be said as a corrective to the excessive verbosity of our religiousness. Contemplation means what we do together in the temple. And when we gather in the temple, it is primarily for silence of the mind. It doesn't mean we can't have chickens and babies and cats and all sorts of comings and goings, such as happen in any temple in India, because you cannot meditate at all unless you can do it in a boiler factory, since all sound is the manifestation of the energy of the universe. Just listen to it as you would listen to classical music. When you listen to the New York Philharmonic playing Beethoven, you don't ask what it means, because music means music. Music is a *symphona spectacale*, an end in itself, and therefore to be likened to the Divine Wisdom as a game, because games are to be played not for anything beyond them, but for their own sake. In the *Book of Proverbs*, Wisdom speaks and says that her delight is to play in the sight of the Almighty, playing among the sons of men. The Divine Wisdom, incidentally, is a lady—Sophia, and she's the other aspect of Logos. Then you make the fundamental discovery that life is not serious—it may be sincere, but not serous. Wouldn't it be awful if God were serious? I always love to quote G. K. Chesterton saying that angels fly because they take themselves lightly. And if they, how much more the Lord of the angels? There would be no reason whatsoever for God to take himself seriously. God doesn't preach, God woos. He speaks in the language of the *Song of Songs*, the language that convinces. That's not the language of "throwing the Book," though people love being scolded, especially in church.

Mental silence does not involve the absence of physical sound. That's why music, chanting and all sorts of sublimely nonsensical activities are supports for contemplation. But remember, in our *mantra* service, I made the distinction between nonsense and claptrap. Nonsense is something of a very high order—that which is transcendent of what is sensible. So we make holy nonsense and joyful noise to the Lord as we have been doing in our marvelous devotions these past days. I think we have all discovered here that in the total silence of contemplation and the sublime "non-sense" of mantric prayer we have arrived at a tacit and firm understanding, which cannot and should not be formulated or defined. Speaking for myself, I have found unity of heart with people whose formal religious concepts are very different from mine. This is not sentimental friendship. We have met at a level of the spirit in which there is nothing to argue about, whether we be Catholics, Protestants, Orthodox, Jews, Muslims, Buddhists, or Hindus. This is, in Christian terms, the Grace of God. It is happening and will go on happening, and it is in this grass-roots, spontaneous and unofficial way that a truly catholic and ecumenical religion is coming into being—a unity that appreciates and fosters our wonderfully different disciplines of meditation and forms of worship. One morning the "official" world will wake up to find that this unity is a fact—in the light of which our ancient disputations have become irrelevant. But it will be so, not through our mutual subscription to vague platitudes such as the Golden Rule, but through exploring together the silent depths of mystical experience and practice. A Zen Buddhist verse puts it, laughingly, this way:

> When two masters meet on the road,
> They need no introduction.
> Thieves recognize one another instantly.

In conclusion, I want to offer my thanks to the monks of St. Benedict of this community, and to say that this place is an island of sanity in a mad world. I am not a monk; I like women too much. But those of you who *are* so called do the most unbelievable service in establishing these islands of constant prayer, scholarship and manual work. It's a very balanced Rule, and you Benedictines, being the most ancient Order in the Church, are like true aristocrats. You don't have to blow your own trumpet. Please keep this going! Do not lose courage. It is such a great service to the rest of us. Naturally there are members here of many other Orders, but I speak particularly to our hosts. It is essential that there be people in the world who are sitting on the mountain peaks, because if there isn't someone around who is contemplating God, the life of the rest of us is absurd. Someone must be there to give the rest of us, as it were, a center.

NOTE

1. [Watts is referring to a typology of sexual identity developed by his father-in-law, Gavin Arthur (1966)—Eds].

REFERENCE

Arthur, G. A. (1966). *The circle of sex*. New Hyde Park, NY: University Books.

PART FIVE

Psychedelics

CHAPTER TWENTY

The Individual as Man/World (1963)

*(P*refatory *note:* The following was originally delivered as an impromptu lecture for the Social Relations Colloquium at Harvard University on April 12, 1963. Although the subject was not discussed in the lecture itself, its theme is closely related to the expansion of consciousness achieved through psychedelic substances. With proper "set and setting," the psychedelics are very frequently successful in giving the individual a vivid sensation of the mutual interdependence of his own behavior and the behavior of his environment, so that the two seem to become one—the behavior of a unified field. Those who uphold the impoverished sense of reality sanctioned by official psychiatry describe this type of awareness as "depersonalization," "loss of ego-boundary," or "regression to the oceanic feeling," all of which, in their usual contexts, are derogatory terms suggesting that the state is hallucinatory. Yet it accords astonishingly well with the description of the individual that is given in the behavioral sciences, in biology and in ecology.

Theoretically, many scientists know that the individual is not a skin-encapsulated ego but an organism-environment field. The organism itself is a point at which the field is "focused," so that each individual is a unique expression of the behavior of the whole field, which is ultimately the universe itself. But to know this theoretically is not to *feel* it to be so. It was possible to calculate that the world was round before making the voyage that proved it to be so. The psychedelics are, perhaps, the ship, the experimental instrument by which the theory can be verified in common experience.)

Reprinted from *The Psychedelic Review*, 1(1), 55–65. Copyright © 1963 by the International Federation for Internal Freedom. Used by permission of Ralph Metzner.

There is a colossal disparity between the way in which most individuals experience their own existence, and the way in which the individual is described in such sciences as biology, ecology, and physiology. The nub of the difference is this: the way the individual is described in these sciences is not as a freely moving entity within an environment, but as a process of behavior that *is* the environment also. If you will accurately describe what any individual organism is doing, you will take but a few steps before you are also describing what the environment is doing. To put it more simply, we can do without such expressions as "what the individual is doing" or "what the environment is doing," as if the individual was one thing and the doing another, the environment one thing and its doing another. If we reduce the whole business simply to the process of doing, then the doing, which was called the behavior of the individual, is found to be *at the same time* the doing that was called the behavior of the environment. In other words, it is quite impossible to describe the movement of my arm except in relation to the rest of my body and to the background against which you perceive it. The relations in which you perceive this movement are the absolutely necessary condition for your perceiving at all. More and more, a "field theory" of man's behavior becomes necessary for the sciences.

Yet this is at complete variance with the way in which we are trained *by our culture* to experience our own existence. We do not, generally speaking, experience ourselves as the behavior of the field, but rather as a center of energy and consciousness, which sometimes manages to control its environment, but at other times feels completely dominated by the environment. Thus there is a somewhat hostile relationship between the human organism and its social and natural environment, which is expressed in such phrases as "man's conquest of nature," or "man's conquest of space," and other such antagonistic figures of speech.

It would obviously be to the advantage of mankind if the way in which we feel our existence could correspond to the way in which existence is scientifically described. For what we feel has far more influence upon our actions than what we think. Scientists of all kinds are warning us most urgently that we are using our technology disastrously, eating up all the natural resources of the earth, creating incredibly beautiful but wholly nonnutritious vegetables by altering the biochemical balances of the soil, spawning unbelievable amounts of detergent froth, which will eventually engulf cities, overpopulating ourselves because of the success of medicine, and thus winning our war against nature in such a way as to defeat ourselves completely. All this advice falls on deaf ears, because it falls on the ears of organisms convinced that war against nature is their proper way of life. They have to be unconvinced, and can be, to some extent, by intellectual propaganda, scientific description, and clear thought. But this moves relatively few people to action. Most are moved only if their feelings are profoundly affected. We need to *feel* this view of our individual identity as including its environment, and this must obviously concern scientists who are trying to find ways of controlling human feelings.

This problem has an important historical background. It is curious how the ancient philosophical debates of the Western world keep coming up again and again in new forms. Any question of the definition of the individual always becomes involved with the old argument between nominalism and realism. I do not wish to insult the intelligence of this learned audience, but, just to refresh your memories, the realistic philosophy of the Middle Ages and of the Greeks was not what today we call realism. It was the belief that behind all specific manifestations of life such as men, trees, dogs, there lies an archetypal, or ideal, form of Man, of Tree, of Dog, so that every particular man is an instance of that archetypal form, and that behind all men is something that can be called Man with a capital M, or the "substance" of man, of "human nature."

The nominalists argued that this was a mere abstraction, and that to regard Man (capital M) as possessing any effective existence was to be deluded by concepts. There are only specific, individual men. This idea is carried on in one of the most remarkable forms of modern nominalism, General Semantics, which argues that such abstractions as "The United States," "Britain," or "Russia," are so much journalistic gobbledygook.

Most people working in the sciences tend to be nominalists. But if you carry nominalism to its logical conclusion, you are involved in awkward problems. Not only would there be no such thing as Man, Mankind, or Human Nature, but it would also follow that there are no individual men, because the individual man is an abstraction, and what really exists is only an enormous amalgamation of particular molecules. If you pursue this further and inquire about the individual entities composing the molecules, there is an interminable array of nuclear and subnuclear realities, and if *these* in turn are to be regarded as the only realities, then the reality that we call a man is simply the association of discontinuous particles. This is the *reductio ad absurdum* of nominalism carried too far. The nominalist and realist viewpoints are actually *limits*—to borrow a term from mathematics. I have often thought that all philosophical debates are ultimately between the partisans of structure and the partisans of "goo." The academic world puts heavy emphasis on structure: "Let's be definite, let's have rigor and precision, even though we are studying poetry." But the poets will reply: "We are for goo, and you people are all dry bones, rattling in the wind. What you need is essential juices, and therefore more goo is necessary to liven you up." But when we want to know what goo is, and examine it carefully, we eventually turn up with a structure, the molecular or atomic composition of goo! On the other hand, when we try to examine the structure itself to study the substance of its bones, we inevitably come up with something gooey. When the microscope focus is clear, you have structure. But when you reach beyond the focus and what confronts you is vague and amorphous, you have goo because you cannot attain clarity. Structure and goo are essentially limits of human thought; similarly, the nominalist-structural and the realist-gooey will always be essential limits in our thinking. We must be aware that today, the particular academic and scientific fashion leans heavily in the direction of structure and nominalism.

To take a specific example, we all know that in modern medicine nominalism and structuralism hold the field. When you go to a hospital, you are liable to go through a process of examination by specialists working upon you from different points of view. They will treat you as a nonperson, from the very moment you enter. You are immediately put in a wheelchair—a symbol of the fact that you are now an object. You will be looked at piecemeal, X-rays will be taken of various organs, and special tests will be made of their functioning. If anything is wrong, you will be taken to a medical mechanic, i.e., a surgeon, who will use his equivalents of wrenches, screwdrivers and blowtorches to make certain mechanical alterations in your organism, and it is hoped you will get along fairly well with these repairs!

But the opposite, minority school of medicine will say: "This is all very well, and the services of the surgeon are sometimes greatly welcomed, but man must be considered as a whole. He has complicated metabolic and endocrine balances, and if you interfere with him seriously at one point, you will affect him unpredictably at many others, for man is an organic whole." Such are accused of being woolly-minded, old-fashioned doctors, mostly from Europe, with a kind of nature-cure background, who will use diet, complicated fasts, and massage. The poor layman doesn't know whether to deliver himself over to these old-fashioned naturalistic doctors or to Mr. Sawbones with his very up-to-date qualifications.

Fortunately, precise science is coming to the rescue of our man-as-whole. More recent studies are showing just how diseases formerly regarded as specific entities, or afflictions of a particular organ or area, are actually brought about by responses of the central nervous system, acting as an integrated whole. We are beginning to see how man, as a complex of organs, is not an *addition* of parts, like an automobile. His various organs are not to be treated as if they were assembled together, but by seeing the physical body as a unified or integrated pattern of behavior—which is just what we mean when we talk about an entity or thing. What happens when we have the feeling that we understand something, when we say, "Oh, I see"? If a child asks, "Why are the leaves green?" and you answer, "Because of the chlorophyll," and the child says, "Oh!" that is *pseudo*-understanding. But when the child has a jigsaw puzzle and sees how it all fits together, then the "Oh!" has a different meaning from the "Oh!" following the chlorophyll explanation. To understand anything is to be able to fit various parts into a system that is an integrated whole, so that they "make sense."

As organic diseases are fitted into a whole, and problems of crime or psychosis in individual behavior are fitted in with a pattern of social behavior that makes sense, that is consistent with those kinds of behaviors, we say "Aha!—*now* I see!"

Fascinating work is being done in studying the ways in which the individual as a system of behavior is related to his biological and social environments, showing how his behavior may be explained in terms of those environments. One of the people who has done very important work in this sphere is our distinguished colleague, B. F. Skinner. I cite his work because it brings out these ideas in a marvelously clear, crucial, and provocative way, and because it is evidence for conclusions that he himself does not seem to have realized. One of his most important statements is in his book, *Science and Human Behavior* (1953):

> The hypothesis that man is not free is essential to the application of scientific method to the study of human behavior. The free inner man who is held responsible for the behavior of the external biological organism is only a prescientific substitute for the kinds of causes which are discovered in the course of a scientific analysis. (p. 447)

He is talking, of course, about the chauffer inside the body, or what Wittgenstein called the little man inside the head: this is for him a prescientific substitute for the kinds of causes for behavior that are discovered in the course of scientific analysis. He continues:

> All these alternative causes lie *outside* the individual. The biological substratum itself is determined by prior events in a genetic process. Other important events are found in the nonsocial environment and in the culture of the individual in the broadest possible sense. These are the things which *make* [italics added] the individual behave as he does. For them he is not responsible and for them it is useless to praise or blame him. It does not matter that the individual may take it upon himself to control variables of which his own behavior is a function or, in a broader sense, to engage in the design of his own culture. He does this only because he is the product of a culture which *generates* [italics added] self-control or cultural design as a mode of behavior. The environment determines the individual even when he alters the environment. (pp. 447–448)

I am not going to quarrel with this finding. I am not a clinical or experimental psychologist and am therefore unqualified to criticize Skinner's evidence. Let's take it for Gospel, simply for the sake of argument.

But there is a rather heavy emphasis upon the individual being the puppet. "All these alternative causes," i.e., the kinds of causes discovered in the course of scientific behavior, "lie outside the individual," i.e., outside this wall of flesh and bag of skin. The individual is therefore passive. This is psychology in terms of Newtonian physics. The individual is a billiard ball upon which other balls impinge, and his seemingly active behavior is only a passive response. Skinner admits the individual does and can alter the environment, but when he does so, he is *being made* to do so. This is put forth in such a way as to make the individual appear passive and the things *really* controlling his behavior outside him.

But the reciprocal relationship between the knower and the known, common to all the sciences, is set aside here although he mentions it elsewhere (Skinner, 1961):

> A laboratory for the study of behavior contains many devices for controlling the environment and for recording and analyzing the behavior of organisms. With the help of these devices and their associated techniques, we change the behavior of an organism in various ways, with considerable precision. But note that the organism changes our behavior in quite as precise a fashion. Our apparatus was designed by the organism we study, for it was the organism which led us to choose a particular manipulandum, particular categories of stimulation, particular modes of reinforcement, and so on, and to record particular aspects of its behavior. Measures which were successful were for that reason reinforcing and have been retained, while others have been, as we say, extinguished. The verbal behavior with which we analyze our data has been shaped in a similar way: order and consistency emerged to reinforce certain practices which were adopted, while other practices suffered extinction and were abandoned. (All scientific techniques, as well as scientific knowledge itself, are generated in this way. A cyclotron is "designed" by the particles it is to control, and a theory is written by the particles it is to explain, as the behavior of these particles shapes the nonverbal and verbal behavior of the scientist.) (p. 543)

In one of his essays, he has a cartoon of a mouse saying to another, "Boy have I got that guy up there fixed! Every time I press this bar, he gives me some food!"

Although Skinner seems in general to be stressing heavily the point of view that the individual is the puppet in the field in which he is involved, he is nevertheless stating here the opposite point, that the individual organism, mouse, or guinea pig, in the experiment is nevertheless determining the environment even when, as in a laboratory, the environment is designed to control the specific organism. The environment of a rat running in a barn is not designed to control the rat, but the more it is so designed, the more the rat is involved in and shaping its environment. He writes elsewhere that what he has been saying

> does not mean that anyone in possession of the methods and results of science can step outside the stream of history and take evolution of government into his own hands. Science is not free, either. It cannot interfere with the course of events; it is simply part of that course. It would be quite inconsistent if we were to exempt the scientist from

the account which science gives of human behavior in general. (Skinner, 1953, p. 446)

Now we might well object: "Look, Professor Skinner, you say we are completely conditioned behavior-systems. We cannot change anything. At the same time, you are calling upon us to embark upon the most radical program of controlling human behavior. How can you write *Walden II*, a utopia? Are you not a monstrosity of inconsistency by calling for responsible human action and at the same time saying that we have no freedom?" But is this actually a contradiction? He is saying two things, both of which can be valid, but he does not provide a framework in which the opposed points of view can make sense. Similarly, the physicist says light can be considered as a wave or as a particle system. These sound mutually exclusive to the nonphysicist. In the same way, the advocacy of a planned development of human resources and potentials, coupled with the idea that the individual is not a self-controlling, skin-encapsulated ego, needs some further concept to help it along. The following passage clinches the problem:

> Just as biographers and critics look for external influences to account for the traits and achievements of the men they study, so science ultimately explains behavior in terms of "causes" or conditions which lie beyond the individual himself. As more and more causal relations are demonstrated, a practical corollary becomes difficult to resist: it should be possible to *produce* behavior according to plan simply by arranging the proper conditions. (Skinner, 1955–1956, p. 47)

There is the contradiction that necessarily arises in a psychology with a language system that incorporates into present scientific knowledge an outmoded conception of the individual—the individual as something bounded by skin, and that is pushed around by an environment that is not the individual. Skinner (1953) is naturally aware that his emphasis on our passive relationship to conditioning causes is rather unpalatable:

> The conception of the individual which emerges from a scientific analysis is distasteful to most of those who have been strongly affected by democratic philosophies . . . it has always been the unfortunate task of science to dispossess cherished beliefs regarding the place of man in the universe. It is easy to understand why men so frequently flatter themselves—why they characterize the world in ways which reinforce them by providing escape from the consequences of criticism or other forms of punishment. But although flattery temporarily strengthens behavior, it is questionable whether it has any ultimate survival value.

If science does not confirm the assumptions of freedom, initiative, and responsibility in the behavior of the individual, these assumptions will not ultimately be effective either as motivating devices or as goals in the design of culture. We may not give them up easily, and we may, in fact, find it difficult to control ourselves or others until alternative principles have been developed. (p. 449)

There the book ends, and there is no suggestion as to what those principles might be, even though they are implied in his conclusions:

When an individual conspicuously manipulates the variables of which the behavior of *another* [italics added] individual is a function, we say that the first individual controls the second, but we do not ask who or what controls the first. When a government conspicuously controls its citizens, we consider this fact without identifying the events that control the government. When the individual is strengthened as a measure of counter-control, we may, as in democratic philosophies, think of him as a starting point.

Isn't this political nominalism?

Actually, however, we are not justified in assigning *to anyone or anything* [italics added] the role of prime mover. Although it is necessary that science confine itself to selected segments in a continuous series of events, it is *to the whole series* [italics added] that any interpretation must eventually apply. (pp. 448–449)

We are now listening to a man who represents himself as a behavioristically oriented, nonmystical, on-the-whole materialistic, hard-headed scientist. Yet this passage is the purest mysticism, which might have come straight from Mahayana Buddhism: "We are not justified in assigning to anyone or anything the role of prime mover." No segment, no particular pattern of integrated behavior within whatever universe we are discussing can be called the prime mover. Now this is the *Dharmadhatu* doctrine of Mahayana Buddhism; that the universe is a harmonious system that has no governor, that it is an integrated organism but nobody is in charge of it. Its corollary is that everyone and everything is the prime mover.

In Skinner's language, the popular conception of the inner self, the little man inside the head who is controlling everything, must be replaced by the whole system of *external* causes operating upon the individual, the whole network of causal relationships. But this language obscures a very simple thing: when there is a certain cause in the external environment whose effect is always a particular individual behavior, you are using very cumbersome language for something you can describe more simply. For when you find these two things going together, you are actually talking about one thing. To say that Event A causes Event B is a laborious way of saying that it is one Event C. If I lift up this book by a corner, all the corners are lifted up at the same time. If I lift up an accordion, there is an interval between cause and effect. Similarly when we study the individual's behavior, we are studying a system of relationships, but we are looking at it too close up. All we see is the atomic events, and we don't see the integrated system that would make them make sense if we could see it. Our scientific methods of description suffer from a defective conception of the individual. The individual is not by any means what is contained inside a given envelope of skin. The individual organism is the particular and unique focal point of a network of relations that is ultimately a "whole series"—I suppose that means the whole cosmos. And the whole cosmos so focused is one's actual self. This is, whether you like it or not, pure mysticism. Skinner is saying that although science is a method of observation, which, by reason of the blinkers of the head, is limited to our one-thing-at-a-time method of thought, science can only look at the world area by area. But science also becomes the method of understanding its own limitations. When you conduct any experiment, you must be careful to exclude variables you cannot measure. When you want to keep something at a constant temperature, you must put it into some kind of heat-and-cold-proof or shock-proof, or cosmic-ray-proof system. So by excluding variables and by having to do it rigorously, you begin to understand how really impossible it is to do except in very special cases. In this way, the scientist, by attempting to isolate events and by looking as rigorously as he can at one segment of the world at a time, becomes aware of the fact that this looking at things simply in segments, although it is a form of very bright, clear, conscious knowledge, is also a form of ignorance. For it is a form of "ignore-ance," ignoring everything that is not in that segment. Therefore he becomes aware of the fact that just this is *ultimately* what you can't do. You *can* do it only to discover you *cannot* do it.

I commend these observations to you simply to show how a scientific thinker whose whole stance is in the direction of mechanism, or regarding the human being as a kind of biological puppet, must be forced by the logic of his own thinking to conclusions of a rather different kind. He states these questions in veiled language, so that neither he nor his colleagues will see their disastrously unrespectable implications!

Suppose, then, it becomes possible for us to have a new sense of the individual, that we all become conscious of ourselves as organism-environment fields, vividly aware of the fact that when we move, it is not simply my self moving inside my skin, exercising energy upon my limbs, but also that in some marvelous way the physical continuum in which I move is also moving me. The very fact that I am here in this room at all is because you are here. It was a common occurrence, a whole concatenation of circumstances that go together, each reciprocally related to all. Would such an awareness be significant? Would it add to our knowledge? Would it change anything, make any difference? Seriously, I think it would; because it makes an enormous difference whenever what had seemed to be partial and disintegrated fits into a larger integrated pattern. It will of course be impossible finally to answer the question, "Why does that satisfy us?" because to answer this question exhaustively I would have to be able to chew my own teeth to pieces. In the pursuit of scientific knowledge, always watch out for that snag. You will never get to the irreducible explanation of anything because you will never be able to explain why you want to explain, and so on. The system will gobble itself up. The Gödel theory has roughly to do with the idea that you cannot have any system that will define its own axioms. An axiom in one system of logic must be defined in terms of another system, etc., etc. You never get to something that is completely self-explanatory. That of course is the limit of control, and the reason why all systems of control have ultimately to be based on an act of faith.

The problem confronting all sciences of human behavior is that we have the evidence (we are *staring* at it) to give us an entirely different conception of the individual than that which we ordinarily feel and that influences our common sense: a conception of the individual not, on the one hand, as an ego locked in the skin, nor, on the other hand, as a mere passive part of the machine, but as a reciprocal interaction between everything inside the skin and everything outside it, neither one being prior to the other, but equals, like the front and back of a coin.

REFERENCES

Skinner, B. F. (1953). *Science and human behavior*. New York, NY: Macmillan.

Skinner, B. F. (1955–1956). Freedom and the control of men. *The American Scholar,* 25(1), 47–65.

Skinner, B. F. (1961). The design of cultures. *Daedalus, 90*(3), 534–546.

CHAPTER TWENTY-ONE

A Psychedelic Experience

Fact or Fantasy (1964)

Since at least 1500 B.C. men have, from time to time, held the view that our normal vision of the world is a hallucination—a dream, a figment of the mind, or, to use the Hindu word that means both art and illusion, a *maya*. The implication is that, if this is so, life need never be taken seriously. It is fantasy, a play, a drama to be enjoyed. It does not really *matter*, for one day (perhaps in the moment of death) the illusion will dissolve, and each one of us will awaken to discover that he himself is *what* there is and *all* that there is—the very root and ground of the universe, or the ultimate and eternal space in which things and events come and go.

This is not simply an idea that someone "thought up," like science fiction or a philosophical theory. It is the attempt to express an experience in which consciousness itself, the basic sensation of being "I," undergoes a remarkable change. We do not know much about these experiences. They are relatively common, and arise in every part of the world. They occur to both children and adults. They may last for a few seconds and come once in a lifetime, or they may happen repeatedly and constitute a permanent change of consciousness. With baffling impartiality they may descend upon those who never heard of them, as upon those who have spent years trying to cultivate them by some type of discipline. They have been regarded, equally, as a disease of consciousness with symptoms everywhere the same, like measles, and as a vision of higher reality such as comes in moments of scientific or psychological insight. They may turn people into monsters and megalomaniacs, or transform them into saints and sages. While there is no sure way of inducing these experiences, a favorable atmosphere may be created by intense concentration, by fasting, by sensory deprivation, by hyper-oxygenation, by prolonged emotional stress, by profound relaxation, or by the use of certain drugs.

Experiences of this kind underlie some of the great world religions—Hinduism, Buddhism and Taoism in particular, and, to a much lesser extent, Judaism, Christianity, and Islam. As expressed in the doctrines of these religions, they purport to be an account of "the way things are" and therefore invite comparison with descriptions of the universe and of man given by physicists and biologists. They contradict common sense so violently and are accompanied with such a powerful sense of authenticity and reality (*more* real than reality is a common description) that men have always wondered whether they are divine revelations or insidious delusions.

This problem becomes all the more urgent now that the general public has become aware that experiences of this type are available, with relative ease, through the use of such chemicals as the so-called psychedelic drugs—LSD-25, mescaline, psilocybin, hashish, and marijuana, to name only the better known. The reality status of the modes of consciousness induced by these chemicals becomes, then, a matter of most serious concern for the guardians of our mental health, for psychiatrists and psychologists, philosophers and ministers, for every scientific investigator of the nature of consciousness, and, above all, for a large section of the general public curious and eager to get "the experience" for reasons of all kinds.

A proper study of the question runs, at the very beginning, into two obstacles. The first is that we know very little indeed about the structure and chemistry of the brain. We do not know enough of the ways in which it gleans information about the outside world and about itself to know whether these chemicals help it (as lenses help the eyes) or confuse it. The second is that the nature and use of these chemicals is surrounded with an immense semantic fog, whose density is increased by people who ought to know better. I mean psychiatrists.

What we know, positively and scientifically, about psychedelic chemicals is that they bring about certain alterations of sense perception, of emotional level and tone, of identity feeling, of the interpretation of sense data, and of the sensations of time and space. The nature of these alterations depends on three variables: the chemical itself (type and dosage), the psycho-physiological state of the subject, and the social and aesthetic context of the experiment. Their physiological side effects are minimal, though there are conditions (e.g., disease of the liver) in which some of them may be harmful. They are not physiologically habit-forming in the same way as alcohol and tobacco, though some individuals may come to depend upon them for other (i.e., "neurotic") reasons. Their results are not easily predictable since they depend so largely upon such imponderables as the setting, and the attitudes and expectations of both the supervisor and the subject. The (enormous) scientific literature on the subject indicates that a majority of people have pleasant reactions, a largish minority have unpleasant but instructive and helpful reactions, while a very small minority have psychotic reactions lasting from hours to months. It has never been definitely established that they have led directly to a suicide. (I am referring specifically here to LSD-25, mescaline, the mushroom derivative psilocybin, and the various forms of *cannabis*, such as hashish and marijuana.)

Thus what we know for certain implies that these chemicals cannot be used without caution. But this applies equally to antibiotics, whisky, household ammonia, the automobile, the kitchen knife, electricity, and matches. No worthwhile life can be lived without risks, despite current American superstitions to the contrary—as that passing laws can prevent people from being immoral and that technological power can be made foolproof. The question is therefore whether the risks involved in using these chemicals are worthwhile, and it seems to me that what is worthwhile should be judged not only in terms of useful knowledge or therapeutic effect, but also in terms of simple pleasure. (I have heard addiction to music described in just the same vocabulary as addiction to drugs.) If it turns out that psychedelics offer valid ways of exploring man's "inner world," the hidden ways of the mind and brain, we should surely admit that new knowledge of this inmost frontier may be worth quite serious risks. Psychoses and compulsive delusions are, after all, no more dangerous than the Indians and the mountain ranges that stood in the way of the first settlers of the American West.

Psychiatrists often wonder why colleagues in other branches of medicine and specialists in other fields of science do not take them quite seriously. A typical reason may be found in their haste to define the nature and effects of these chemicals in terms that are simply prejudicial, and that boil down to nothing more than gobbledygook with an authoritative rumble. For example, the chemicals in question are commonly classified as "hallucinogenics" or "psychotomimetics." The first word means that they generate hallucinations, and the second that their effects resemble, or mimic, certain forms of psychosis or insanity. Only rarely do they give the impression of events in the external world that are not actually happening (i.e., hallucinations) and the 10-year-old notion that they induce "model psychoses" such as temporary schizophrenia has long been abandoned by those who are still in active research. But even if these findings were to be contested, the words "hallucination" and "psychosis" are loaded: they designate *bad* states of mind, whereas a clean scientific language should say only that these chemicals induce different and unusual states of mind.

It is almost a standard joke that psychiatry has pejorative or "put-down" words for every human emotion, as "euphoric" for happy, "fixated" for interested, and "compulsive" for determined. The discussion of psychedelic chemicals, both in the scientific literature and the public press, is thoroughly swamped with question-begging language of this kind in articles that purport to be impartial and authoritative. Right from the start the very word "drug," when used in this connection, evokes the socially reprehensible image of people who are "drugged" or "doped"—glassy-eyed, staggering, or recumbent wrecks of humanity, withdrawn from reality into a diabolic paradise of bizarre or lascivious dreams. The image of the Fu Manchu opium den, with screaming meemies at the end of the line.

Thus it is most common to find the action of psychedelics called "toxic" (i.e., poisonous), and the sensory and emotional changes induced referred to as "distortions," "delusive mechanisms," "dissociations," and "regressions," or as "loss of ego structure" and "abnormal perception of body image." This is the language of pathology. Used without explicit qualification, it implies that a consciousness so changed is sick. Likewise, when—in the context of a scientific article—the writer reports, "Subjects experienced religious exaltation, and some described sensations of being one with God," and leaves it at that, the implication is plainly that they went crazy. For in our own culture, to feel that you are God is insanity almost by definition. But, in Hindu culture, when someone says, "I have just found out that I am God," they say, "Congratulations! You at last got the point." Obviously, the word "God" does not mean the same thing in both cultures. Yet psychiatrists toss off such utterly damning remarks without scruple, and feel free to use their diagnostic jargon of mental pathology for states of consciousness that many of them have never even bothered to experience. For they expect to get accurate information about these states from subjects untrained in scientific description, fearing that if they themselves entered into any new mode of consciousness it would impair their scientific objectivity. This is pure scholasticism, as when the theologians said to Galileo, "We will not look through your telescope because we already know how the universe is ordered. If your telescope were to show us anything different, it would be an instrument of the devil."

Similarly, so many practitioners of the inexact sciences (e.g., psychology, anthropology, sociology) let it be known most clearly that they already know what reality is, and therefore what sanity is. For these poor drudges reality is the world of nonpoetry: it is the reduction of the physical universe to the most banal and desiccated terms conceivable, in accordance with the great Western myth that all nature outside the human skin is a stupid and unfeeling mechanism. There is a sort of "official psychiatry" of the army, state mental hospital, and of what, in California, they call "correctional facility" (i.e., prison), which defends this impoverished reality with a strange passion.

To come, then, to any effective evaluation of these chemicals and the changed states of consciousness and perception that they induce, we must begin with a highly detailed and accurate description of what they do, both from the standpoint of the subject and of the neutral observer, despite the fact that in experiments of this kind it becomes startlingly obvious that the observer cannot be neutral, and that the posture of "objectivity" is itself one of the determinants of the outcome. As the physicist well knows, to observe a process is to change it. But the importance of careful description is that it may help us to understand the kind of level of reality upon which these changes in consciousness are taking place.

For undoubtedly they are happening. The dancing, kaleidoscopic arabesques that appear before closed eyes are surely an observation of *some* reality, though not, perhaps, in the physical world outside the skin. But are they rearranged memories? Structures in the nervous system? Archetypes of the collective unconscious? Electronic patterns such as often dance on the TV screen? What, too, are the fern-like structures that are so often seen—the infinitude of branches upon branches upon branches, or analogous shapes? Are these a glimpse of some kind of analytical process in the brain, similar to the wiring patterns in a computer? We really have no idea, but the more carefully observers can record verbal descriptions and visual pictures of these phenomena, the more likely that neurologists or physicists or even mathematicians will turn up the physical processes to which they correspond. The point is that these visions are not *mere* imagination, as if there had ever been anything mere about imagination! The human mind does not just perversely invent utterly useless images out of nowhere at all. Every image tells us something about the mind or the brain or the organism in which it is found.

The effects of the psychedelics vary so much from person to person and from situation to situation that it is well nigh impossible to say with any exactitude that they create certain particular and invariable changes of consciousness. I would not go so far as to say that the chemical effects are simply featureless, providing no more than a vivid mirror to reflect the fantasies and unconscious dispositions of the individuals involved. For there are certain types of change that are usual enough to be considered characteristic of psychedelics: the sense of slowed or arrested time, and the alteration of "ego boundary"—that is, of the sensation of one's own identity.

The feeling that time has relaxed its pace may, to some extent, be the result of having set aside the better part of a day just to observe one's own consciousness, and to watch for interesting changes in one's perception of such ordinary things as reflected sunlight on the floor, the grain in wood, the texture of linen, or the sound of voices across the street. My own experience has never been of a distortion of these perceptions, as in looking at oneself in a concave mirror. It is rather that every perception becomes—to use a metaphor—more resonant. The chemical seems to provide consciousness with a sounding box, or its equivalent, for all the senses, so that sight, touch, taste, smell, and imagination are intensified like the voice of someone singing in the bathtub.

The change of ego boundary sometimes begins from this very resonance of the senses. The intensification and "deepening" of color, sound and texture lends them a peculiar transparency. One seems to be aware of them more than ever as vibration, electronic and luminous. As this feeling develops it appears that these vibrations are continuous with one's own consciousness and that the external world is in some odd way inside the mind-brain. It appears, too, with overwhelming obviousness, that the inside and the outside do not exclude one another and are not actually separate. They go together; they imply one another, like front and back, in such a way that they become polarized. As, therefore, the poles of a magnet are the extremities of a single body, it appears that the inside and the outside, the subject and the object, the self and the world, the voluntary and the involuntary, are the poles of a single process that is my real and hitherto unknown self. This new self has no location. It is not something like a traditional soul, using the body as a temporary house. To ask *where* it is, is like asking where the universe is. Things in space have a where, but the thing that space is in doesn't need to be anywhere. It is simply what there is, just plain basic isness!

How easily, then, an unsophisticated person might exclaim, "I have just discovered that I am God!" Yet if, during such an experience, one retains any critical faculties at all, it will be clear that anyone else in the same state of consciousness will also be God. It will be clear, too, that the "God" in question is not the God of popular theology, the Master Technician who controls, creates, and understands everything in the universe. Were it so, a person in this state should be able to give correct answers to all questions of fact. He would know the exact height of Mount Whitney in millimeters. On the other hand, this awareness of a deeper and universal self would correspond exactly with that other type of God that mystics have called the "divine ground" of the universe, a sort of intelligent and super-conscious space containing the whole cosmos as a mirror contains images . . . though the analogy fails in so far as it suggests something immense: we cannot picture sizelessness.

Anyone moving into completely unfamiliar territory may at first misunderstand and misinterpret what he sees, as is so evident from the first impressions of visitors to foreign lands where patterns of culture differ radically from their own. When Europeans depicted their first impressions of China, they made the roofs of houses exaggeratedly curly and people's eyes slanted at least 45 degrees from the horizontal. Contrariwise, the Japanese saw all Europeans as red-haired, sunken-eyed goblins with immensely long noses. But the unfamiliarities of foreign cultures are nothing to those of one's own inner workings. What is there in the experience of clear blue sky to suggest the structure of the optical nerves? Comparably, what is there in the sound of a human voice on the radio to suggest the formation of tubes and transistors? I raise this question because it is obvious that any chemically induced alteration of the nervous system must draw the attention of that system to itself. I am not normally aware that the sensation of blue sky is a state of the eyes and brain, but if I see wandering spots that are neither birds nor flying saucers, I know that these are an abnormality within the optical system itself. In other words, I am enabled, by virtue of this abnormality, to become conscious of one of the instruments of consciousness. But this is most unfamiliar territory.

Ordinarily, we remain quite unaware of the fact that the whole field of vision with its vast multiplicity of colors and shapes is a state of affairs inside our heads. Only eyes within a nervous system within a whole biological organism can translate the particles and/or waves of the physical world into light, color and form, just as only the skin of a drum can make a moving hand go "Boom!" Psychedelics induce subtle alterations of perception that make the nervous system aware of itself, and the individual suddenly and unaccustomedly becomes conscious of the external world as a state of its own body. He may even go so far as to feel a confusion between what other people and things are doing, on the one hand, and his own volition, on the other. The particular feeling, or "cue," attached to thoughts and actions normally understood to be voluntary may then be attached to what is ordinarily classified as involuntary. (Similarly, in *déjà vu* or "hasn't-this-happened-before?" experiences, perceptions of the immediate here and now come through with the cue or signal usually attached to memories.)

Under such circumstances the naive observer might well take these impressions so literally as to feel that the universe and his own body are *in fact* one and the same, that he is willing everything that happens, and that he is indeed the God of popular theology. If that were all, the psychedelics might certainly be dismissed as hallucinogens. We might conclude that they merely confuse the "wiring" of the nervous system in such a way that volition or "I-am-doing-this" signals get mixed up with messages about the external world.

Yet the problem cannot be set aside so simply. Let us suppose that a biologist wants to make a very detailed and accurate description of the behavior of some particular organism, perhaps of a sea bird feeding on the beach. He will be unable to describe the behavior of the bird without also describing the behavior of the water, of the sandworms or shellfish that the bird is eating, of seasonal changes of tide, temperature, and weather, all of which go together with behavior of the bird. He cannot describe the behavior of the organism without also describing the behavior of its environment. We used to attribute this to the fact that organisms are always reacting to things that happen in their environments, and are even determined by their environments in all that they do. But this is to speak as if things were a collection of perfectly separate billiard balls banging against one another. Today, however, the scientist tends more and more to speak of the behavior of the organism and the behavior of the environment as the behavior of a single "field," somewhat awkwardly named the "organism/environment." Instead of talking about actions and reactions between different things and events, he prefers to speak of transactions. In the transaction of buying and selling, there is no selling unless there is simultaneous buying, and vice versa. The relation of organism to environment is also considered a transaction, because it has been found that living creatures exist only in a balanced relationship to one another. The present natural state of this planet "goes with" the existence of human beings, just as buying goes with selling. In any radically different environment, man could survive only by becoming a different type of being.

The implications of this organism/environment relationship are somewhat startling, for what is really being said is this: The entity we are describing is not an organism *in* an environment; it is a unified field or process, because it is more simple and more convenient to think of what the organism does and what the environment does as a single "behavior." Now substitute for "entity we are describing" the idea of the self. I myself am not just what is bounded by my skin. I myself (the organism) am what my whole environmental field (the universe) is doing. It is, then, simply a convention, a fashion, an arbitrary social institution, to confine the self to some center of decision and energy located within this bag of skin. This is no more than the rule of a particular social game of cops and robbers, that is, of who shall we praise and reward, and who shall we blame and punish? To play this game, we pretend that the origin of actions is something inside each human skin. But only force of long ingrained habit makes it hard to realize that we could define and actually *feel* ourselves to be the total pattern of the cosmos as focused or expressed *here*. This would be a sense of our identity consistent with the scientific description of man and other organisms. It would involve, too, the sensation that the external world is continuous with and one with our own bodies—a sensation very seriously needed in a civilization where men are destroying their environment by misapplied technology. This is the technology of man's *conquest* of nature, as if the external world were his enemy and not the very matrix in which he is brought forth and sustained. This is the technology of the dust bowls, of polluted air, poisoned streams, chemical chickens, pseudo-vegetables, foam-rubber bread, and the total Los Angelization of man.

Yet how is this long-ingrained sense of insular identity to be overcome? How is twentieth-century man to gain a feeling of his existence consistent with twentieth-century knowledge? We need very urgently to know that we are not strangers and aliens in the physical universe. We are not dropped here by divine whim or mechanical fluke out of some other universe altogether. We did not arrive, like birds on barren branches; we grew out of this world, like leaves and fruit. Our universe "humans" just as a rosebush "flowers." We are living in a world where men all over the planet are linked by an immense network of communications, and where science has made us theoretically aware of our interdependence with the entire domain of organic and inorganic nature. But our ego-feeling, our style of personal identity, is more appropriate to men living in fortified castles.

There seems to me a strong possibility that the psychedelics (as a medicine rather than a diet) may help us to "trigger" a new sense of identity, providing the initial boost to get us out of the habit of restricting "I" to a vague center within the skin. That they make us aware that our whole knowledge of the external world is a state of our own bodies is not a merely technical and trivial discovery. It is the obverse of the fact that our own bodies are functions, or behaviors, of the whole external world. This—at first—weird and mystical sensation of "unity with the cosmos" has been objectively verified. The mystic's subjective experience of his identity with "the All" is the scientist's objective description of ecological relationship, of the organism/environment as a unified field.

Our general failure (over the past 3,000 years of human history) to notice the inseparability of things, and to be aware of our own basic unity with the external world, is the result of specializing in a particular kind of consciousness. For we have very largely based culture and civilization on concentrated attention, on using the mind as a spotlight rather than a floodlight, and by this means analyzing the world into separate bits. Concentrated attention is drummed into us in schools; it is essential to the three Rs; it is the foundation of all careful thought and detailed description, all high artistic technique and intellectual discipline. But the price we pay for this vision of the world in vivid detail, bit by bit, is that we lose sight of the relationships and unities between the bits. Furthermore, a form of attention that looks at the world bit by bit doesn't have time to examine all possible bits; it has to be programmed (or prejudiced) to look only at *significant* bits, at things and events that are relevant to certain preselected ends—survival, social or financial advancement, and other fixed goals that exclude the possibility of being open to surprises, and to those delights that are extra special because they come without being sought.

In my own experience, which is shared by very many others, the psychedelics expand attention. They make the spotlight of consciousness a floodlight that not only exposes ignored relationships and unities but also brings to light unsuspected details—details normally ignored because of their lack of significance, or their irrelevance to some prejudice of what ought to be. (For example, the tiniest hairs on people's faces and blotchy variations of skin color, not really supposed to be there, become marvelously visible.) There is thus good reason to believe that the psychedelics are the opposite of hallucinogens insofar as they decrease the selectivity of the senses and expose consciousness to events beyond those that are supposed to deserve notice.

Time after time, this unprogrammed mode of attention, looking *at* things without looking *for* things, reveals the unbelievable beauty of the everyday world. Under the influence of programmed attention, our vision of the world tends to be somewhat dusty and drab. This is for the same reason that *staring* at things makes them blurred, and that trying to get the utmost out of a particular pleasure makes it something of a disappointment. Intense beauty and intense pleasure are always gratuitous, and are revealed only to senses that are not seeking and straining. For our nerves are not muscles; to push them is to reduce their efficiency.

What, finally, of the strong impression delivered both by the psychedelics and by many forms of mystical experience that the world is in some way an illusion? A difficulty here is that the word "illusion" is currently used pejoratively, as the negative of everything real, serious, important, valuable, and worthwhile. Is this because moralists and metaphysicians are apt to be personality types lacking the light touch? Illusion is related etymologically to the Latin *ludre*, to play, and thus is distinguished from reality as the drama is distinguished from "real life." In Hindu philosophy, the world is seen as a drama in which all the parts—each person, animal, flower, stone, and star—are roles or masks of the one supreme Self, which plays the *lila* or game of hide and seek with itself for ever and ever, dismembering itself as the Many and remembering itself as the One through endless cycles of time, in the spirit of a child tossing stones into a pond through a long afternoon in summer. The sudden awakening of the mystical experience is therefore the one Self remembering itself as the real foundation of the seemingly individual and separate organism.

Thus the Hindu *maya*, or world illusion, is not necessarily something bad. *Maya* is a complex word signifying the art, skill, dexterity, and cunning of the supreme Self in the exercise of its playful, magical, and creative power. The power of an actor so superb that he is taken in by his own performance. The God-head amazing itself, getting lost in a maze.

Classical illustrations of *maya* include the apparently continuous circle of fire made by a whirling torch, and of the continuity of time and moving events by the whirring succession of *ksana*, or atomic instants. Physicists use similar metaphors in trying to explain how vibrating wavicles produce the illusion of solid material. The impenetrability of granite, they say, is something like the apparently solid disk made by the blades of an electric fan: it is an intensely rapid motion of the same minute orbits of light that constitute our fingers. Physics and optics have also much to say about the fact that all reality, all existence is a matter of relationship and transaction. Consider the formula

$$\frac{a \qquad b}{c} = \text{Rainbow,}$$

where *a* is the sun, *b* is moisture in the atmosphere, and *c* is an observer, all three being at the same time in a certain angular relationship. Deduct any one term, *a*, *b*, or *c*, or arrange them in positions outside the correct angular relationship, and the phenomenon "rainbow" will not exist. In other words, the actual existence of rainbows depends as much upon creatures with eyes as it depends upon the sun and moisture in the atmosphere. Common sense accepts this in respect to diaphanous things like rainbows that back off into the distance when we try to reach them. But it has great difficulty in accepting the fact that chunky things like apartment buildings and basic things like time and space exist in just the same way—*only* in relation to certain structures known as organisms with nervous systems.

Our difficulty in accepting for ourselves so important a part in the actual creation or manifestation of the world comes, of course, from this thorough habituation to the feeling that we are strangers in the universe—that human consciousness is a fluke of nature, that the world is an external object that we confront, that its immense size reduces us to a pitiful unimportance, or that geological and astronomical structures are somehow more real (hard and solid?) than organisms. But these are actually mythological images of the nineteenth and early twentieth centuries—ideas that, for a while, seemed extremely plausible, mostly for the reason that they appeared to be hardboiled, down to earth and tough-minded, a currently fashionable posture for the scientist. Despite the lag between advanced scientific ideas and the common sense of even the educated public, the mythology of man as a hapless fluke trapped in a mindless mechanism is breaking down. The end of this century may find us, at last, thoroughly at home in our own world, swimming in the ocean of relativity as joyously as dolphins in the water.

CHAPTER TWENTY-TWO

Psychedelics and Religious Experience (1968)

The experiences resulting from the use of psychedelic drugs are often described in religious terms. They are therefore of interest to those like myself who, in the tradition of William James, are concerned with the psychology of religion. For more than thirty years I have been studying the causes, consequences, and conditions of those peculiar states of consciousness in which the individual discovers himself to be one continuous process with God, with the Universe, with the Ground of Being, or whatever name he may use by cultural conditioning or personal preference for the ultimate and eternal reality. We have no satisfactory and definitive name for experiences of this kind. The terms "religious experience," "mystical experience," and "cosmic consciousness" are all too vague and comprehensive to denote that specific mode of consciousness, which, to those who have known it, is as real and overwhelming as falling in love. This article describes such states of consciousness as and when induced by psychedelic drugs, although they are virtually indistinguishable from genuine mystical experience. It then discusses objections to the use of psychedelic drugs that arise mainly from the opposition between mystical values and the traditional religious and secular values of Western society.

The idea of mystical experiences resulting from drug use is not readily accepted in Western societies. Western culture has, historically, a particular fascination with the value and virtue of man as an individual, self-determining, responsible ego, controlling himself and his world by the power of conscious effort and will. Nothing, then, could be more repugnant to this cultural tradition than the notion of spiritual or psychological growth through the use of drugs.

From *California Law Review*, 1968, 56(1), 74–85. Copyright © 1968 by *California Law Review*. Reprinted with permission of *California Law Review*, Inc.

A "drugged" person is by definition dimmed in consciousness, fogged in judgment, and deprived of will. But not all psychotropic (consciousness-changing)
chemicals are narcotic and soporific, as are alcohol, opiates, and barbiturates.
The effects of what are now called psychedelic (mind-manifesting) chemicals
differ from those of alcohol as laughter differs from rage or delight from depression. There is really no analogy between being "high" on LSD and "drunk" on
bourbon. True, no one in either state should drive a car, but neither should
one drive while reading a book, playing a violin, or making love. Certain creative activities and states of mind demand a concentration and devotion that
are simply incompatible with piloting a death-dealing engine along a highway.

I myself have experimented with five of the principle psychedelics: LSD-
25, mescaline, psilocybin, dimethyltryptamine (DMT), and cannabis. I have
done so, as William James tried nitrous oxide, to see if they could help me in
identifying what might be called the "essential" or "active" ingredients of the
mystical experience. For almost all the classical literature on mysticism is vague,
not only in describing the experience, but also in showing rational connections
between the experience itself and the various traditional methods recommended
to induce it—fasting, concentration, breathing exercises, prayers, incantations,
and dances. A traditional master of Zen or Yoga, when asked why such-and-such
practices lead or predispose one to the mystical experience, always responds,
"This is the way my teacher gave it to me. This is the way I found out. If
you're seriously interested, try it for yourself." This answer hardly satisfies an
impertinent, scientific-minded, and intellectually curious Westerner. It reminds
him of archaic medical prescriptions compounding five salamanders, powdered
gallows-rope, three boiled bats, a scruple of phosphorous, three pinches of
henbane, and a dollop of dragon dung dropped when the moon was in Pisces.
Maybe it worked, but what was the essential ingredient?

It struck me, therefore, that if any of the psychedelic chemicals would
in fact predispose my consciousness to the mystical experience, I could use
them as instruments for studying and describing that experience as one uses a
microscope for bacteriology, even though the microscope is an "artificial" and
"unnatural" contrivance that might be said to "distort" the vision of the naked
eye. However, when I was first invited to test the mystical qualities of LSD-25
by Dr. Keith Ditman of the Neuropsychiatric Clinic at UCLA Medical School,
I was unwilling to believe that any mere chemical could induce a genuine
mystical experience. I thought it might at most bring about a state of spiritual
insight analogous to swimming with water wings. Indeed, my first experiment with LSD-25 was not mystical. It was an intensely interesting aesthetic
and intellectual experience that challenged my powers of analysis and careful
description to the utmost.

Some months later, in 1959, I tried LSD-25 again with Drs. Sterling Bun-
nell and Michael Agron, who were then associated with the Langley-Porter
Clinic in San Francisco. In the course of two experiments I was amazed and

somewhat embarrassed to find myself going through states of consciousness that corresponded precisely with every description of major mystical experiences I had ever read.[1] Furthermore, they exceeded both in depth and in a peculiar quality of unexpectedness the three "natural and spontaneous" experiences of this kind that I had had in previous years.

Through subsequent experimentation with LSD-25 and the other chemicals named above (with the exception of DMT, which I find amusing but relatively uninteresting) I found I could move with ease into the state of "cosmic consciousness," and in due course become less and less dependent on the chemicals themselves for "tuning in" to this particular wavelength of experience. Of the five psychedelics tried, I found LSD-25 and cannabis suited my purposes best. Of these two, the latter, which I had to use abroad in countries where it is not outlawed, proved to be the better. It does not induce bizarre alterations of sensory perception, and medical studies indicate that it may not, save in great excess, have the dangerous side effects of LSD, such as psychotic episodes.

For the purpose of this study, in describing my experiences with psychedelic drugs, I avoid the occasional and incidental bizarre alterations of sense perception that psychedelic chemicals may induce. I am concerned, rather, with the fundamental alterations of the normal, socially induced consciousness of one's own existence and relation to the external world. I am trying to delineate the basic principles of psychedelic awareness. But I must add that I can speak only for myself. The quality of these experiences depends considerably upon one's prior orientation and attitude to life, although the now voluminous descriptive literature of these experiences accords quite remarkably with my own.

Almost invariably, my experiments with psychedelics have had four dominant characteristics. I shall try to explain them—in the expectation that the reader will say, at least of the second and third, "Why, that's obvious! No one needs a drug to see that." Quite so, but every insight has degrees of intensity. There can be obvious$_1$ and obvious$_2$—and the latter comes on with shattering clarity, manifesting its implications in every sphere and dimension of our existence.

The first characteristic is a slowing down of time, a *concentration in the present*. One's normally compulsive concern for the future decreases, and one becomes aware of the enormous importance and interest of what is happening at the moment. Other people, going about their business on the streets, seem to be slightly crazy, failing to realize that the whole point of life is to be fully aware of it as it happens. One therefore relaxes, almost luxuriously, in studying the colors in a glass of water, or in listening to the now highly articulate vibration of every note played on an oboe or sung by voice.

From the pragmatic standpoint of our culture, such an attitude is very bad for business. It might lead to improvidence, lack of foresight, diminished sales of insurance policies, and abandoned savings accounts. Yet this is just the corrective that our culture needs. No one is more fatuously impractical than the "successful" executive who spends his whole life absorbed in frantic paperwork with the objective of retiring in comfort at sixty-five, when it will be all too late. Only those who have cultivated the art of living completely in the present have any use for making plans for the future, for when the plans mature they will be able to enjoy the results. "Tomorrow never comes." I have never yet heard a preacher urging his congregation to practice that section of the Sermon on the Mount, which begins, "Be not anxious for the morrow. . . ." The truth is that people who live for the future are, as we say of the insane, "not quite all there"—or here: by overeagerness they are perpetually missing the point. Foresight is bought at the price of anxiety, and, when overused, it destroys all its own advantages.

The second characteristic I will call *awareness of polarity*. This is the vivid realization that states, things, and events that we ordinarily call opposite are interdependent, like back and front or the poles of a magnet. By polar awareness one sees that things that are explicitly different are implicitly one: self and other, subject and object, left and right, male and female—and then, a little more surprisingly, solid and space, figure and background, pulse and interval, saints and sinners, and police and criminals, ingroups and outgroups. Each is definable only interns of the other, and they go together transactionally, like buying and selling, for there is no sale without a purchase, and no purchase without a sale. As this awareness becomes increasingly intense, you feel that you yourself are polarized with the external universe in such a way that you imply each other. Your push is its pull, and its push is your pull—as when you move the steering wheel of a car. Are you pushing it or pulling it?

At first, this is a very odd sensation, not unlike hearing your own voice played back to you on an electronic system immediately after you have spoken. You become confused, and wait for *it* to go on! Similarly, you feel that you are something being done by the universe, yet that the universe is equally something being done by you—which is true, at least in the neurological sense that the peculiar structure of our brains translates the sun into light and air vibrations into sound. Our normal sensation of relationship to the outside world is that sometimes we push it, and sometimes it pushes us. But if the two are actually one, where does the action begin and responsibility rest? If the universe is doing me, how can I be sure that, two seconds hence, I will still remember the English language? If I am doing it, how can I be sure that, two seconds hence, my brain will know how to turn the sun into light? From such unfamiliar sensations as these the psychedelic experience can generate confusion, paranoia, and terror—even though the individual is feeling his relationship to the world exactly as it would be described by a biologist, ecologist, or physicist, for he is feeling himself as the unified field of organism and environment.

The third characteristic, arising from the second, is *awareness of relativity*. I see that I am a link in an infinite hierarchy of processes and beings, ranging from molecules through bacteria and insects to human beings, and, maybe, to angels and gods—a hierarchy in which every level is in effect the same situation.

For example, the poor man worries about money while the rich man worries about his health: the worry is the same, but the difference is in its substance or dimension. I realize that fruit flies must think of themselves as people, because, like ourselves, they find themselves in the middle of their own world—with immeasurably greater things above and smaller things below. To us, they all look alike and seem to have no personality—as do the Chinese when we have not lived among them. Yet fruit flies must see just as many subtle distinctions among themselves as we among ourselves.

From this it is but a short step to the realization that all forms of life and being are simply variations on a single theme: we are all in fact one being doing the same thing in as many different ways as possible. As the French proverb goes, *plus ça change, plus c'est la même chose*—"the more it varies, the more it is one." I see, further, that feeling threatened by the inevitability of death is really the same experience as feeling alive, and that as all beings are feeling this everywhere, they are all just as much "I" as myself. Yet the "I" feeling, to be felt at all, must always be a sensation relative to the "other," to something beyond its control and experience. To be at all, it must begin and end. But the intellectual jump that mystical and psychedelic experience make here is in enabling you to see that all these myriad I-centers are yourself—not, indeed, your personal and superficial conscious ego, but what Hindus call the *paramatman*, the self of all selves.[2] As the retina enables us to see countless pulses of energy as a single light, so the mystical experience shows us innumerable individuals as a single Self.

The fourth characteristic is *awareness of eternal energy*, often in the form of intense white light, which seems to be both the current in your nerves and that mysterious e that equals mc^2. This may sound like megalomania or delusion of grandeur—but one sees quite clearly that all existence is a single energy, and that this energy is one's own being. Of course there is death as well as life, because energy is a pulsation, and just as waves must have both crests and troughs the experience of existing must go on and off. Basically, therefore, there is simply nothing to worry about, because you yourself are the eternal energy of the universe playing hide-and-seek (off-and-on) with itself. At root, you are the Godhead, for God is all that there is. Quoting Isaiah just a little out of context: "I am the Lord, and there is none else. I form the light and create the darkness: I make peace, and create evil. I, the Lord, do all these things."[3] This is the sense of the fundamental tenet of Hinduism, *Tat tvam asi*—"THAT (i.e., "that subtle Being of which this whole universe is composed") art thou."[4] A classical case of this experience, from the West, is in Tennyson's (1898) *Memoirs*:

A kind of waking trance I have frequently had, quite up from boyhood, when I have been all alone. This has generally come upon me thro' repeating my own name two or three times to myself silently, till all at once, as it were out of the intensity of the consciousness of individuality, the individuality itself seemed to dissolve and fade away into boundless being, and this not a confused state, but the clearest of the clearest, the surest of the surest, the weirdest of the weirdest, utterly beyond words, where death was an almost laughable impossibility, the loss of personality (if so it were) seeming no extinction but the only true life. (p. 320)

Obviously, these characteristics of the psychedelic experience, as I have known it, are aspects of a single state of consciousness—for I have been describing the same thing from different angles. The descriptions attempt to convey the reality of the experience, but in doing so they also suggest some of the inconsistencies between such experience and the current values of society.

Resistance to allowing use of psychedelic drugs originates in both religious and secular values. The difficulty in describing psychedelic experiences in traditional religious terms suggests one ground of opposition. The Westerner must borrow such words as *samadhi* or *moksha* from the Hindus, or *satori* or *kensho* from the Japanese, to describe the experience of oneness with the universe. We have no appropriate word because our own Jewish and Christian theologies will not accept the idea that man's inmost self can be identical with the Godhead, even though Christians may insist that this was true in the unique instance of Jesus Christ. Jews and Christians think of God in political and monarchical terms, as the supreme governor of the universe, the ultimate boss. Obviously, it is both socially unacceptable and logically preposterous for a particular individual to claim that he, in person, is the omnipotent and omniscient ruler of the world—to be accorded suitable recognition and honor.

Such an imperial and kingly concept of the ultimate reality, however, is neither necessary nor universal. The Hindus and the Chinese have no difficulty in conceiving of an identity of the self and the Godhead. For most Asians, other than Moslems, the Godhead moves and manifests the world in much the same way that a centipede manipulates a hundred legs: spontaneously, without deliberation or calculation. In other words, they conceive the universe by analogy with an organism as distinct from a mechanism. They do not see it as an artifact or construct under the conscious direction of some supreme technician, engineer, or architect.

If, however, in the context of Christian or Jewish tradition an individual declares himself to be one with God, he must be dubbed blasphemous (subversive) or insane. Such a mystical experience is a clear threat to traditional religious concepts. The Judaeo-Christian tradition has a monarchical image of God, and monarchs, who rule by force, fear nothing more than insubordination. The Church has therefore always been highly suspicious of mystics because they seem to be insubordinate and to claim equality or, worse, identity with God. For this reason John Scotus Erigena and Meister Eckhart were condemned as heretics. This was also why the Quakers faced opposition for their doctrine of the Inward Light, and for their refusal to remove hats in church and in court. A few occasional mystics may be all right so long as they watch their language, like Saint Teresa of Avila and Saint John of the Cross, who maintained, shall we say, a metaphysical distance of respect between themselves and their heavenly King. Nothing, however, could be more alarming to the ecclesiastical hierarchy than a popular outbreak of mysticism, for this might well amount to setting up a democracy in the kingdom of heaven—and such alarm would be shared equally by Catholics, Jews, and fundamentalist Protestants.

The monarchical image of God with its implicit distaste for religious insubordination has a more pervasive impact than many Christians might admit. The thrones of kings have walls immediately behind them, and all who present themselves at court must prostrate themselves or kneel because this is an awkward position from which to make a sudden attack. It has perhaps never occurred to Christians that when they design a church on the model of a royal court (basilica) and prescribe church ritual, they are implying that God, like a human monarch, is afraid. This is also implied by flattery in prayers:

> O Lord our heavenly Father, high and mighty, King of kings, Lord of lords, the only Ruler of princes, who dost from thy throne behold all the dwellers upon earth: most heartily we beseech thee with thy favor to behold . . .

The Western man who claims consciousness of oneness with God or the universe thus clashes with his society's concept of religion. In most Asian cultures, however, such a man will be congratulated as having penetrated the true secret of life. He has arrived, by chance or by some such discipline as Yoga or Zen meditation, at a state of consciousness in which he experiences directly and vividly what our own scientists know to be true in theory. For the ecologist, the biologist, and the physicist know (but seldom feel) that every organism constitutes a single field of behavior, or process, with its environment. There is no way of separating what any given organism is doing from what its environment is doing, for which reason ecologists speak not of organisms in environments but organism-environments. Thus the words "I" or "self" should properly mean what the whole universe is doing at this particular "here-and-now" called John Doe.

The kingly concept of God makes identity of self and God, or self and universe, inconceivable in Western religious terms. The difference between Eastern and Western concepts of man and universe, however, extends beyond strictly religious concepts. The Western scientist may rationally perceive the idea of organism-environment, but he does not ordinarily *feel* this to true. By cultural and social conditioning, he has been hypnotized into experiencing himself as an ego—as an isolated center of consciousness and will inside a bag of skin, confronting an external and alien world. We say, "I came into this world." But we did nothing of the kind. We came *out* of it in just the same way as fruit comes out of trees.

Such a vision of the universe clashes with the idea of a monarchical God, with the concept of the separate ego, and even with the secular, atheist-agnostic mentality, which derives its common sense from the mythology of nineteenth-century scientism. According to this view, the universe is a mindless mechanism and man a sort of accidental micro-organism infesting a minute globular rock that revolves about an unimportant star on the outer fringe of one of the minor galaxies. This "putdown" theory of man is extremely common among such quasi-scientists as sociologist, psychologists, and psychiatrists, most of whom are still thinking of the world in terms of Newtonian mechanics, and have never really caught up with the ideas of Einstein and Bohr, Oppenheimer and Schrödinger. Thus to the ordinary institutional-type psychiatrist, any patient who gives the least hint of mystical or religious experience is automatically diagnosed as deranged. From the standpoint of the mechanistic religion he is a heretic and is given electro-shock therapy as an up-to-date form of thumbscrew and rack. And, incidentally, it is just this kind of quasi-scientist who, as consultant to government and law-enforcement agencies, dictates official policies on the use of psychedelic chemicals.

Inability to accept the mystic experience is more than an intellectual handicap. Lack of awareness of the basic unity of organism and environment is a serious and dangerous hallucination. For in a civilization equipped with immense technological power, the sense of alienation between man and nature leads to the use of technology in a hostile spirit—to the "conquest" of nature instead of intelligent cooperation with nature. The result is that we are eroding and destroying our environment, spreading Los Angelization instead of civilization. This is the major threat overhanging Western technological culture, and no amount of reasoning or doom-preaching seems to help. We simply do not respond to the prophetic and moralizing techniques of conversion upon which Jews and Christians have always relied. But people have an obscure sense of what is good for them—call it "unconscious self-healing," "survival instinct," "positive growth potential," or what you will. Among the educated young there is therefore a startling and unprecedented interest in the transformation of human consciousness. All over the Western world publishers are selling millions of books dealing with Yoga, Vedanta, Zen Buddhism, and the chemical mysticism of psychedelic drugs, and I have come to believe that the whole "hip" subculture, however misguided in some of its manifestations, is the earnest and responsible effort of young people to correct the self-destroying course of industrial civilization.

The content of the mystical experience is thus inconsistent with both the religious and secular concepts of traditional Western thought. Moreover, mystical experiences often result in attitudes that threaten the authority not only of established churches but also of secular society. Unafraid of death and deficient in worldly ambition, those who have undergone mystical experiences are impervious to threats and promises. Moreover, their sense of the relativity of good and evil arouse the suspicion that they lack both conscience and respect for law. Use of psychedelics in the United States by a literate bourgeoisie means than an important segment of the population is indifferent to society's traditional rewards and sanctions.

In theory, the existence within our secular society of a group that does not accept conventional values is consistent with our political vision. But one of the great problems of the United States, legally and politically, is that we have never quite had the courage of our convictions. The republic is founded on the marvelously sane principle that a human community can exist and prosper only on a basis of mutual trust. Metaphysically, the American Revolution was a rejection of the dogma of Original Sin, which is the notion that because you cannot trust yourself or other people, there must be some Superior Authority to keep us all in order. The dogma was rejected because if it is true that we cannot trust ourselves and others, it follows that we cannot trust the Superior Authority that we ourselves conceive and obey, and that the very idea of our own untrustworthiness is unreliable!

Citizens of the United States believe, or are supposed to believe, that a republic is the best form of government. Yet, vast confusion arises from trying to be republican in politics and monarchist in religion. How can a republic be the best form of government if the universe, heaven, and hell are a monarchy?[5] Thus, despite the theory of government by consent, based upon mutual trust, the peoples of the United States retain, from the authoritarian backgrounds of their religions or national origins, an utterly naïve faith in law as some sort of supernatural and paternalistic power. "There ought to be a law against it!" Our law-enforcement officers are therefore confused, hindered, and bewildered—not to mention corrupted—by being asked to enforce sumptuary laws, often of ecclesiastical origin, which vast numbers of people have no intention of obeying and, which, in any case, are immensely difficult or simply impossible to enforce—for example, the barring of anything so undetectable as LSD-25 from international and interstate commerce.

There are two specific objections to use of psychedelic drugs. First, use of these drugs may be dangerous. However, every worthwhile exploration is dangerous—climbing mountains, testing aircraft, rocketing into outer space, skin diving, or collecting botanical specimens in jungles. But if you value knowledge and the actual delight of exploration more than mere duration of uneventful life, you are willing to take the risks. It is not really healthy for monks to practice fasting, and it was hardly hygienic for Jesus to get himself crucified, but these are risks taken in the course of spiritual adventures. Today the adventurous young are taking risks in exploring the psyche, testing their mettle at the task just as, in times past, they have tested it—more violently— in hunting, dueling, hot-rod racing, and playing football. What they need is not prohibitions and policemen but the most intelligent encouragement and advice that can be found.

Second, drug use may be criticized as an escape from reality. However, this criticism assumes unjustly that the mystical experiences themselves are escapist or unreal. LSD, in particular, is by no means a soft and cushy escape from reality. It can very easily be an experience in which you have to test your soul against all the devils in hell. For me, it has been at times an experience in which I was at once completely lost in the corridors of the mind and yet relating that very lostness to the exact order of logic and language, simultaneously very mad and very sane. But beyond these occasional lost and insane episodes, there are the experiences of the world as a system of total harmony and glory, and the discipline of relating these to the order of logic and language must somehow explain how what William Blake called that "energy which is eternal delight" can consist with the misery and suffering of everyday life.[6]

The undoubted mystical and religious intent of most users of the psychedelics, even if some of these substances should be proved injurious to physical health, requires that their free and responsible use be exempt from legal restraint in any republic that maintains a constitutional separation of Church and State. I mean "responsible" in the sense that such substances be taken by or administered to consenting adults only. The user of cannabis, in particular, is apt to have peculiar difficulties in establishing his "undoubtedly mystical and religious intent" in court. Having committed so loathsome and serious a felony, his chances of clemency are better if he assumes a repentant demeanor, which is quite inconsistent with the sincere belief that his use of cannabis was religious. On the other hand, if he insists unrepentantly that he looks upon such use as a religious sacrament, many judges will declare that they "dislike his attitude," finding it truculent and lacking in appreciation of the gravity of the crime, and the sentence will be that much harsher. The accused is therefore put in a "double-bind" situation in which he is "damned if he does, and damned if he doesn't." Furthermore, religious integrity—as in conscientious objection—is generally tested and established by membership in some church or religious organization with a substantial following. But the felonious status of cannabis is such that grave suspicion would be cast upon all individuals forming such an organization, and the test cannot therefore be fulfilled. It is generally forgotten that our guarantees of religious freedom were designed to protect precisely those who were *not* members of established denominations, but rather such screwball and (then) subversive individuals as Quakers, Shakers, Levellers, and Anabaptists. There is little question that those who use cannabis, or other psychedelics, with religious intent are now members of a persecuted religion that appears to the rest of society as a grave menace to "mental health," as distinct from the old-fashioned "immortal soul," but it's the same old story.

To the extent that mystical experience conforms with the tradition of genuine religious involvement, and to the extent that psychedelics induce that experience, users are entitled to some constitutional protection. Also, to the extent that research in the psychology of religion can utilize such drugs, students of the human mind must be free to use them. Under present laws, I, as an experienced student of the psychology of religion, can no longer pursue research in the field. This is barbarous restriction of spiritual and intellectual freedom, suggesting that the legal system of the United States, is, after all, in tacit alliance with the monarchical theory of the universe and will, therefore, prohibit and persecute religious ideas and practices based on an organic and unitary vision of the universe.[7]

NOTES

1. An excellent anthology of such experiences is *Watcher on the Hills* (Johnson, 1959).

2. Thus Hinduism regards the universe, not as an artifact, but as an immense drama in which the One Actor (the *paramatman* or *brahman*) plays all the parts, which are his (or "its") masks, or *personae*. The sensation of being only this one particular self, John Doe, is due to the Actor's total absorption in playing this and every other part. For fuller exposition, see Radhakrishnan (1927) and Zimmer (1951, pp. 355–463). A popular version is in Watts (1966).

3. *Isaiah* 45:6. 7.

4. *Chandogya Upanishad* 6.15.3.

5. Thus, until quite recently, belief in a Supreme Being was a legal test of valid conscientious objection to military service. The implication was that the individual objector found himself bound to obey a higher echelon of command than the President and Congress. The analogy is military and monarchical, and therefore objectors who, as Buddhists or naturalists, held an organic theory of the universe often had difficulty in obtaining recognition.

6. This is discussed at length in Watts (1962).

7. Amerindians belonging to the Native American Church, who employ the psychedelic peyote cactus in their rituals, are firmly opposed to any government control of this plant, even if they should be guaranteed the right to its use. They feel that peyote is a natural gift of God to mankind, and especially to natives of the land where it grows, and that no government has the right to interfere with its use. The same argument might be made on behalf of cannabis, or the mushroom *Psilocybe mexicana Heim*. All these things are natural plants, not processed or synthesized drugs, and by what authority can individuals be prevented from eating them? There is no law against eating or growing the mushroom *Amanita pantherina*, even though it is fatally poisonous and only experts can distinguish it from a common edible mushroom. This case can be made even from the standpoint of believers in the monarchical universe of Judaism and Christianity, for it is a basic principle of both religions, derived from *Genesis*, that all natural substances created by God are inherently good, and all evil can arise only in their misuse. Thus laws against mere possession, or even cultivation, of these plants are in basic conflict with Biblical principles. Criminal conviction of those who employ these plants should be based on proven misuse. "And God said, 'Behold, I have given you *every* herb bearing seed, which is upon the face of all the earth, and every tree, in the which is the fruit

of a tree yielding seed; to you it shall be for meat.' . . . And God saw everything that he had made, and, behold, it was very good" (*Genesis* I:29, 31).

REFERENCES

Johnson, R. C. (1959). *Watcher on the hills*. New York, NY: Harper.

Radhakrishnan, S. (1927). *The Hindu view of life*. New York, NY: Macmillan.

Tennyson, H. T. (1898). *Alfred Lord Tennyson: A memoir by his son* (Vol. I). New York, NY: Macmillan.

Watts, A. W. (1962). *The joyous cosmology: Adventures in the chemistry of consciousness*. New York, NY: Pantheon.

Watts, A. W. (1966). *The book: On the taboo against knowing who you are*. New York, NY: Pantheon.

Zimmer, H. (1951). *Philosophies of India*. New York, NY: Pantheon.

CHAPTER TWENTY-THREE

Ordinary Mind Is the Way (1971)

In talking about experiences under the influence of lysergic acid (LSD-25) and other psychedelic chemicals, everyone must speak for himself. It is very hard to generalize, because the quality of these experiences depends only partially on the chemical reaction: of special importance are the mental state of the person taking such chemicals and the circumstances under which the experiment is conducted, that is to say, the set and the setting.

Therefore, so far as I am concerned, I have found experiments with psychedelics both like and unlike what I understand as the flavor of Zen, and find them more akin to the approaches of Vajrayana. I say "approaches" advisedly, because I am sure that the culmination of Vajrayana, as exemplified in *zogchen* meditation in the Nyingmapa school of Tibetan Buddhism, is essentially the same as Zen. If there is any difference one would have to be experiencing nondualistic differences!

As I have experienced them, the changes in consciousness stimulated by LSD go through a more-or-less regular pattern. There is first a slowing down of the sense of passing time. This moment becomes of supreme importance, and one seems able to savor its nuances to the utmost. In this state of mind, the future-oriented strivings of ordinary people seem to be somewhat insane: they appear frantic—missing the whole point of life—and for such people one feels sorrow rather than contempt.

Next there are subtle changes in sense-perception. Colors become intensely bright and vivid. Sounds, especially of music, acquire astonishing resonance. Light seems to come from inside things—not to shine upon them from outside—and

---

From *The Eastern Buddhist* (New Series), 1971, 4(2), 134–137. Copyright © 1971 by the Eastern Buddhist Society. Reprinted with permission of the Eastern Buddhist Society.

the whole world acquires that peculiar luminosity that is normally seen at dawn and twilight. Both to sight and touch, objects seem to undulate or breathe, and it is difficult to decide whether this is a hallucination, or whether one has merely ceased to ignore some constant and normal input arising from the natural fluidity of our organs of sense. Perhaps a world sensed by a breathing organism should seem to breathe, except that ordinary consciousness screens out this impression because of its very constancy. At this stage, and for some time later during the total 8 to 10 hours of the experience, closing the eyes will reveal extraordinary visions of highly colored, arabesque-like designs, which, for me, have raised the question that I may be seeing patterns of energy related to the basic structure of my nerves.

In the stage following, the "influence" passes into the thinking process, as if the chemical were spiraling through different levels of one's being to get at the inmost center. Here, the discriminating mind is confounded because it becomes completely clear that all so-called opposites imply each other and go together in somewhat the same way as the two sides of a single coin. Yes indeed, form is very much emptiness, and emptiness is very much form! And the same goes for "self" and "other," as also for what you *do* voluntarily and what *happens* to you involuntarily: it's all the same process. Before, you may have known it intellectually, but now it comes to you with full clarity and certainty that because you can't experience the feeling "self" without the contrast of the feeling "other," (or of solid without space) these supposed "opposites" imply each other mutually, and this leads on to recognition of the *ji-ji-mu-ge* principle that every identifiable thing or event implies and "goes with" all others, whether past, present, or future.

But here there is a danger-point in the experience, especially for those who have not had previous training in Zen, Yoga, or some similar discipline. It may appear, on the one hand, that you are the helpless victim of everything that happens, a total puppet of fate. How can you trust it? What guarantee is there that you will be able to think and behave rationally five minutes from now? On the other hand, it may appear that you yourself, like God, are doing and are personally responsible for everything that happens. Paranoia or megalomania may result from siding with either aspect of this experience—in other words, from failing to see that these are two opposite ways of looking at the same state of affairs, the state of *tzu-jan* or *shizen* in which everything is happening "of itself." This, then, is liable to be the point at which the inexperienced experimenter with psychedelics is in real danger of a psychotic episode. He may get the feeling that there is absolutely nothing to be relied upon, for if all comes from impersonal fate, how is that to be trusted? And if all depends upon his own self . . . well, "when I look for it I can't find it." Nothing in this whole universe is more unreliable than ego.

But if this stage is passed without panic—and the passage requires an attitude of profound faith or letting-go to you know not what—the rest of the experience is total delight, *sat-chit-ananda, mahasukha, sambhoga*. For there follows what, in Buddhist terms, would be called an experience of the world as *dharmadhatu*, of all things and events, however splendid or deplorable from relative points of view, as aspects of a symphonic harmony, which, in its totality, is gorgeous beyond all belief. And it is here that one may often have an apprehension of consciousness itself, of Mind, of the current inside the nervous-system, as vivid, electric-blue light such as is described in the Tibetan *Bardo Thödol* or in Hakuin Zenji's vision of total transparency.

But, in my own experience, the most interesting thing seems to happen just at the moment when the effect of the chemical wears off and you "descend" from these exalted and ecstatic experiences into your ordinary state of mind. For here, in "the twinkling of an eye," there is the realization that so-called everyday or ordinary consciousness is the supreme form of awakening, of Buddha's *anuttara-samyak-sambodhi*. It is so simple, so self-evident, so clear that nothing that makes any sense can be said about it. The *problem* vanishes, for the problem was the ever-impossible one of representing reality consistently in the forms of ideas and words, or of looking for something beyond and above this eternal here-and-now. This is where Zen language makes perfect sense. The ultimate meaning of Buddhism is MU!—or "the-sound-of-one-hand"—or my old worn-out sandals.

Of course, if you arrive at this by using LSD you remember it quite clearly, but the true feeling of it passes off. It is thus that many of us who have experimented with psychedelic chemicals have left them behind, like the raft that you used to cross a river, and have found growing interest and even pleasure in the simplest practice of *za-zen*, which we perform like idiots, without any special purpose. Perhaps we are not overly impressed with the "attainments" and the "spiritual status" of great Zen-masters, but we deeply appreciate their ordinary way of life.

PART SIX

Psychology and Psychotherapy

CHAPTER TWENTY-FOUR

Asian Psychology and Modern Psychiatry (1953)[1]

At the basis of Asian culture there are certain traditions and ways of life that have the outward appearance of religions. However, when one investigates such phenomena as the Vedanta, Yoga, Buddhism, and Taoism more deeply, and becomes familiar not so much with their popular application as with the thought and practice of their most advanced exponents, one discovers disciplines that are neither religion nor philosophy in the Western sense. For, unlike Christianity or Judaism, they only rarely involve "beliefs"—that is to say, adherence to positive, formulated opinions about the nature and destiny of man and the universe based on revelation or intuition. And, unlike Western philosophy, their *modus operandi* is only quite secondarily the construction of a verbal and logical description or explanation of man's experience.

Oriental "philosophy" is, at root, not concerned with conceptions, ideas, opinions, and forms of words at all. It is concerned with a transformation of experience itself, and it would seem that one of the things most akin to it in Western culture—akin by form rather than content—is psychotherapy. For this is the one major area in which the West has developed disciplines that aim at transforming the actual processes of the mind, and, through them, of the ways in which we experience the world, usually without commitment to any metaphysical or philosophical theory. Thus the curing of a psychotic or neurotic person, the transformation of the way in which he thinks and feels, is to a large extent the best Western analogy of the special concerns of Oriental philosophy. In many respects, then, it is more accurate to speak of such

From *The American Journal of Psychoanalysis*, 1953, *13*(1), 25–30. Copyright © 1953 by the Association for the Advancement of Psychoanalysis. Reprinted with permission of the *American Journal of Psychoanalysis*.

a phenomenon as Buddhism as psychology, rather than philosophy or religion. But this requires at least two reservations: that in *popular* practice it has many of the characteristics of a religion, and that its ultimate concerns are, as yet, hardly within the scope of Western psychology.

From the outset, there is one notable difference between the "psychotherapy," the transformation of the mind, envisaged by an Oriental psychology, on the one hand, and Western psychiatry, on the other. In the West we are chiefly preoccupied with the transformation of mental states that are peculiar to relatively few individuals, and that arise out of certain special conditioning circumstances of the individual's history. But Asian psychology interests itself in the transformation of states that are common to mankind as a whole, and is thus, as it were, a psychotherapy of the "normal" man. It proposes to change patterns of thought and feeling that are characteristic of the society as well as of the individual, though this does not amount in practice to an attempt to change the society as a whole. For it is recognized that in any given society relatively few individuals seem to have the capacity and the interest to liberate themselves from patterns of conditioning common to all.

It follows that for an Oriental psychology, "normalcy" could never be a standard of mental health—where "normalcy" means the ways of thinking and feeling, the conventions and life-goals, acceptable to the majority of persons in a particular culture. Likewise, the diseases of the mind are not recognized in terms of deviation from the normal. From this (Oriental) standpoint, there is a clear absurdity in trying to achieve the "happy adjustment" of an individual to the conventions of a society that is largely composed of unhappy people. Thus an Oriental psychology such as Buddhism is concerned, not with the peculiar frustrations of the neurotic individual, but with the general frustration, the common unhappiness (*duhkha* in Sanskrit), which afflicts almost every member of the society.

Buddhist and Hindu psychology agree in ascribing this general unhappiness to *avidya*—the Sanskrit term for a special type of ignorance or unconsciousness, which is the failure to perceive that certain desires and activities are self-contradictory and "viciously circular." The victims of *avidya* are thus described as being in the state of *samsara*—the "round" or "whirl"—a life pattern that, having set itself a self-contradictory goal, resolves or oscillates interminably to the increasing discomfiture of those involved. Thus self-contradiction rather than deviation from the cultural norm becomes the criterion of mental disease, for which reason this basic difference between Oriental and Western psychology requires some explanation.

Self-contradiction is technically described in Buddhist and Hindu psychology as the human mind in a state of *dvaita*, which is duality or dividedness, a concept rather more inclusive than the approximate Western equivalent of "internal conflict." One of the simplest examples of *dvaita* and its attendant self-contradiction is the making of one's life-goal the acquisition of pleasure and the avoidance of pain. It is pointed out that pleasure and pain are relative experiences, such that a life consisting wholly or even principally of pleasure is as far beyond any possibility of experience as a world in which "everything is up" and nothing down. To the degree that one avoids pain one also eliminates pleasure, and so achieves a way of life that is merely indifferent and boring. Consequently a life devoted to the pursuit of pleasure or happiness is devoted to a self-contradictory goal, because, in so far as one succeeds in gaining pleasure, there is necessarily a proportionate increase in some form of pain—often the simple, but most unpleasant, anxiety of losing what one has gained.

Buddhist psychology, in particular, emphasizes as perhaps *the* major form of self-contradiction a division of experience into subject and object, thinker and thought, feeler and feeling. According to Buddhist psychology, the notion that "I" am in some way different from the feelings that I now feel or the thought that I now think, the notion that man's psycho-organism contains an ego as the enduring subject of a changing panorama of sensations, is an illusion based on memory (*smrti*). The notion of the ego arises because of the apparent phenomenon of self-consciousness, of knowing that one knows, or feeling that one feels. But it is pointed out that, in fact, we are never actually self-conscious. While thought A exists, we are not aware *that* we are aware of thought A. "I am aware that I am aware of thought A" is no longer thought A, but thought B. Every attempt to be aware of being aware is an infinite regress, a vicious circle, like trying to bite one's own teeth. Thought B is not thought A; it is the memory of *having had* thought A, so that one is never aware of an ego that actually "has" (tense present) an experience. There are simply memory-traces of past experiences, and these suggest a continuous ego as a whirled light suggests a continuous circle of fire.

Thus the self or ego of which we claim to be conscious is in fact an abstraction from memory. The real substratum or content of the ego-experience is the memory of what has been, and not the knowledge of what *is*. In fact, then, I am not different from my present complex of thought-feeling-sensation. The difference between "I" and "my experience" is a misinterpretation of the difference between two kinds of experience—memory and immediate awareness. In fact, there is no "I" *apart* from the present, immediate experience. But contradiction arises when we try to make the abstract, conventional, and actually nonexistent "I" *do* something. For example, let us suppose that the present feeling is one of acute anxiety. If I "feel" that, apart from this anxiety, there is some separate, subjective ego that "has" this state of mind, efforts of will are made to fight the anxiety or to escape from it; the "I" is opposed to the anxiety. The result, however, is the familiar vicious circle of worry, because the effort to get rid of the anxiety is not the work of some independent, controlling "I": it is the anxiety itself—in a state of self-contradiction that only aggravates it.

THE "EGO" AS AN ABSTRACTION

But when it is realized that in fact there is no "I" to be rescued from anxiety, there follows a psychic relaxation in which the anxiety itself subsides. This realization is not, of course, a matter of mere theoretical perception, for it arises, not so much through intellectual self-analysis, as through a total awareness (*samyaksmrti*) of what and how one actually feels *now*. Buddhist "psychotherapy" values nothing more than simple attention to the actual, immediate content of sensation and feeling—as distinct from the verbalized abstractions that thought constructs *about* it. Thus it is understood that "ego" is an abstraction, and not a content of the immediately perceived world. It is a convenient abstraction if treated, like the equator, as imaginary. But if treated as real, as an effective agent, it is only a source of confusion and psychic self-contradiction.

From the foregoing it might seem that there is one respect in which Buddhist psychology contradicts itself. It states that the pursuit of pleasure and the flight from pain is an illusory and impossible life-goal, and yet it proposes a deliverance from the "general unhappiness" called *duhkha*. This reveals an important aspect of the technique of Buddhist psychology. Stated verbally and formally its "goal" is release from *duhkha*, but in actual practice it dispenses with psychological goals entirely. "Goal" implies futurity, and the object of Buddhist psychology is not future. The object is complete attention to what one feels *now*, complete *presence* of mind. This involves the falling away of any notion of a psychological goal, because it dissipates the sense of the "I" distinct from the present feeling, and hence of the possibility of changing or escaping from it. Finding itself "trapped," totally unable to choose to be other than the "now-state" of the mind, the "I" gives up or expires (*nirvana*). But this is a case of *stirb und werde* (die and come to life), of the familiar paradox of the law of reversed effort, of the creative freedom that comes through "self-surrender."

In our seminar, participants trained in some forms of Western psychotherapy often objected that this "surrender" of the ego would imply the mere abandonment of the psyche to the lawless direction of the unconscious, and that it was an attempted reversion to the undifferentiated state of "primitive mentality" in which the conscious and the unconscious are still confused. But such an objection rests on a confusion between "ego" and "consciousness." For in practice this dissipation of the ego comes about, not through unconsciousness, but through very intense consciousness, through the clearest awareness of the present realities of psychic life. Furthermore, the various types of Oriental psychology are not at all afraid of the "lawless direction" of an "unconscious," which has become capable of so great a clarity of consciousness. This may sound paradoxical if it is not understood that in Oriental psychologies such as the Hindu, Buddhist, and Taoist the unconscious is recognized as the source of consciousness, as *that* which is conscious. There should be no difficulty in understanding this when put into its simple physical parallel: we are conscious *with* the brain but not *of* the brain. We simply do not know how we are conscious, how we remember, how we reason, abstract, and perceive *gestalten*. We only know that the autonomic nervous system, for example, effects miracles of organization so complex that the conscious intellect is baffled in attempting to understand them. Oriental psychology feels, then, that the direction of life is basically from those unconscious processes that have thus far organized the marvelous complexity of the human form, and that constellate not only the autonomic nervous system but consciousness, memory, and reason itself. One might ask, then, *what* directions we are to trust if we cannot trust these!

The following quotations from the Chinese Taoist philosopher Chuang-Tzu (c. 400 B.C.) aptly express the Oriental attitude to this unconscious process (*Tao*):

> Your body is not your own: it is the delegated image of Tao. Your life is not your own: it is the delegated harmony of Tao. Your individuality is not your own: it is the delegated adaptability of Tao. You move, you know not how; you are at rest, you know not why. These are the operations of the laws of Tao.
>
> Things are produced around us, but no one knows the whence. They issue forth, but no one sees the portal. Men one and all value that part of knowledge which is known. They do not know how to avail themselves of the unknown in order to reach knowledge. Is not this misguided?

Tao is not "God" in the personified or conceptualized sense of the West—not a definite *thing*, but a negative concept analogous to the *un*conscious. Chuang-Tzu's mentor, Lao-Tzu, said: "The Tao which can be defined (lit., tao-*ed*, made its own object) is not the regular Tao." Tao is thus the total process of life that cannot be defined nor made conscious because no standpoint of observation exists outside it.

The foregoing considerations, which were but a few of the topics reviewed in our seminar, suggested two points of application for Western psychotherapy. The first was the therapeutic value of the subjective abandonment of any psychological goals, in the future, coupled with the gentle but persistent focusing of attention on the immediately present totality of feeling-sensation—without any attempt to explain, diagnose, judge, or change it. Oriental psychologies do not particularly value rationalized explanations of *how* a person has come to feel the way he feels, in terms of his past history and conditioning. They do not stress the idea that the perception or understanding of a causal chain, running from the past to the present, effects release from it. For the task of unraveling the conditioning of the present by the past is infinite, since it leads not only to conditioning of the child by parents, but also to the conditioning of the parents—and the child—by their entire social context. By such means, a thorough psychoanalysis would have to go back to Adam and Eve!

WESTERN "WRONG-AWARENESS"

Their feeling is rather that we are conditioned unconsciously by the past because of an incomplete and incorrect awareness of the present. Such "wrong-awareness" (*avidya*) underlies, in their opinion, one of the basic assumptions of Western thought and science: namely, the whole notion that the past contains the entire explanation of the present, that the understanding of what-is-now is complete in its mere history. For Oriental thought, the past exists only conventionally. It has no real existence, being a logical inference from present memory—an abstraction, and not a real, concrete experience. Therapy consists in releasing the mind from treating the abstract as the concrete, without, however, losing the power of abstraction.

The second point of application goes hand-in-hand with the first. Clear awareness, clear feeling, of one's real and present experience involves, as we saw, the realization that the ego—the continuing "I" as the substratum of changing experiences—is an abstraction and thus not an effective agent.[2] It can no more perform an action or effect a psychological change than, say, an inch or the number three. Yet Western science, and especially applied science (technology), is based on the assumption that its immediate objective is always the understanding and *control* of the environment by the ego. Western culture as a whole rests on the feeling that man, as ego, is the independent observer and potential controller of a world that he experiences as profoundly *other* than himself. Yet it is for this reason that Western technology leads us repeatedly into vicious circles. For if this split between the ego and the environment is unreal, the whole effort of technology is like the attempt of a hand to grasp itself. Its ultimate issue is the (almost) totally controlled or planned society— the totalitarian state—which is precisely the breakdown of society because it is based on mutual mistrust. It is the maximum effort of everyone to control everyone and everything else. "Am I my brother's policeman?"

Generally speaking, psychiatry shares most of the unexamined assumptions of Western science. Thus it tends to represent the unconscious as a mass of irrational and chaotic "drives" that have to be organized and controlled by the ego, the conscious. However, the method of control is not that of Protestant Puritanism or Catholic moral theology—the method of whip and spur. It is the much improved method of the humane horse-trainer, who "loves his animals" and gently coaxes them into obedience with lumps of sugar rather than whippings. But from the standpoint of Oriental psychology this is still a quasi-schizoid state of mind. It gives inadequate practical recognition to the fact that consciousness is a function of the unconscious, however much this may be admitted in theory. Man is not dual, the horse and its rider. The relationship of conscious and unconscious is perhaps better represented by the centaur. For it is surely absurd to conceive the unconscious as an unintelligence, a generator of nothing but colossal blind urges with which "we" must somehow come to terms, for we do not actually know *how* we reason or "will," or attain creative insight—which is only to say that these are, at root, unconscious functions.

"INSPIRED SPONTANEITY"

The second point of application is, then, a recognition of the fact that therapy is not the increase of conscious control over the unconscious by the ego. It is rather an integration of conscious and unconscious, preparatory to a type of living, thinking, and acting, which in Zen Buddhism is called *mushin* (*mu* "no," *shin* "mind'). *Mushin* is a kind of "inspired spontaneity." It is the art of making the appropriate responses to life without the interruption of that wobbling and indecisive state that we call "choosing." In other words, *mushin* is when acts and decisions are "handed over" to the same unconscious processes, which organize the ingenious structure of the body. Ordinarily, our breathing, circulation, hearing, and seeing all happen *mushin*—without the necessity of conscious direction and control. But there are also times when we make a witty remark or get an extremely important idea by the same mysterious process. We did not "try"; it just "came."

Buddhist psychology proposes to facilitate this process to the point where inspired spontaneity is not the exceptional but the usual mode of thought and action. But as in many other arts, this comes about through a process of growth and a subtle kind of "effortless discipline." It is by no means to be confused with acting wildly—saying or doing the first thing that comes into one's head. Yet thinking or acting "wild" or at random is indeed the starting point, though, like free-association in the analyst's office, it occurs in a context (i.e., some sort of *ashram* or school) where the resultant vagaries are accepted. In due course, one learns to use *mushin* as a way of action just as one learns the use of any other instrument or faculty, which, at first try, seems erratic and unreliable.[3]

In Western psychology, free-association—the nearest thing to *mushin*—has a different objective. The Freudian or Jungian analyst is primarily interested in *what* associations, symbols, and other diagnostic materials are produced in free-association. It is a way of exploring the unconscious in order to control it. In Buddhist psychology the point of interest is rather *that* spontaneous images and symbols are produced. The preliminary vagaries of *mushin* are not analyzed, for *mushin* is being brought into play as a way of life rather than a diagnostic technique. Herein, I believe, is reflected the wide difference between Eastern and Western psychology, the one trusting the unconscious and attempting to liberate the full depth of its wisdom, and the other trying to arrange a treaty wherein the unconscious accepts the control of the ego in return for certain recognition of its blind demands. But there are many signs that this difference is decreasing. Of late many of us have noted the growth of a remarkable humility and readiness to admit ignorance in Western psychiatric circles. For in the course of scientific research there is a long preliminary stage of rapid progress and easy overconfidence, until a point is reached where every addition to our knowledge reveals, at the same time, a new universe of ignorance. Through such knowledge we come to the place of which Chuang-Tzu said, "He who knows that he is a fool is not a great fool."

NOTES

1. This article arose out of an experimental seminar on "The Application of Asian Psychology to Modern Psychiatry," conducted during 1951 at the American Academy of Asian Studies in San Francisco under the direction of three members of the faculty: Frederic Spiegelberg, PhD, Haridas Chaudhuri, PhD, and the author. Dr. Spiegelberg is director of Studies at the Academy, and assistant professor in the Department of Asiatic and Slavic Studies at Stanford University. Dr. Chaudhuri was, before coming to the Academy, professor of philosophy at Krishnagar Government College in India, and is a noted exponent of the philosophy of the late Sri Aurobindo Ghose. Alan W. Watts is a professor at the Academy in the field of comparative philosophy and psychology, and author of many books on East-West relations in religion, philosophy, and psychology, including *The Spirit of Zen* (1936), *The Meaning of Happiness* (1940), *The Supreme Identity* (1950), and *The Wisdom of Insecurity* (1951). He is now working on a research fellowship in Oriental Philosophy under the Bollingen Foundation.

In a note to the [*Journal*] editor, Dr. Watts writes, "You will recognize, of course, that this is an enormous subject, such that in eleven-and-a-half typewritten pages I have only been able to sketch some of the general issues. I would have liked to have had space to give adequate recognition to the fact that there are many exceptions to some of my generalizations about Western psychiatry. But just because these are still exceptional, I felt it might be better to omit them in an article dealing with preliminary, large-scale considerations."

2. It must be understood that we are not here using the term "I" or "ego" to designate the total human organism. In ordinary speech, as well as in psychological jargon, they are seldom so used, but refer rather to a supposed center of consciousness for which other parts of the organism, such as the glands or the limbs, are objects that the "I" *has* or *uses*.

3. For further information about the techniques of *mushin* see Suzuki (1938, chap. 4; 1949). Interesting discussions of the same phenomenon from the standpoint of Western psychology will be found in three articles by E. D. Hutchinson (1939, 1940, and 1941).

REFERENCES

Hutchinson, E. D. (1939). Varieties of insight. *Psychiatry, 2*, 323–332.

Hutchinson, E. D. (1940). The period of frustration in creative endeavor. *Psychiatry, 3*, 351–359.

Hutchinson, E. D. (1941). The nature of insight. *Psychiatry, 4*, 31–43.

Suzuki, D. T. (1938). *Zen Buddhism and its influence on Japanese culture.* Kyoto, Japan: Eastern Buddhist Society.

Suzuki, D. T. (1949). *The Zen doctrine of no-mind.* London, UK: Rider.

CHAPTER TWENTY-FIVE

Convention, Conflict, and Liberation

Further Observations on Asian Psychology and Modern Psychiatry (1956)

When we compare some of the trends in modern psychotherapy with certain practical disciplines of Asian philosophy, we begin to discover a most instructive clarification of the whole function of therapy, and especially of its relation to social institutions. Among social institutions we must understand conventions of every type; not only the family, marriage, legal codes, and systems of language, but also ideas of motion, time, space and personality, which are generally understood to be properties of the physical world rather than conventions of social origin.[1] But it would seem that the rigorous procedures of mathematics and physics are confirming the intuition of Indian and Chinese thinkers as to the essentially conventional character of our conceptions of the physical world.

In Indian philosophy the world as we conceive it is termed *maya*—a much misunderstood word derived from the Sanskrit root *matr*—, "to measure," and from which we have in turn derived such words as meter, matrix, and material. Stated rather baldly, the theory of *maya* is that the world as we conceive it is a mental construct as distinct from an "objective" reality. This is not to be confused with Western views of subjective idealism. It is rather the more easily verifiable notion that the world as we conceive it (e.g., as a multiplicity of "things" in relative motion) is not to be identified with the world as it is, in the same way that one does not identify the measure with what is measured. One does not confuse the cloth with the yard, since it would be impossible to make clothing from merely abstract yards. Thus a person is said to be spellbound by

From *The American Journal of Psychoanalysis*, 1956, *16*(1), 63–67. Copyright © 1956 by the Association for the Advancement of Psychoanalysis. Reprinted with permission of *The American Journal of Psychoanalysis*.

maya when he confuses the concrete with the abstract, when he is hypnotized into believing that the world of immediate experience is precisely the system of concepts (*vikalpa*) and measures that he employs to manipulate that world, and to make reconstructions of it in terms of the symbols of thought. These concepts and measures are our social institutions, and include, as here defined, so-called laws of nature, ideas of "human nature," of matter, of things, and of events—all of which are held to be fundamentally arbitrary conventions of measurement and classification into which the real world is "fitted" as water is poured into jars, bottles and conduits of varying shapes and uses.

It is as if the real world corresponded to the amorphous ink blot of the Rorschach Test, and the world-as-conceived to the picture that the subject projects upon it. The actual ink blot is *satyam* or *brahman*, the immeasurable reality, and in this case the "blot" includes both the perceiver and the perceived. The subject's projection upon the blot is *maya*, but in this case the subject—every individual in a society—does not fabricate his own projection. He learns it from society in the course of his upbringing, and is taught to regard it, not as a projection, but as "what really is."

In every society, Western and Eastern, upbringing and education is the process of learning the conventions, a process that entails many types of difficulty and conflict. For social conventions are like the bed of Procrustes: those too short for it have to be stretched, and those too long have to be cut down. Since all these conventions are in some sense types of language, of symbolic classification and representation of the world, the difficulties in learning them are the same as those encountered in mastering the complex vocabulary and grammar of an unfamiliar tongue.

Here are two immediate sources of conflict. Because every system of "language" is an attempt to represent the world in terms of a static and usually linear system of signs, it appears that the world is, in itself, frustratingly complex. But the complexity lies in the language rather than the reality, and is analogous to the complexity of trying to drink water with a fork. Nothing is simpler than to breathe; it becomes complex only when one tries to represent how it is done in communicable signs, that is, to *think* about it. Furthermore, all such systems must of necessity have a static—because generally accepted—character that makes the real world appear bewilderingly changeable.

Conventional systems necessarily involve rather rigid conceptions of what man is, whether as the knowing subject or ego, as possessing a human nature with more-or-less fixed and "proper" characteristics, or as having a defined role in society that the individual is obliged to identify with "himself." Such concepts do not necessarily correspond with what we feel ourselves to be, in ways that we cannot easily formulate.[2] This, together with misunderstandings as to what the rules of the system are supposed to be, leads to the most excruciating conflicts between the individual and the system, or rather, between the individual's version of what he is and his version of what the system requires of him. To the extent that he identifies the rules of the system with the laws of nature, or of God, he feels himself to be at odds with reality itself, and to be faced with the choice of an intolerable submission or foolhardy rebellion against "iron facts."

Still another source of conflict is that the confusion of the abstract formulation with the concrete reality leads to the pursuit of goals that, because they exist in the abstract alone, cannot be attained or do not give satisfaction when attained. The ideal of a state of pleasure or happiness unalloyed with pain, or the goal of success, of wealth measured in the symbolic terms of money, are obvious examples of such abstract mirages. So, too, are life-goals conceived in terms of future time, as in the feeling that life is insupportable without a promising future, however agreeable the immediate present.

The idea of motion in time is perhaps the most problematic of all conventions, since it appears to be at once the source of our highest culture and our deepest misery. It is not difficult to see that there is an important sense in which only the present is real, even though constantly eluding our grasp. There seems to be no way of measuring it, of determining how "long" it lasts, and it cannot be regarded as infinitesimally "short" since this would seem to make any experience of it impossible. Likewise we feel that the present experience cannot be held in consciousness, and the more we try to retain it, the more we are aware of its evanescence. But this appears to be a special case of the whole problem of trying to define or measure the real world in terms of conventional structures. The problem of defining or grasping the present is essentially the same as that of trying to write a law without loopholes, or of formulating an exhaustively accurate description of a simple event.

By the convention of time we identify ourselves, collectively and individually, with history, with a linear series of past events projected into a future. This series is conventional not only in the sense that the present alone has actuality, but also in that the events constituting the history are a selection of "significant" events from an infinite possibility, just as there are infinitely many ways of projecting pictures into the Rorschach ink blots. To be identified with a history is to be identified with an abstraction, and thus to have the constant, gnawing sense that one lacks reality, that one is perpetually and ineluctably "falling apart," that one is everlastingly inadequate. But the definition, the description, is always inadequate to the reality. Therefore, to be identified with such an abstraction (e.g., a social role), or, worse, to be *in search* of security in terms of such an abstraction, is to be self-condemned to inadequacy.

The foregoing may sound as if social conventions were under attack. On the contrary, they are the *sine qua non* of human communication, the foundations of all culture. But, like every useful and creative instrument, they involve costs and dangers. There is certainly no doubt that every member of society must be disciplined in its conventions. But it must be recognized that the disciplinary process brings about inner conflicts, and almost inevitably warps the indefinable naturalness and spontaneity that every adult envies in the child.[3]

Therefore certain Asian societies provide optional means for relieving people of the warping effects of their acculturation and upbringing, which give them inward liberation (*moksha*) from the conventions that they have been compelled to learn. This liberation is, however, utterly different from rebellion against the conventions, since rebellion always implies a bondage to that against which one rebels. Liberation enables a man to be the master instead of the slave of his social conventions, and requires not that he condemn them as wrong, but that he "see through them" as arbitrary, like the rules of the game.

The process of acculturation and liberation is reflected in the outward structure of ancient Hindu society. The society as such consisted of four castes or role-groups: *brahmana* (priesthood), *kshatriya* (temporal power), *vaishya* (merchant), and *shudra* (laborer). By virtue of membership in one of these castes an individual possessed an identity. But, whenever he had completed his responsibilities, he might abandon caste to follow the way of liberation, giving up his identity and becoming a *sanyassin*, or homeless monk. The *sanyassin* was an "upper outlaw," just as the Untouchable was a "lower outlaw," for as the latter was beneath the law the former was above it. Ideally, the *sanyassin* was a *jivan-mukta*—one who, though still appearing to be an individual from the standpoint of social convention (*maya*), is from his own standpoint "no one," since he no longer identifies himself with a role, a *persona*, but with concrete reality, which is nonconceptual (*nirvikalpa*).[4]

In Chinese society, the process of acculturation is represented by Confucianism, and of liberation by Taoism or Buddhism, since the typical Taoist is the old man who has retired from the world to live alone in the mountains.

> I will cast out Wisdom and reject Learning.
> My thoughts shall wander in the Great Void.
> (Chi K'ang, A.D. 223–262, as cited in Waley, 1947)

In common with the *sanyassin*, the Taoist sage is a superior outlaw who has freed his mind from distinctions, from good and evil, life and death, pleasure and pain. But the Chinese view differs from the Indian in that the sage need not necessarily abandon his worldly duties, for as "king without and sage within" he can continue in outward observance of the conventions though inwardly free from their compulsions. "If the mind is without wind and waves, everywhere are blue mountains and green trees" (*Saikontan*, 291).[5]

In Chinese and Indian culture the "superior outlaw" was in the social order but not of it in the sense that society itself usually recognized him and even honored him. For the culture admitted the relativity and the limitations of its own conventions, and could assent in theory to the validity of a viewpoint beyond its understanding, as one might extrapolate an outside to a closed space of which one knows only the inside boundaries. But the cultures of the West, both Christian and secular, have never really had a place for the "upper outlaw," a fact that has surprisingly far-reaching and disastrous results. Christian theology has persistently identified the system of conventions—the moral order—not only with the will but also with the very nature of the Absolute, and has been resolutely opposed to any idea of God as beyond good and evil. The secular cultures of the West are in an even worse state, for having abandoned the belief in God there remains absolutely nothing but the system of conventions. Thus the secular state recognizes nothing outside its jurisdiction, nothing that "is not Caesar's." The Church admitted a degree of supra-conventionality in God through the doctrine of his infinite love and forgiveness. Behind the Law stood the Person who made the Law, an understanding heart rather than a blind principle. But the secular state cannot admit anything higher than Law, and thus is ever in danger of becoming a mechanism without mercy.

To identify the system of conventions with the Absolute is to weight them with excessive authority, and is actually a danger to the system, somewhat as an electric wire will burn out when the current is too strong for it. The Western mind seems to have difficulty in thinking in other terms than extremes—true or false, right or wrong—and thus finds it hard to see that a conventional principle can be true and important without being absolutely true and absolutely important. Thus when there arise between the man and system, the types of conflict described above there is no release save through catastrophic revolt against the whole system. But such revolutions "throw out the baby with the bath water," and usually establish worse tyrannies than those that they remove, since they go to the opposite extreme, and every extreme is a tyranny.

This Asian parallel suggests, then, that the most important function of a psychotherapy is to deliver people from the inevitable warping and the inevitable violence done to them in the course of their upbringing and education. It is not simply to ease the process of acculturation for intractable individuals, to "adjust them to the group." We must recognize that acculturation is at once a blessing and a curse, that it is both a necessity and a positively splendid achievement, which, however, entails the price of damage and danger. But as meat salted for preservation may be unsalted for eating, so the wise society provides a cure for the ill effects of social discipline—an initiation, a therapy, for the fully cultured adult, which releases him from compulsive identification with the system of conventions.

One may ask whether Western psychotherapy is in a position to fulfill this function. In some respects it begins to be so, as, for example, in its emphasis on self-acceptance and in its faith in the self-healing properties of the psyche. But its official "schools" seem, as yet, to have a long way to go, and this not only because of the still prevalent notion that its role is to provide adjustment to social norms. The chief difficulty is that the standard systems of psychotherapy—Freudian, Jungian, and Adlerian, as well as the more physiologically oriented systems of "orthodox" psychiatry—are still all too unconscious of their own identification with some of the more basic social conventions. One might say that these systems have an unanalyzed Unconscious whose contents are primarily intellectual, consisting of unexamined assumptions and premises derived from the philosophy and scientific theory of the nineteenth century. These include those conceptions of time, motion, causality, progress, history, and human nature that appear all too easily to be laws of nature rather than conventions of thought. For many years it has been fashionable to underrate the power of ideas as factors in producing neurosis, and the emphasis has been laid on the traumatic experiences of childhood, a fashion reflecting the theoretical assumption that physiology is more "real" than ideology. But the therapist can no longer neglect the force of ideas, and especially of unconsciously accepted ideas. He must be a philosophical analyst as well as a psychoanalyst—and this he cannot be unless he is himself philosophically "analyzed." He must be able to reveal the conflicts arising from the patient's unconscious self-identification with his conventional history, with his identity in time, with his conventionally delineated "body,"[6] and with many other conceptual entities.

Little can be done in this direction unless Western thought can overcome its characteristic fear that the only alternative to the conventional systems is total chaos. Thus many readers of the above may have formed the impression that the real, concrete, and nonconceptual world (corresponding in our analogy to the Rorschach blot) is in fact a disorder, a lawless and directionless waste-land. But this, again, is but another symptom of unconscious acceptance of a conventional pattern of thought that provides "con" as the only alternative to "pro." Both order and disorder belong to *maya*, to the category of conceptual projections upon a real world that altogether escapes the dualistic definitions of our thinking. Thus the one indispensable prerequisite for a therapy of this kind is the realization that man's concrete identity can *never* be an object of formal knowledge, definition, and control. This realization forces him into a psychological trap where nature—in her kindness—virtually compels him to see that he has no other alternative than a leap into the dark. And this is that "leap of faith" that is essential to every creative action: not belief in a formally defined God or philosophical dogma, but trust in that most concrete unknown that is the *atman*, the actual self.

NOTES

1. For this extension of the concept of a social institution I am largely indebted to the work of my colleague, Leo Johnson of Berkeley, California, from research in the field of the history of science.

2. As witness the intense difficulty of most patients in trying to describe the "peculiar feelings" that occasion their neurosis.

3. In the child this naturalness is still embryonic, and is similar in kind but not in quality to the naturalness of a "twice-born" adult who has "become again as a child."

4. And thus "supernatural" and "meta-physical" in the proper sense of being above

nature or *physis* when the word refers primarily to class, as in asking, "Of what *nature* is this?" Similarly, the immaterial is that which escapes the abstract category of matter or meter, and cannot be defined. Occidental conceptions of spirit relate it to the abstract rather than the concrete.

5. [*Saikontan* (Chinese—Caigentan) is a collection of aphorisms by Hong Zicheng, a Ming Dynasty scholar writing in the late 1500s. See Aitken and Kwok (2006) for a contemporary English translation—Eds.].

6. Since it is really a matter of opinion that I am "this" body as distinct from, e.g., a group of bodies (family or community), or that I am effectively confined within my skin.

REFERENCES

Aitken, R., & Kwok, D. W. Y. (Trans.). (2006). *Vegetable roots discourse: Wisdom from Ming China on life and living: The caigentan* by Hong Zicheng. Emeryville, CA: Shoemaker & Hoard.

Waley, A. (Trans.). (1947). *One hundred and seventy Chinese poems.* London, UK: Constable.

CHAPTER TWENTY-SIX

Eternity as the Unrepressed Body (1959)

The work of Sigmund Freud and his disciples is one of the most striking examples of the miscarriage of the romantic and naturalist movements of the nineteenth century. For it was presumably the intention of these movements to bring man to himself by overcoming the ancient dualism of mind and body, spirit and matter, reason and instinct, which for so long had been the religious and philosophical expression of the human being's mistrust of himself. Self-consciousness has almost always involved the dilemma and the vicious circle of every delicate system of control: *quis custodiet custodies*—who guards the guards, or rather, how do we control the controller, particularly when the controlled and the controller are one? How can man govern his bodily appetites if his mind and will are the same as his body? How can a hand hold onto itself? The problem seemed to be solved if man could be considered a duality—a mind in a body like a driver in a car. This was all very well so long as the controlling mind, soul, will, or ego could be trusted. But one of the main insights of Christianity, of Jesus, St. Paul, and St. Augustine, was that the root of evil lay in the spiritual sphere, in the perversion of the controlling will.

This insight actually destroyed the usefulness of the soul-body dualism, though it was not effectively questioned until the materialistic and naturalistic viewpoints of nineteenth-century science suggested a theory of man in which mind and will could be considered as operations of the body. Freud played an enormous part in constructing this unitary view of man. From his early days he had been convinced that mental processes could ultimately be explained in terms of neurology, but his contribution to the unitary view was not to lie along

From *ETC.: A Review of General Semantics*, 1959, 16(4), 486–494. Copyright © 1959 by the Institute for General Semantics. Reprinted with permission of the Institute for General Semantics.

these lines. It came through psychology, through a reduction of the motivations of the conscious will to irrational bodily instincts, or at least to instincts that had always been associated with flesh rather than spirit.

But this unitary, naturalistic view of man miscarried in a number of ways. It seemed impossible to take it seriously since for all practical purposes human beings had to feel themselves to be conscious wills directing and mastering nature both inside and outside their own organisms. Through the technology that arose from nineteenth-century science, men succeeded in controlling nature as never before, and this very success confirmed the feeling that, more and more, the rational will has to stand in opposition to natural spontaneity, and that the future development of man can no longer be left to the unmanaged process by which our species, our brains, and our consciousness have evolved. Here, at once, is seen the difference between the theory of evolution and the idea of human progress that the theory was originally supposed to justify. Evolution was the result of spontaneous natural selection; progress, of controlled mechanical direction. The terminology of man's separation from his body and his physical environment had changed, but the feeling, and modes of action expressing it, became stronger than ever. Scientific objectivity became the new distance between man and his nature.

In Freud and psychoanalysis this miscarriage is the more remarkable just because it was Freud's discovery that mental disease came about through man's repression of his own nature, and especially of that erotic energy that Freud felt to be the basic character of all living matter. Psychoanalysis, if it was to be something more than a system of investigation and description, that is, if it were to be a clinical technique for healing mental disease, had therefore to do something to reconcile the conscious will to its own erotic foundations—in short, to accept them instead of disowning them. But I have always wondered why Freud and his school have described the erotic processes of life with a curiously obscene nomenclature. Why call the erotic energy *libido*, suggesting "libidinous"? Why call the total distribution of erotic feeling over an infant's body "polymorphous *perversity*"? What is the final effect of being able to speak of literary, artistic, and philosophical productions as manifestations of "anal eroticism"? It is hard to avoid the conclusion that this is yet another symptom of disgust with oneself, and that Freud was at heart a moralist who, despite his brilliant diagnosis, did not like what he found and could not bring himself to that *love* of his own nature that would be the necessary condition for reconciling man to himself.

There is another, though related, respect in which the Freudian philosophy stands in the way of letting psychoanalysis be an effective cure of man's division against himself. This has been brought out and quite marvelously developed in a book that should certainly turn out to be one of the great philosophical works of our time, Professor Norman O. Brown's (1959) *Life against Death: The*

Psychoanalytical Meaning of History. This is a sympathetic critique of the Freudian movement, written largely from a sociological standpoint, by a professor of classics at Wesleyan University in Middletown, Connecticut, a man of obviously considerable learning in many fields—philosophy, literature, economics, political science, and sociology. With humor, scholarship, and philosophical sophistication, Professor Brown proposes the outrageous thesis that Freud's diagnosis be taken seriously, and that we actually face the practical possibility of doing without repression. It is his carefully argued opinion that civilization as we know it is an almost total denial of the human organism and its needs, a system of habitual and organized repression that is not biologically viable since it will destroy itself through pent-up hostility. He suggests that the lifting of repression will unveil many surprises: that exclusively genital sexuality is itself a repression, that death so far from something to be dreaded, is the foundation of individual personality, and that bodily existence is a form of bliss, which, if we would allow ourselves to experience it fully, would result in an almost mystical awareness of our union with the whole natural universe.

Professor Brown begins by asking why Freud ended his life on a note of pessimism, and why, in effect, his final position was to take the side of the ego and the superego against the id. For if the function of psychoanalysis has to be to square the pleasure-principle of the libido with the reality-principle of civilization, to adjust erotic energy to practical human relations and their moral imperatives, surely it must fail as a means of healing the basic human sickness. If this is to be the final position of psychoanalysis, then, says Professor Brown, we need a psychoanalysis of psychoanalysis, which is what his book begins to provide.

He traces Freud's pessimism to his dual theory of the instincts, to the idea that in all living creatures there is a necessary and ingrained conflict between Eros and Thanatos, between the love of life and the wish to die. If this is so, says Professor Brown, "all organic life is then sick; we humans must abandon hope of cure." He goes on, however, to reexamine Freud's theory of the instincts, skillfully arguing that the pleasure-principle and the death-wish constitute not an irresolvable situation of conflict but a polarity or dialectical unity. He argues that the death-wish is not necessarily at variance with the pleasure-principle, for fear of death arises precisely from the repression of Eros, from living a life that at every present moment is so unsatisfactory that the only hope seems to lie in an indefinitely prolonged future in which we seek repeatedly for lost delights of a past infancy.

> The difference between men and animals is repression. Under conditions of repression, the repetition-compulsion establishes a fixation to the past, which alienates the neurotic from the present and commits him to the unconscious quest of the past in the future. (p. 92)

The lifting of repression reveals that life, to which Eros presses, is life-and-death, and that death can be accepted when life has been fully lived, quoting Nietzsche's, "What has become perfect, all that is ripe—wants to die." "The precious ontological uniqueness which the human individual claims," says Professor Brown, "is conferred on him not by possession of an immortal soul but by possession of a mortal body. . . . At the simplest organic level, any particular animal or plant has uniqueness and individuality because it lives its own life and no other—that is to say, because it dies" (p. 104). Perhaps this is another way of saying that if an individual is unrecognizable without certain limits in space, it must also have limits in time, if time and space are actually inseparable. Freud's dualism of the instincts, he says elsewhere,

> leads to a suicidal therapeutic pessimism, because it results in representing conflict not as a human aberration but as a universal biological necessity; our modification of Freud's ontology restores the possibility of salvation. It is the distinctive achievement of man to break apart the undifferentiated or dialectical unity of the instincts at the animal level. Man separates the opposites, turns them against each other, and, in Nietzsche's phrase, sets life cutting into life. It is the privilege of man to revolt against nature and make himself sick. But if man has revolted from nature, it is possible for him to return to nature and heal himself. Then man's sickness may be, again in Nietzsche's phrase, a sickness in the sense that pregnancy is sickness, and it may end in a birth and a rebirth. (p. 84)

The repression of Eros and its sublimation into the abstract and bodiless ends of human culture that are always somewhere off in the future, representing an unconscious quest for the past, is thus what gives man a history. His concern with his history, personal or social, is the measure of his failure to be alive in the real present, becoming the fatuous pursuit of an ever-receding goal. Professor Brown quotes the economist J. M. Keynes' *Essays in Persuasion:*

> Purposiveness means that we are more concerned with the remote future results of our actions than with their own quality or their immediate effects on our environment. The "purposive" man is always trying to secure a spurious and delusive immortality for his acts by pushing his interest in them forward into time. He does not love his cat, but his cat's kittens; nor, in truth, the kittens, but only the kitten's kittens, and so on forward for ever to the end of cat-dom. For him jam is not jam unless it is a case of jam tomorrow and never jam today. Thus by pushing his jam always forward into the future, he strives to secure for his act of boiling it an immortality. [cited in Brown, 1959, p. 107]

The ending of repression, and thus the success of psychoanalysis, would therefore mean a recovery from history and a deliverance from spurious time. "Unrepressed life," Professor Brown says, "would be timeless or in eternity. Thus again psychoanalysis, carried to its logical conclusion and transformed into a theory of history, gathers to itself ageless religious aspirations . . . [It] comes to remind us that we are bodies, that repression is of the body, and that perfection would be the realm of Absolute Body; eternity is the mode of unrepressed bodies" (p. 93).

Much of Professor Brown's book is devoted to a discussion of what the life of the unrepressed body would be—something very different from the normal expectation of a life of unrestrained lust, hatred, and self-interest. His argument is that we should return (though why must he use this phrase?) to the "polymorphous perversity" of the infant, to a state in which the whole body is, as it were, an erogenous zone, resulting in a constant erotic communion with itself and the external world. He points out that though this may sound like the remotest utopian ideal, such a state of affairs has in fact occasionally been realized by mystics, both Western and Eastern, and may, indeed, descend out of the blue for brief periods upon very ordinary people—invariably carrying with it the conviction that this way of seeing things is reality, and that the so-called sober reality of the world as seen on Monday morning is a socially inculcated sham, based upon repressed senses. In such a state of open sensitivity, the most ordinary circumstances are so intensely marvelous that there is no conceivable necessity to go out seeking the enormous "kicks" of lust and violence. He argues, further, that if the Eros in us is indeed ultimately ineradicable, we have no choice but to be utopian, and to employ all our scientific resources, psychological and technological, in that direction.

> There is an attack on the great god Science in psychoanalysis; but the nature of the attack needs careful explanation. What is being probed, and found in some sense morbid, is not knowledge as such, but the unconscious schemata governing the pursuit of knowledge in modern civilization—specifically the aim of possession or mastery over objects (Freud), and the principle of economizing in the means (Ferenczi). . . . In contrast, what would a nonmorbid science look like? It would presumably be erotic rather than (anal) sadistic in aim. Its aim would not be mastery over but union with nature. And its means would not be economizing but erotic exuberance. And finally, it would be based on the whole body and not just a part; that is to say, it would be based on the polymorphous perverse body. (p. 236)

How is such a state of affairs to be brought about, and how are we to answer the obvious "practical" objections, let alone religiomoral objections, to the unrepressed life? It is here, I feel, that Professor Brown's book leaves something to be desired; he does not really tackle these problems save, perhaps, to point out the enormous practical objections to continuing in the ways society believes to be realistic. Apparently Professor Brown has only slight faith in the psychoanalysis of couch and consulting room, seeing rightly enough that these problems are not to be solved by *talking*, and agreeing with Trigant Burrow in feeling that they are really social rather than individual. By this he does not appear to mean that the solution lies through such political measures as the abolition of capitalism or monogamy, but rather, I would gather, through the recognition that such social institutions as our concepts of time, the ego, money, success, status, personality-role, and even death, have only a conventional reality.

> Psychoanalysis . . . transformed into a science of culture would, of course, be able to dispense with its mysterious rites of individual initiation. The necessity, on which Freud insisted, of undergoing individual analysis in order to understand what psychoanalysis is talking about would be eliminated: the problem and the data would no longer be individual but social. I am not criticizing psychoanalytical therapy as a technique for restoring broken-down individuals to a useful role in society. (p. 155)

> There is a certain loss of insight reflected in the tendency of psychoanalysis to isolate the individual from culture. Once we recognize the limitations of talk from the couch, or rather, once we recognize that talk from the couch is still an activity in culture, it becomes plain that there is nothing for psychoanalysis to psychoanalyze except these (cultural) projections—the world of slums and telegrams and newspapers—and thus psychoanalysis fulfills itself only when it becomes historical and cultural analysis. (p. 170)

So far so good, but surely Professor Brown does not mean historical and cultural analysis solely in the form of books and public discussions.

At this point the author becomes vague, and this criticism seems to me well worth making because it is hard to believe that so cogent a thinker has not a great deal more to say about this aspect of the problem. It is almost impossible in a review to do justice to the complexity of the argument and the multiplicity of topics in this extraordinary book—the fascinating digressions into literature and economics, history and religion. All in all, the great contribution of this work is Professor Brown's spirited and learned defense of the supreme reality and value of the organic human body and its physical environment. But one should not, I feel, jump to the conclusion that he is in any ordinary sense a mere materialist with a dreary mechanical-causal view of the physical world. He would certainly agree with Blake, whom he so often quotes, that "Energy is the only life, and is from the Body. . . . Energy is Eternal Delight." And again,

"If we could cleanse the doors of perception, we should see everything as it is—infinite." Indeed, as Professor Brown himself says, "The mentality which was able to reduce nature to 'a dull affair, soundless, scentless, colorless; merely the hurrying of material endlessly, meaninglessly'—Whitehead's description—is lethal. It is an awe-inspiring attack on the life of the universe" (p. 316).

If I may put this philosophy of trust in one's own body and one's own nature in my own words, I would say that if our senses could be sufficiently open, what we call the physical world, mortal and changing as it is, would give us all and perhaps more than we have ever asked of any spiritual world that we can possibly imagine. There have been times when, by various chances, my own senses have been opened far enough to see it, and to know that the process within us that Freud called libido is a love that comprises within itself at once everything from the earthiest sexuality, through the most human endearment, to Dante's "love that moves the sun and other stars." Perhaps the thing that is most deeply repressed in the Freudian system is that Eros is the same as Logos, that the supposedly blind and unconscious id is profoundly intelligent.

REFERENCE

Brown, N. O. (1959). *Life against death: The psychoanalytical meaning of history.* Middleton, CT: Wesleyan University Press.

CHAPTER TWENTY-SEVEN

Oriental and Occidental Approaches to the Nature of Man (1962)

It is a common assumption among the most educated people in the Western world that the peoples of Asia are more primitive than we, and therefore represent within the scale of evolution a standpoint that for us would be regressive. It is furthermore understood that they do not in these cultures place much value upon individual personality and have ideas of man in which the individual tends to be merged in the collective, whether the collective be social or cosmic. It is understood that the ideal, say, of Indian spirituality is to enter into a state of consciousness in which the individual ego disappears into the undifferentiated esthetic continuum (courtesy of Dr. Northrup).

Now this, of course, is a travesty, but historically it is rather interesting that this view of essential differences between East and West, a view to a large extent espoused by psychoanalysis, arose at just the time when the West was busy colonizing other peoples, particularly those in Asia. It thus became an extraordinarily convenient doctrine, for purpose of colonization, to suppose that this was not mere rapacity, but bringing the benefits of a higher order of civilization and culture to less developed peoples.

Greater knowledge in the course of time shows us to what an enormous degree all these suppositions were unfounded and shows us furthermore that the typical contrasts that we believe to exist between East and West are to a large extent imaginary. Nevertheless, to make some of these contrasts is instructive just for theoretical discussion. I'm not, at the moment, going to point out by

From L. N. Solomon (Ed.). (1962). A symposium on human values (pp. 107–110). *Journal of Humanistic Psychology*, 2(2), 89–111. Copyright © 1962 by the Association of Humanistic Psychology. Reprinted by permission of Sage Publications, Inc.

detailed facts and illustrations how wrong these contrasts were, but to try to carry the discussion to a more constructive level.

Now, I suppose it is true that the Western view, by which I mean largely the Anglo-Saxon-Protestant view of the nature of man, does set an enormous value upon integrity and the uniqueness of the individual. We have, of course, seen in this country a great epoch for so called rugged individualism, which has now collapsed. And, it is curious as one looks around even in such an intelligent assembly as this to notice an extraordinary uniformity of appearance. In other words, what individualism led to was an increasing conformity and loss of individuality, because when the value of each individual finger is so emphasized that it amounts to the severance of the finger from the hand, the finger begins to lose its life.

I believe we are seeing the consequence of this individualism by the fact that it is swinging over into its opposite—that is to say into simple collectivism—because actually the individualist and the collectivist doctrine, the capitalist doctrine and the Marxist doctrine, rest upon the same misconception of man's nature: the conception of man as something that is not truly natural. That may sound odd because the flavor of scientific thought in the nineteenth century, from which Marxism and Capitalism and, of course, much of psychotherapeutic doctrine emerges, was a philosophy of scientific naturalism or monism. It was felt that the human psyche was a naturalistic phenomenon and not a soul imprisoned in flesh from another world. But the behavior of Western man has belied this theory altogether. For it is out of a climate of scientifically naturalistic opinion that there arose a technology whose avowed aims were "the conquest of nature" and an attack of major dimensions on the physical world.

For the feeling was no longer that man was a supernatural soul embodied but that he was a natural freak—an accident of nature—a completely spontaneous and unreliable emergence of intelligence resulting from the process of natural selection that could not be relied upon to perpetuate the phenomenon. Therefore, man as the intelligent accident had to seize the initiative and defend his intelligence and his culture against all forces of natural erosion. Thus, the natural freak took the place of the supernatural creation, but the two doctrines are in practice identical.

Now we contrast this, though the contrast is a flagrant generalization, with such conceptions of man as we find especially in China, in the doctrine known as "Taoism," and to some extent in India, in conceptions of man that are found in Buddhism and Hinduism. Here we find, I think, something of enormous importance. It is generally understood that the view of man's identity among Buddhists and Taoists is based on some terrifying regressive experience called "mysticism" or the "oceanic feeling," and I think much misunderstanding arises from the use of such words. Generally speaking, the content of this sort of experience is that the boundaries that are ordinarily established between the ego, or the individual, and the rest of the world are not rigid boundaries at all and that they are not boundaries in the sense of being walls but rather boundaries in the sense of being bridges. In other words, in these types of thought the human being inside the skin and the world outside the skin are regarded as having in the skin a common boundary that belongs to both. We know this in our own behavioral sciences, especially in human ecology and social psychology. We know very well that if we try to describe accurately the behavior of the human organism, whether that behavior be called psychic or physical, we have only to go a few steps before it becomes necessary for us to describe the behavior of the environment—and vice versa. In other words, you can't go very far in talking about the behavior of an individual person, or of a social group, or of a species, without talking about the behavior of the environment: thus you are beginning to describe the behavior of a unified field.

Although, in these sciences, it is perfectly clear theoretically that this is what we are talking about, there is no parallel as yet between this theoretical conception of man and our personal feeling of our own identity. We still feel ourselves to be what I have called skin-encapsulated egos, and whatever value this feeling may have, carried too far it leads to a chronic alienation, a sense of loneliness, of being isolated intelligent organisms in a blind, unintelligent universe. This drives us to seek security in a herd-like social structure. Therefore, there are two views of man that are not contradictory, but that should stand to each other in a hierarchical order. (1) The Eastern view of man as a node in a unified field of behavior, because, after all, this so called mystical experience is nothing other than a direct sensation of man-and-the-universe as a single pattern of behavior. That's all it is. You don't need to invoke any spooky business whatsoever. (2) The Western view, which stresses the special value of each organism and its unique character.

These two views of man go together in a hierarchical pattern. They are not mutually exclusive. I have sometimes said that it is characteristic of maturity to be able to distinguish what is more important from what is less important, without making what is less important unimportant. I feel that it is quite basic that we need a conception of man coupled with a sensation of man as really belonging in his natural and cosmic environment. We cannot assume that we are unique islands of intelligence in a completely capricious world. For a world in which man evolves must be an environment *itself* evolved to the point where it can ecologically sustain the human organism. An intelligent organism argues an intelligent environment.

It is of capital importance for the Western world to find some means of sensing ourselves in this way unless we are to run amuck completely and abuse and exploit our natural resources and animal, insect, and bacteriological fellow-beings. We shall never use this world correctly without the concrete definite experience that it is as much our own body as what is inside our skin. But this universal feeling of man's nature is not antithetical to Western values concerning the importance of the individual and its personality. As a matter of fact, not only is there no conflict between them but they are mutually essential. To return to the finger: the fingers of the hand can move separately. They are plainly articulated and quite different, but their life, their difference, their individuality, depends upon their belonging to one organism—to having beneath their individual difference a common ground.

These Eastern views of man have emphasized our common ground, what in Hindu philosophy is called the Atman, the super-individual self that is always underlying our individual selves. To go back down into that ground is not a regression. It is recovering again the foundation of one's house. To use the French phrase, it is *reculer pour mieux sauter*—going back to take a better jump. Childhood and the maternal basis of nature is not something that we leave and quit in becoming adult. It is something from which we grow up as a tree grows up from the soil.

CHAPTER TWENTY-EIGHT

The Woman in Man (1963)

If I am asked, "What is a woman?" I must reply, "I know, but when you ask me, I don't." As soon as we become analytical and definite about things, familiar objects tend to disappear. Under the microscope, human flesh seems to disintegrate into an unfamiliar arabesque of cells. This is why scientific investigation seems so often to be a debunking of popularly held notions, for when we examine things closely and carefully, we realize that the world is a lot less easily categorizable than we might imagine.

Attention has been drawn to the unsoundness of hard and fast distinctions between male and female, masculine and feminine, based upon a bifurcation of the innate and the acquired. In the past the physiologist and biologist were expected to tell us what a woman *really* is; that is to say, how she was made by nature. Then came the anthropologist and the historian, and later the psychologist and psychoanalyst, to tell us how she has been distorted by culture, as if there were some fundamental difference between what man is biologically and physically, and what he becomes through cultural or self-conditioning. This would argue a basic distinction between nature and culture, between natural and artificial, and between the biological and animal on the one hand, and the human on the other. I think that this is a distinction from which our culture is actually suffering, and one to be made only with great care, realizing that it is entirely for purposes of discussion.

We make distinctions between things in order to be able to talk about them. The human body is, after all, a unity; it goes continuously all the way

From *The Potential of Woman*, edited by S. M. Farber & R. H. L. Wilson, 1963, New York: McGraw-Hill. Copyright renewed © 1991 by S. M. Farber & R. H. L. Wilson. Reprinted by permission of Katherine Neubauer and the S. M. Farber estate.

from top to bottom. It has some interesting parts in it, and if I want to talk about those, I describe it in the digital system of language; I have to cut the body into bits. I have to say it has a head, a neck, and shoulders, and speak about these things almost as though they were parts of a machine, which as a matter of fact they are not. This is because we have to cut things up in order to digest them, in the same way that you get a cutup fryer in the store but you don't get cutup fryers ready chopped out of eggs.

The differences, then, between what is masculine and what is feminine must be thought of from many points of view. There are things that are typically masculine and typically feminine, using the word "typically" in a very strict and special sense, since things that are typically masculine or typically feminine have no necessary connection with biologically identifiable males or females.

For example, in psychoanalytic symbolism all long things are male and all round things are female. Aggressiveness is typically male; passivity is typically female. But we are only speaking here in a kind of symbolism that is highly useful, so long as we don't confuse it with actual individuals, and what they are supposed to be and how they are supposed to behave. I want, then, to draw attention to a strong tendency in the Anglo-Saxon subculture of the United States to identify all value with certain stereotypes of the male and to put down and devaluate certain stereotypes of the female. This is quite a different matter from exalting men and debasing women.

I want to talk about things, attitudes, and ways of thinking that are *typically* male or female rather than biologically male or female.

It seems that the human mind, whatever that is—I would prefer perhaps to say the human organism—is equipped with two modes of sensitivity, which I will compare respectively to the spotlight and the floodlight or to something like central and peripheral vision in the eye. According to our system of typical symbols, the spotlight, being a pinpoint sort of thing, will be male, and the floodlight, being diffused, will be female. This is interesting, since our culture puts these two kinds of knowing in a hierarchy of values whereby the spotlight is considered much more important than the floodlight.

To be specific, the spotlight mode of consciousness is what we call conscious attention. It is the kind of attention that we use when we read or when we notice things. For example, a husband can come home from a committee meeting and his wife will say, "Well, what was Mrs. Smith wearing?" And he will say, "I didn't notice," even though she happened to be sitting right opposite him at the conference table. He indeed saw, his eyes registered optically what the dress was, and what its color was, but it was not noticed.

All knowledge upon which science is based, and upon which the careful description, study, and organization of the world is based, depends on noticing, or "spotlight knowledge," and it is characteristic of this that it focuses on certain areas of experience. To the degree that it illuminates those areas brightly and comprehends them, it ignores what lies outside.

Conversely, there is the method of knowing like the floodlight. This is a way of understanding that does not notice but somehow manages to take in a whole variety of things simultaneously. In other words, you can drive your car into town without even thinking about it, using that kind of knowledge. You regulate your breathing, the secretions of your glands, the circulation of your blood, and all the homeostatic balances of the organism by this kind of diffused sensitivity. It is a curious thing that there is really no scientific name for this mode of knowing. It has been called the preconscious, the subconscious, the unconscious, the superconscious, but these are all very vague terms, lacking in precision. Yet there is quite definitely underneath the spotlight kind of attention this diffused knowledge, or awareness of all that is going on, without which we should be completely and totally lost.

However, in a culture that underestimates the value of this mode of knowledge, the academic world does almost nothing to develop it. Lynn Whyte pointed out some years ago that the academic world values only three kinds of intelligence: mnemonic intelligence, that is, good memory; computational intelligence, being able to figure; and verbal intelligence, being able to read and write. It does not, he said, develop social intelligence or kinesthetic intelligence.

Social intelligence is something that is exceedingly difficult to teach by any system of verbal instruction; you have to get it by osmosis. But the scientific temper as we have known it undervalues that sort of knowledge, because of its vagueness and uncontrollability. Therefore, we tend instead to value conceptual knowledge, and through that we get a wholly conceptual orientation toward life.

I would like to discuss what seem to me to be four principle symptoms of this one-sided orientation. Firstly, there is a tendency for symbols to be valued more highly than what they represent. For example, money becomes much more important than wealth. In other words, the symbol, or notation, for goods becomes more valuable than the goods themselves, and the *reporting* of things that happen becomes more valuable than the events themselves. It is a byword in the academic world today that how you are recorded in the registrar's office is much more important than anything you did by way of study, because it is your record that counts. If you present yourself in a government office and say, "Here I am," they say you do not exist unless you produce a piece of paper such as a birth certificate to prove that you do exist, and in the same way a lot of people don't feel that they are really alive unless they can read about it in the newspaper.

I believe that this is the basis of a great deal of juvenile delinquency. Because you can read all about it, you can be a hero and see that you really do exist, because the record of history has put you down as being really here. So in this sense, we come to what somebody has recently called pseudo-events: the arrangement of meetings, of parties, of all sorts of affairs simply for the purpose of being written about in the newspapers or shown on television.

I am not quite sure this symposium is a pseudo-event at the moment or not, but I want to point out that the style of evaluating things so that what is on the label is more important than what is in the bottle, that the skinny cover of one's automobile is more important than what is under the hood—that whole feeling of the symbol having primacy over the what the symbol signifies—is the result of giving an excessive valuation to noticing. In this way it is characteristic of our culture that when you get a menu in a restaurant it is far more interesting to read it than actually to eat what it stands for. This is the difference between our menus and other people's: a French menu just gives the bare name of the dish. But here we go on to say "garnished with crispy toasted slivers of fresh farmhouse potatoes"—a long, long mouthwatering description of something that may well turn up uncooked in rancid axle grease.

Secondly, we tend to notice *things* and ignore their contexts or backgrounds. Often with a group I draw a circle on the blackboard and ask, "What have I drawn?" In the vast majority of cases people will say I have drawn a circle or a ball or something like that; very few will ever suggest that I have drawn a wall with a hole in it, because again we tend to notice a small figure enclosed and to ignore the background. While this gives us enormous power of description, it also is a serious disadvantage for human survival in that it makes us blind to the environmental factors of all things and events. We regard what is inside the boundary of one's skin as being much more important than what is outside. This is a familiar problem to architects, because they know that most of their clients think of a house in terms of a person rattling around in a space. But the architect sees the space and the person as an integrated unit and therefore does something more than just provide him with a cubic box to rattle around in; he wants the house related to all that that particular person does within the house, because he sees the house and the person as one activity, a single process.

When human beings do not notice this, and regard the earth that surrounds them, the hills, the forests, the vegetables, the birds, and the waters as a kind of grocery store where you simply expect things to be on the shelves to be exploited and plundered, they become unaware of the solid fact that the earth around them is an integral part of their own body. It is just as much *you* as your hands and your feet, and as soon as you neglect that, you begin to get deteriorated products in the soil, you begin to get problems of water shortage, air pollution, imbalances of insect life, epidemics, and God knows only what. This comes as an exaggeration of this typically masculine way of thinking, which notices the figure and ignores the ground.

The third thing is rather intimately related to that—a conception of the human personality as something *inhabiting* the body, so that each one of us senses himself as a center of consciousness in a bag of skin, confronting an alien world of more or less stupid mechanisms. The primitive science of the nineteenth century has become twentieth-century common sense, and thus it seems generally plausible that value, love, and intelligence exist only within man, within the human organism, and that therefore outside in the world of nature there is an impersonal, mechanical process that has absolutely nothing in common with human values. That estrangement is again a result of noticing only one-half of one's own existence, to notice the half inside the skin and ignore the "better-half" outside.

A fourth way in which this kind of valuation appears in our culture, is that the male tends to become mistrustful of all within him that is feminine, and tends therefore to insist on his masculinity in extremely exaggerated ways and to identify with stereotypes of what it is to be a man, which are quite absurd.

You will notice in current magazines an advertisement sponsored by the United States Marine Corps. It shows enormous phallic rockets standing at Cape Canaveral and a boy in a helmet talking anxiously on the telephone, and the caption says, "What does it take to feel like a man?" Now I don't want to discourage the Marine Corps, but that is not the way to go about it; you won't get real men in the Marine Corps that way. If you want to get real men to join the Marine Corps, there is a very simple formula—I leave it to your imagination. But phallic rockets are going to attract a man who is afraid that he is not a male and therefore compensates by identifying himself with exaggerated male stereotypes. As a result of this we get the general feeling that there is something weak about feminine characteristics and the fear that it would be "sissy" for a man to incorporate within his personality elements of grace and charm. To be uncharming, to be gruff, grubby, and tough has been considered the quintessence of maleness.

I was recently reading an anecdote about that great pirate and admiral, Sir Francis Drake, entertaining a Spanish nobleman for dinner aboard ship. He had actually captured the Spanish nobleman and was negotiating for fat ransom, but he did it in a gentlemanly way. Here was this tough old sea captain entertaining at dinner, dressed in lavish silks, with gold plate on the table and a trio with violins and flutes. As a parting gift Sir Francis presented the Spaniard with several bottles of fine perfume. Imagine being entertained in such style aboard a United States aircraft carrier.

The person who has no reason to doubt his masculine potency can really afford feminine graciousness, but in this culture he may be thought homosexual or sissy because he does so. But this exaggerated worship of the male gives itself away.

These are four symptoms that show, in various ways, how something that we might call feminine in the typical sense is neglected, undeveloped, unused.

Let me repeat them: Firstly, the symbol has more value than the thing, and Logos more value than Eros.

Secondly, the seed is valued more than the soil and the word more valued than context.

Thirdly, the individual is more valued than the individual's own extended body, which is his whole natural environment.

Fourthly, a special form of the symbol being more important than the fact, the symbols of maleness are confused with genuine maleness.

It is an ancient tradition that man is completed only by developing the feminine within himself. This underlies such forms of oriental self-development— Tantra in India and Taoism in China. Lao-tse, great philosopher of Taoism, in his classic, the *Tao Te Ching*, the book of the way and its power, says, "While being a male one should cleave to the female, and so doing one will become a universal channel and be possessed of a power that one will never call upon in vain." Taoism is the whole art of completing the masculine by the feminine. He says elsewhere, "Man at his birth is supple and tender, but in death he is rigid and hard. Therefore suppleness and tenderness are the marks of life, but rigidity and hardness are the marks of death." This is illustrated by the parable of the willow and the pine. Under the weight of snow the springy branches of the willow give way and the snow falls off them, but the pine stands there with tough strong branches, and as the weight of the snow increases they finally crack. Every engineer knows in building a bridge that it must sway in the wind and be flexible; a rigid bridge is a collapsed bridge. This is equally true of psychological and cultural rigidity, and thus symbolic overmaleness is profoundly weak and unsound.

It is not, then, without reason that in old theological writings the soul is always "she," the anima, the *ewig Weiblichkeit*, the muse, the feminine source of inspiration. You don't hear much about that today because souls are out of fashion. We think of the soul as some kind of anthropoid or maybe gynecoid spook, whereas the soul is precisely what I called our generalized sensitivity, our floodlight awareness, as distinct from our spotlight awareness. It is our innate, natural intelligence, completely structured like our bodies, which are at root a form of thinking, of unbelievably subtle intelligence. The academic fallacy is that what cannot be described in words is neither intelligent nor intelligible. Yet the neurologist is unable to figure out the complexity of the very brain with which he thinks, and such a man tends to become humble through realizing that he is more intelligent than he knows! He is more intelligent than he can explain himself as being, in flat contradiction to the erstwhile scientific fashion of considering rational intelligence more intelligent than subconscious intelligence.

To value and use this hidden feminine aspect is peculiarly important in the problem of bringing about constructive change in human behavior. If history has one monotonous lesson, it is this: that human behavior has never been changed by preaching. Violence, whether physical or moral, does not truly move the human being. Even so great an apostle of nonviolence as Gandhi was still a violent man, because his appeal was a serious and earnest call to duty. Why is it that nobody has yet tried to change human behavior by the force of enchantment? Would you, as a woman, get very far by saying to some man, "It is your duty to raise children and bring up a family; you *must* love me! Come on now, get to work!"

You go about it in an entirely different way, on the principle that you catch flies with honey. In the same way, educators, ministers, legislators, or whoever is interested in changing human conduct must realize that they need to go to charm school and to be like the musician Orpheus, who was supposed to tame the wild beasts and calm the winds by playing on his lyre. He is the archetypal symbol of the man who developed his feminine aspect and became a universal enchanter, commanding the obedience of the world because it just loved to follow. That is the secret power of the feminine. I don't think I am "giving the show away" about the secret of feminine power. Nor am I trying to advocate a greater respect for, and use of, this power by warnings of doom—that we are going to be annihilated by atomic bombs, overpopulation, and ecologic imbalances if we don't pay attention to this principle. The point is rather that it is a way of living that is a delight, not a duty. For it will never be worth surviving if we *must* survive, but only if continuing to live is an expression of joy.

CHAPTER TWENTY-NINE

An Interview with Alan Watts (1969)

(with Philip D. Ungerer)

U NGERER: What sorts of things are you thinking about now in comparison to the days of *The Spirit of Zen*?

WATTS: Well, I'm fundamentally interested today in the problems of human ecology, the double situation of our technological development on the one hand and our sense of human identity on the other. Because our technology in the hands of a man or being who feels alienated from his environment is an extremely dangerous thing. We are actively fouling our own nests at the moment, using technology to destroy and pollute the planet. I feel the reason we are doing that is because we have a hallucinatory sense of identity. Man experiencing himself as a skin-encapsulated ego is a completely false feeling. It's against the facts of biology and ecology. I'm interested in talking in that sort of language because the scientific and academic community, as well as the political one, cannot understand the language of mysticism.

UNGERER: Are you saying that this is the first time that man cannot identify the problem? He knows the symbols.

WATTS: Yes. His problems have become all too real. Therefore, you get to the point where the man who regards himself as extremely hard-nosed and practical is forced by the logic of his condition to face up to the mystical.

UNGERER: How is it more real today than, say, the things that confronted the individual in the Middle Ages?

WATTS: Simply because technology has amplified everything we do. It's like turning up the volume on the radio. So, the things we think we want and our strategy for getting them—here's a situation which, in other words, has simply

From *Existential Psychiatry* (1969), 7(summer–fall), 109–117. Copyright © 1969 by Seven Bridges Publishing. Reprinted by permission of Jordan M. Scher, editor of *Existential Psychiatry*.

been turned up. So we see it so devastatingly clearly that it simply cannot be dodged. There's no escape anymore. You can't get away from civilization anymore. There are no far-off frontiers. People think about getting out into space, but more and more one sees there is no escape. So you have to turn around and face the fundamental questions: Who am I and what do I want? Everyone has to face this because there is nowhere else to go.

UNGERER: What sorts of things are you examining within this context?

WATTS: A number of things. The philosophy of war, for example. That's a nitty-gritty question.

UNGERER: What can we do to further our self-knowledge on some of these things?

WATTS: It's a matter of consistently thinking through your feelings. In other words, I was asked by the Air Force weapons research center in New Mexico a few years ago to be on a panel to discuss the question of what is your basis for personal morality. This was started by the chaplains because none of the senior officers indicated any religious preference. Apparently, this disturbed the chaplains. So they thought they'd better expose these senior officers to some sort of religious thinking. They had an Episcopalian, Jesuit, etc. I said to these people that my basis for personal morality, and I'll tell you quite frankly because you people are supposed to be realistic people, my basis is that I am out for me. But I'm not going to be crude about it. I'm not going to trouble people. I'm going to make a pretense that I'm very nice and I'm all for them and that I love everybody and I'm ready to cooperate. But, I told them, I have a couple of problems. The two problems are, first of all, what do I want? The more I think about it, the more I realize that I don't know. There are two situations in which you don't know what you want. The first is one in which you really haven't thought about it at all. You think you want the things that Madison Avenue tells you you ought to want. The second situation is where you've been through all that. You've thought out what other things go with all the things you say you want and then you realize you cannot relate yourself to the world in the position of saying I want certain things out of this world because there are no things in this world. There are no separate things. Everything goes with everything else. Then you ask the question, you love yourself, you say, but who are you? And you find that you cannot ever find a separate definable entity that can be called you.

UNGERER: You are with the world?

WATTS: You are with it. You're a symptom of the world. Fundamentally, you are the universe, as the universe is centered at a particular place one calls here and now. The universe centers itself at every center. It's like on the surface of a sphere, every point on the surface can be regarded as the center of that surface. In the same way, the universe is an energy system centered wherever there is a center. The human organism is a center. So you discover that your whole notion of yourself as an ego inhabiting a bag of skin is an illusion or a social institution actually of a high civilization which has defined people in that way. People are hoaxed into believing that a social institution is a physical reality. So we get this situation of people actually feeling themselves in a sensory way of being this ego inside the bag of skin. They do not realize that this is simply brain washing imposed upon them in childhood.

UNGERER: Given this state of affairs, what can man do about it?

WATTS: The question is the trouble. Because what can I do about it simply aggravates the situation of thinking in terms of a separate ego. So we've got a situation today when everybody feels powerless. We feel that things are out of control, that civilization is much too complicated, that nobody understands it. That even the President of the United States doesn't know what he's doing—and indeed he doesn't. But the meaning of that situation is that we feel out of control because the individual we think ourselves to be is unreal. Of course you can't control everything as an ego because you don't exist as an ego. You exist as the total organism-environment-energy field that's you. We've got models of the world that are hopelessly out of date. The Christian-Jewish model of the world is political. It's the king. The God-King who is in charge of everything and rules it by spiritual violence. And that's a totally obsolete model in a universe which is organic or at least quantum mechanics as distinguished from Newton's mechanics. That's why we are feeling our powerlessness. So to ask the question "what can we do about it?" is to ask the wrong question.

UNGERER: I remember one time you talking about the cork in the water. Isn't what you're saying now quite different from that?

WATTS: Yes. If you think of yourself as a cork in the water, that implies that you are completely passive, that you are a victim of circumstances and are moved around by your environment like a puppet. But that's simply the other pole of the idea that you are separate from your environment and that you should dominate it. Both are based on the same false premise that you are separate from your environment. You're only a puppet so long as you define yourself that way. But when you realize that what you are truly is that you are your whole physical organism, and that includes your brain and nervous system and all the rest—And the human brain is far more intelligent than any human ego because it is an organized system which we cannot yet describe in language yet—it is far too complicated.

UNGERER: How so the ego?

WATTS: The ego is merely a social institution. It's a way of defining the mask, what role you play. But the brain, which is in a way what you are to begin with, organically, has as yet escaped full description. And because, therefore, it has a higher order of complexity than the most complex language we can use to describe it, it is more intelligent. So what we've got to do, as we say, is use your head. And that doesn't mean think. It means use your nervous system, which is to say we have to relearn being spontaneous. A person only thinks when he doesn't trust himself.

UNGERER: You've said, though, that when one is confronted by the command "Be You," one finds it impossible. I see a departure in what you're saying now.

WATTS: Yes, but the danger is with people who think they are going to be spontaneous, that they imitate their preconception of spontaneous behavior. We think that our culture is defined as nonspontaneous so we think spontaneous behavior must be the opposite of the way we normally behave. When you get an encounter group, for example, people say they are going to take off their social masks. Immediately, they start being hostile to each other because they think that's more real. It isn't necessarily. We see it only as too alternatives. We have to learn a new dimension: What do you really feel like? And to do that you have to stop categorizing, stop thinking. You have to be quiet. You have to look for you, whatever that is. It's possible.

UNGERER: We're trapped in words here, obviously.

WATTS: Of course, but the point is that we are completely spontaneous in growing hair, breathing, all that's going on all the time. It's highly intelligent, but it's unpremeditated.

UNGERER: We really are there already?

WATTS: Yes, it's a question of realization.

UNGERER: What, by the way, do you think of the approaches in psychiatry today?

WATTS: The whole domain of psychiatry is very exciting because in some ways it's sharply divided between custodial psychiatry and adventurous psychiatry. Custodial psychiatry is a terrifying priesthood which is perpetrating in contemporary terms everything that was done by the Spanish Inquisition. In 1600, a person who had deviant religious opinions was considered an exceptionally dangerous person. Because he would, as a result of his unbelief, be damned eternally. And the people who said that had the same kind of authority in their culture as the professor of pathology at the University of Chicago. So if the professor of pathology says somebody has cancer there's no question about it. He has cancer. If, in 1600, the professor of theology said someone had heresy, it too was a serious problem. And they were asking out of a sense of mercy; that this person had to be cured because he is going to suffer for all eternity. And anybody he infects is likewise going to suffer. So we are first going to reason with him and if he won't listen to reason, we are going to put pressure on him and finally, we are going to burn him. Because just at the last moment, that might get a repentance out of him. These people were acting in a fully responsible sense that they were after mental health for the good of everybody. Today, religion is not important. In a sense, all religion is phony. People really don't believe in it, but they think they ought to. The moment you get sermons on the subject of how one ought to have faith, religion is dead. Because the assumptions of religion have not become unquestioned common sense. So what has taken the place of heresy is not deviant opinion about religion, but a deviant state of consciousness. So a schizophrenic is a heretic because he is experiencing the world in an irregular way. So we can't stand it. When we get this behavior, we say that fellow is all mixed up because he doesn't go along with our feeling of what isn't mixed up, what is straight conduct. So we put them in an institution where they are depersonalized. They become nonpeople. And then everything done to these people in the institution helps to confirm that. In order to get attention, he has to become violent. But that defines him as sick. So the whole thing is a vicious circle. They subject these people to torture—shock treatment, deprivation of all civil rights. You have the inquisition all over again.

UNGERER: And the adventuresome kind?

WATTS: A great many people in psychotherapy realize that's not the answer. They may quarrel with the whole model of mental illness as being an illness at all. The work of a psychiatrist, many of these people think, is not to cure sick people, but to cure normal people. Get rid of the normal hallucinations that are fouling up the whole of human society. You can call a number in Chicago, for example. It's called "Let Freedom Ring." You get a taped spiel against sensitivity training, encounter groups, all these things, equating them to Chinese Communist techniques of self-criticism, where everybody gets themselves into a group and reduces themselves to a common denominator. These Bircher people haven't the faintest idea of the difference of that on the one hand and on the other hand a group that has nothing to do with self-criticism at all. It's self-realization. You can only have self-criticism in relation to some preconceived standard of how you ought to be. Here, a truly operating encounter group is one where you don't know where you are going. No preconceived idea of what you ought to be.

UNGERER: Do you find this perhaps the most hopeful technique?

WATTS: That's rather the wrong question, again. The only truly hopeful thing for the future is people who know how to live in the present. The schizophrenic is somebody who feels that there is something wrong, but doesn't know what it is. Beyond schizophrenia is the same sort of person who is enlightened, like a Buddha, and he knows what's the matter, he knows how to negotiate with society. The schizophrenic doesn't know how to negotiate with society because he cannot live both on his level of consciousness and pretend to live on the level of consciousness of ordinary people.

UNGERER: In a sense they are both wearing masks.

WATTS: Sure, but in the latter case you've got a conscious mask instead of an unconscious one. You know what you're doing. I said earlier that the only people who have a hopeful future are those who can live in the present. Because plans are only useful to people who know how to live in the present. Because if your plans materialize, that materializing of those plans can be useful only if you can enjoy them. If, when plans mature, you always are making other plans, you never get there. So now, we should realize there is no place to be except the present. It's even nonsense to talk about exercises to live in the present because you can't do anything else. So we have to see that's the situation. In the same way it's not a question of how do I overcome my egocentricity. You are not an ego in a real sense. So it's a matter of simply seeing what is already is the case. So, in this sense, everything I'm trying to do is not to be understood in the context of preaching. Of saying you should. I'm only interested in what's happening. If one can show to people in government, in terms of, say, military strategy, that what is happening is in flat contradiction to what they say they want, we say to them you are not immoral, you are simply stupid. Because you don't know what you want and what you think you want you aren't getting. Take the war in Viet Nam. It would be a perfectly understandable war if we were over there to capture the territory and carry off all those beautiful girls and bring them back to the United States and screw them. Because if that were our intention, it would be perfectly understandable, human and merciful, for we'd be careful to preserve the territory and keep the girls in good shape. As it is, we are fighting for a pure abstraction. We are fighting an ideology called Communism in the name of another ideology called Free Enterprise, neither of which actually exist in reality. But because we are fighting for an ideology, not anything real, we are absolutely ruthless. There can be no agreement, no compromise because we are just as hung up on our ideology as they are on theirs. Until we get away from these ideologies and go back to being ordinary, scurrilous human beings, we'll never understand each other.

UNGERER: I'd like to get you back to therapy for a moment. Could you elaborate a bit on your feelings about the encounter approach?

WATTS: I think on the whole this sort is better than the couch approach, the psychoanalysis ritual because it's focused on the here and now. Psychoanalysis has always considered that what you are today is the result of your past and, therefore, you have to go back into the past. That's like saying the wake drives the ship. What I think is developing, and what I think many therapists under-stand today, is that you're not the consequence of an abstract past, but that right now you are creating your problems. Therefore, let's watch the problem in the act of being created.

UNGERER: And the use of drugs?

WATTS: I think this is not a new situation because drugs have been used for centuries because, after all, we are what we eat. When we find what we are is somehow not right, we eat a little something to adjust our feelings. So we take medicine when we get sick and all drugs are medicine rather than diet because they are correctives. So we have to beware of living on drugs as diet. The drugs like LSD, etc. are correctives. You don't need to take LSD very often. Two or three times in a lifetime may be quite adequate. That can give a person a completely different perspective about who he is and what's going on. That should be enough. Once you get the message, you hang up the phone. It can be very helpful, but not just by itself. LSD is not bottled wisdom. We've found that what it does to them is proportional to what they bring to it. If you give LSD to a very creative person, it helps him be more than he already is. But if you give it to someone who is basically an adolescent, he doesn't get much out of it. I know a lot of kids who are saying they are through with the drug scene because there was nothing in it. Well, the point is, there wasn't enough in them. If you do know how to use it, LSD can be as valuable to an investigator of the mind as a microscope is to a biochemist.

UNGERER: What do you consider to be the most insidious things being done in psychiatry today?

WATTS: Things like lobotomies, shock treatments. All those things that are done to normalize people forcibly. It doesn't work. It's a frantic passion to maintain reality in the form of the world as seen on a bleak Monday morning. It's a matter of not having any expectations. You see, that's the whole problem of education today. The university thinks they know what the future is for which they should prepare these children. The truth of the matter is the world is changing so rapidly, we don't know what the future is. So the function of an educational institution is to put young people into a situation where they learn how to face the unknown or unpredictable. That means that everybody in the university, faculty, that is, or students, are all students engaged in a cooperative opening of our minds to not what we know but what we don't know. Everybody's engaged in research. You ask questions. The Socratic method is the model. The highest compliment, by the way, that you can pay to a scholar's book is not that he has the answers, but that he asks the right questions.

UNGERER: Do reviewers say that about your books?

WATTS: I don't very often get reviewed. I don't know why. Whenever, for example, I've written books that start from a theological basis, you see what I do in my books is go around a wheel and approaching the hub along different spokes. The spokes can be theology, logical positivism, psychiatric assumptions, it makes no difference where I start, but because I'm headed for that hub which is the point about man's identity that he is not this separate thing, but that he is the whole universe. Now, when I write a theological book, the theologians never will review it except that they'll misrepresent it entirely and then argue against that misrepresentation. Niebuhr did this with one of my books years ago. He simply stated that the case presented by the book was the exact opposite of the case that the book did, in fact, represent. Then he attacked it. I wrote a book about the relationship between Christianity and Hinduism and the reviewer in the *Christian Century* said it's about Christianity and Buddhism. He hadn't even read it! I find this occurs quite often. I really don't get reviewed. For example, the last book I wrote was called *The Book: On the Taboo Against Knowing Who You Are,* and sold thousands and thousands of copies. It's hardly been reviewed at all.

UNGERER: Do you still consider yourself an exponent of Zen? You seemed to have moved away from it in many ways.

WATTS: I don't use a label. I try to say I'm not any kind of religionist. Zen is something like ophthalmology. It's correction of conception. I don't say Zen is what I'm trying to sell. Because to Western ears, that sounds exotic, like an imported fad. I want to think and talk within the framework of Western science and discourse so that we don't have to appeal to any kind of exotic mumbo-jumbo, although at the same time, I want to say that, from studying these things in Oriental culture, I have learned a great deal. They've been very valuable to me. But what I have learned is not something that I should come on with like a missionary. Missionaries have the preconceived idea that they know what's right without examining, except in the most patronizing way, that what we believe is right.

UNGERER: Do you think there is a growing awareness at the so-called grass-roots about what you are trying to get at?

WATTS: Yes, I do.

UNGERER: The trouble in this country. What is your view about it?

WATTS: Don't forget, we are the richest country in the world. People are bothered because they are not rich enough and they think everything will be solved if they get enough. Then they get it and they start worrying about their health. There's always something to worry about. When you compare the U. S. with India, India is in the most ghastly poverty. Even our slum dwellers are rich beyond the dreams of a Calcutta slum dweller. But we have a different worry. The technology we have has just amplified this worry so that it becomes extraordinarily dangerous. So our particular problems are about the ghettos, race, and one of the great problems, the older people hating the young people. They actually want to get rid of them. There are too many of them. The population is increasing. This manifests itself with all sorts of rationalizations to divert attention from the actual fact that older people want to get rid of their kids—don't take them to a party, get a sitter, get them out of sight, etc. So we send them to Viet Nam to get killed off. And this lies behind the whole Chicago incident during the convention. The police today stand as the hired agents of the people who feel that they have only certain security and don't want anybody to rock the boat. So they get these unconscious homosexuals, the tough guy types, the over-specialized males, to beat up the so-called sissies. Because, you see, that kind of man, when he sees the long hair and the flower power stuff thinks it's sissified. They feel that way about the kids. Because these kids characteristically are quiet. They are only moved to aggression by the sorts of things that happened in Chicago. This goes back, of course, to some very fundamental questions in our culture. The paradox in American culture is that we are a republic which is a form of government in which the people are supposed to rule themselves, but our metaphysical presuppositions are monarchical. Any Christian or Jew believes the universe is a monarchy. Well, then, how can you say the republic is the best form of government? So when we take the republic seriously, the monarchy people feel threatened. We have, in other words, a very serious problem about the conflict of church and state. What has created the crime problem is basically that we are asking the police to be armed clergymen and enforce laws against prostitution, gambling, fornication, etc., which primarily are a matter of personal morals. Now a question that needs no answer is what kind of person would volunteer to serve on a vice squad? What kind of man would volunteer to peek through holes in toilets to detect homosexual acts? We know the only kind of persons who could possibly volunteer are creeps. So, you can't reform the police. You can't say let's upgrade training, etc.; you can't do it. But what you can do with one stroke of the pen is take all matters of private morals out of the hands of their jurisdiction.

UNGERER: Do you think we are coming to that?

WATTS: Well, it's got to happen because the police are overburdened. Their energies are vitally needed to control traffic, prevent ordinary street muggings, etc. If they were restricted to that, we wouldn't have the police problem we have today.

UNGERER: Is it a matter of doing some of these things or we'll all go under?

WATTS: Yes it is. One of the people running around the U.S. today and talking about these things and one with whom I have a great deal of personal sympathy is Buckminster Fuller. He's the most hopeful man talking today and I very much agree with him. He has the idea that he calls *synergy*. This means that in any complex organization the intelligence of the whole organization is greater than any one of its parts. Therefore, organic man may be a great deal more intelligent than conceptual man. Man, as he is, the brain, the nervous system, is more intelligent than man as he conceives himself to be ideologically, religiously, politically, psychologically. So, through the extension of the nervous system, through radio communication, jet aircraft, everything is being tied together. Thus, an organization is developing that is not being controlled by any kind of conscious programming, but by its own nature. And he's saying that that organization is more intelligent. An example. It's the nature of jet planes that they must keep flying or they will deteriorate. So we have a tremendous interest in maintaining this transportation system. Now all customer barriers, passport barriers are in the way of the air lines. They are a nuisance. They are going to have to go. Also, any sort of war interferes with the schedule. People want to travel. Wars get in the way. What technology is doing is that it's a process where we progressively realize where we were in the first place. The bat has something like radar. The human being temporarily has lost his instincts and is creating them technologically. Then he may rediscover that he had them all the time.

UNGERER: And then we'll talk to the porpoise.

WATTS: Sure. I was talking to John Lilly, who knows more about the porpoise than anybody. He was saying, look, this creature does not need any appliances. It lives in the water with the grocery right in front of it and if it isn't right there, it's just a matter of a short swim away. It doesn't need clothes, a house, books, records, because the body of the creature is its culture. These are highly intelligent, essentially playful beings. Their only problem is that they cannot stay under the water very long. They have to keep surfacing, therefore, they have to stay alert. Beyond that, they have it made.

UNGERER: And man's problems?

WATTS: His problems seem to lie largely in his system of thinking. That is to say, thinking is a method of representing events in the physical world with symbols. Now this has great advantages, but its disadvantage is that one confuses the world as symbolized with the world that is. You can't confuse the map with the territory, the menu with the meal. We have to get back to a direct relationship with the physical world. Even when one says "physical world," that is a concept. Physical is an Aristotelian idea about the nature of things. The problem is in confusing the world thought about with the world that is; we eat the menu and not the dinner. We've created a culture which has a reputation for being materialistic and isn't materialistic at all. It's sort of the reverse of Plato's cave, where the people are looking at the shadows on the walls.

CHAPTER THIRTY

Psychotherapy and Eastern Religion

Metaphysical Bases of Psychiatry (1974)

Perhaps I should first explain that I have been involved with psychotherapy for years, and talking to the staffs of psychiatric institutions has been one of the main things I do. Something that has constantly worried me about almost all the schools of psychotherapy is what I'm going to call a lack of metaphysical depth, a certain shallowness that results from having a philosophical unconscious that has not been examined. Now, I'm a philosopher, and as a philosopher I am grateful to some of the great pioneers in psychotherapy like Freud, Jung, and Adler, for pointing out to us philosophers the unconscious emotional forces that underlie our opinions. In a way, I'm also a theologian, but not a partisan theologian. I don't belong to any particular religion because I don't consider that to be intellectually respectable. We are grateful for their showing us how our unconscious and unexamined emotional tendencies influence the ideas that we hold. It's a very valuable insight. Be we, in our turn, are interested in the unconscious intellectual assumptions that underlie psychotherapy.

Psychotherapy is a product of the philosophy of nature of the nineteenth century. From my point of view, that is not an exact science but a mythology that is taken for granted. The philosophy of nature of the nineteenth century has become the common sense of the twentieth century, and is widely accepted in the medical profession, in the psychotherapeutic professions, and in sociology. From the point of view of a physicist or an advanced mathematician or biologist, however, there is a serious question as to whether psychiatry is a genuine

Reprinted from the *Journal of Transpersonal Psychology*, 1974, 6(1), 19–31. Copyright © 1974 by the Association for Transpersonal Psychology. Used by permission of the Association for Transpersonal Psychology.

science, and even whether medicine is a genuine science. These professions have not caught up with quantum theory and are still holding Newtonian views of the universe, thinking about their subjects in terms of mechanical models. We hear constant reference to "unconscious mental mechanisms." What on earth are we talking about? Psychoanalysis is to a very large degree psychohydraulics—an analogy or model of the behavior of the so-called psyche based on Newtonian analysis of the mechanics of water—and so we hear of a basic notion of psychic energy as libido. Now libido means "blind lust," and it operates according to the pleasure principle that comes into conflict with something else called the reality principle. One of the difficulties of the human being is that the whole length of the spinal cord separates the brain from the genitals, and so they're never quite together. . . .

We are looking at the basic models underlying the practice of psycho-therapy. There are exceptions to this and you must always understand that I'm going to make exaggerations and outrageous generalizations for purposes of discussion rather than laying down the law. Our practice is based on the world view of nineteenth-century scientific naturalism, which has as its fundamental assumption that the energy that we express is basically stupid—blind energy, libido—and it's called the unconscious. The assumption of this philosophy of nature was that the psychobiology of human nature was a stupid mechanism, a fluke that had arisen in a mechanical universe, and if we were to maintain this fluke and its values, it would be necessary for us to enter into a serious fight with nature. Scientific naturalism was in fact against nature, believing nature to be foolish and blind, and therefore in need of being dominated by our intelligence that, paradoxically enough, was the product of this foolishness. But the fluke had happened.

Let's go back into the history of this idea. Western man, whether he was a Jew, a Moslem or a Christian, had always considered the natural universe to be an artifact, something made, and a child in this culture very naturally seems to ask its parents, "How was I made?" To make something is to create an artifact; you make a table out of wood or a sculpture out of stone. This is the basic mythology underlying our common sense. We are mostly unconscious of the basic images in which we think. That is why I say that we have an intellectual unconscious. We are mostly unconscious of the basic belief systems within which we think and behave. So here is this basic belief system—we are all made. It would be unnatural for a Chinese child to ask, "How was I made?" He might instead ask, "How did I grow?" The idea of our being manufactured objects is basic to almost all Western thought. In the course of history, when we got rid of the idea of God as the maker, we were stuck with the idea of the universe as a mechanism.

People today who believe in God don't really believe in God; they believe that they ought to believe in God, and therefore are somewhat fanatical about it because of their doubt. The strong believer always profoundly doubts what he believes and therefore wants to compel other people to believe, to bolster up his own courage. A person who truly believes in God would never try and thrust the idea on anyone else, just as when you understand mathematics, you are not a fanatical proponent of the idea that two and two are four. . . . Nevertheless we have been stuck with the assumption that the universe is a mechanical construct.

Now, what is the difference between a mechanism and an organism? A mechanism is an arrangement of parts that are put together, gathered, as it were, from separate places and assembled. No organism comes into being that way. An organism starts as a seed, or a cell, a little small . . . I'm at a loss for words, because I won't call it an object, and I won't call it a thing, and I won't even call it an entity. All these words misdescribe what an organism is. Anyway, it starts tiny, and it swells, and as it swells, it becomes more complicated, not by the addition of parts that are screwed on or welded together, but it has this marvelous capacity of growth . . . and that's how we came into being. An organism is incredibly intelligent, and its intelligence surpasses anything we might call mechanical intelligence. In physics, where there are millions of variables, we manage to understand them by statistical methods and then predict what will happen. But in the ordinary situations of life where we are dealing with perhaps several hundred thousand variables, we haven't the ghost of a notion how to handle them.

For example, you can't possibly keep up with the literature that you need to know in the field of psychotherapy. It's endless, and most of it boring. We all become scanning lines, because conscious attention is the brain's radar, and you know how radar works. It is the propagation of a beam with a bounce factor in it that feeds back to the scope, and you keep scanning the environment for changes. If a rock should come up, if a storm should come up, if another vehicle should come up, the radar picks it up. Our conscious attention is only a minimal part of our total psychic functioning, because the brain as a whole, the nervous system as a whole, regulates and organizes all kinds of psychic and physical functioning without thinking about it. You don't know how you beat your heart. You don't know how you make a decision. You don't know how you breathe. You may, if you're a physiologist, have some idea of it, but that doesn't enable you to do it any better than somebody who doesn't know. All this incredibly intricate functioning is carried on unconsciously. Oh, we say, it's by the brain. But what is the brain? Nobody really knows.

One of my great friends is Karl Pribram, who is a professor of neuropsychiatry at Stanford. He has a marvelous understanding of the brain, but he is the first person to admit that he doesn't really understand it at all. He's fascinated, and he shows us most amazing things—how the brain creates the world that it sees. If you want a simple explanation of this, read J. Z. Young's (1960) book, *Doubt and Certainty in Science*. He begins with the brains of octopuses, which are very simple brains and fairly easy to understand, and then he goes on to the human brain and shows how we are what we are by creating the kind of world that we think we live in. The brain, the nervous system, evokes the world, but is also something in the world. What an egg-and-hen situation that is! He is stating in very sophisticated language some ancient philosophical problems. When Bishop Berkeley explained that the world is entirely in our minds, he had a very vague idea of the mind. Everybody used to think that the mind was something like space. It had no form of its own but was able to contain forms, like a mirror that has no color but reflects all colors, like the eye lens that has no color but is able to see all colors. This was a vague idea of the mind. Now the neurologist studying the brain gets a very precise idea of the mind. He can say it has all these neurons, dendrites and what have you, pathways. But in the end, he comes to exactly the same thing. He's saying, the world is what your brain evokes. So we're back where we started, only in a more complicated and more rigorous way. Nature is assumed to be complex. We say, the world is complicated, not only in its biology, in its geology, in its astronomy, but also in its politics, its economics. Actually the world isn't complicated at all. What is complicated is the attempt to translate the world into linear symbols.

What I'm developing is the idea that *what we are physically is far more intelligent than what we are intellectually*. Behind our minds and our books and our schedules and our laws and our mathematics, there is something far more intelligent than anything we can record. So naturally, when you get into the practice of psychotherapy, you have first of all gone through school, and you've read a lot of textbooks, and you've seen a lot of procedures and heard a lot of explanations. Incidentally, do you know what "explained" means? It means "to lay out flat, to put it on a plain." It's like those slices people take of fetuses, and enlarge them and so on, to see what a fetus really is. You've got it *explained*. But a fetus "laid out flat" is no fetus, just like blood in a test tube is not the same process as blood in the veins—because it's out of context. Blood in the veins is in a certain situation. It is what it is because of its relationship to a vast system. But in a test tube where it's isolated, it's not the same thing. A thing is also *where* it is.

Let us begin to realize that we have identified ourselves with a process of mentation or consciousness that is not really ourselves at all. Let's have the humility to see that. We don't trust ourselves because of this, and therefore scientists are sometimes saying today, "Human civilization has come to the point where we've got to take our own evolution in hand. We can no longer leave it to the spontaneous processes of nature." Well, these people are idiots. Like a conference of geneticists that I recently attended: they summoned for advice several philosophers and theologians—that showed they were pretty desperate—and they said, "We have just realized that we're within reach of the power to control human character by genetic manipulation. We want to know what you people think about this. What sort of human character should we produce?" Wowee! There were various views offered, and I said, "Of course

you can't know, because you yourself are genetically unregenerate. You yourself
are the product of the random selection of nature, and therefore by your own
showing, you must be a mess. You, as a mess, cannot decide what should be
the proper order of things. The only thing you can do is to ensure that there
be as many different kinds of human being as possible."

We don't know what kinds of human beings we need. At one period,
we need people who cooperate and who are good team-workers. At another
period, we need rugged individualists who have their own ideas and go ahead
and persuade everybody else to follow them. We're in a teamwork situation
right now. Everybody is always looking out of the corner of their eye to see
what everybody else is doing. What is the right way to proceed evolutionarily?
We haven't the faintest idea. We all seem to agree that we should survive. I'm
not at all sure about this. There are two schools of thought about life. Take
the analogy of fire: some people think a good fire is a colossally bright blaze
that is a flash, like lightning. Other people say, "Oh, no, no, that's a waste of
energy. Cool it. Keep it down to a dull glow that goes on for a long, long time,
so that 'this is the way the world ends, not with a bang but a whimper.'" What
should life be? Suppose you were confronted with a choice: you could spend
one night with the most beautiful woman imaginable, or man, and have the
most incredible orgiastic experience, and then die. Or, you could be with some
rather indifferent, not very exciting companion for a long, long time, so that
you would be bored. Which would you choose? We find that very difficult to
decide. In the ordinary way, we are not really aware of life because we're using
our conscious attention too much. We think we are our opinion of ourselves,
our image of ourselves, and therefore feel reduced to linear symbolism, and
that's a kind of strung-out, skinny thing. It's starved. It's all skin and bones and
no flesh. When you think of yourself as your ego, as your personality, this is
an entirely fictitious account of yourself, lacking in richness; if you are identified with that, you feel impoverished, and you have to go to a psychiatrist. You
say, I feel frustrated. Of course you do. The psychiatrist also feels frustrated,
because, by and large, he has the same opinion of himself; he thinks he's an ego.

Freedom is the only thing that works. If I don't trust you, I can't live with
you. I've got to make the gamble, even though it will sometimes be betrayed.
I've got to make the gamble of trusting you. I can't go out of my door without
a fundamental sense that I can trust my neighbors. So in the same way, I cannot make a single decision without the fundamental sense of trusting my own
brain. If I don't know how my brain works, how the hell do I know if I'm not
crazy? I have no way of determining. I may be absolutely nutty as a fruitcake,
but nevertheless, I have to trust my brain. The trouble with most people we
call crazy is that they can't trust themselves. Clinically, one has somehow or
other to get these people to trust themselves again. You can't do that if you're
uptight. If you, in the company of a so-called crazy person, feel ill-at-ease, and
feel that you've got to get this person to conform and do things according to

the book, you're going to get nowhere. You've got to be able, yourself, to be as crazy as a crazy person in order to be a therapist.

The therapist must, above all things, have a basic trust in life, in the unconscious. The unconscious shouldn't be a noun. It's a verb, the unconscious aspect of process, of nature. If you don't trust it, you get clutched up in the situation where you can't really do anything. Our technology is basically a mistrust of nature and, clever as it is, it's not going to work in the long run. Our technology is going to destroy us, unless we upend it, and base it on trust in the processes of life.

The basis of what we're going into is what I have called the intellectual unconscious. Nowadays it's customary, especially in psychological circles, to put down intellectual considerations. Such words are used as being "overcerebral," as being on a "head trip," as dismissing it all as "a lot of talk," but the fact remains that those comments on intellectualization are an expression of a philosophy— and at that, an unexamined one. You will often come across a type who says, "I'm just a practical businessman. I don't give a shit about philosophy. I've got to get things done." And so that fellow is advertising himself as a member of a particular philosophical school called pragmatism. He doesn't know this, and because he doesn't know it he's bad pragmatist. He says, "I want to get things done." Or, he's the sort of person who says, "You can't stop progress." But what is being practical? This is a very, very undecided question, and for a lot of people, their only idea of what is practical is what enables them to survive. Well, this can be thoroughly called into question.

I mean, is it a good idea to survive? Most people have never thought about that at all. Albert Camus (1960), in his book, *The Myth of Sisyphus*, starts out by saying, "The only serious philosophical question is whether or not to commit suicide." Now, in your profession, suicide is a major evil. I once went to a conference held by the American Academy of Psychotherapists on the subject of "Failure in Psychotherapy," and various papers were presented. The first paper contained a case study of someone who had been under therapy for five years and then committed suicide. So I said, "This is rather a funny case because, after all, you kept the guy alive for five years, and in the treatment of cancer that would have been counted as a cure. The statistics on cancer treatment always reckon five years' survival as a cure. What's so bad about suicide? After all, we're overpopulated, and if someone doesn't want to be around anymore, that's their privilege. All I'm saying is that that assumption is questionable. Furthermore, what are you afraid of about death?"

This is a real hospital hang-up. We don't know how to treat dying people. The literature on the psychotherapy of the dying has only just begun to come into existence, and a doctor is in a very tough position because he's supposed to keep you alive, at all costs. The most heroic measures are used to keep people alive, and there they suffer, linked up with all kinds of tubes and kidney machines and various systems—because at all costs while there is life there is hope, and often while there is life there is pain. The doctor is sort of out of the role when he knows in his heart that the patient will not live, and then all kinds of lying starts up. He may tell the patient's relatives that the case is hopeless, but he says to them, "Don't tell the patient." For some reason, knowing that you're going to die is supposed to be bad for you. It's supposed to depress you. It's supposed to perhaps cut down the recuperative forces of nature that are at work in your organism.

But the most important thing for anybody to know is that he's going to die. Oh, we can put it off and say, "Well, we'll think about that later." But we don't realize that the certainty of death is an extremely liberating experience. I've never been a doctor of medicine, but I've been a "doctor of divinity" . . . under rather strange circumstances. I've often been called in when people are dying, because when the doctor gives up, he calls the clergyman, and the clergyman feels in role at this point, although he may be a silly idiot and make all sorts of consolations and tell you about heaven and hell and such things. But that's not the way to work. Dying is a splendid opportunity, and the sooner one can realize fully the certainty of death the better.

The hospital is, by and large, a terrible place, although its intentions are very good. But the last place I would send anyone is to a mental hospital, and if possible, not even to a physical hospital. I had a friend recently who was dying of cancer—he had a brain tumor. And here he was in a Kaiser Hospital, in the most horrible surroundings. You know what hospital rooms are—colorless, healthy, hygienic, awful. And here he was, you know, he could hardly look out of the window even. And I said to him, "Harry, listen, I don't know, I haven't talked to your doctor, and I don't know what your condition really is, so don't take anything I say about your condition as being true, but let's just suppose for the sake of argument that it's hopeless. Suppose you're going to die. You may not be, but suppose it is so. Now you know enough, because you're well educated in Oriental philosophy, to realize that the best thing that could possibly happen to you is to lose your ego and be liberated. After all, that's what you've been concerned with all your life, the sense of transcending the narrow bounds of self-consciousness and feeling one with the universe, with the eternal energy behind all this, and the only way to get that feeling is to give yourself up." I said, "Here's the opportunity. There's no question of holding on to yourself anymore, because it's going to go away, and nothing can stop it, so get with it. Just give up, and get out of this place, and rent yourself a beach cottage and look out at the ocean, and stop all this concern to hang on."

Hanging onto oneself is self-strangulation. It's like smother-love. When a mother hangs on to her child too long and doesn't let it be independent because of her concern, or alleged love, the child becomes warped. Well, it's the same, you can smother-love yourself. You can hang on. You can be full of anxiety. I know and you know, for many people this is a regular program. They're anxious because they don't have enough money, and they think, If only I could double my income, everything would be okay. And they succeed. They do it. So they have plenty of money. Then the next thing they worry about is their health. They go to the doctor and they get a complete medical examination, and the doctor says, "As far as I can see, you're all right." Well, they think there's something probably wrong, because this person is a born worrier and maybe should go to a psychiatrist. So he looks you over and yes, "I can't see anything wrong." Well, then, you worry about politics. Is the revolution coming? Are the tax people going to take away all your money? Will you be robbed? I mean, there are endless contingencies you can worry about.

And finally, death. Am I going to die? Of course. How soon? Does that matter? What are you waiting for? There's a song, you know, which used to go . . . "There's a good time coming, be it ever so far away," and everybody thinks there is one far off divine event to which all creation moves, and maybe that'll turn up between now and your death . . . or even perhaps after death. Everybody's looking for *that thing* somewhere else than now. But if you accept death, a funny thing happens—you discover how good *now* is, and that's really where you're supposed to be. Very often people may get into these states when they're threatened by death, when they've given themselves up for dead, or sometimes, too, in convalescing from a long illness. In those transformed states of consciousness in which we see this, there's a sudden enlightenment about now.

When you see that *the whole point of life is this moment*, most other people seem objects of pity. You're rather sorry for them. Because they are rushing around, madly intent on something. They look insane on the streets. Going somewhere. Wow, it's important to get there. And their noses seem to be longer than usual, sort of prodding into the future, and their eyes staring. They rush about in cars. Looking out of the window I see all these cars streaming down Lake Shore Drive into Chicago. They're intent on something. What? Well, we have to go to work. Why? Well, to make money. Why? Well, I mean one must live. You *must*? If you say to any spontaneous process—and life is a spontaneous process—"You must happen," it's like saying to someone, "You must love me." But we all do that to our children. The basic rule for bringing up a child—which every child learns—is, "You are required and commanded to do that which will be acceptable only if you do it voluntarily." That is known as the double-bind. So we say to our spouses "You must love me," and if I don't feel like loving my spouse anymore, I'm made to feel guilty, and when I feel guilty, I feel I have to make an effort to be loving—but nobody wants to be loved on purpose. I don't want to be loved out of somebody's sense of duty. I want them to love me because they can't help loving me. Then I feel okay.

Ever so many people are thoroughly confused by being commanded to do that which is only any good if it's natural—and living *is* such a thing. If I say to myself, "I must live," then life is a drag. Or I say, "I must live because I have children and I'm responsible." But then all I do is teach my children to have the same feeling, and they will teach their children to have the same feeling, and life will continue to be a drag for everybody concerned. So life can only not be a drag when you understand it's gravy. That is to say, it happens unnecessarily, not under orders, but for kicks. Then you are free from the oppressive duty to go on living. And so the physician, and especially the psychiatrist, should be the first person to understand this. Jung once made a joke, "Life is a disease with a very bad prognosis. It lingers on for years and invariably ends with death." . . . So, death is most important, but of course, Westerners, particularly, are scared of it. It's the one awful awful that mustn't happen, because, well . . . why are we afraid of it? Some of us say, "It's not death I'm afraid of, it's dying." Well, that makes sense, but then medicine doesn't help: medicine prolongs dying. It doesn't really prolong life, I mean, it does sometimes, but for old people particularly, it prolongs dying. Terminal cancer is prolonged dying.

Still, there is something real spooky about death. Even if you're not religious and you don't believe in an afterlife that might be awful, I mean, who knows? But supposing death is like going to sleep and never waking up. That's quite something to think about. I find thinking about death is one of the most creative things one can do. To go to sleep and never wake up. Fancy that. It won't be like going into the dark forever. It won't be like being buried alive forever. There'll be no problems at all; there's nothing to regret. It will be as if you had never existed at all, and not only you, but everything else as well. It never was there. No further problems. But wait a minute. I seem to remember something like that. That was just the way it was before I was born. And yet, here I am. I exist, and once, I didn't. Nor did anything else, so far as I am concerned. And I always figure in life that a thing that happened once can always happen again. So I came out of nothing. But we say, "You couldn't have done that, because there's nothing in nothing to produce something, and we believe in the Latin precept, *ex nihilo nihil fit*, which means 'out of nothing comes nothing.'" But it's not true. It's a fault in our logic. If you had Chinese logic, you would see it differently. You would see that you have to have nothing in order to have something, because the two go together.

Well, isn't that obvious? Where would the stars be without space? There would be nowhere for them to be . . . and they shine out of space. Physicists are just beginning to realize that it is precisely space that is the creative matrix, the womb of creation. So in the same way, look at your head. What color is it? I can't even find mine. You all have heads, but I don't: I can't see my head. And I also don't feel with my eyes that there is a back blob in the middle of everything I experience. It isn't even fuzzy. It just isn't there, although neurologically speaking, all that I call outside is a state of the optic nerves that are located in the back of the head. So I'm looking at the inside of my head. It's pretty weird. So out of this nothingness comes my sight. Out of the space come the stars. So, you can regard death as the origin of life, for how would you know you are alive unless you had once been dead. Think that one over.

We think we are alive, don't we?—Something we can't quite put our finger on, but we know there is such a thing as reality, as existence. We're here. And everything we know is known by contrast. You know you can see light against a background of darkness, hot as compared with cold, pain compared with pleasure. So we know we're alive. Obviously we must have once been dead. This seems to me very plain.

So, you say, "Well now, wait a minute. When I come back again, if this does happen again, this sense of existence, in what form will I come back?" I hope I could be a human being again, or an angel, but perhaps I'll come back as a fruit fly, or a hippopotamus." But be assured it won't make any difference. All beings think they're human. We don't like to admit that because we think we're top species, but that doesn't follow at all. That's just our opinion, and we're very conceited. We say of somebody who is very ill, "Oh, it's too bad. He's just become a vegetable" . . . with the most extraordinary ignorance of vegetables. We think vegetables are unintelligent, unfeeling, but vegetables are highly intelligent organisms, and tests with electroencephalograms show that they feel. Now, if you came back as a vegetable, you would have vegetable consciousness, and you would think that was entirely normal . . . in fact, civilized, the usual thing, the regular thing. You would understand your fellow vegetables and the bees that visited you, and that would be the normal routine. You would think human beings were ridiculous. Human beings, in order to consider themselves civilized, have to accumulate enormous quantities of rubbish. They have to have clothes, cars, libraries, houses . . . all this junk. Whereas, look at us vegetables—our bodies are our culture, and we're not ashamed of them. Look at the flower. Isn't *that* something? Fish would have the same view. We think sharks are terrible, but they at least stay in the ocean. Human beings go everywhere, into the sky, into the ocean, and all over the earth catching their prey. But the civilized shark stays in the water at least. Look at the dolphins. Why, they are quite probably more intelligent than we. But they decided that our game was stupid. Stay in the water because the groceries are right there, and you can spend most of your time playing. And so that's just what the dolphins do. They gambol all over the place, and, for example, they'll follow a human ship and swim circles around it; then they'll set their tail at a twenty-six degree angle and let the bow-wake carry them. No effort, see . . . just keep your tail that way and the ship will take you along. Where to? Who cares?

Everywhere is the place to go, to be at. It's like a king. When a king walks, he is stately. Why? Because he has nowhere to go to. Because he is where he is at. He's the place, wherever he moves. So he walks in a stately way. He doesn't march, he doesn't hurry—he's there. Everybody must learn, then, to walk like a king. You can remember this because, in Sanskrit, your real self is called *atman*. Making a pun that scholars would deplore, that means the "man where it's at," and where it's at is where you are. But we're all under the illusion that we should be someone and somewhere else. So we're not seated properly. That's why, when you practice yoga, the first thing you have to learn is to sit in such a way that you're really there. So, by the acceptance of death, one overcomes the necessity for a future, and that in both senses of the word is a *present*.

You can see this more clearly perhaps if you would imagine what it would be like to regress, as it's called in psychotherapeutic language, to babyhood. And, here you are. You really don't know anything about anything. All you know is what you feel. You've no sense of time. You don't know the difference between who you are and what you see. You're in what Freud called the "oceanic state." You don't know anything. You don't know any language, no words in your head. Now consider what it would be like to stop thinking, stop talking to yourself, and simply be aware. You hear all the sound going on but you don't put names on them. You see all these colors and forms buzzing at you, but you don't call them anything. You just experience.

That's a pretty crazy state of consciousness because there's no past, there's no future, there's no difference between you and what you're aware of. It's all one, or none, or both, or neither—there are no words. You would be in a state that in yoga is called *nirvikalpa samadhi,* a very high consciousness in which illusions vanish—Eternal Now. Incidentally, a very therapeutic state of consciousness. But that is a kind of metaphorical death. It is the death of your self-image, your idea of yourself, your concept of yourself. Literal death, or the immediate prospect thereof, can bring a person into that state of consciousness. This state of consciousness is highly invigorating, because all the energy that you were wasting on worrying is now available for other things. All the energy you were wasting on trying to hold onto yourself is now available for things that can be done, and so people, paradoxically it would seem, are very pepped up by the acceptance of death in its various senses. So a hospital, where many people are in one way or another dying, should be a place of immense joy. But we don't allow it to be that, because we have the fixed idea that people in the hospital are in trouble, and we show them by the way in which we attend and relate to them emotionally: "Yes, you are in trouble." Well then, of course they feel in trouble. They have to play that role.

There is nothing that causes more trouble to people than helping them. There's a famous saying, "Kindly let me help you or you'll drown," said the monkey, putting the fish safely up a tree. The moment you take this attitude of "You are sick," people learn to eat pity, and thrive on it, and play sick as a profitable role for getting attention, sympathy, care, and to indulge in the masochism of gaining a sense of identity through being in peril, in misfortune. It's like the phrase, "nursing a grievance." I once had a woman come to me who had had a very serious tragedy. Her husband had died of a heart attack and a year later her son was struck by lightning and killed. She was beside herself with grief. Understandably. Well, at the time, I was a clergyman. And I took a look at this woman and I thought, I'm not going to give her any bullshit, she's too intelligent. So I asked her to explore grief. What is it to grieve? Where do you feel grief? What part of your body is it in? What sort of a feeling is it? What images are connected with it? In every way we explored grief. And by God, she got over it. Because eventually, concentrating on it as a sensation, she stopped talking to herself and saying, "Poor little me, I've lost my son, I've lost my husband," and repeating all these words over and over that hypnotize you and perpetuate the feeling of being important because you're in a state of grief. And she became an extremely creative and active person.

So it seems to me that anybody in the hospital professions, the healing professions, must get the hang of this somehow, and stop running desultory institutions. There's no reason why hospitals should be designed the way they are. Hospitals should be arranged in such a way as to make being sick an interesting experience. One learns a great deal sometimes from being sick. Dying only happens to you once, so it should be a great event. Special sanitariums, not hospitals—"sanitarium" means "a place of sanity"—should be arranged for different methods of dying. How would you like to die? Do you want a very, very marvelous religious ceremony? Do you want to invite all your friends to a champagne party? Do you want to be among flowers? How would you like to die if you really had your choice? Would you like to be drowned in a barrel of wine? You could take an extremely positive attitude to death as the greatest opportunity you'll ever have to experience what it's like to let go of yourself . . . than which there is no greater bliss.

REFERENCES

Camus, A. (1960). *The myth of Sisyphus, and other stories.* New York, NY: Vintage.

Young, J. Z. (1960). *Doubt and certainty in science.* New York, NY: Oxford University Press.

Academic and Literary Reviews
of Watts' Major Texts

THE SPIRIT OF ZEN: A WAY OF LIFE, WORK,
AND ART IN THE FAR EAST (1936)

Lea, A. (1937). [Review of the book *The spirit of Zen*]. *Journal of the Royal Central Asian Society, 24*(2), 332–343.

Lewin, B. (1959). [Review of the book *The spirit of Zen*]. *Orientalistische Literaturezeitung, 54*, 82.

[Review of the book *The spirit of Zen*]. (1936). *Asiatic Review, 32*(110), 452.

[Review of the book *The spirit of Zen*]. (1959). *Middle Way, 34*, 48.

Shyrock, J. T. (1937). [Review of the book *The spirit of Zen*]. *Journal of the American Oriental Society, 57*(2), 204–205.

Wright, L. L. (1936). [Review of the book *The spirit of Zen*]. *Theosophical Forum, 9*(1), 71.

THE LEGACY OF ASIA AND WESTERN MAN:
A STUDY OF THE MIDDLE WAY (1937)

[Review of the book *The legacy of Asia and Western man*]. (1937, October 22). *Times of India,* 6.

Smith, M. (1938). [Review of the book *The legacy of Asia and Western man*]. *Journal of the Royal Asiatic Society of Great Britain and Ireland, 70*(2), 326–327.

Speigelberg, F. (1938). [Review of the book *The legacy of Asia and Western man*]. *Review of Religion, 13*, 176–178.

Tyberg, J, (1938). [Review of the book *The legacy of Asia and Western man*]. *Theosophical Forum, 12*(1), 67.

THE MEANING OF HAPPINESS:
THE QUEST FOR FREEDOM OF THE SPIRIT IN
MODERN PSYCHOLOGY AND THE WISDOM OF THE EAST (1940)

Colum, M. M. (1940). Life and literature: Poets and psychologists. *Forum and Century, 103*(6), 322–326.

Hinkle, B. M. (1940). [Review of the book *The meaning of happiness*]. *Review of Religion, 5*, 484–487.

Holmes, J. H. (1940, July 14). Out of life. *New York Herald Tribune*, H6.

Ponsonby, I. R. (1940). Freedom of the spirit. *Theosophical Forum, 17*, 39–42.

[Review of the book *The meaning of happiness*]. *Crozer Quarterly, 17*, 225.

Richards, H. (1941, June 17). [Review of the book *The meaning of happiness*]. *Main Currents in Modern Thought*, 1–2.

Rowell, T. (1940). [Review of the book *The meaning of happiness*]. *Journal of Bible and Religion, 8*(4), 214–215.

BEHOLD THE SPIRIT:
A STUDY IN THE NECESSITY OF MYSTICAL RELIGION (1947)

Akhilanada, S. (1948). [Review of the book *Behold the spirit*]. *Journal of Bible and Religion, 16*(3), 185–186.

Burke, T. P. (1972). [Review of the book *Behold the spirit*, 2nd ed.]. *Commonweal, 96*, 413–415.

Crabbe, C. V. (1948). [Review of the book *Behold the spirit*]. *Interpretation, 2*(2), 267–268.

Gowen, H. H. (1949). [Review of the book *Behold the spirit*]. *Anglican Theological Review, 31*(1), 46–47.

Hardy, E. R. (1948). [Review of the book *Behold the spirit*]. *Review of Religion, 13–14*, 405–409.

Kepler, T. S. (1949). [Review of the book *Behold the spirit*]. *Religious Education, 44*, 312.

Reinhold, H. A. (1948, August 20). [Review of the book *Behold the spirit*]. *Commonweal*, 454–455.

[Review of the book *Behold the Spirit*]. (1947). *Liturgical Arts, 16*, 78.

Steere, D. V. (1949). [Review of the book *Behold the Spirit*]. *Journal of Religion, 29*(4), 321–322.

EASTER: ITS STORY AND MEANING (1950)

Enslin, M. S. (1950). [Review of the book *Easter: Its story and meaning*]. *Review of Religion, 15–16*, 210–211.

Fildey, V. S. (1951). [Review of the book *Easter: Its story and meaning*]. *Religious Education, 46*, 120.

Symbolism of a Yearly Feast. [Review of the book *Easter: Its story and meaning*]. (1951, March 11). *New York Harold Tribune*, E18.

THE SUPREME IDENTITY: AN ESSAY ON ORIENTAL METAPHYSIC AND CHRISTIAN RELIGION (1950)

Brinton, H. H. (1952). [Review of the book *The supreme identity*]. *Review of Religion, 17*(1), 77.

Christian, W. (1950). Some varieties of religious belief. *Review of Metaphysics, 4*(4), 595–616.

Keene, J. C. (1952). [Review of the book *The supreme identity*]. *Journal of Bible and Religion, 20*(2), 132.

Kitagawa, J. (1951). [Review of the book *The supreme identity*]. *Journal of Religion, 31*(3), 225.

Martin, J. A. (1951). [Review of the book *The supreme identity*]. *Theology Today, 8*(1), 134.

Morris, C. (1951). [Review of the book *The supreme identity*]. *Philosophy East and West, 1*(1), 77–79.

Nance, J. (1950). [Review of the book *The supreme identity*]. *Hibbert Journal, 49,* 96.

Niebuhr, R. (1950, December 2). Redemption by negation. *The Nation,* p. 511.

[Review of the book *The supreme identity*]. (1950). *The Middle Way, 25,* 92.

[Review of the book *The supreme identity*]. (1950). *New Blackfriars, 31*(366), 411.

[Review of the book *The supreme identity*]. (1950). *Islamic Review, 38*(9), 42.

[Review of the book *The supreme identity*]. (1950, September 29). *The Times of India,* 6.

[Review of the book *The supreme identity*]. (1958). *Psychiatric Quarterly, 32,* 210.

Waterhouse, E. S. (1953). [Review of the book *The supreme identity*]. *Philosophy, 28*(107), 273–274.

Wheelwright, P. (1953). The philosophy of Alan Watts. *Sewanee Review,* 493–500.

Wilson, P. W. (1950, October 22). [Review of the book *The supreme identity*]. *New York Times Saturday Review of Books and Art,* 20.

THE WISDOM OF INSECURITY: A MESSAGE FOR AN AGE OF ANXIETY (1951)

[Review of the book *The wisdom of insecurity*]. (1954). *Middle Way, 29,* 39.

Sherrill, L. J. (1952). [Review of the book *The wisdom of insecurity*]. *Pastoral Psychology, 3,* 61–62.

Wheelwright, P. (1953). The philosophy of Alan Watts. *Sewanee Review,* 493–500.

MYTH AND RITUAL IN CHRISTIANITY (1953)

Brandon, S. G. F. (1953). [Review of the book *Myth and ritual in Christianity*]. *Hibbert Journal, 52,* 404.

Burger, N. K. (1954, April 18). [Review of the book *Myth and ritual in Christianity*]. *New York Times Saturday Review of Books and Art,* 16.

Every, G. (1954). [Review of the book *Myth and ritual in Christianity*]. *Theology, 57*(408), 229–230.

James, E. O. (1954, May). [Review of the book *Myth and ritual in Christianity*]. *Man*, 54, 77.

Paul, D. (1954). Transformations of eros. *Encounter*, 2(5), 86.

Perennial Philosophy [Review of the book *Myth and ritual in Christianity*]. (1954, June 5), *Irish Times*, 6.

[Review of the book *Myth and ritual in Christianity*]. (1954). *Church Quarterly Review*, 155, 409.

[Review of the book *Myth and ritual in Christianity*]. (1954). *Middle Way*, 29, 44.

Seager, R. (1957). [Review of the book *Myth and ritual in Christianity*]. *Midwest Folklore*, 7(1), 43–45.

Watts, H. H. (1954). [Review of the book *Myth and ritual in Christianity*]. *Journal of Bible and Religion*, 22(4), 265.

Weisinger, H. (1957). [Review of the book *Myth and ritual in Christianity*]. *Journal of American Folklore*, 70(276), 195–197.

THE WAY OF ZEN (1957)

Burden, J. (1958). Why is a mouse when it spins? [Review of the book *The way of Zen*]. *Prairie Schooner*, 32(2), 79–81.

Campbell, J. (1957, August 4). [Review of the book *The way of Zen*]. *New York Times Saturday Review of Books and Art*, 5.

Curran, C. E. (1959). [Review of the book *The way of Zen*]. *ETC: A Review of General Semantics*, 16(2), 232–236.

Hurvitz, L. (1958). [Review of the book *The way of Zen*]. *Journal of Asian Studies*, 17(3), 487–489.

Marlow, N. (1958). [Review of the book *The way of Zen*]. *Hibbert Journal*, 57, 208.

McCarthy, H. E. (1957). [Review of the book *The way of Zen*]. *Philosophy East and West*, 7(1–2), 70–73.

Patterson, R. L. (1958). [Review of the book *The way of Zen*]. *Encounter*, 19, 353–355.

[Review of the book *The way of Zen*]. (1959). *Humanist*, 19, 315.

[Review of the book *The way of Zen*]. (1962). *Middle Way*, 37, 91.

[Review of the book *The way of Zen*]. (1962). (1958). *Psychiatric Quarterly*, 32, 191.

Sangharakshita, B. (1960). [Review of the book *The way of Zen*]. *Maha Bodhi*, 68, 25–26.

NATURE, MAN AND WOMAN (1958)

Adams, R. M. (1958). Man and nothing: Earthbound comments. *Hudson Review*, 11(4), 626–631.

Curran, C. E. (1960). Man's exile from nature. [Review of the book *Nature, man and woman*]. *ETC.: A Review of General Semantics*, 17(4), 502–504.

Humphreys, C. (1958). [Review of the book *Nature, man and woman*]. *Middle Way*, 33, 166.

Mahoney, S. (1958). The prevalence of Zen. *Nation*, 187(14), 311–314.

MacGreggor, G. (1958). [Review of the book *Nature, man and woman*]. *Living Church*, 137, 25–26.

THIS IS IT, AND OTHER ESSAYS ON ZEN
AND SPIRITUAL EXPERIENCE (1960)

Barrett, W. (1960, December 18). [Review of the book *This is IT, and other essays on Zen and spiritual experience*]. *New York Times Saturday Review of Books and Art*, 6.

Eden, P. (1979). [Review of the book *This is IT, and other essays on Zen and spiritual experience*]. *Middle Way*, 54(1), 38.

Gundry, D. W. (1962). [Review of the book *This is IT, and other essays on Zen and spiritual experience*]. (1961). *Theology*, 65(506), 337.

[Review of the book *This is IT, and other essays on Zen and spiritual experience*]. (1961). *Middle Way*, 36, 135.

Shahani, R. (1960, December 24). All roads lead to Nirvana. *Saturday Review*, 21–22.

Weber, J. (1967). [Review of the book *This is IT, and other essays on Zen and Spiritual experience*]. *Literature East and West*, 11, 469.

PSYCHOTHERAPY EAST AND WEST (1961)

Books Notes. (1963). *Journal of Individual Psychology*, 19(1), 106.

Burton-Bradley, B. G. (1972). [Review of the book *Psychotherapy, East and West*]. *Australian and New Zealand Journal of Sociology*, 8(2), 136–137.

Clare, A. (1971, August 14). The new neurosis. *Irish Times*, 8.

Curry, A. E. (1962). [Review of the book *Psychotherapy, East and West*]. *Psychoanalysis and the Psychoanalytic Review*, 49(3), 128.

Eichler, R. M. (1963). [Review of the book *Psychotherapy, East and West*]. *Teachers College Record*, 65(1), 89–90.

Enroth, B. (1973). [Review of the book *Psychotherapy, East and West*, 2nd ed.]. *Sociologisk Forskning*, 10(2), 61–62.

Henderson, J. L. [Review of the book *Psychotherapy, East and West*]. *Journal of Analytical Psychology*, 8(2), 186–187.

Levy, N. J. (1967). [Review of the book *Psychotherapy, East and West*]. *American Journal of Psychoanalysis*, 27(2), 211–212.

Moffett, J. (1962). Turning language upon itself. [Review of the book *Psychotherapy, East and West*]. *ETC: A Review of General Semantics*, 28(4), 486–490.

[Review of the book *Psychotherapy, East and West*]. *MANAS*, 41(28), 6–7.

Rioch, M. J. (1963). [Review of the book *Psychotherapy, East and West*]. *Psychiatry*, 26(1), 107–110.

Ruesch, J. (1962). [Review of the book *Psychotherapy, East and West*]. *Archives of General Psychology*, 6(3), 254–255.

Salzman, L. (1963). [Review of the book *Psychotherapy, East and West*]. *Journal of Pastoral Care*, 17(3), 172–173.

Skynner, A. C. R. (1971). [Review of the book *Psychotherapy, East and West*, 2nd ed.]. *Group Analysis*, 4(3), 192–193.

Zaehner, R. C. (1971). [Review of the book *Psychotherapy, East and West*, 2nd ed.]. *Spectator*, 227(7466), 179.

THE JOYOUS COSMOLOGY: ADVENTURES IN THE
CHEMISTRY OF CONSCIOUSNESS (1962)

Gorham, D. R. (1963). The new world of superconsciousness. [Review of the book *The joyous cosmology*]. *Contemporary Psychology, 8*(1), 22–24.

Peerman, D. (1962, August 1). Instant mysticism. [Review of the book *The joyous cosmology*]. *Christian Century*, 938–939.

Rexroth, K. (1962). [Review of the book *The joyous cosmology*]. *Foot, 2*, 22–23.

THE TWO HANDS OF GOD: THE MYTHS OF
POLARITY [PATTERNS OF MYTH SERIES, VOL. 2] (1963)

Bharati, A. (1964). [Review of the *Patterns of myth* series]. *Journal of Bible and Religion, 32*(3), 277–279.

Luomala, K. (1964). [Review of the *Patterns of myth* series]. *American Anthropologist* (New Series), *66*(4), 960–962.

[Review of the *Patterns of myth* series]. *Virginia Quarterly Review, 40*(1), 43–44.

[Review of the book *The two hands of God*]. *Diologist, 2*, 68.

Rice, S., & Rice, M. (1965). Other sets of glasses. [Review of *The patterns of myth* series]. *Etc: A Review of General Semantics, 22*(4), 515–520.

Scharbach, A. (1965). [Review of the book *The two hands of God*]. *Journal of American Folklore, 78*(310), 354–355.

Sullivan, H. P. (1965). The truth of myths. [Review of *The patterns of myth* series]. *Contemporary Psychology, 10*(5), 208–211.

Wade, D. V. (1964). [Review of *The patterns of myth* series]. *Canadian Journal of Theology, 10*, 217–218.

BEYOND THEOLOGY: THE ART OF GODMANSHIP (1964)

Flew, A. (1965). Hip homiletics. *New York Review of Books*. Retrieved from http://www.nybooks.com/articles/archives/1965/jan/14/hip-homiletics/

Lee, P. (1965). [Review of the book *Beyond theology*]. *The Psychedelic Review, 5*, 126–127.

Limper, P. F. (1965). [Review of the book *Beyond theology*]. *Review of Metaphysics, 18*(4), 779.

[Review of the book *Beyond theology*]. (1964). *Kirkus Reviews*. Retrieved from https://www.kirkusreviews.com/book-reviews/alan-watts/beyond-theology

Vahanian, G. (1965). God without God. *Christian Century, 82*(23), 745.

THE BOOK: ON THE TABOO AGAINST
KNOWING WHO YOU ARE (1966)

Danser, J. (1971). Where there is "oneness." [Review of the book *The book: On the taboo against knowing who you are*]. In D. Fairfield (Ed.), *Modern man in search of utopia* (pp. 96, 99). San Francisco, CA: Alternatives Foundation.

[Review of the book *The book: On the taboo against knowing who you are*]. (1967). *Review of Metaphysics, 21*(2), 381–382.

[Review of the book *The book: On the taboo against knowing who you are*]. (1967). *Virginia Quarterly Review, 43*(2), 42.

[Review of the book *The book: On the taboo against knowing who you are*]. (1966). *Kirkus Reviews*. Retrieved from https://kirkusreviews.com/book-reviews/alan-watts-2/the-book-2

Ross, N. W. (1966, December 31). The self as dangerous delusion. *Saturday Review, 23*, 40.

Southall, D. (1969). [Review of the book *The book: On the taboo against knowing who you are*]. *Middle Way, 44*(2), 92.

Weber, J. (1967). [Review of the book *The book: On the taboo against knowing who you are*]. *Literature East and West, 11*, 340.

TAO: THE WATERCOURSE WAY (1975)

Burton-Stibbon, A. (1976). [Review of the book *Tao: The watercourse way*]. *Middle Way, 51*, 91–92.

Hewitt, C. (1976). [Review of the book *Tao: The watercourse way*]. *Middle Way, 51*, 92–93.

Manning, G. (1976). Tao. *Library Journal, 100*(18), 1729.

[Review of the book *Tao: The watercourse way*]. (1975). *Kirkus Reviews*. Retrieved from https://www.kirkusreviews.com/book-reviews/alan-al-chung-liang-huang-watts/tao-the-watercourse-way/

[Review of the book *Tao: The watercourse way*]. (1976). *San Francisco Review of Books, 2*, 12–13.

Ryback, D. (1976, July 4). From Zen to Tao with Alan Watts. *Atlanta Constitution*, 14C.

Sadler, A. W. (1976). [Review of the books *Tao: The watercourse way* and *Alan Watts*]. *Horizons, 3*, 301–304.

Versfeld, M. (1977). [Review of the book *Tao: The watercourse way*]. *Philosophical Papers, 6*(1), 57–58.

Contributors

PETER J. COLUMBUS is administrator of Shantigar Foundation for Theater, Meditation and Healing, adjunct professor of psychology at Assumption College and Greenfield Community College, and serves on the Board of Directors of Valley Zendo—a Soto Zen Buddhist temple in the lineage of Kodo Sawaki and Kosho Uchiyama. Co-editor (with Don Rice) of *Alan Watts—Here and Now: Contributions to Psychology, Philosophy, and Religion* (2012) and *Psychology of the Martial Arts* (1988), he holds a PhD in experimental psychology from the University of Tennessee, and an MA in humanistic psychology from the University of West Georgia.

DONADRIAN L. RICE is professor and chair of psychology at the University of West Georgia. Co-editor (with Peter Columbus) of *Alan Watts—Here and Now: Contributions to Psychology, Philosophy, and Religion* (2012) and *Psychology of the Martial Arts* (1988), he has published more than 50 papers on martial arts, dreams, hypnosos, organizational development, psychotherapy, and mind-body studies He holds a PhD from Saybrook Graduate School, received training from R. D. Laing at the Philadelphia Association Clinic in London, and is a licensed psychotherapist.

ALAN W. WATTS (1915–1973) was one of widest read twentieth-century religious philosophers. He was an Episcopal priest and chaplain at Northwestern University, professor of comparative philosophy at the American Academy of Asian Studies, visiting scholar at Harvard University, and freelance philosopher. A graduate of King's School in Canturbury, he held a master's degree in sacred theology from Seabury-Western Theological Seminary and an Honory

Doctorate of Divinity from the University of Vermont for his contributions to comparative religion. Watts published more than 20 books during his lifetime, including *The Wisdom of Insecurity*; *The Way of Zen*; *Psychotherapy East and West*; *The Book*; and *Tao—The Watercourse Way*.

Index

Made in the USA
Monee, IL
03 April 2021